Transnational Nazism

In 1936, Nazi Germany and militarist Japan built a partnership that culminated in the Tokyo–Berlin Axis. This study of interwar German-Japanese relations is the first to employ sources in both languages. Transnational Nazism was an ideological and cultural outlook that attracted non-Germans to become adherents of Hitler and National Socialism, and convinced German Nazis to identify with certain non-Aryans. Because of the distance between Germany and Japan, mass media was instrumental in shaping mutual perceptions and spreading transnational Nazism. This work surveys the two national media to examine the impact of transnational Nazism. When Hitler and the Nazi movement gained prominence, Japanese newspapers, lectures and pamphlets, nonfiction, and language textbooks transformed to promote the man and his party. Meanwhile, the ascendancy of Hitler and his regime created a niche for Japan in the Nazi worldview and Nazified newspapers, films, nonfiction, and voluntary associations.

RICKY W. LAW is Associate Professor of History at Carnegie Mellon University. He has received grants and fellowships from the Alexander von Humboldt Foundation, the Japan Foundation, and the Royster Society of Fellows. In 2013, he received the Dean's Distinguished Dissertation Award at the University of North Carolina at Chapel Hill, where he earned his PhD, and the Fritz Stern Dissertation Prize of the Friends of the German Historical Institute.

T0381718

Publications of the German Historical Institute

Edited by

Simone Lässig
with the assistance of David Lazar

The German Historical Institute is a center for advanced study and research whose purpose is to provide a permanent basis for scholarly cooperation among historians from the Federal Republic of Germany and the United States. The Institute conducts, promotes, and supports research into both American and German political, social, economic, and cultural history; into transatlantic migration, especially during the nineteenth and twentieth centuries; and into the history of international relations, with special emphasis on the roles played by the United States and Germany.

A full list of titles in the series can be found at:
www.cambridge.org/pghi

Transnational Nazism

Ideology and Culture in German-Japanese Relations, 1919–1936

Ricky W. Law
Carnegie Mellon University

GERMAN HISTORICAL INSTITUTE

Washington, DC

and

CAMBRIDGE
UNIVERSITY PRESS

University Printing House, Cambridge CB2 8BS, United Kingdom

One Liberty Plaza, 20th Floor, New York, NY 10006, USA

477 Williamstown Road, Port Melbourne, VIC 3207, Australia

314-321, 3rd Floor, Plot 3, Splendor Forum, Jasola District Centre, New Delhi - 110025, India

79 Anson Road, #06-04/06, Singapore 079906

Cambridge University Press is part of the University of Cambridge.

It furthers the University's mission by disseminating knowledge in the pursuit of education, learning and research at the highest international levels of excellence.

www.cambridge.org
Information on this title: www.cambridge.org/9781108465151
DOI: 10.1017/9781108565714

© Ricky W. Law 2019

First published 2019
First paperback edition 2020

A catalogue record for this publication is available from the British Library

Library of Congress Cataloging in Publication data
NAMES: Law, Ricky W., 1979- author.
TITLE: Transnational nazism : ideology and culture in German-Japanese relations, 1919-1936 / Ricky W. Law, Carnegie Mellon University, Pennsylvania.
OTHER TITLES: Ideology and culture in German-Japanese relations, 1919–1936
DESCRIPTION: First edition. | New York : Cambridge University Press, [2019] | SERIES: Publications of the German Historical Institute | Includes bibliographical references and index.
IDENTIFIERS: LCCN 2019004780| ISBN 9781108474634 (hardback : alk. paper) | ISBN 9781108465151 (pbk. : alk. paper)
SUBJECTS: LCSH: Germany–Foreign public opinion, Japanese. | National socialism in popular culture–Japan. | National socialism–Germany. | Japan–Foreign public opinion, German. | Japan–Civilization–German influences. | Germany–Civilization–Japanese influences. | Japan–Relations–Germany. | Germany–Relations–Japan. | Public opinion–Germany. | Public opinion–Japan.
CLASSIFICATION: LCC DS849.G4 L39 2019 | DDC 303.48/24305209042–dc23
LC record available at https://lccn.loc.gov/2019004780

ISBN 978-1-108-47463-4 Hardback
ISBN 978-1-108-46515-1 Paperback

To my parents

Contents

Figures

Acknowledgments

Though writing this book has mostly been a solitary, late night endeavor for well over a decade, I could not have completed it without the assistance of many individuals and organizations.

Foremost, I had two superb *Doktorväter*, Christopher Browning and Miles Fletcher, at the University of North Carolina (UNC) at Chapel Hill. Their steadfast support, encouragement, and confidence in me created the perfect environment for tackling a sprawling dissertation covering two countries and historical traditions. They continued to guide me after the dissertation defense and shared with me their thoughts on the manuscript. I learned much from them and am only now beginning to appreciate some of their wisdom and insights on teaching and research. The other dissertation committee members each left their intellectual marks on me and the project. Konrad Jarausch inspired me to have a vision and challenged me to view my work in a broader perspective. Dominic Sachsenmaier gave suggestions on issues in East–West interactions and global history methodologies. Daniel Botsman led me to think more about continuities in Japanese-German interactions from the nineteenth century. Cemil Aydin showed me Pan-Asianism's impact in pre-1945 Japan. Beyond the committee, Richard Talbert indulged me in my fascination with Roman history. Jan Bardsley offered much kindness and valuable practical advice on researching in Japan. Jennifer Smith and Paul Roberge introduced me to basic Japanese and German linguistics.

Several institutions furnished indispensable material support. The German Chancellor Fellowship of the Alexander von Humboldt Foundation funded my research stay in Germany. I not only collected the necessary historical sources but also learned much about German society, economy, culture, and politics. This book and I personally greatly benefited from the fellowship's interdisciplinary ethos. The Doctoral Fellowship of the Japan Foundation enabled my research in Tokyo. Kitaoka Shin'ichi of the Graduate Schools for Law and Politics at the University of Tokyo supervised my work. Suzuki Tamon familiarized me with the National Diet Library. The Royster Society at UNC Chapel Hill granted me a dissertation fellowship that let me concentrate on writing. I am also grateful to the UNC Graduate School for the Dean's Distinguished Dissertation Award. The History Department at Carnegie Mellon University (CMU) gave me leave so that I could finish the manuscript. I was honored to be awarded the Fritz Stern Dissertation Prize by the Friends of the German Historical Institute. I thank prize committee members Ann Goldberg, Paul Lerner, and Jesse Spohnholz for the recognition. David Lazar of the German Historical Institute invited me to submit my manuscript and shepherded the project throughout the publication process. Editor Liz Friend-Smith of Cambridge University Press and content manager Ian McIver have been very patient and accommodating to this first-time book author. Elizabeth Stone of Bourchier meticulously copy-edited the manuscript. I thank Berghahn Books for permission to reuse a previously published piece.

Talented, committed archivists and librarians facilitated my research. In the United States, the librarians of Davis Library at UNC, especially those of the interlibrary loan department, deserve high praise for their patience and responsiveness. Kris Troost of Perkins Library at Duke University was generous with her time and always ready to answer my questions from the beginning to the end of the project. Andrew Marshall of Hunt Library at CMU distinguished himself with his attention to detail and resourcefulness. In Germany, the archivists at the Federal Archives in Berlin, Koblenz, and Freiburg were all professional, helpful, and knowledgeable. Sven Schneidereit and Herr Klein at Berlin-Lichterfelde patiently handled my requests for obscure documents and located them without fail. David Parrett of the film collection taught me much about pre-1945 motion pictures. The Political Archives of the Foreign Office, Berlin State Archives, and the library of Humboldt University of Berlin also proved rich depositories of sources. I spent months at the German National Library in Leipzig, where the librarians were thorough and efficient. I also appreciate the assistance of the staffs of the library and archives of Leipzig University. In Japan, the National Diet Library is a model of accessibility, innovation, and user-friendliness. I thank especially the rotating staffs at the microfiche and rare books reading rooms and copy services.

My colleagues at CMU have been supportive and engaged ever since I joined the History Department. They asked profound, insightful questions at my first presentation of the project. Donna Harsch helped me revise crucial portions of the manuscript. Nico Slate read and commented on the entire manuscript, many parts repeatedly. Stephen

Brockmann and Elisabeth Kaske were great company. Ema Grama was always available for emotional support.

The outside reviewers invited by the CMU History Department encouraged me to reorient the project and elevate its theoretical aspect. I thank the two anonymous referees solicited by my editor for their extremely useful feedback. They are my teachers. Of course, I am solely responsible for any remaining errors.

Speaking of teachers, I am endlessly grateful to Michael Grüttner at Technical University of Berlin for two decades of wisdom, mentoring, and friendship. I owe much of what I know in German history to him. I have the deepest appreciation for Erich Gruen at the University of California, Berkeley. His gentle but forceful exhortations to interpret evidence more critically and creatively were never far from my mind when I wrote this book.

I am thankful for opportunities to present my findings and grow from comments and questions at conferences at the Association for Asian Studies, German Studies Association, University of Southern California ("Approaches to Wartime Japan: Militarism, Fascism and Religion," convened by John Person and Clinton Godart), University of California, San Diego ("Germans in the Pacific World from the Late 17th to 20th Century," convened by Hartmut Berghoff, Frank Biess, and Ulrike Strasser), Seton Hall University ("Encounters: Travel and Tourism in Historical Perspective," convened by Sarah Fieldston), and Berlin Program of Advanced German and European Studies at Free University of Berlin ("Strange Bedfellows/Unexpected Allies," convened by Deborah Barton, Jeremy DeWaal, Karin Goihl, Thomas Haakenson, and Carol Hager).

Along the journey from Chapel Hill to Germany to Japan to Pittsburgh, numerous people took care of me. Michael Meng, Sarah and Ben Vierra, Rebecca Archer, Pearl Chang, Michael Smith, Philipp Stelzel, Megan Kassabaum, and others made my time in graduate school pleasant and stimulating. Michael Meng in particular was a great *senpai* and model. In Germany, fellow "Buka" Andrea Stith was a caring listener and good friend. The Kuschminder, Albani, and Eck families opened their doors and let me celebrate holidays with them. Fellow graduate students Mari Webel, Stephen Gross, Dan Bullard, and Stephen Scala provided solidarity and tips during my stay. In Japan, I very much appreciated the intelligent, enjoyable company of Max Ward, Nick Kapur, and Benjamin Uchiyama at the Modern Japan History Workshop. Kari Shephardson-Scott and Anne Giblin Gedacht showed me the wonders of Jinbōchō. Meghen Jones educated me about Japanese art museums and accessing collections. Birgit Schneider is a fine fellow student of German-Japanese relations. The Iwata family and everyone in Atsuta-mura again treated me as one of their own. In Jacksonville, Florida, Charles Closmann, David Courtwright, and Chau Kelly took time to listen to me as a beginning academic. In the last days of revision, I met a group of conscientious educators from around Pittsburgh through Classrooms without Borders, made possible by the indefatigable Tsipy Gur and Patti Askwith Kenner. I had the honor to meet and learn from Howard Chandler, who reminds me why I am a historian.

During this project and beyond, Brian Mathias put up with me through his gentleness and ability to see the best in people. May we have many more years of good food and togetherness. I dedicate this work to my parents, May-lan Lau and Kwai Law, whose sacrifice and love made me the person I am.

Note on Languages

All non-English quotations are translated by the author, unless an English translation is cited. German words retain the spelling prevalent in the interwar years. Japanese words are romanized according to the modified Hepburn system. Japanese surnames precede given names, except in citations of works in European languages. Long vowels in familiar terms such as Tokyo or Showa are not marked with macrons other than in titles of publications or organizations.

Abbreviations

AEPM	Allgemeiner Evangelisch-Protestantischer Missionsverein
BArch	Bundesarchiv
BLA	*Berliner Lokal-Anzeiger: Zentral-Organ für die Reichshauptstadt*
BTH	*Berliner Tageblatt und Handels-Zeitung*
DAZ	*Deutsche Allgemeine Zeitung*
DJAG	Deutsch-Japanische Arbeitsgemeinschaft
DJG	Deutsch-Japanische Gesellschaft
DTW	*Deulig-Tonwoche*
EE	Evening edition
EW	*Emelka-Woche*
G	*Germania: Zeitung für das deutsche Volk*
IPA	International Phonetic Alphabet
JTM	*The Japan Times and Mail*
K	*Kokumin shinbun*
KAZ	*Königsberger Allgemeine Zeitung*
ME	Munich edition
NGE	North German edition
NPK	*Neue Preußische (Kreuz)-Zeitung*
NSKK	Nationalsozialistisches Kraftfahrkorps
OM	*Ōsaka mainichi shinbun*
PA AA	Politisches Archiv des Auswärtigen Amts
RF	*Die Rote Fahne: Zentralorgan der Kommunistischen Partei Deutschlands*
RM	Reichsmark
S	*Sekki*
TA	*Tōkyō asahi shinbun*
TN	*Tōkyō nichinichi shinbun*
UAL	Universitätsarchiv Leipzig
Ufa	Universum Film AG
UTW	*Ufa-Tonwoche*
V	*Vorwärts: Berliner Volksblatt, Zentralorgan der Sozialdemokratischen Partei Deutschlands*

VB   *Völkischer Beobachter: Kampfblatt der nationalsozialistischen*
         Bewegung Großdeutschlands
VZ   *Vossische Zeitung: Berlinische Zeitung von Staats- und gelehrten*
         Sachen
Y   *Yomiuri shinbun*

Introduction

In 1934, a Japanese businessman in Osaka hit upon a clever advertising gimmick. He applied to trademark "Hitler" in the Latin alphabet and Japanese kana as a brand name for bicycles and tricycles. The Patent Office publicized his application in early June. Within days, the German Embassy reacted to the taking of the Führer's name in vain by asking the Japanese Foreign Ministry to intervene. It invoked Japanese laws barring trademarks that infringed personal names or might disrupt public order. It asserted that Chancellor Adolf Hitler had not authorized such use of his name. Moreover, "in Germany the name 'Hitler' enjoys a reputation and profound veneration that far exceeds the typical significance attached to the name of a leading statesman. Approving the registration would thus provoke widespread resentment in Germany ... but also upset Japan's international relations."[1] The embassy pressed its case in person the next month and designated its general counsel to follow up.[2] It reported to Berlin in November that the application had been rejected and the issue resolved.[3]

This book explores how nationalists in Japan and Germany became mutual admirers in the 1930s. The Hitler bicycle affair is a small but telling illustration of Germany and Japan's political and cultural entanglements before their entente through the Anti-Comintern Pact of 1936. It also exemplifies two major arguments of this book. First, many Japanese shared Germans' excitement about Hitler. The word Hitler was evidently popular enough in Japan to be considered a marketing ploy. The bicycle maker proposed the trademark not to offend but to claim a valuable brand from fellow Japanese admirers of Hitler. I argue that this admiration is evidence of a "transnational Nazism" that enabled Japanese and Germans to identify with each other and imagine a binational

---

[1] Bundesarchiv (hereafter: BArch), R 43II/1454, German Embassy's *note verbale* to Japanese Foreign Ministry, June 12, 1934.
[2] BArch, R 43II/1454, Herbert von Dirksen to Foreign Office, July 27, 1934.
[3] BArch, R 43II/1454, Willy Noebel to Foreign Office, November 21, 1934.

community before their governments forged the alliance. Transnational Nazism was an ideological outlook. Its Nazism centered on Hitler's personality and elemental National Socialism as a worldview that combined emphasis on the nation and communal sharing of benefits and sacrifice. This Nazism was transnational because Hitler and his messages resonated with non-Germans on the one hand, and because German Nazis and their movement allowed for the limited accommodation of non-Aryan foreigners, in this case the Japanese, on the other. Transnational Nazism's emergence in both countries was eased by reciprocal cultural appreciation in their media throughout the interwar era.[4]

This last point brings forth the second major argument: words and activities in civil society helped shape German-Japanese mutual perceptions and so promote transnational Nazism. Christening bicycles, a luxury good, "Hitler" was meant to be honorific and convey Hitler's atypical significance; other models included "Hegemon" and "Tokyo Fuji."[5] But the bicycle maker's clumsy, even if sincere, adulation did not amuse German officialdom. The Third Reich could not countenance any profaning of the "Hitler myth" and touchily defended the Führer's honor, even against an irreverent but harmless commercial appropriation far away.[6] Yet Germany only had tenuous control of Hitler's image in Japan because Japan also invested words with importance. The embassy had to act indirectly through politely petitioning the foreign ministry and citing domestic laws. In denying the registration, the patent office conceded the violation of an individual's name, but not the transnational disorder that naming rides after the Führer would allegedly spark.

Public discourse and perceptions mattered in interwar Japanese-German relations because few could afford firsthand interactions. To move between the countries, one needed 46 hours on an experimental flight, 102 hours on a zeppelin, 12 days by rail, two weeks via Lufthansa, or one to two months by ship.[7] A Friedrichshafen to Tokyo ticket on the

---

[4] There appears to be only one other use of "transnational Nazism," defined as "a dialogue between Nazism's classic form (Nazi Germany) and its various reformulations." Rebecca Wennberg, "Ideological Incorrectness Beyond 'Political Religion': Discourse on Nazi Ideology among Scandinavian National Socialist Intellectuals" (PhD diss., Royal Holloway, University of London, 2015), 159–160. This definition approximates mine in that Japanese commentators attempted to interpret Nazism. But it also differs because German and Japanese Nazis did not debate ideological correctness.

[5] *Tōkyō asahi shinbun* (hereafter: TA), June 8, 1933.

[6] Ian Kershaw, *The "Hitler Myth": Image and Reality in the Third Reich* (Oxford: Clarendon Press, 1987); Rudolph Herzog, *Dead Funny: Humor in Hitler's Germany*, trans. Jefferson Chase (New York: Melville House, 2011).

[7] Joachim Wachtel, *As Time Flies By: The History of Lufthansa since 1926*, rev. ed. (Frankfurt am Main: Deutsche Lufthansa AG, 2002), 44–47; Deutsche Lufthansa AG Firmenarchiv, "Lufthansa pioneers paved the way to the Far East," 1959.

zeppelin in 1929 cost almost ¥20,000, or 38,000 Reichsmark (RM).[8] Junior office workers in Japan and Germany earned about ¥70 and 150 RM monthly in the 1930s.[9] Steamships were more common but their prices were still prohibitive. On the day the zeppelin landed near Tokyo, Norddeutscher Lloyd advertised its 55-day service from Yokohama to Hamburg on the "intermediate class" for around ¥500.[10] Germans could travel to Japan and China, "from time immemorial full of mysteries to us Europeans," on the tourist class of Canadian Pacific in 1934 for approximately 770 RM.[11] Hamburg America Line offered a discount fare of roughly 270 RM for passengers' "colored domestic help" in 1939; European servants counted as family members and so were charged full prices.[12] The Trans-Siberian Railway, since reopening for international traffic in 1927, was touted by the Soviet travel agency Intourist as "the shortest, most comfortable and cheapest way between Europe and the Far East" with "considerably reduced fares."[13] Still, intercontinental rail journeys were expensive. An unpadded cot on an eastbound train in 1935 set one back about 370 RM, a padded berth 590 RM, and a bed 630–870 RM, while the westbound third, second, and first classes cost ¥333, ¥600, and ¥877.[14] The higher westbound fares indicate that demand for traffic from Japan to Europe was heavier than vice versa.

Germans and Japanese could connect through words – handwritten, spoken, or printed – but long distances hampered communications too. Sending a postcard from Japan to Germany via the zeppelin cost ¥2.50 and a letter ¥5.00.[15] Regular international mail cost as little as ¥0.20 but moved only as fast and frequently as surface transportation.[16] Telegraph was typically reserved for exigencies, commerce, or government

[8] *Yomiuri shinbun* (hereafter: Y), August 22, 1929.
[9] Obama Toshie, "Shoninkyū shirabe," *Chūō kōron* 45, no. 7 (1930): 295–301; Landesarchiv Berlin A Rep 001–02/1278, Grundvergütung in Jahres- und Monatssätzen für Angestellte im Alter von mehr als 20 Jahren, June 23, 1938.
[10] *The Japan Times and Mail* (hereafter: JTM), August 19, 1929.
[11] *Über Kanada nach Ostasien und Australien: Der neue Expreßdienst mit Riesenschnelldampfern* (Hamburg: Canadian Pacific, 1934), 3, 13–14.
[12] *Überfahrts- und Gepäckbestimmungen: Ostasien, Niederländisch-Indien, Australien* (Hamburg: Hamburg-Amerika-Linie, 1939), 5–6.
[13] Intourist, *Der transsibirische Express ist der kürzeste, bequemste und billigste Weg zwischen Europa und dem fernen Osten* (Moscow: Wneschtorgisdat, 1935), 6–7; JTM, June 24, 1935.
[14] Westbound ticket prices dropped to ¥313, ¥499, and ¥713 in 1937. *The Japan-Manchoukuo Year Book 1937* (Tokyo: The Japan-Manchoukuo Year Book Co., 1937), front leaf.
[15] TA, August 22, 1929.
[16] Shūkan Asahi, ed., *Nedanshi nenpyō: Meiji Taishō Shōwa* (Tokyo: Asahi Shinbunsha, 1988), 26.

business. Technology enabled conversations across continents by 1935, but at a price.[17] To facilitate year-end greetings in 1935 and 1936, the Japanese Communications Ministry cut telephone rates to Europe by half, so the first three minutes of a call to Berlin cost just ¥50.[18] Of course, these stipulations applied only to the privileged few with acquaintances abroad. Those without personal ties had to settle for two-way radio broadcasts, available from late 1933. Audience sizes were limited by radio prices, then about ¥50 in Japan and up to 400 RM in Germany before the Nazi regime introduced the "People's Receiver" starting at 35 RM.[19] Western classical music permeated the programming because few Japanese and even fewer Germans understood each other's language.

Space, time, and money made mass media the primary tool with which Japanese and Germans related to each other. Opinion makers with command of foreign knowledge and the means to propagate their views influenced their countrymen's mutual impressions – the bicycle maker must have been swayed by the Japanese media's portrayals of Hitler. It may seem doubtful that words could paper over the gulf separating the nations, but such leaps of imagination are actually performed rather blithely. The phrase "German-Japanese" visually and conceptually bridges the two with a hyphen. At once convenient and dangerous because of its power to condense distance, the hyphen can summarize transnational bonds (personal, cultural, ideological, commercial, etc.) but also mask difficulties, ambiguities, contradictions, and transformations in interactions. Tokyo and Berlin were so mindful of public words and perceptions that each put itself first in its version of the "Japanese-German/German-Japanese Agreement against the Communist International."

As the bicycle maker's scheme suggests, many Germans and Japanese were already united by their enthusiasm for Hitler before and independently of their governments' compact. Both states had long guarded diplomacy as a prerogative. But conditions in Taisho Japan and Weimar Germany were especially conducive to the proliferation of public rhetoric and imagery that affected popular views of the world and even foreign relations. Political liberalization, cultural experimentation, and technological innovation in the 1920s and early 1930s created an opening for

---

[17] JTM, March 1, 1935.

[18] TA, December 12, 1935; TA, December 16, 1936, evening edition (hereafter: EE).

[19] Morinaga Takurō, *Bukka no bunkashi jiten: Meiji Taishō Shōwa Heisei* (Tokyo: Tenbōsha, 2009), 214; Wolfgang Schneider, ed., *Alltag unter Hitler* (Berlin: Rowohlt, 2000), 78; Jeremy Noakes and Geoffrey Pridham, eds., *Nazism 1919–1945, Volume 2: State, Economy and Society 1933–1939* (Exeter: University of Exeter Press, 2000), 192.

civil society to engage in public affairs. Neither in Germany nor Japan could the authoritarian regime of the 1930s shut that door completely. Official neglect of bilateral ties until the Anti-Comintern Pact left latitude for determined individuals and organizations to advance their foreign-policy agendas, maintain contacts abroad, and conduct foreign relations. Whether in the democratic 1920s or the authoritarian 1930s, access to foreign knowledge and mass media was also a tool for international liaisons.

Opinion makers' discourse and activities in both countries reflected and propagated transnational Nazism. In Japan, the media shifted from appreciating Germany to admiring Hitler and his ideology in the early 1930s as the Nazi movement expanded and attained power. Commentators emerged from previous indifference toward Germany, converted from the political left, or radicalized from the traditional right to promote rapprochement with the Third Reich. Before 1933, journalists across the ideological spectrum already obsessed over a rightist Germany and downplayed Weimar's achievements. From 1933, successive newspapers abandoned misgivings about Nazism to lionize the Führer and gravitate toward Germany's viewpoints. Pamphleteers catering to the masses embraced Nazi populism wholeheartedly, while lecturers speaking to the elites found Nazi anticommunism reassuring. Authors and translators imported German knowledge in all fields. As Nazism gained currency, publishers inaugurated a trend in nonfiction about Nazi deeds and in Hitler biographies. And linguists, already overwhelmingly partial to a conservative Germany, increasingly incorporated Nazi-speak in language textbooks from the mid-1930s. The Japanese media succumbed to Hitler and Nazism's appeal much as the Germans did: a galvanized minority acclaimed the Führer; ever more conservatives and centrists joined the approving chorus; and only diminishing leftist outlets remained hostile. The media celebrated Nazi exploits even if they did not benefit Japan. Thrilled by Nazi attacks on liberal democracy, communism, and capitalism, many pundits missed the rhetoric's racist undertones and only superficially grasped the content of National Socialism. Overt Nazi racism was sporadically criticized, deemed inapplicable to Japan, or simply ignored.

In Germany, transnational Nazism took shape as Japan's elevation to a respectable, nuanced, and visible niche within the Nazi worldview and Nazified public sphere. The media affirmed Japan's status as a great power like Germany throughout the interwar era. But in the last Weimar years, domestic polarization began to fuse with external affairs and politicize attitudes toward East Asia: leftists sympathized with China while rightists sided with Japan. At the Nazi regime's outset, the media replaced a generally apolitical, positive stance toward Japan with ideological partisanship. Formerly fringe voices that heroized Japan and urged collaboration entered the mainstream or semi-officialdom. Before 1933, newspapers of different political leanings covered Japan as a noteworthy nation. From 1933, the Nazi-dominated press cheered Japanese aggression and challenges to the Versailles–Washington system. Interwar German film tended to present a stereotyped vision of Japan. But Third Reich cinema magnified aspects of Japanese culture that aligned with the Nazi glorification of war, martial ethos, and masculinity. Popular and academic nonfiction articulated Japan favorably and described modern traits familiar to Germans. Writers influenced by Nazism selectively highlighted this modernity and old clichés as proof of the two peoples' shared characters and destinies. And voluntary associations founded to foster civil society bonds mutated under Nazi rule into power-hungry organizations lobbying for Japan and themselves. Nazi media outlets demarcated a position for Japan within their weltanschauung by praising its racial purity and admitting its superiority to Germany in certain areas.

Transnational Nazism contributes to several historiographies. The history of German-Japanese convergence deserves and has attracted attention. Ever since the Anti-Comintern Pact, interpreters of the entente have underscored the members' similarity. Contemporary Japanese and German publicists boasted of common values and struggles.[20] Critics branded the two regimes equally cynical and mutually exploitative.[21] The American wartime documentary *Why We Fight* declared of the Axis: "Although these countries are far apart and different in custom and in language, the same poison made them much alike."[22] Postwar trials, memoirs, and opening of records provided sources for diplomatic histories that remain standards today.[23] Written in the totalitarian theory's

---

[20] Erin L. Brightwell, "Refracted Axis: Kitayama Jun'yū and Writing a German Japan," *Japan Forum* 27, no. 4 (2015): 431–453; Danny Orbach, "Japan through SS Eyes: Cultural Dialogue and Instrumentalization of a Wartime Ally," *Yōroppa kenkyū* 7 (2008): 115–132.

[21] Freda Utley, "Germany and Japan," *The Political Quarterly* 8, no. 1 (1937): 51–65; Freda Utley, *Japan's Feet of Clay* (New York: W. W. Norton, 1937).

[22] *Why We Fight: Prelude to War*, dir. Frank Capra, Department of War, 1943; Michaela Hoenicke Moore, *Know Your Enemy: The American Debate on Nazism, 1933–1945* (New York: Cambridge University Press, 2010), 157–159.

[23] F. C. Jones, *Japan's New Order in East Asia: Its Rise and Fall, 1937–45* (London: Oxford University Press, 1954); Frank Iklé, *German-Japanese Relations, 1936–1940* (New York: Bookman Associates, 1956); Ernst L. Presseisen, *Germany and Japan: A Study in Totalitarian Diplomacy, 1933–1941* (The Hague: Martinus Nijhoff, 1958); Theo Sommer, *Deutschland und Japan zwischen den Mächten, 1935–1940: Vom Antikominternpakt zum Dreimächtepakt, eine Studie zur diplomatischen Vorgeschichte des Zweiten Weltkriegs* (Tübingen: J. C. B. Mohr, 1962); Haruki Takeshi, *Sangoku Dōmei*

heyday, several such histories describe the two states' diplomacy as similarly authoritarian. Other scholars, often but not only Marxists, argue that both regimes were fascist.[24] Since social history's rise in the 1960s, the "latecomer" theory identifies Italy, Germany, and Japan as late modernizing, "have-not" upstarts that jointly assaulted the entrenched empires.[25] From the 1970s, neorealists in international relations further reduce differences among nations by treating them as quantitatively defined "like units."[26] After new diplomatic history's emergence in the 1980s, researchers have been examining culture's role in Japanese-German rapprochement through public opinion, ideology, and knowledge transfer.[27]

But narratives that revolve around the diplomatic alliance and attribute it to national commonalities can introduce a hindsight bias and skew our

no hyōka (Tokyo: Aoyama Gakuin Daigaku Hōgakukai, 1964); Johanna Menzel Meskill, *Hitler and Japan: The Hollow Alliance* (New York: Atherton Press, 1966); Miyake Masaki, *Nichi-Doku-I Sangoku Dōmei no kenkyū* (Tokyo: Nansōsha, 1975).

[24] Karl Drechsler, *Deutschland-China-Japan, 1933–1939: Das Dilemma der deutschen Fernostpolitik* ([East] Berlin: Akademie-Verlag, 1964); Xunhou Peng, *China in the World Anti-Fascist War* (Beijing: China Intercontinental Press, 2005).

[25] Barrington Moore Jr., *Social Origins of Dictatorship and Democracy: Lord and Peasant in the Making of the Modern World* (Boston: Beacon Press, 1966); Robert A. Scalapino, *Democracy and the Party Movement in Prewar Japan: The Failure of the First Attempt* (Berkeley: University of California Press, 1953), 396–397; Peter Weber-Schäfer, "Verspätete Demokratie: Parlamentarismus in Japan und Deutschland," in *Japan und Deutschland im 20. Jahrhundert*, eds. Klaus Kracht, Bruno Lewin, and Klaus Müller (Wiesbaden: Harrassowitz, 1984), 137–149; Mark R. Thompson, "Japan's 'German Path' and Pacific Asia's 'Flying Geese,'" *Asian Journal of Social Science* 38, no. 5 (2010): 697–715; Akira Kudō, Nobuo Tajima, and Erich Pauer, eds., *Japan and Germany: Two Latecomers on the World Stage, 1890–1945*, 3 vols. (Folkestone: Global Oriental, 2009). Curiously, the original, Japanese, edition of the last work does not mention "latecomers": see Kudō Akira and Tajima Nobuo, eds., *Nichi-Doku kankeishi 1890–1945*, 3 vols. (Tokyo: Tōkyō Daigaku Shuppankai, 2008).

[26] Kenneth N. Waltz, *Theory of International Politics* (New York: McGraw-Hill, 1979); Randall L. Schweller, *Deadly Imbalances: Tripolarity and Hitler's Strategy of World Conquest* (New York: Columbia University Press, 1998).

[27] Josef Kreiner, ed., *Deutschland-Japan: Historische Kontakte* (Bonn: Bouvier, 1984); Nakano Yoshiyuki, *Doitsujin ga mita Nihon: Doitsujin no Nihonkan keisei ni kansuru shiteki kenkyū* (Tokyo: Sanshūsha, 2005); Christian W. Spang and Rolf-Harald Wippich, eds., *Japanese-German Relations, 1895–1945: War, Diplomacy and Public Opinion* (London: Routledge, 2006); John W. M. Chapman, *Ultranationalism in German-Japanese Relations, 1930–45: From Wenneker to Sasakawa* (Folkestone: Global Oriental, 2011); Nichi-Doku Kōryūshi Henshū Iinkai, ed., *Nichi-Doku kōryū 150-nen no kiseki* (Tokyo: Yūshōdō Shoten, 2013); Qinna Shen and Martin Rosenstock, eds., *Beyond Alterity: German Encounters with Modern East Asia* (New York: Berghahn Books, 2014); Joanne Miyang Cho, Lee Roberts, and Christian W. Spang, eds., *Transnational Encounters between Germany and Japan: Perceptions of Partnership in the Nineteenth and Twentieth Centuries* (New York: Palgrave Macmillan, 2016); Sven Saaler, Akira Kudō, and Nobuo Tajima, eds., *Mutual Perceptions and Images in Japanese-German Relations, 1860–2010* (Leiden: Brill, 2017).

understanding of German-Japanese relations overall. Many works confine their accounts of the entente's origins to the span of the Third Reich's existence.[28] The years between the Anti-Comintern Pact in 1936 and the Tripartite Pact in 1940 enjoy particularly dense coverage.[29] The individuals directly responsible for the Anti-Comintern Pact, Joachim von Ribbentrop and Ōshima Hiroshi, and even those marginally involved, the geopolitics theorist Karl Haushofer and the military intelligence chief Wilhelm Canaris, are topics of books.[30] In contrast, socio-economic studies take a decades-long view beginning in the late nineteenth century, when Germany's impact on Japanese Westernization was palpable and both powers pursued aggressive imperialism. They then skip to the mid-1930s, when talks and moves toward cooperation intensified.[31] Whether seen from the short- or long-term perspective, a narrow topical focus on the strategic partnership enhances an appearance of historical inevitability or teleological determinism on the route to joint Japanese-German world domination.

[28] Gerhard Krebs and Bernd Martin, eds., *Formierung und Fall der Achse Berlin-Tōkyō* (Munich: Iudicium Verlag, 1994); Bill Maltarich, *Samurai and Supermen: National Socialist Views of Japan* (New York: Peter Lang, 2005); Iwamura Masashi, *Senzen Nihonjin no tai Doitsu ishiki* (Tokyo: Keiō Gijuku Daigaku Shuppankai, 2005); Till Philip Koltermann, *Der Untergang des Dritten Reiches im Spiegel der deutsch-japanischen Kulturbegegnung 1933–1945* (Wiesbaden: Harrassowitz, 2009); Hans-Joachim Bieber, *SS und Samurai: Deutsch-japanische Kulturbeziehungen 1933–1945* (Munich: Iudicium, 2014).

[29] Tokushirō Ōhata, "The Anti-Comintern Pact, 1935–1939," in *Deterrent Diplomacy: Japan, Germany, and the USSR 1935–1940*, ed. James William Morley (New York: Columbia University Press, 1976), 1–112; Chihiro Hosoya, "The Tripartite Pact, 1939–1940," in Morley, ed., *Deterrent Diplomacy*, 179–258; John P. Fox, *Germany and the Far Eastern Crisis 1931–1938: A Study in Diplomacy and Ideology* (Oxford: Clarendon Press, 1985); Wolfgang Michalka, "From the Anti-Comintern Pact to the Euro-Asiatic Bloc: Ribbentrop's Alternative Concept of Hitler's Foreign Policy Programme," in *Aspects of the Third Reich*, ed. H. W. Koch (New York: St. Martin's Press, 1985), 267–284; David Stuart Morris and Robert H. Haigh, "Japan, Italy, Germany and the Anti-Comintern Pact," in *Rethinking Japan, Volume II: Social Sciences, Ideology and Thought*, eds. Adriana Boscaro, Franco Gatti, and Massimo Raveri (New York: St. Martin's Press, 1990), 32–42.

[30] Wolfgang Michalka, *Ribbentrop und die deutsche Weltpolitik, 1933–1940: Aussenpolitische Konzeption und Entscheidungsprozesse im Dritten Reich* (Munich: W. Fink, 1980); Carl Boyd, *The Extraordinary Envoy: General Hiroshi Ōshima and Diplomacy in the Third Reich, 1934–1939* (Washington, DC: University Press of America, 1980); Christian W. Spang, *Karl Haushofer und Japan: Die Rezeption seiner geopolitischen Theorien in der deutschen und japanischen Politik* (Munich: Iudicium, 2013); Tajima Nobuo, *Nachizumu Kyokutō senryaku: Nichi-Doku Bōkyō Kyōtei wo meguru chōhōsen* (Tokyo: Kōdansha, 1997).

[31] Bernd Martin, *Japan and Germany in the Modern World* (New York: Berghahn Books, 1995); Miyake Masaki, *Nichi-Doku seiji gaikōshi kenkyū* (Tokyo: Kawade Shobō Shinsha, 1996); Mochida Yukio, ed., *Kindai Nihon to Doitsu: Hikaku to kankei no rekishigaku* (Kyoto: Mineruva Shobō, 2007).

Transnational Nazism builds on but also departs from the extant scholarship. It devotes full attention to the medium-term interactions between Germany and Japan from the end of World War I through the mid-1930s. Because the two governments did not conduct vigorous bilateral diplomacy or exchange voluminous documents then, the period is usually dismissed as uneventful or tangential. The one exception is analysis of the 1927 commerce treaty based on evidence from its archival record.[32] Otherwise, diplomatic and military histories refer only cursorily to the years between the Versailles Treaty and the diplomatic maneuvering that led to the Anti-Comintern Pact. Studies grounded in political-economic structures or the latecomer theory also downplay the 1920s. Interpretations that argue that both states implemented generic fascism or met a "fascist minimum" pay some, but not much more, attention to these years.[33] Weimar and Taisho democracies and internationalisms, however flawed, do not fit well with accounts that highlight long-term authoritarian tendencies. Frank Iklé identified this lacuna in our knowledge in the 1970s:

Weimar diplomacy toward Japan and Japan's interest in Germany in the 1920s are unknown factors ... There is need for research on Japan's interest in a revived Germany and Japan's attitudes towards Hitler's *Machtergreifung* [seizure of power] in 1933. Especially important might be an attempt to see what connections, if any, existed between the rise of Nazi ideology in Germany and nascent militarism in Japan, and to what degree, consciously or otherwise, there was some kind of intellectual cross-fertilization.[34]

Since then, scholars have only partly filled this gap.[35] Moreover, some comparative and analytical frameworks have been overturned in the newer literature. Few studies still call mid-1930s Japanese or German policy making totalitarian. Fascism's historical presence in Japan remains contested. And the latecomer theory's assumption of a model modernization from which Germany and Japan deviated on their own "special

---

[32] Akira Kudō, *Japanese-German Business Relations: Cooperation and Rivalry in the Inter-War Period* (London: Routledge, 1998).

[33] Joseph P. Sottile, "The Fascist Era: Imperial Japan and the Axis Alliance in Historical Perspective," in *Japan in the Fascist Era*, ed. E. Bruce Reynolds (New York: Palgrave Macmillan, 2004), 1–48.

[34] Frank W. Iklé, "Japan's Policies toward Germany," in *Japan's Foreign Policy, 1868–1941: A Research Guide*, ed. James W. Morley (New York: Columbia University Press, 1974), 305–306.

[35] Peter Pantzer, "Deutschland und Japan vom Ersten Weltkrieg bis zum Austritt aus dem Völkerbund (1914–1933)," in Kreiner, ed., *Deutschland-Japan*, 141–160; Josef Kreiner and Regine Mathias, eds., *Deutschland-Japan in der Zwischenkriegszeit* (Bonn: Bouvier, 1990).

paths" has been questioned.[36] If either nation was not totalitarian, fascist, or late-developing, interpretations hinging on these theories must be revised. Certainly, Tokyo and Berlin had overlapping goals. But they do not account for the mutual esteem and solidarity that arose between Germans and Japanese in the 1930s. Similarities in development did not bring Meiji Japan and Imperial Germany together. Just the opposite. The Kaiserreich reversed Japanese expansion through the Triple Intervention in 1895 and Wilhelm II warned Europe of the "Yellow Peril." In World War I, Japan conquered Germany's Asian-Oceanic colonies. Likeness and common interests are not sufficient to explain the rapprochement of Nazi Germany and Showa Japan.

This book argues that a cultural-historical perspective that focuses on the entire interwar era helps make sense of the diplomatic entente. The turn to culture leads the historian to rich, diverse sources created in the relatively liberal, open 1920s and early 1930s. Opinion makers in each country expressed their views in newspapers, pamphlets, lectures, films, books, language textbooks, and interest clubs. These outlets reveal the reciprocal interpretations and ideological adaptations by Japanese and German journalists, speakers, writers, translators, and filmmakers as they encountered information from the other country. *Transnational Nazism* consults these sources to present an ideologically and culturally context-ualized history of German-Japanese convergence rather than a narrative focused on short-term power politics or reliant on generalizations of structural similarity. Essentially, for diplomatic history the Anti-Comintern Pact is the cornerstone of the Axis, but for cultural history it is the keystone capping years of ideological resonance and positive mutual depictions.

The case for transnational Nazism's existence intersects with debates on 1930s Japan's transition from liberalism to authoritarianism. Adven-turism overseas, insurrectionary junior officers, and their suppression by the military establishment subverted parliamentary democracy and pushed Japan rightward even before the onset of full-scale war against China. Researchers concur that from the mid-1930s Japan was militarist. Alfred Vagts's 1937 definition of "militarism" fits Japan: "a domination of the military man over the civilian, an undue preponderance of military demands, an emphasis on military considerations, spirit, ideals, and

---

[36] Bernd Martin, ed., *Japans Weg in die Moderne: Ein Sonderweg nach deutschem Vorbild?* (Frankfurt: Campus Verlag, 1987); Wolfgang Streeck and Kozo Yamamura, *The Origins of Nonliberal Capitalism: Germany and Japan in Comparison* (Ithaca: Cornell University Press, 2001).

scales of value."[37] The Anti-Comintern Pact itself materialized from militarist diplomacy – Major General Ōshima overstepped his authority as military attaché and bypassed regular channels to negotiate with Ribbentrop. Yet scholars disagree about whether Japan ever turned fascist. Guided by Maruyama Masao's thesis of "fascism from above" imposed by the state after it crushed radical officers' "fascism from below," academics trained in Japan generally conclude that Japan, especially in wartime, was fascist.[38] Western opinions vary: specialists on fascism mostly rule against its existence in Japan while Japanologists are divided.[39] The Tokyo–Berlin–Rome Axis and the similarities enumerated to explain it have been cited as causes or effects of Japanese fascism.[40] As the war escalated, the state became more compulsive, expansive, and intrusive, but many Japanese, commoners and apostate Marxists in the "conversion" (tenkō) phenomenon alike, rallied of their own volition around the "national polity" (kokutai).[41] Ascertaining fascism in Japan is difficult because armed conflict erupted in 1931 when Japan conquered Manchuria and triggered repercussions that can be seen as fascist or war-related regimentation and mobilization.

---

[37] Alfred Vagts, *A History of Militarism: Civilian and Military*, rev. ed. (New York: The Free Press, 1967), 14.

[38] Masao Maruyama, *Thought and Behavior in Modern Japanese Politics*, ed. Ivan Morris, expanded ed. (London: Oxford University Press, 1963), 25–83.

[39] John Weiss, *The Fascist Tradition: Radical Right-Wing Extremism in Modern Europe* (New York: Harper & Row, 1967), 130–132; Roger Griffin, *The Nature of Fascism* (New York: Palgrave Macmillan, 1991); Stanley G. Payne, *A History of Fascism, 1914–1945* (Madison: University of Wisconsin Press, 1995), 336; Robert O. Paxton: *The Anatomy of Fascism* (New York: Alfred A. Knopf, 2004), 200; E. Bruce Reynolds, ed., *Japan in the Fascist Era* (New York: Palgrave Macmillan, 2004). For an excellent overview of the debate on fascism in Japan, see: Stephen S. Large, "Oligarchy, Democracy, and Fascism," in *A Companion to Japanese History*, ed. William M. Tsutsui (Malden: Blackwell Publishing, 2007), 156–171.

[40] There is no precise definition of Japan's membership in the Axis, an inexact label. Benito Mussolini first described Italian-German accord as an "Axis" after a secret memorandum in 1936. Berlin and Rome were not treaty-bound until 1937 when Italy acceded to the Anti-Comintern Pact or 1939 at the latest through the Pact of Steel. Japan called itself an Axis power after it joined the Tripartite Pact in 1940. I think "Axis" can be applied broadly to German-Japanese convergence from 1936 just as it is to Italian-German rapprochement. Japan and Germany closed ranks officially, publicly through the Anti-Comintern Pact, which grew to be a Rome–Berlin–Tokyo alliance before the Tripartite Pact.

[41] Yoshiaki Yoshimi, *Grassroots Fascism: The War Experience of the Japanese People*, trans. and ed. Ethan Mark (New York: Columbia University Press, 2015); Patricia G. Steinhoff, *Tenkō: Ideology and Societal Integration in Prewar Japan* (New York: Garland, 1991); Germaine A. Hoston, *Marxism and the Crisis of Development in Prewar Japan* (Princeton: Princeton University Press, 1990); Max Ward, *Thought Crime: Ideology and State Power in Interwar Japan* (Durham: Duke University Press, 2019).

In contrast, Fascist Italy and Nazi Germany spent more time at peace than war and demonstrate what "unadulterated" fascism looks like.[42] Because wartime Japan – without a charismatic leader, mass movement, and comprehensive ideology – differs markedly from the European fascist regimes, scholars who argue that fascism existed in Japan qualify it as "imperial," "bureaucratic," "military," or "restoration" fascism.[43] But any "fascism with Japanese characteristics" seems so sui generis that the label "fascism" loses its synthesizing purpose.

To paraphrase Vagts, I posit that the essence of fascism is a domination of the ideological man over the civilian and even military man.[44] Miles Fletcher, Alan Tansman, Janis Mimura, and Aaron Moore have established that there were such ideological men among intellectuals, writers, and the technocrats who administered Japan's empire.[45] They were Japanese fascists even if they did not necessarily make Japan fascist. *Transnational Nazism* argues that just as there were Japanese fascists, some Japanese became adherents of Hitler and Nazism, though of course Japan did not turn Nazi. Just as Japanese fascists adapted generic fascism or Italian Fascism, Japanese transnational Nazis purposefully tailored Hitler's personality and National Socialism so they shed their native and nativist baggage to resonate in Japan.[46] Without prompting from Germany, Japanese opinion makers sold Hitler and the "Nazi brand" to media consumers.[47] These intermediaries were not powerful enough to make Japan Nazi, but their pro-Nazi discourse and activities laid the cultural groundwork for Tokyo's accord with Berlin. The Anti-Comintern Pact resulted also from transnational Nazi diplomacy – Ōshima, characterized by William Shirer as "more Nazi than the Nazis"

---

[42] Cf. Paul Brooker, *The Faces of Fraternalism: Nazi Germany, Fascist Italy, and Imperial Japan* (New York: Oxford University Press, 1991).

[43] Large, 167; Andrew Gordon, *Labor and Imperial Democracy in Prewar Japan* (Berkeley: University of California Press, 1987); Rikki Kersten, "Japan," in *The Oxford Handbook of Fascism*, ed. R. J. B. Bosworth (New York: Oxford University Press, 2009), 543.

[44] The military remained a source of some resistance in Italy and Germany, unlike in Japan.

[45] William Miles Fletcher, *The Search for a New Order: Intellectuals and Fascism in Prewar Japan* (Chapel Hill: The University of North Carolina Press, 1982); Alan Tansman, *The Aesthetics of Japanese Fascism* (Berkeley: University of California Press, 2009); Janis Mimura, *Planning for Empire: Reform Bureaucrats and the Japanese Wartime State* (Ithaca: Cornell University Press, 2011); Aaron Stephen Moore, *Constructing East Asia: Technology, Ideology, and Empire in Japan's Wartime Era, 1931–1945* (Stanford: Stanford University Press, 2013).

[46] Reto Hofmann, *The Fascist Effect: Japan and Italy, 1915–1952* (Ithaca: Cornell University Press, 2015).

[47] Nicholas O'Shaughnessy, *Selling Hitler: Propaganda and the Nazi Brand* (London: Hurst & Company, 2016).

and nicknamed in Japan "the German ambassador to Germany," was not only a Germanophile but an advocate of the Third Reich.[48]

Transnational Nazism also complicates our understanding of interwar German external affairs and ideology. In light of World War II and the Holocaust, pre-1945 German views and behaviors toward those deemed alien are subjects of a vast literature. The Kaiserreich's imperialism, war, and genocide in Africa, and especially the Third Reich's own in Europe, have drawn the most scrutiny.[49] German interactions with Asia have only recently begun to be discussed concertedly in conferences and publications. Asian-German studies emerged alongside the global turn in the early 2000s to add a dimension to Germany's international history beyond transatlantic ties and imperialism. Suzanne Marchand and others have shown that German orientalism was a distinct variant derived more from imagination and projection than contact or experience.[50] Cultural interest and intellectual study predominated because Germany had limited presence beyond its infiltration in the Near East and short-lived empire in China and Oceania.[51] Todd Kontje observes that German postures toward "the east," stretching from Eastern Europe to the Far East, fluctuated historically between estrangement and identification.[52] Such was the case with India, whose mystery and history elicited broad curiosity in the Kaiserreich and Weimar Republic.[53] The xenophobic

---

[48] William L. Shirer, *The Rise and Fall of the Third Reich: A History of Nazi Germany* (New York: Simon & Schuster, 1990), 872; Hayashi Shigeru, *Nihon no rekishi 25: Taiheiyō Sensō* (Tokyo: Chūō Kōronsha, 1967), 119.

[49] Shelley Baranowski, *Nazi Empire: German Colonialism and Imperialism from Bismarck to Hitler* (Cambridge: Cambridge University Press, 2010).

[50] Suzanne L. Marchand, *German Orientalism in the Age of Empire: Religion, Race, and Scholarship* (New York: Cambridge University Press, 2009); Lee M. Roberts, ed., *Germany and the Imagined East* (Newcastle upon Tyne: Cambridge Scholars Publishing, 2009); Veronika Fuechtner and Mary Rhiel, eds., *Imagining Germany Imagining Asia: Essays in Asian-German Studies* (Rochester: Camden House, 2013).

[51] Malte Fuhrmann, *Der Traum vom deutschen Orient: Zwei deutsche Kolonien im Osmanischen Reich 1851–1918* (Frankfurt am Main: Campus Verlag, 2006); Peter H. Christensen, *Germany and the Ottoman Railways: Art, Empire, and Infrastructure* (New Haven: Yale University Press, 2017); George Steinmetz, *The Devil's Handwriting: Precoloniality and the German Colonial State in Qingdao, Samoa, and Southwest Africa* (Chicago: University of Chicago Press, 2007); Nina Berman, Klaus Mühlhahn, and Patrice Nganang, eds., *German Colonialism Revisited: African, Asian, and Oceanic Experiences* (Ann Arbor: University of Michigan Press, 2014); Joanne Miyang Cho and Douglas T. McGetchin, eds., *Gendered Encounters between Germany and Asia: Transnational Perspectives since 1800* (New York: Palgrave Macmillan, 2017).

[52] Todd Kontje, *German Orientalisms* (Ann Arbor: University of Michigan Press, 2004).

[53] Douglas T. McGetchin, *Indology, Indomania, and Orientalism: Ancient India's Rebirth in Modern Germany* (Madison: Fairleigh Dickinson University Press, 2009); Perry Myers, *German Visions of India, 1871–1918: Commandeering the Holy Ganges during the Kaiserreich* (New York: Palgrave Macmillan, 2013); Joanne Miyang Cho, Eric Kurlander, and Douglas T. McGetchin, eds., *Transcultural Encounters between Germany and India:*

Third Reich continued this fascination but subsumed it under occultism and Aryanism.[54] Such was also the case with Japan, which through its breathtaking rise impressed Germany alternately as the Yellow Peril or "Prussians of the East."[55] The racist Nazi regime even invented the extraordinary label "honorary Aryan" for Japan and treated it as a counterparty, though not quite a counterpart.

Transnational Nazism expands these insights on German orientalism. It argues that Nazism's complex conceptualization of Japan prepared the cultural and ideological groundwork for bilateral convergence. I have been particularly inspired by Kris Manjapra's work on German-Indian intellectual entanglements in response to British hegemony and by Andrew Zimmerman's on German cooperation with African American experts on an imperialist venture.[56] Transnational Nazism resembled but also exceeded the traditional German engagement with Asia. German opinion makers and "Nazis of the East" jointly imagined a community for the Nazi project of German-Japanese collaboration. Nazi racist arrogance was tempered by admiration for and envy of Japanese homogeneity, because there can be no racial hierarchy without racial purity.[57] Unlike other "undesirables," the Japanese did not seek integration into and so did not threaten the "national community" (*Volksgemeinschaft*). Nazi commentators recognized Japanese Westernization both for its progress and essence as confirmation of Western leadership. They replaced some stereotypes of Japan such as geisha, beauty, and refinement with others such as samurai, physical fitness, and fighting spirit for ideology's sake. What under Weimar had been outlandish foreign policy

Kindred Spirits in the Nineteenth and Twentieth Centuries (New York: Routledge, 2014); Vishwa Adluri and Joydeep Bagchee, *The Nay Science: A History of German Indology* (New York: Oxford University Press, 2014); Elija Horn, *Indien als Erzieher: Orientalismus in der deutschen Reformpädagogik und Jugendbewegung 1918–1933* (Bad Heilbrunn: Verlag Julius Klinkhardt, 2018).

[54] Stefan Arvidsson, *Aryan Idols: Indo-European Mythology as Ideology and Science*, trans. Sonia Wichmann (Chicago: University of Chicago Press, 2006); Wolfgang Kaufmann, *Das Dritte Reich und Tibet: Die Heimat des "östlichen Hakenkreuzes" im Blickfeld der Nationalsozialisten* (Ludwigsfelde: Ludwigsfelder Verlagshaus, 2009); Eric Kurlander, *Hitler's Monsters: A Supernatural History of the Third Reich* (New Haven: Yale University Press, 2017).

[55] Sepp Linhart, *"Dainty Japanese" or Yellow Peril? Western War Postcards 1900–1945* (Vienna: LIT Verlag, 2005); Sarah Jordan Panzer, "The Prussians of the East: Samurai, Bushido, and Japanese Honor in the German Imagination, 1905–1945" (PhD diss., University of Chicago, 2015).

[56] Kris Manjapra, *Age of Entanglement: German and Indian Intellectuals across Empire* (Cambridge: Harvard University Press, 2014); Andrew Zimmerman, *Alabama in Africa: Booker T. Washington, the German Empire, and the Globalization of the New South* (Princeton: Princeton University Press, 2010).

[57] Roger Eatwell, *Fascism: A History* (New York: Viking Penguin, 1996), 180–181.

thinking was implemented by Nazism. Contrary to realist interpretations of Nazi diplomacy, I stress that the entente with Japan was ideologically driven and consistent, not pragmatic. Germany did not merely grant Japan practical concessions, which all Axis powers received. Rather, and significantly, the "racial state" created a niche for Japan – perhaps only Japan – in its worldview.[58] To be sure, Japan was not always depicted positively or as Germany's equal. But it only needed to be perceived as good enough to be a collaborator. Few, if any, other Axis states occupied a comparable position in Nazi ideology. The minor members were an afterthought. Hitler's affection for one Italian – Mussolini – but not the Italians, dictated Germany's attitudes toward Italy.[59] In contrast, Hitler did not know any Japanese leaders but thought well of the Japanese collectively.

Transnational Nazism was a nationalistic reaction to existential concerns. Japanese transnational Nazis believed approaching, though not necessarily emulating, Hitler's Germany would deliver Japan from its predicament. German transnational Nazis fancied engaging but not mingling with racially pure Japan. My depiction of transnational Nazism as an "imagined community" invokes Benedict Anderson's thesis on nationalism.[60] Germans and Japanese did not jointly build a nation, but factors essential for nationalism identified by Anderson facilitated their transnational solidarity. Print capitalism empowered opinion makers in presses and publishers, amplified by radio stations, lecture circuits, film studios, and interest clubs, to share and spread ideas across continents.[61] Transnational Nazis admired one leader – Hitler, adhered to one "political religion" – National Socialism, and adopted one imagery and vocabulary – Nazi symbols and Nazified German.[62] Global history's rise in the early 2000s has caused nationalism to be examined in

---

[58] Michael Burleigh and Wolfgang Wippermann, *The Racial State: Germany 1933–1945* (Cambridge: Cambridge University Press, 1991); Devin O. Pendas, Mark Roseman, and Richard F. Wetzell, *Beyond the Racial State: Rethinking Nazi Germany* (New York: Cambridge University Press, 2017).

[59] F. W. Deakin, *The Brutal Friendship: Mussolini, Hitler, and the Fall of Italian Fascism* (New York: Harper & Row, 1962); Elizabeth Wiskemann, *The Rome-Berlin Axis: A Study of the Relations between Hitler and Mussolini* (London: Collins, 1966).

[60] Benedict R. Anderson, *Imagined Communities: Reflections on the Origin and Spread of Nationalism*, rev. ed. (New York: Verso, 1991); Max Bergholz, "Thinking the Nation: Imagined Communities: Reflections on the Origin and Spread of Nationalism, by Benedict Anderson," *The American Historical Review* 123, no. 2 (April 2018): 518–528.

[61] Cf. Nicholas O'Shaughnessy, *Marketing the Third Reich: Persuasion, Packaging and Propaganda* (New York: Routledge, 2018).

[62] Michael Burleigh, *The Third Reich: A New History* (New York: Hill and Wang, 2000).

international contexts.[63] The inherent tension can be challenging but also generate exciting results, including John Fousek's "nationalist globalism" and Jens-Uwe Guettel's "imperial liberalism."[64] Transnational Nazism describes a similarly tension-filled, paradoxical phenomenon; I use "transnational" to capture Nazism's mobility, direction, and fluidity.[65] International movements are usually associated with the political left, such as struggle for liberation, world peace, or communism.[66] But as Manjapra, Zimmerman, Fousek, Guettel, and others demonstrate, transnational engagements are not inevitably progressive or cosmopolitan.[67] Fascism also travels, through universal fascism or imitative regimes.[68] Nazism, with its dogmatic anti-Semitism, German chauvinism, and adoration of Hitler, may seem too peculiar to resonate outside German circles. But the Nazification of some Japanese proves that its tenets crossed borders and adapted to local habitats.[69] *Transnational Nazism*

---

[63] Glenda Sluga, *Internationalism in the Age of Nationalism* (Philadelphia: University of Pennsylvania Press, 2013); Sebastian Conrad, *What Is Global History?* (Princeton: Princeton University Press, 2016), 79–89.

[64] Akira Iriye, *Global and Transnational History: The Past, Present, and Future* (London: Palgrave Macmillan, 2013), 15–16; John Fousek, *To Lead the Free World: American Nationalism and the Cultural Roots of the Cold War* (Chapel Hill: The University of North Carolina Press, 2000); Jens-Uwe Guettel, *German Expansionism, Imperial Liberalism, and the United States, 1776–1945* (New York: Cambridge University Press, 2012).

[65] Dominic Sachsenmaier, *Global Perspectives on Global History: Theories and Approaches in a Connected World* (New York: Cambridge University Press, 2011), 76; Diego Olstein, *Thinking History Globally* (New York: Palgrave Macmillan, 2015), 16–18; Conrad, 44–48.

[66] Michael Seidman, *Transatlantic Antifascisms: From the Spanish Civil War to the End of World War II* (New York: Cambridge University Press, 2018).

[67] Paul A. Kramer, "Power and Connection: Imperial Histories of the United States in the World," *The American Historical Review* 116, no. 5 (December 2011), 1348–1391; Martin Durham and Margaret Power, eds., *New Perspectives on the Transnational Right* (New York: Palgrave Macmillan, 2010); Daniel Brückenhaus, *Policing Transnational Protest: Liberal Imperialism and the Surveillance of Anticolonialists in Europe, 1905–1945* (New York: Oxford University Press, 2017); Graham Macklin and Fabian Virchow, eds., *Transnational Extreme Right Networks* (New York: Routledge, 2018).

[68] Federico Finchelstein, *Transatlantic Fascism: Ideology, Violence, and the Sacred in Argentina and Italy, 1919–1945* (Durham: Duke University Press, 2010); *Fascism: Journal of Comparative Fascist Studies* 2, no. 2 (2013); Madeleine Herren, "Fascist Internationalism," in *Internationalisms: A Twentieth-Century History*, eds. Glenda Sluga and Patricia Clavin (Cambridge: Cambridge University Press, 2017), 191–212; Arnd Bauerkämper and Grzegorz Rossoliński-Liebe, eds., *Fascism without Borders: Transnational Connections and Cooperation between Movements and Regimes in Europe from 1918 to 1945* (New York: Berghahn Books, 2017).

[69] Cf. Maria Framke, *Delhi -Rom -Berlin: Die indische Wahrnehmung von Faschismus und Nationalsozialismus 1922–1939* (Darmstadt: Wissenschaftliche Buchgesellschaft, 2012); Benjamin Zachariah, "A Voluntary Gleichschaltung? Perspectives from India towards a Non-Eurocentric Understanding of Fascism," *Transcultural Studies* 5, no. 2 (2014): 63–100; Sandrine Kott and Kiran Klaus Patel, eds., *Nazism Across Borders: The Social Policies of the Third Reich and Their Global Appeal* (Oxford: Oxford University Press, 2019).

sheds light on how extremism can mutate, migrate, disperse, and endure. It offers an "asymmetrical comparison": German ideas influenced more recipients in Japan than Japanese ideas in Germany, and German Nazis determined who would be incorporated in their weltanschauung.[70] It is a study of foreign relations but not of diplomacy – political, cultural, or public – that is coordinated and executed by the state.[71] Although it is incontrovertible that in theory perception affects behavior in international relations, attributing any act to an impression is much less straightforward.[72] Hitler's belief in Jewish hostility toward Japan and praise for Japan's imperial system do not conclusively explain the Axis.[73] Cultural history does not aim to pinpoint the cause of a specific event but to situate it within a milieu, as Akira Iriye does for Japan–US relations and John Dower for the Pacific War.[74]

Transnational Nazism contextualizes the interwar German-Japanese entente by reconstructing the cultural traffic and ideological projection between citizens that preceded the diplomatic compacts.[75] Its narrative begins in 1919, with the emergence of a new Japan and new Germany, and ends in 1936, when the Anti-Comintern Pact formalized bilateral convergence as policy and reduced the latitude of civil society therein.[76] German and Japanese intermediaries deployed specialist knowledge not

---

[70] Jürgen Kocka, "Asymmetrical Historical Comparison: The Case of the German *Sonderweg*," *History and Theory* 38, no. 1 (February 1999): 40–50.

[71] "Diplomacy" can refer strictly to engagements between national governments and "foreign relations" broadly to interactions between governments, civil societies, economies, and individuals. Some activities of the opinion makers, especially influential Nazis in party publications or organizations, may qualify as "Track Two diplomacy," defined loosely as non-state actors' involvement in international relations and negotiations, distinct from Track One or official diplomacy. Peter Jones, *Track Two Diplomacy in Theory and Practice* (Stanford: Stanford University Press, 2015).

[72] Richard Ned Lebow, *A Cultural Theory of International Relations* (New York: Cambridge University Press, 2010); Robert Jervis, *Perception and Misperception in International Politics*, new ed. (Princeton: Princeton University Press, 2017); Robert Jervis, *How Statesmen Think: The Psychology of International Politics* (Princeton: Princeton University Press, 2017).

[73] Adolf Hitler, *Mein Kampf* (Munich: Franz Eher Nachf., 1927), 723–724; Adolf Hitler, *Monologe im Führerhauptquartier 1941–1944*, ed. Werner Jochmann (Munich: Orbis Verlag, 2000), 174 (January 3–4, 1942).

[74] Akira Iriye, *Power and Culture: The Japanese-American War, 1941–1945* (Cambridge: Harvard University Press, 1981); John W. Dower, *War without Mercy: Race and Power in the Pacific War* (New York: Pantheon Books, 1986).

[75] Angela M. Crack, *Global Communication and Transnational Public Spheres* (New York: Palgrave Macmillan, 2008); John M. Owen IV, *The Clash of Ideas in World Politics: Transnational Networks, States, and Regime Change, 1510–2010* (Princeton: Princeton University Press, 2010).

[76] Frederick R. Dickinson, *World War I and the Triumph of a New Japan, 1919–1930* (New York: Cambridge University Press, 2013).

to subjugate but to elevate and accommodate each other. They used diminishing Weimar and Taisho freedoms of expression and association to advocate illiberal ideas such as Nazism and aggression. The revelation that civil society under authoritarianism conducted its own foreign relations illuminates how individuals and groups exerted unofficial influence within and between states.[77]

This book is one of very few monographs on Japanese-German relations that pays balanced attention to both nations. Because of the nature of the subject, most works favor German or Japanese sources, or are edited volumes by multiple authors discussing different aspects of each country. The resulting knowledge landscape is fragmented and uneven, obscures linkages, and hinders comparisons. *Transnational Nazism* uses primary sources from diverse segments of the Japanese and German media. It is divided into two substantive halves: the first examines Germany through Japanese eyes, the second Japan through German ones. Chapters One to Four analyze the portrayals of Germany in Japanese newspapers, lectures and pamphlets, nonfiction and translations, and language textbooks. Chapters Five to Eight study the depictions of Japan in German dailies, films, nonfiction, and interest and advocacy groups. The survey of the media is broad but not exhaustive. The main missing component is periodicals such as *Chūō kōron*, *Kaizō*, *Simplicissimus*, or *Kladderadatsch*. I have replaced them with Japanese lectures and pamphlets and German films because these sources are less frequently consulted. Moreover, contributors to journals also wrote newspaper articles and books so that their viewpoints are expressed through these venues.[78] The chapters treat outlets that are highly comparable in some cases (newspapers and nonfiction) but less so in others (language textbooks, cinema, associations). They cover media formats of various qualities and with different customer bases. Together they demonstrate the ubiquity and influence of relatively few opinion makers who molded intercultural perceptions through prolific, skillful production of words.

---

[77] Davide Rodogno, Bernhard Struck, and Jakob Vogel, eds., *Shaping the Transnational Sphere: Experts, Networks and Issues from the 1840s to the 1930s* (New York: Berghahn Books, 2014).

[78] Miyake Masaki, "Hitorā seiken no shōaku to Nihon no rondan—zasshi *Kaizō* to *Chūō kōron* wo chūshin to suru kōsatsu," in *Berurin Wīn Tōkyō: 20-seiki zenhan no Chūō to Higashi Ajia*, ed. Miyake Masaki (Tokyo: Ronsōsha, 1999), 191–249. The inclusion of German films introduces a group of opinion makers with a wide-reaching platform who are rarely examined for their influence in foreign relations.

German-Japanese Relations, 1914–1945

Indeed, because of the distance between Japan and Germany, words rather than people or objects were the main instrument for interaction and exchange from just before World War I to the end of World War II. On the eve of the former, the two states maintained formal, correct ties; improving relations was not a priority in their foreign-policy establishments. Germany was far more obsessed with its security in Europe and "place in the sun" overseas. Japan acted in self-interest by maximizing its diplomatic flexibility without violating the Anglo-Japanese Alliance. Tokyo did not depend on any one foreign supplier for arms, and some in its military and bureaucracy entertained the idea of coming to terms with Germany in the early 1910s.[79] Outside government, the two populations treated each other with appreciation rather than partiality. Many Japanese studied in Germany, but more went to America. German expatriates in Japan were always outnumbered by English-speaking ones.[80] Germany's constitution, army, and universities served as models for Meiji Japan, but America, Britain, and France influenced Japan's agriculture, industry, banking, commerce, navy, and public administration.[81] For Japan, Germany was just one among several Western competitors. Germany, to the extent it thought of Japan at all, saw it as part of the "Far East."

Tokyo declared war on Berlin in August 1914, soon after war broke out in Europe. Japan expelled and expropriated most resident Germans. It captured many of Germany's Asian-Oceanic possessions with little bloodshed. German prisoners of war were interned in Japan and treated humanely.[82] Germany unsuccessfully explored a separate peace with

[79] Frederick R. Dickinson, *War and National Reinvention: Japan in the Great War, 1914–1919* (Cambridge: Harvard University Press, 1999), 45.

[80] Naikaku Tōkeikyoku, ed., *Nihon Teikoku tōkei nenkan* (Tokyo: Tōkyō Tōkei Kyōkai, 1919–1937). In the interwar era, the number of Japanese in Germany seldom exceeded 1,000, while more than 100,000 Japanese nationals were in America, many as emigrants. The German community in Japan never reached 2,000 and was smaller than the British or the American one.

[81] James R. Bartholomew, *The Formation of Science in Japan: Building a Research Tradition* (New Haven: Yale University Press, 1989); Gerhard Krebs, ed., *Japan und Preußen* (Munich: Iudicium Verlag, 2002); Karl Anton Sprengard, Kenchi Ono, and Yasuo Ariizumi, eds., *Deutschland und Japan im 20. Jahrhundert: Wechselbeziehungen zweier Kulturnationen* (Wiesbaden: Harrassowitz, 2002); Morris Low, ed., *Building a Modern Japan: Science, Technology, and Medicine in the Meiji Era and Beyond* (New York: Palgrave Macmillan, 2005).

[82] Narashino-shi Kyōiku Iinkai, ed., *Doitsu heishi no mita Nippon: Narashino Furyo Shūyōjo 1915–1920* (Tokyo: Maruzen, 2001); Tomita Hiroshi, *Bandō Furyo Shūyōjo: Nichi-Doku Sensō to zainichi Doitsu furyo* (Tokyo: Hōsei Daigaku Shuppankyoku, 2006); Mahon

Japan in 1915 and 1916.[83] Then in 1917, Germany, desperate to resume unrestricted submarine warfare in the Atlantic despite American warnings, proposed in the Zimmermann Telegram an alliance with Mexico to deter America from entering the war. The scheme further called for inviting Japan to the anti-American partnership. What negligible chance of the plot succeeding vanished when British Intelligence decoded and published the note.

Japan's contribution to Allied victory earned it a seat at the negotiations of the Versailles Treaty in 1919. Japan received some German warships as spoils and a tiny portion of reparations. Japanese control of the Marshall, Mariana, and Caroline Islands was legally confirmed as mandates of the League of Nations. Germany's concessions in China were transferred to Japan, even though China had expected their abolishment upon joining the Allies in 1917. China thus refused to sign the treaty and instead ended hostilities with Germany separately.

Berlin and Tokyo ratified the treaty and restored official ties in 1920. Germany treated Japan as a great power by reopening its embassy in Tokyo – one of Germany's nine embassies and its only one outside the West.[84] But meaningful relations took much longer to repair. Cooperation came about coincidentally, as when Japanese troops in Siberia and German Freikorps militiamen in Eastern Europe fought the Red Army during the Russian Civil War. Otherwise, the two states had divergent foreign-policy objectives. The Weimar Republic spent its diplomatic capital on rehabilitating and reintegrating Germany in the world. Reconciling distant Japan was at best an afterthought. And it found a likeminded partner, China, which also resented the postwar settlement.[85] China and Germany, both cash-strapped, developed symbiotic barter arrangements. Germany's loss of colonies gave its merchants and military advisers in China a political and moral advantage over Western and Japanese competitors. Meanwhile, Japan channeled its diplomatic energy into multilateral instruments such as the League of Nations and

Murphy, *Colonial Captivity during the First World War: Internment and the Fall of the German Empire, 1914–1919* (New York: Cambridge University Press, 2018), 169–179.

[83] Frank W. Iklé, "Japanese-German Peace Negotiations during World War I," *The American Historical Review* 71, no. 1 (October 1965): 62–76.

[84] Christoph M. Kimmich, *German Foreign Policy, 1918–1945: A Guide to Current Research and Resources*, 3rd ed. (Lanham: Scarecrow Press, 2013), 7.

[85] Donald S. Sutton, "German Advice and Residual Warlordism in the Nanking Decade: Influences on Nationalist Military Training and Strategy," *China Quarterly* 91 (September 1982): 386–410; William C. Kirby, *Germany and Republican China* (Stanford: Stanford University Press, 1984).

Washington Treaties, and managing the delicate relations with America and China.[86] Japanese-German traffic was so neglected that Berlin and Tokyo took until 1927 to conclude a new commerce and navigation treaty to replace the one nullified by war in 1914.[87]

Civil society assumed responsibility for nurturing bilateral ties in this vacuum of official attention. Japanese academics and traders were already returning to Germany to resume studies or commerce in 1919.[88] In Japan, many released German internees reestablished their previous positions in academia and business. The German Embassy advised the Foreign Office in 1922 that "as we mean little to Japan politically and even our trade with Japan is threatened, it is especially necessary that we do everything to retain our trump card, the respect and love for German culture and science, and to look after the cultural bond."[89] It pointed out that of the 425 students abroad sponsored by the Japanese Education Ministry, 130 were in Germany, 55 in America, 80 in Britain, and 58 in France. Although few Germans visited Japan, luminaries who did, such as the Nobel laureates Albert Einstein in 1922 and Fritz Haber in 1924, were received enthusiastically and spoke highly of Japan upon their return.[90] Haber became an especially vocal, active advocate of German cooperation with Japan.[91] Even Ambassador Wilhelm Solf invested much of his time in Japan from 1920 to 1928 in intercultural endeavors rather than diplomacy.[92] Several binational voluntary associations were founded in both countries with Solf's participation or endorsement. Additionally, the 1920s saw the popularization of international tourism for the affluent, facilitated by the Trans-Siberian Railway's reopening and excess capacities on ocean liners

---

[86] Ian Hill Nish, *Japanese Foreign Policy in the Interwar Period* (Westport: Praeger Publishers, 2002); Thomas W. Burkman, *Japan and the League of Nations: Empire and World Order, 1914–1938* (Honolulu: University of Hawai'i Press, 2008).

[87] Erich Pauer, "Die wirtschaftlichen Beziehungen zwischen Japan und Deutschland 1900–1945," in Kreiner, ed., *Deutschland-Japan*, 161–210.

[88] Wada Hirofumi et al., *Gengo toshi Berurin 1861–1945* (Tokyo: Fujiwara Shoten, 2006), 7–34.

[89] Politisches Archiv des Auswärtigen Amts (hereafter: PA AA), R 85846, Martin Renner to Foreign Office, August 11, 1922.

[90] Ippei Okamoto, "Albert Einstein in Japan: 1922," trans. Kenkichiro Koizumi, *American Journal of Physics* 49, no. 10 (October 1981): 930–940; Albert Einstein, *The Travel Diaries of Albert Einstein: The Far East, Palestine, and Spain, 1922–1923*, ed. Ze'ev Rosenkranz (Princeton: Princeton University Press, 2018).

[91] Hideko Tamaru Oyama, "Setsuro Tamaru and Fritz Haber: Links between Japan and Germany in Science and Technology," *The Chemical Record* 15, no. 2 (April 2015): 535–549.

[92] Eberhard von Vietsch, *Wilhelm Solf: Botschafter zwischen den Zeiten* (Tübingen: Wunderlich Verlag, 1961); Peter J. Hempenstall and Paula Tanaka Mochida, *The Lost Man: Wilhelm Solf in German History* (Wiesbaden: Harrassowitz, 2005).

made available by the end of mass immigration to America.[93] Technology seemed poised to revolutionize intercontinental traffic when the airship *Graf Zeppelin* flew nonstop from Germany to Japan in 1929.

The outbreak of the world economic crisis the same year marked a turning point in Japanese-German relations. The Versailles–Washington system in which Berlin and Tokyo had sought to operate started to collapse. Most crippling for Germany was the withdrawal of foreign capital, and for Japan the erection of trade barriers. Squabbling politicians seemed incapable of meeting these existential challenges. So radical individuals and ideologies gained a wider following and resonated across borders. Hitler and Nazism's ascent caught the imagination of ever more Japanese observers. They propagated Nazi ideology through the media and called for closer relations with Germany from the early 1930s. In Germany, Hitler's rise gave an opening to loyally Nazi but amateurish diplomats, self-styled foreign-policy experts, or geopolitics theorists who admired Japan, in contradiction to the practice of cultivating China.

Despite the more favorable conditions, rapprochement did not come early or easily. In one of its last diplomatic acts, the Weimar Republic contributed to a League of Nations commission in 1932 investigating Japan's seizure of Manchuria. The critical Lytton Report caused Japan to storm out of the league the next year.[94] Though Hitler became chancellor in 1933, conservatives who maintained the arrangements with China largely continued to run the Foreign Office and War Ministry. And Hitler very much preferred an alliance with Britain to one with Japan. Only after an accord with London no longer seemed imminent did he authorize Joachim von Ribbentrop in 1935 to bypass the Foreign Office and approach Tokyo in earnest. The Japanese Foreign Ministry likewise had reservations about international reactions to a settlement with the Third Reich, pushed ardently by Japanese transnational Nazis such as Ōshima Hiroshi and many opinion makers. But Japan had left itself few diplomatic options by the mid-1930s. Its incursions into China from 1931, withdrawal from the league in 1933, and abrogation of the London and Washington Naval Treaties in 1934 alienated the liberal democratic West. Its internal suppression of communists and aggressive stance in Manchuria antagonized the Soviet Union.[95] And civilian rule had been undermined through political violence by radical officers.

---

[93] Lorraine Coons and Alexander Varias, *Tourist Third Cabin: Steamship Travel in the Interwar Years* (New York: Palgrave Macmillan, 2003).

[94] Jessamyn R. Abel, *The International Minimum: Creativity and Contradiction in Japan's Global Engagement, 1933–1964* (Honolulu: University of Hawai'i Press, 2015), 25–53.

[95] Tajima Nobuo, *Nihon Rikugun no taiso bōryaku: Nichi-Doku Bōkyō Kyōtei to Yūrashia seisaku* (Tokyo: Yoshikawa Kōbunkan, 2017).

These factors combined to enable the two regimes to finally converge in the Anti-Comintern Pact in 1936.

The agreement, ostensibly a high point in bilateral ties, in fact manifests uneasiness in Japanese-German diplomacy. It was not an exclusive partnership. Italy acceded in 1937. Britain, Poland, and China, too, were invited to join the front. Because neither Berlin nor Tokyo was prepared to confront Moscow explicitly, the Comintern was settled on as a proxy boogeyman – never mind that the suppression of communists in both countries had rendered "anti-Comintern" hollow. The pact was thus a vague commitment they could agree on while risking upsetting the fewest number of nations. Japan still hoped to negotiate with the Soviet Union over Pacific fisheries. Some Germans kept fantasizing about recruiting Britain into the alliance. Even after Japan launched all-out war against China in 1937, Germany still attempted to maintain its pragmatic affair with China while staying politically married to Japan. Oskar Trautmann, the ambassador to China, strained to balance Germany between the belligerents until his recall by the Nazified Foreign Office in 1938.[96] For both Japan and Germany, prioritizing their ideological partnership incurred negative practical consequences.

The pact encouraged pundits who had agitated for closer cooperation and now churned out more self-fulfilling prophesies explaining and predicting German-Japanese solidarity. Propagandistic pronouncements, high-profile visits, and official exchanges followed. On the accord's second anniversary in 1938, Japan and Germany signed a compact to facilitate cultural interactions. It coincided with the technological feat of a German aircraft flying to Japan in 46 hours with only three refueling stops. But it crash-landed in the Philippines on its return leg.

German actions before the outbreak of World War II in Europe in 1939 nearly ruptured bilateral relations. Germany did not inform Japan of its determination to attack Poland despite British and French warnings. In violation of a secret protocol of the Anti-Comintern Pact, Berlin concluded a nonaggression pact with Moscow in August 1939, just when Japanese soldiers were dying in a disastrous clash with the Red Army on the Mongolian-Manchurian border.[97] Germany's about-face, along with the Kwantung Army's defeat, undercut the pro-German faction in the Japanese government and military, altered Japan's diplomatic stance

[96] Gerhard L. Weinberg, *Hitler's Foreign Policy 1933–1939: The Road to World War II* (New York: Enigma Books, 2010), 263–270.

[97] Gerhard L. Weinberg, "Die geheimen Abkommen zum Antikominternpakt," *Vierteljahrshefte für Zeitgeschichte* 2 (1954): 193–201.

toward the Soviet Union, and conceivably made Western possessions in Southeast Asia more attractive targets.[98]

The tide of war in Europe ultimately kept Japanese-German partnership afloat. Germany had defeated the Netherlands and France by late 1940, and seemed on the verge of invading Britain. Japan saw an urgent opportunity to seize their "orphaned" colonies in Southeast Asia, possibly before their eventual annexation by a new, much-expanded German empire.[99] It browbeat Vichy France into accepting Japanese occupation of northern Indochina in September. The same month, Italy, Germany, and Japan forged the Tripartite Pact, a defensive treaty for mutual military assistance. Tokyo, taking a cue from Berlin, also signed a non-aggression pact with Moscow in April 1941 to secure its continental frontiers.

Yet two months later, Germany attacked the Soviet Union, having again kept its plans hidden from Japan and Italy. The Tripartite Pact did not dictate that Japan join an offensive war, so Japan remained neutral, having resolved to expand southward. Most damaging for Japanese-German traffic, the invasion severed the last unobstructed artery, the Trans-Siberian Railway. The railroad had been shuttling personnel and goods between the ends of the Axis, but from June 1941 both parties had to count on blockade runners. The seas were made even more inhospitable in December when Japan returned Germany's favor and attacked Pearl Harbor and Western colonies in Asia without forewarning. The Tripartite Pact did not mandate that Germany open hostilities, but Hitler had assured Japan of his support in a hypothetical war against America.[100] Berlin and Rome declared war on Washington four days after Pearl Harbor, and the three main Axis powers pledged not to seek a separate peace. In January 1942, they at last signed a convention to formally coordinate military operations.

---

[98] Chihiro Hosoya, "The Japanese-Soviet Neutrality Pact," in *The Fateful Choice: Japan's Advance into Southeast Asia, 1939–1941*, ed. James William Morley (New York: Columbia University Press, 1980), 13–114; Alvin D. Coox, *Nomonhan: Japan against Russia, 1939* (Stanford: Stanford University Press, 1985), 1078; Stuart D. Goldman, *Nomonhan, 1939: The Red Army's Victory That Shaped World War II* (Annapolis: Naval Institute Press, 2012).

[99] Jeremy A. Yellen, "Into the Tiger's Den: Japan and the Tripartite Pact, 1940," *Journal of Contemporary History* 51, no. 3 (2016): 555–576.

[100] As late as a month before Pearl Harbor, doubts were raised at an imperial conference about Germany's trustworthiness should Japan attack America – specifically, whether Germany would honor its "paper agreements" with Japan or side with the white race. Nobutaka Ike, *Japan's Decision for War: Records of the 1941 Policy Conferences* (Stanford: Stanford University Press, 1967), 237.

But the agreements had no discernible impact.[101] The Axis members devoted almost all their resources to what Mussolini called "parallel wars" for the duration of the conflict. Japan diligently observed neutrality vis-à-vis the Soviet Union and watched as shiploads of American matériel flowed to Vladivostok, to be hurled at German forces on the Eastern Front. Germany fought America in the Atlantic largely to destroy supplies for Britain and the Soviet Union. It sent some merchant raiders and submarines to the Indian Ocean with Japanese consent, but they were not there to help the Japanese war effort, only to cut off shipments bound for Britain.[102] Not until January 1943 did Germany and Japan conclude an economic arrangement to organize trafficking technology and materials, long after regular contact had become all but impossible to uphold.

The compacts from 1936 to 1943, one annually except 1939, in fact show that the two regimes were struggling to accept that words – pacts, speeches, and propaganda – could not shrink the distance between them.[103] Transportation on land was ruled out; grand visions of Axis armies meeting in India never came close to reality. Only one round-trip flight between Europe and East Asia was undertaken, by an Italian crew and aircraft in 1942. Germany and Italy had planned a few more such stunts, but Japan demurred because it did not want to flaunt violations of Soviet air space.[104] Blockade runners slipped supplies into German-controlled ports, but these possibilities dwindled as the Allies established supremacy at sea. The only remaining transportation option was ultra-long-range submarines. Some completed the obstacle course between occupied France and East Indies, ferrying from Europe blueprints and parts for advanced weapons, and from Asia raw materials such as rubber. These voyages took three months each way and became increasingly hazardous as the Allies perfected antisubmarine warfare. But the pile of goods so smuggled was overshadowed by the mountain shipped from the Arsenal of Democracy. A single Allied convoy carried more materials

---

[101] Hugo Dobson, "The Failure of the Tripartite Pact: Familiarity Breeding Contempt between Japan and Germany, 1940–45," *Japan Forum* 11, no. 2 (1999): 179–190; Richard L. DiNardo, *Germany and the Axis Powers: From Coalition to Collapse* (Lawrence: University Press of Kansas, 2005).

[102] Paul Schmalenbach, *German Raiders: A History of Auxiliary Cruisers of the German Navy, 1895–1945* (Annapolis: Naval Institute Press, 1979); Hans-Joachim Krug et al., *Reluctant Allies: German-Japanese Naval Relations in World War II* (Annapolis: Naval Institute Press, 2001).

[103] The compacts are the Anti-Comintern Pact in 1936, Italy's accession to it in 1937, cultural agreement in 1938, Tripartite Pact in 1940, agreement precluding a separate peace in 1941, agreement on military coordination in 1942, and economic arrangement in 1943.

[104] Peter Herde, *Der Japanflug: Planungen und Verwirklichung einer Flugverbindung zwischen den Achsenmächten und Japan 1942–1945* (Stuttgart: Franz Steiner Verlag, 2000).

than all Axis cargo submarines combined. Particularly detrimental to an alliance that mostly led a verbal existence, word of mouth and the airwaves too were made unsafe. Richard Sorge, a German Comintern operative posing as a correspondent in Japan, relayed to Moscow in late 1941 Tokyo's decision not to attack the Soviet Union, thereby freeing the Red Army to amass around the capital.[105] And Allied code-breakers deciphered Ōshima's transmissions to Japan detailing German defenses in coastal France before D-Day.[106] Fundamentally, the Tokyo–Berlin Axis lived by words and died by words.

[105] Chalmers Johnson, *An Instance of Treason: Ozaki Hotsumi and the Sorge Spy Ring*, expanded ed. (Stanford: Stanford University Press, 1990).
[106] Carl Boyd, *Hitler's Japanese Confidant: General Ōshima Hiroshi and MAGIC Intelligence, 1941–1945* (Lawrence: University Press of Kansas, 1993).

Part I

Transnational Nazism in Japan

1   Germany in Newspapers

Newspapers were unrivaled in disseminating information and molding opinions in interwar Japan. Major chains such as the *Mainichi* and the *Asahi* were comprehensive publications that interceded between the governing and the governed. The state already recognized the impact of the printed word in 1875 and claimed authority to discipline any newspaper. It made an example of the largest by punishing the *Asahi* in 1918 for reporting the Rice Riots and denouncing the Siberian Intervention. Then in 1925, the Diet enacted the Peace Preservation Law to make certain leftist topics taboo. Still, the press adapted to these parameters. As businesses, they did not necessarily shirk but could profit from antigovernment rhetoric. They even mobilized crowds that helped fell three prime ministers in the 1910s.[1] Days after the Peace Preservation Law, the press celebrated the Diet's promulgation of universal male suffrage. The *Asahi* and the *Mainichi* groups each churned out 2 million copies every day by 1927, and subscriptions in Tokyo exceeded households by 130,000.[2] The two chains made and sold their own news through sponsoring such spectacles as sports competitions and endurance flights. They ran airplanes and telephone and telegraph operations to relay breaking stories. Supported by legions of customers, newspapers organized fund drives for the needy or disaster victims.[3] Yet they also raised money for warships and warplanes. When Japan seized Manchuria in 1931, they rallied around the army and fed the jingoist fever to hawk extras and copies.[4]

Echoing debates on pre-1945 Japanese liberalism and authoritarianism, scholars of the media disagree about the scope and nature of newspapers' clout. Some emphasize their limitations under tightening

---

[1] James L. Huffman, *Creating a Public: People and Press in Meiji Japan* (Honolulu: University of Hawai'i Press, 1997), 364–365.

[2] Ibid., 363.

[3] Bunshirō Suzuki, *Japanese Journalism* (Tokyo: The Japanese Council Institute of Pacific Relations, 1929), 13–14.

[4] Louise Young, *Japan's Total Empire: Manchuria and the Culture of Wartime Imperialism* (Berkeley: University of California Press, 1998), 55–114.

censorship, while others interpret the same state control as reactions to their expansion.[5] Contemporaries certainly treated the press as a source of real but unofficial power, derived from its daily contact with the masses and function in public commentary. A commoner aspiring to enter politics might start by working as a journalist to raise his profile before running for a seat in the Diet or joining a state ministry.[6] One such newsman turned parliamentarian, Takekoshi Yosaburō, reflected that power had shifted from the Diet to the press.[7] Ōta Masataka, a bureaucrat turned newspaperman, boasted in 1923 that the 150,000 workers in his industry "constitute one third of the teachers of civil culture," along with as many Buddhist priests or elementary schoolteachers.[8] The American sociologist Harry Emerson Wildes observed in 1929 that "most Japanese ... agree in stating that the press should be regarded as the influential factor working toward improvement in social and political conditions."[9] A former newsman might even become prime minister under favorable circumstances, as Hara Takashi did in 1918 and Inukai Tsuyoshi in 1931. Their cabinets were coincidentally the first and the last with a parliamentary majority before 1945 and the symbolic bookends of Taisho democracy. Conversely, newspapering was deemed a worthwhile occupation for statesmen rotating out of office. Katō Takaaki and Ashida Hitoshi both presided over a daily after leaving the Foreign Ministry, before becoming prime ministers in 1924 and 1948. Hara and Inukai perhaps best embody newspapers' potent but precarious position – both their premierships were cut short by assassins.

Newspapers, the most available and affordable segment of the media, were the prime channel for commenting on Germany and Japanese-German relations. Extending James Huffman's argument that the Meiji press "created a public" distinct from the state, this chapter makes the case that newspapers maintained civil society's stance toward Germany in an absence of articulated policy until late 1936. Pundits praised

---

[5] Lawrence Ward Beer, *Freedom of Expression in Japan: A Study in Comparative Law, Politics, and Society* (Tokyo: Kodansha International, 1984); Jung Bock Lee, *The Political Character of the Japanese Press* (Seoul: Seoul National University Press, 1985). On censorship: see Richard H. Mitchell, *Thought Control in Prewar Japan* (Ithaca: Cornell University Press, 1976); Richard H. Mitchell, *Censorship in Imperial Japan* (Princeton: Princeton University Press, 1983). On the media's influence: see Gregory J. Kasza, *The State and the Mass Media in Japan, 1918–1945* (Berkeley: University of California Press, 1988); Dickinson, *New Japan*.

[6] Kasza, 28–29.

[7] Takekoshi Yosaburō, introduction to *Shinbungaku: Ō-Bei shinbun jigyō*, by Matsumoto Kunpei (Tokyo: Hakubunkan, 1899), 1.

[8] M. Ohta, *Society and the Newspaper* (Tokyo: Hōchi Shinbun Shuppanbu, 1923), 1.

[9] Harry Emerson Wildes, *The Press and Social Currents in Japan* (Chicago: University of Chicago Press, 1927), 53.

Germany, then Nazism, and then Japanese-German rapprochement. Newsmen and readers alike shared a substantial interest in and familiarity with Germany and its people. Germany basked in attentive, overwhelmingly positive coverage throughout the 1920s and 1930s. Germans were collectively portrayed as possessing a national character that made their culture, politics, science, and economy noteworthy even after World War I. Famous and ordinary German individuals received personal, sympathetic attention in their role as protagonists to enliven and humanize conditions in Germany. Above this baseline of focus, Germany experienced three episodes of heightened publicity. In the immediate postwar years, newspapers indulged in expectant speculations over a monarchist restoration and dismissed the Weimar Republic's prospects. In summer 1929, the press enthusiastically welcomed the *Graf Zeppelin* and celebrated German technological breakthroughs that linked the two countries. After the Third Reich's onset in 1933, some of its aspects initially made negative headlines. But as newspapers raced to report developments in Germany, they often blurred the line between publicizing and promoting Nazism. Opinion makers used the remaining liberalism in Japan to applaud rising authoritarianism in Germany. Hitler and his messages increasingly resonated in the press because of its preexisting partiality for a rightist Germany and personality-driven style. Transnational Nazism emerged as successive journalists voluntarily transformed from observers or skeptics to adherents of Nazism and advocated approaching Germany.

Germany as Fine Print

Germany's preeminent quality in the press was its ubiquity. Newspapers discussed Germany almost daily, in morning and evening editions, special or Sunday supplements, and extras. It was depicted in news articles, opinion columns, cartoons, advertisements, and photographs. In the morning paper, Germany could appear on the first page, reserved for advertisements; the second, for major news; the third, for editorials and opinions; and the fourth, for the economy.[10] Subsequent sections on sports, science, diversion, advertisements, family and women, and local happenings also mentioned Germany frequently. In short, journalists and readers alike found Germany a topic from which they could hardly avert their gaze.

---

[10] This description applied mostly to mainstream newspapers.

That Germany should make news may seem self-evident, but it did not have to, especially from Japan's perspective after World War I. Germany emerged from the conflict with a far smaller presence in East Asia thanks to Japan's wartime measures against German properties and individuals.[11] Meanwhile, Japanese nationals had been barred from Germany, embassies and consulates shuttered, and commerce halted. The war, Versailles Treaty, and postwar upheavals so reduced Germany that one could not assert with certainty that it would again matter to Japan as before. How then did Germany come to consume so much newsprint and attention?

The press found German attributes worth highlighting regardless of international relations or relevance to Japan. One recurring theme was "Germanness" and its myriad manifestations. Whether during the post-1918 chaos or the Nazi revolution from 1933 on, Japanese newsmen seldom missed a chance to interpret conditions in Germany as expressions of the Germans' innate qualities. The intellectual Tokutomi Sohō used three consecutive columns in 1920 in his *Kokumin shinbun* to diagnose "defects of the German national character" and to disabuse his countrymen of their illusions of proverbial German strengths such as "order, science, industry, research, and thoroughness."[12] He conceded that Germany had repulsed attacks on all sides, but its vaunted "indomitable perseverance" was sustained only by a promised victory. So when the true extent of Germany's military catastrophe was exposed, German will, too, imploded. The Germans, he concluded, strutted like tigers in triumph, but in defeat they only resembled cats.

That Tokutomi spent three days trying to dispel the myths of German superiority reveals how widely shared and deeply rooted these beliefs were. But he failed even to convince his fellow critics, who throughout the interwar era introduced and reviewed intellectual and artistic expressions of the German essence. Works warranted exposure simply for being German, so essays titled "German Music," "German Cinema," and the like appeared regularly. But interest in culture did not necessarily translate into awareness of current events. The *Yomiuri shinbun* misidentified *Deutschland über Alles* as a banned song until Paul von Hindenburg became president in 1926, when in reality it was designated the national anthem in 1922.[13] Still, most articles were written knowledgeably by connoisseurs. Newspapers at times marveled at innovative German photographers and dramatists. But more frequently commentators revered German classical masterpieces. Bach,

[11] TA, November 14, 1919.   [12] *Kokumin shinbun* (hereafter: K), March 26–28, 1920.
[13] Y, July 27, 1926.

Goethe, and Wagner needed no introduction because readers were expected to be already familiar with them.

This personality-driven exultation of the German spirit permeated the press. Goethe and Wagner deserved the attention lavished on them when the papers revisited their legacies on the anniversaries of their deaths.[14] But many other people appeared in the dailies chiefly for being German. There were Germans coming to Japan, for example a scholar seeking to enter a university and a stowaway on a liner.[15] There were Germans who left Japan, namely, a Go master.[16] There were Germans married to Japanese, including a pair who met while the Japanese was studying in Berlin.[17] There were Germans only partly so, such as a Japanese German biologist relocating to Japan and a Japanese German schoolgirl.[18] There were Germans living in Japan, for example a sailor who opened a beer hall after his internment, naturalized Japanese citizens, and a graduate of a women's medical college.[19] There were even Germans who nearly died in Japan, for instance a woman who poisoned herself.[20]

These human interest stories enabled the newspapers to illustrate and comment on conditions in Germany and make comparisons with Japan. The attempted suicide was revealed to be triggered by Nazi anti-Semitism because she feared being barred from marrying her Jewish lover even in Japan. The Japanese-German couple decided to leave Hitler's Germany to flee harassment. The Japanese Germans moving to Japan since 1933 all cited racism abroad as motivation. These articles indicated that the Third Reich had little room for non- and semi-Germans especially, and contrasted Japanese hospitality with German intolerance. The *Yomiuri* cheered the "triumph of international love" over Nazi persecution when biracial individuals or pairs found refuge in Japan.[21] The Germans who became Japanese to different degrees, by living in Japan for decades, learning Go, or gaining citizenship, were seen as proof of Japan's parity with the West. The foreign students surely appeared to validate Japanese academics: even the Germans were study-ing – medicine no less – at Japanese institutions. On politics, the beer hall owner explained that he preferred expatriation to repatriation because of the "bizarre government" in Germany after 1919. The man trafficking himself to Japan in 1933 was reported to despair of circumstances in Nazi Germany. The lives of these otherwise ordinary Germans provided

---

[14] TA, March 22, 1932; *Tōkyō nichinichi shinbun* (hereafter: TN), February 13, 1933.
[15] TA, October 7, 1933; K, July 14, 1933.   [16] K, April 2, 1932.
[17] K, September 1, 1934.   [18] TA, June 28, 1934, EE; K, January 20, 1934.
[19] TA, November 1, 1936; Y, March 4, 1920; Y, October 30, 1922; K, March 24, 1934.
[20] Y, July 29, 1933.   [21] Y, October 4, 1933.

a gauge for readers to assess Japan's place in the world and interpret events in Germany and between Japan and Germany.

In a similar vein, the dailies delved into German newsmakers' personal details. When Tokyo and Berlin restored formal ties in 1920, the press reflexively gravitated toward the new ambassador Wilhelm Solf. The *Ōsaka mainichi shinbun* took the lead in approving of his appointment. It noted his familiarity with Pacific affairs through his governorship of German Samoa.[22] The *Tōkyō asahi shinbun* responded by dispatching its Berlin correspondent, Nagura Mon'ichi, to interview Solf before his departure for Japan.[23] Smaller papers had to wait until after the Solf family's arrival but made up for the delay with an intimate angle. The *Yomiuri* published a scoop on Solf's daughter.[24] The *Kokumin* answered within a week with a tribute to Solf's wife.[25] The respect for Solf continued throughout his tenure as ambassador and even after his retirement to Germany in 1928. His congratulations to Japan on the birth of Prince Akihito in 1933 still commanded newsprint.[26]

Even if the doting on the Solfs seems tabloidesque, Solf's reception was instrumental in rehabilitating Germany's reputation in Japan. After the initial enthusiasm subsided, Solf continued to receive favorable treatment in the newspapers and leveraged it as one of his few tools. His effort paid off in 1923 when France and Belgium occupied Germany's Ruhr industrial region over missed reparations payments. Instead of clarifying the dispute, the *Asahi* granted Solf, hardly a disinterested observer, space to describe Allied demands viscerally as "squeezing blood from Germany."[27] After Hindenburg's election in 1925, Solf was again given a platform to defend his government and explain that he knew Hindenburg personally, and that the president-elect had no intention to restore monarchy but would uphold the constitution.[28] When very few traversed borders, a country's standing could well hinge on individuals such as Solf.[29]

Several other German notables enjoyed such currency in Japan that they formed part of a corpus of shared knowledge between newspapermen and readers. Such an imagined community was most defined in politics, where German ideologues were tasked with personifying their ideologies and movements. Readers of the Communist Party organ *Sekki* must have already grasped Germany's significance for communism, so it

---

[22] *Ōsaka mainichi shinbun* (hereafter: OM), January 23, 1920, EE.   [23] TA, July 7, 1920.
[24] Y, August 6, 1920.   [25] K, August 12, 1920.   [26] K, December 25, 1933.
[27] TA, January 15, 1923.   [28] TA, April 28, 1925, EE.
[29] Inge Hoppner and Fujiko Sekikawa, eds., *Brückenbauer: Pioniere des japanisch-deutschen Kulturaustausches* (Munich: Iudicium Verlag, 2005).

needed to refer to Liebknecht and Luxemburg simply as Karl and Rosa, just as the German Communist organ did.[30] *Sekki* even venerated the pair alongside Vladimir Lenin as the "Three Ls."[31] When Hitler arrested communists en masse in 1933, *Sekki* voiced solidarity with its German comrades by repeatedly demanding the release of their leader Ernst Thälmann.[32] Likewise, the mainstream dailies used the deaths of the industrialist Hugo Stinnes in 1924 and President Friedrich Ebert in 1925 as shorthand for the vicissitudes in Weimar Germany.

The far more iconic Hindenburg and Hitler received sustained coverage that sometimes resembles personality cults. Nazi propaganda spun the Hitler myth in Germany and provided a template for newspapers to enhance the Führer's charisma and Nazism's respectability in Japan. Hindenburg's appeal is even more remarkable because he did not lead a mass party. After the 1925 election, he was revered as a patriotic savior and embodiment of Germanness, with a mystique that enticed the *Yomiuri* to misstate that he rehabilitated *Deutschland über Alles*.[33] The hero worship climaxed in 1934 when journalists competed to lament his death. The *Japan Times and Mail* mourned the field marshal as the "great leader of German Reich."[34] The *Yomiuri* declared that "Germany's father has fallen."[35] The liberal *Asahi* and the nationalistic *Kokumin* feted him respectively as "the archetypal warrior and incarnation of the German spirit who saved his nation" and "the world-renowned general and president with the unyielding German spirit."[36] His funeral in Germany was extraordinarily broadcast live on radio in Japan.[37] A few days later, Hirohito's brother Prince Chichibu attended a memorial in Tokyo, and Japanese warships flew their flags half-mast for three days.[38] All this attention was for someone who led an enemy during the war, occupied a non-executive presidency, and had nothing to do with Japan. Why did Japan care so much about Hindenburg?

Hindenburg fascinated the newspapers because he was associated with the literal king of German personalities, the ex-Kaiser Wilhelm II. More than Hindenburg or Hitler, Hohenzollern was the one German most featured in the press, though the emperor was just a celebrity without memorable achievements even before his abdication in 1918. Yet the newspapers, except of course *Sekki*, reported even minute trivia of his life

---

[30] *Sekki* (hereafter: S), January 21, 1932; *Die Rote Fahne: Zentralorgan der Kommunistischen Partei Deutschlands* (hereafter: RF), January 15, 1932. All cited *Sekki* material is found in *Akahata: Hi gōhō jidai no Nihon Kyōsantō chūō kikanshi* (Kyoto: San'ichi Shobō, 1954).

[31] S, January 10, 1933.   [32] S, December 21, 1934.   [33] TA, April 28, 1925, EE.

[34] JTM, August 3, 1934.   [35] Y, August 3, 1934.

[36] TA, August 2, 1934, EE; K, August 12, 1934, Sunday supplement.

[37] TN, August 6, 1934.   [38] Y, August 8, 1934, EE.

such as his remarriage, illness, rumored sickness, and daily routine.[39] The *Tōkyō nichinichi shinbun* exclusively published his memoirs in an 85-part series in 1922.[40] Other papers made do with his old letters released by the Weimar Republic.[41] Journalists mulled over Wilhelm's utterances regarding Japan, from rehashing the Yellow Peril to recanting it to appreciating Japan as an anticommunist bulwark.[42] The press indulged in speculations over Wilhelm returning to Germany or reclaiming the throne, in November 1923, April 1925, February 1933, and August 1934.[43] Besides Wilhelm, his wife and sons, particularly the eldest, made the news regularly.[44] Even Hindenburg, who as wartime commander had already sidelined the Kaiser and as president should be considered his equal, was often mentioned in subordination to royalty. When Hindenburg entered the presidential race in 1925, the *Nichinichi* shifted its characterization of the contest from between "rightists and republicans" to between "monarchy and republic."[45] After his death, newspapers published Wilhelm's message of condolence and Hindenburg's will favoring personally the "restoration of Kaiserdom."[46]

Headlined by Wilhelm, German individuals such as Hindenburg, Hitler, Solf, and ordinary men and women acted out tidings from Germany on Japanese newsprint. The many foreign names readers needed to juggle attest a threshold of familiarity with Germany and its people, but this journalistic practice tends to oversimplify and trivialize complex situations. The obsession with Wilhelm caused political changes to be interpreted as openings for imperial restoration, including the Hitler Putsch in 1923, Hindenburg's election in 1925, Hitler's chancellorship from 1933, and Hindenburg's death in 1934. But Hitler barely concealed his contempt for the nobility and royalty. The arch-conservative Hindenburg undermined the republic but did not revive the Kaiserreich. He even handed power to the belittled "Austrian corporal" Hitler rather than reestablishing the monarchy. In lieu of sober analysis, the focus on Wilhelm skewed the newspapers' portrayals of German current events.

[39] TA, April 29, 1925, EE; TA, January 15, 1934, EE; Y, April 21, 1935; TA, July 10, 1935, EE.
[40] TN, September 24–December 17, 1922. The *Tōkyō asahi* even serialized the former crown prince's memoirs. TA, May 15, 1922.
[41] K, January 6, 1920.
[42] TA, April 22, 1934; TA, December 9, 1925; Y, June 12, 1934, EE.
[43] JTM, November 14, 1923; TN, April 27, 1925; Y, February 1, 1933; JTM, August 16, 1934.
[44] TA, February 20, 1933; TN, November 12, 1923.
[45] TN, April 3, 1925; TN, April 27, 1925.
[46] K, August 3, 1934; JTM, August 16, 1934.

Well-known personalities boosted the profile of German science too. As Tokutomi Sohō noted in his critique of the German character, the Japanese associated Germany with technology. When Albert Einstein and Fritz Haber visited Japan, newspapers needed little encouragement to welcome those icons of German research.[47] Businesses named after Germans, such as the lens maker Zeiss, auto parts producer Bosch, and airship pioneer Zeppelin, all evoked traits such as precision and strength.[48] The drugmaker Bayer inundated readers with advertisements for treatments for pain, hangover, or insomnia.[49] Other supplements were touted as cures for such ills as weak libido or unwanted hair.[50] All these drugs were promoted as German imports as a guarantee of quality. German medicine was so trusted in Japan that native pharmaceutical manufacturers mentioned German physicians while pushing their own drugs, including inexplicably the Meiji emperor's doctor Erwin Bälz for a syphilis treatment.[51] Other peddlers sold concoctions that supposedly relieved Goethe of tuberculosis and Wilhelm of ulcers.[52] Some scammers even mislabeled drugs as German.[53] Besides pharmacology, German shipbuilding and aviation were admired. The *Kokumin*, perhaps with an eye on Japan's obligations under the Washington and London Naval Treaties, praised Germany's "pocket battleships" for complying with but outsmarting Versailles restrictions.[54]

Commentators used the respect for German science to measure Japan's progress. The press celebrated German recognition of Japanese technology, as when Bosch acquired the rights to a Japanese invention or when Yebisu Brewery exported beer to Germany.[55] When Japan decided to increase production of synthetic oil, it was said to be setting its sights on superseding "advanced Germany."[56] But the adulation elicited some nativist backlash. One Japanese drugmaker complained that its products had been dismissed offhand abroad until Germany was convinced of their efficacy.[57] Another declared that its potion from a "miracle spring" shocked foreigners by outperforming German remedies.[58] A professor articulated this resentment clearly when he scolded not only patients for splurging on Western medications over equally effective domestic counterparts, but also doctors for "blindly worshipping Germany."[59]

[47] Y, November 17, 1922; Y, October 29, 1924.
[48] TA, October 10, 1933, EE; JTM, October 26, 1936; TA, November 20, 1934.
[49] TN, January 19, 1933; TN, May 18, 1933; TA, August 13, 1929.
[50] TN, August 17, 1929, EE; K, June 13, 1935.   [51] TA, January 30, 1936.
[52] TA, June 25, 1932; TA, May 27, 1932.   [53] K, July 19, 1934.   [54] K, April 1, 1935.
[55] TA, November 16, 1933; K, June 10, 1935, EE.   [56] TN, November 6, 1936.
[57] TN, November 27, 1936.   [58] TN, March 20, 1935, EE.   [59] TA, May 8, 1933.

Indeed, while the science section marveled at German technology, the business section perceived German industry as a competitor. The papers at times accused Germany of dumping goods.[60] More frequently they grumbled about obstacles for Japanese exports, especially when Nazi Germany steered its economy toward autarky and increasingly rejected or taxed Japanese wares.[61] Still, barriers to Japanese-German trade threatened the livelihood of very few Japanese. Business journalists were in fact far keener to learn from Germany for Japan the very concepts of controlled economy and self-sufficiency that were hurting Japanese exports.[62]

Despite the inherently self-interested coverage of international trade, overall the press discussed Germany positively. Germany and its people, even after World War I, were deemed noteworthy. The Germans collectively were believed to exhibit perseverance in life, creativity in art, and inventiveness in science. Individual Germans also commanded attention, so much so that discussion of their nation revolved around personalities such as Solf, Hindenburg, Hitler, and principally Wilhelm. Hohenzollern exerted such gravity that even Hindenburg and Hitler, massively significant in their own right, orbited the ex-Kaiser in the Japanese journalistic cosmos. The dailies never needed to explain why they were so infatuated with the celebrity irrelevant in post-imperial Germany because Wilhelm, like Karl and Rosa in *Sekki* or Bosch and Bayer in technology, existed in a universe of shared assumptions between newsmen and readers. Commentators leaped at every political change, especially rightward ones such as Hindenburg's election and Hitler's appointment, to predict a return of the Kaiser. Their misconception may perhaps be excused because Japan the modern nation-state had known only the Kaiserreich, while the shaky republic replacing it seemed only an interregnum. But as professionals claiming responsibility for national enlightenment, the newspapermen owed it to their countrymen for analyses beyond stereotypes, preconceptions, and infatuation.

The Last Emperor

Above this baseline of familiarity with Germany, the press entered its first episode of heightened attention during Weimar's infant years until late 1923. Japan and Germany had much to catch up on, because four years

---

[60] TA, September 21, 1935.   [61] TN, October 1, 1933.
[62] Y, March 16, 1934; Y, June 26, 1936; Osamu Yanagisawa, *European Reformism, Nazism and Traditionalism: Economic Thought in Imperial Japan, 1930–1945* (Frankfurt am Main: Peter Lang, 2015).

of war had severed communications and fundamentally transformed Germany and even Japan. At the outset, postwar chaos hurt the quality of reporting because the dailies had to relay stories from sources in London and Paris. This filter added delay and hearsay. Headlines appeared late, sometimes even overtaken by changes in Germany. Rumors were related and then had to be refuted. But correspondents as private employees were allowed into Germany sooner than officials. The *Asahi*'s Nagura Mon'ichi was already wiring reports from Berlin in late 1919, but Japanese diplomats had to wait until the reestablishment of formal relations the next year. Thereafter, more Japanese expatriates entered Germany and wrote about their experiences there.

Germany was mostly depicted in short news articles and lengthier commentaries in the first interwar years. Often as first-person impressions, the commentaries described Germany with concrete details. But because they took longer to prepare, they tended to dwell on lasting trends transcending the war rather than volatile developments. Nagura wrote relatively few columns on parliamentary politics but many more on the economy, society, and culture across the country, such as theaters in Berlin or sightseeing in Leipzig. Their quality and subjects attracted such demand that they were collected and republished in book form in 1922. Japanese seeking to learn more about Germany could scarcely begin with a better place than newspapers, especially the *Asahi*'s opinion page.

Casual readers had only incidental contact with Germany, mainly through brief news articles and their briefer headlines. Likely because of the war's aftereffects, coverage suffered from generalization, superficiality, and even sensationalism. These features were sharpened by the dominant theme, the last Hohenzollern emperor. The press compulsively publicized any gossip or trivia about Wilhelm and his family, such as his aging and deteriorating bodily functions.[63] The uneventful passing of the ex-monarch's birthday was elevated to a reportable item in the eventful times.[64] The *Nichinichi* was so blinded by fixation on royalty that in 1919 it printed two contradictory articles side by side.[65] One announced the exiled former crown prince's return to Germany; the other denied the very same proclamation.

Newspapers indulged in speculations for months after the war on whether Wilhelm might be handed over to the Allies and held accountable for Germany's military conduct. The *Nichinichi* and the *Mainichi* conjectured that the wartime chancellor Theobald von Bethmann-Hollweg, Hindenburg, or Wilhelm's second son could stand in for him

---

[63] TN, January 9, 1920; K, January 10, 1920.   [64] OM, January 31, 1920.
[65] TN, July 3, 1919.

in a war crimes trial.[66] The dailies strayed from dispassionate reporting and vociferously, repeatedly opposed any proposal from abroad for punishing the Kaiser.[67] The *Yomiuri* quoted the Japanese constitution's enshrinement of the emperor's sacrosanctity to argue that other monarchs should be similarly preserved.[68] The *Kokumin* emphasized international ethics and humanitarianism as rationale for sparing Wilhelm.[69] Others cited foreign-policy experts' opinions against extradition and a tribunal. All shared Tokyo's official resistance to setting a precedent of hauling a monarch to court, grounded supposedly in the Taisho emperor's personal objection, and possibly because the Meiji Constitution was modeled on the Kaiserreich's constitution. It mattered little to the papers that the question of trying Wilhelm occupied few minds outside Japan and had little relevance in the postwar world. But because they invested the Kaiser with significance, they felt obliged to report and worry about his fate.

This misguided focus on Wilhelm may be dismissed as a distraction but for the shadow it cast on Japanese analyses of the Weimar Republic. Any right-wing upheaval was interpreted as a potential catalyst for Wilhelm's comeback or at least royalist restoration. When ultraconservatives attempted to overthrow the republic through the Kapp Putsch in 1920, the newspapers jumped to the conclusion that the rebels conspired to resurrect the Kaiserreich.[70] Yet the putschists never proclaimed any such goal but were instead striving for an authoritarian regime. When the Nazis launched their putsch in 1923, the press reprised their mistake of depicting any coup leaders as restorationists. The *Yomiuri* added the error of calling Hitler a general, when his coconspirator Erich Ludendorff was the real general.[71] The dailies' misbelief was reinforced by the coincidence that, independently of the Nazi scheme, the crown prince entered Germany around the time of the coup. Months later, when the conspirators were put on trial, the papers had still learnt nothing and continued to label the clique "monarchist," even though Hitler used the defendant's stand to propagate his revolutionary National Socialist weltanschauung.[72] The journalists allowed their prejudice to distort current affairs to such an extent that they refused to acknowledge clear evidence to the contrary.

The newsmen's faith in Wilhelm's return mirrored their belief in the strength of German science. The issue became tangible just after

[66] TN, July 6, 1919; TN, July 10, 1919; OM, July 10, 1919, EE.
[67] TN, July 1, 1919; OM, January 28, 1920; TA, February 21, 1920; Y, January 28, 1920; K, January 17, 1920.
[68] Y, July 9, 1919.   [69] K, January 21, 1920.
[70] TA, March 15, 1920; K, March 15, 1920.   [71] Y, November 11, 1923.
[72] JTM, February 27, 1924; OM, February 29, 1924.

World War I when victorious Japan was allotted German warships as spoils. The delivery of seven submarines in July 1919 caused such sensation that the Taisho emperor, Crown Prince Hirohito, various princes and princesses, and ordinary citizens all went to see for themselves the vaunted U-boats.[73] The submersibles whetted appetite for more German technology. The *Kokumin* looked forward to Japan learning from Germany's "first-rate shipbuilding and gunnery" by divvying up what remained of its navy.[74] The *Nichinichi* reported that Japanese officers were heading to Germany to study military aviation.[75] Germany's capitulation changed little of the newspapers' belief in its martial prowess. If anything, its ability to stave off defeat for so long only enhanced its reputation.

German intellectual and technological achievements also continued to receive favorable treatment. Less than a year after the Armistice, the *Kokumin* already spoke confidently of Germany's "robust regenerative power."[76] German universities continued to be held in high regard. The papers were dismayed when Japanese applicants were rejected to save room for demobilized German veterans.[77] The *Nichinichi* quoted a physician's fear that Japanese pharmacology would suffer from being severed from Germany, though the *Yomiuri* saw it as a blessing in disguise that could spur domestic research.[78] Perhaps the strongest proof of Japan's esteem for "German quality" is the admittance of goods such as automobiles, electronics, and especially books as reparations payments.[79] In contrast, France and Belgium certainly would have rejected substitution of German coal by books.

In sum, newspapers' portrayal of early Weimar Germany was positive but peculiar. Although the *Asahi* published several lengthy series on postwar Germany, it is unclear how many readers perused and understood the treatises. News articles and commentaries had to compete with contents in the rest of the morning paper and perhaps another daily, followed hours later by the evening edition. Few Japanese were equipped with the knowledge or experience to fully appreciate the information. Most other readers likely stopped after the news headlines and articles that reduced developments in Germany to their relevance to Wilhelm, real or imagined. Instead of looking forward to what would become of the new Germany, the press did their customers a disservice by being mostly entranced by the old.

---

[73] OM, July 10, 1919, EE; Y, July 12, 1919; Y, July 22, 1919; TN, July 11, 1919.
[74] K, November 4, 1919.   [75] TN, July 10, 1919.   [76] K, August 10, 1919.
[77] Y, January 4, 1920.   [78] TN, January 29, 1920; Y, January 30, 1920.
[79] Y, July 4, 1926; Y, October 10, 1926.

What the newspapers left unsaid also reveals Japanese attitudes toward Germany. Even though the two nations emerged from four years of belligerency, the press showed very little hostility toward the former foe. Because many longer essays were written from a personal angle by expatriates who thought highly enough of Germany to live there, they often sympathized with the human suffering and lamented Germany's fall from the Kaiserreich's glory days. In a newspaper's finite space, each word wasted on Wilhelm was one deprived from the republic. When the dailies mentioned Weimar, they did so to wonder how it would be overthrown by monarchist putsches. Intentionally or not, Japanese journalists colluded in a conspiracy of silence against German democracy.

Despite the favorable stance in the press, interwar Japan and Germany did not face a straight, short path toward rapprochement. The two countries habitually portrayed each other positively, but the entente through the Anti-Comintern Pact came only in 1936. That is, the depictions acted as a constant while changes in Japan and Germany in the early 1930s acted as the variables that made the alliance possible. A bilateral arrangement was so far out of mind in Japan in 1919 that newsmen busied themselves with denying chatter in America and Europe of Japanese-German collusion.[80] Allegations by foreign pundits that Japan as a "second Germany" or "Germany in the East" had inherited the Kaiserreich's mantle of imperialism, chauvinism, authoritarianism, and militarism so incensed the *Yomiuri* that it attacked them as "fantastical," "prejudicial," and part of a smear campaign when anti-Japanese sentiments ran high in America.[81] Such quick rejections of the prospect of Japanese-German convergence would begin to moderate in the late 1920s.

Solidarity through the Air

If the ideas of Germany and approaching it had seemed remote to Japan in the first postwar years, the arrival of the airship *Graf Zeppelin* in August 1929 shrank the feeling of distance and triggered another wave of celebration of the German national character, personalities, and genius. In the meantime, good news in Germany was no news in Japan, as the Weimar Republic outlasted challenges to its legitimacy and eked out a few "golden years." This German resurgence loomed over Japan and the world when the *Graf Zeppelin* became the first dirigible to circumnavigate Earth. The American press magnate William Randolph Hearst partly

---

[80] OM, July 15, 1919, EE; TA, July 9, 1919.
[81] Y, March 26, 1920; Y, March 28, 1920; Y, October 22, 1920; Y, May 21, 1922.

bankrolled the stunt to make and sell news, a move that the managers of the *Asahi* and the *Mainichi* would have admired and envied.[82] The zeppelin first flew to New York City in late July for the official start of the journey and then recrossed the Atlantic for the sentimental departure from Germany.[83] Lifting off from Friedrichshafen, the *Graf Zeppelin* arrived 102 hours later in Kasumigaura near Tokyo for its only stop outside America and Germany. It unleashed the most sensational media moments in Japanese-German relations between 1919 and 1936.

The dailies used the long lead time preceding the arrival to drum up enthusiasm for the German machine and what it represented. The weeks of anticipation and later the afterglow well exceeded the zeppelin's four-day stay. Japan did not sponsor the flight beyond serving as a way station, but some newspapers invested in the venture by buying a seat on the Hearst–Zeppelin bandwagon. The *Nichinichi* and the *Asahi* each paid about ¥20,000 to place its reporter on board, when a daily copy cost merely ¥0.05 and a monthly subscription a mere ¥1.00. The *Yomiuri* and the *Kokumin* could not match such extravagance but managed to publish accounts by other passengers.[84] Both the profit motive and journalistic ethics demanded that the dailies push themselves as near to the airship as possible. And the *Asahi* and the *Mainichi* each had to sell many more copies and advertisements just to break even.[85] By hitching their fortune to the dirigible and betting on its success, the papers acted as beneficiaries and benefactors rather than dispassionate observers of the zeppelin's feat.

In this spirit, the newspapers competed to anoint themselves with the zeppelin aura and convince readers that they had the latest or best scoop. The *Asahi* and the *Nichinichi*, and to a lesser extent the *Kokumin* and the *Yomiuri*, built human bonds to the airship. They depicted the flight from first-person perspectives through their own correspondents or other travelers. The dailies characteristically articulated news in personal terms and showered attention on the airshipmen. The Zeppelin company head and the *Graf Zeppelin*'s commander Hugo Eckener catapulted to stardom as one of the most recognizable Germans in Japan. His family and personal details became objects of curiosity, an appetite the *Nichinichi*

[82] Peter Fritzsche, *A Nation of Fliers: German Aviation and the Popular Imagination* (Cambridge: Harvard University Press, 1992), 145.
[83] Guillaume de Syon, *Zeppelin! Germany and the Airship, 1900–1939* (Baltimore: The Johns Hopkins University Press, 2002), 136.
[84] Y, August 20, 1929; K, August 21, 1929, EE.
[85] Mainstream newspapers derived just over half of their revenue from circulation and the rest from advertisements in the early 1920s. Neither source alone could cover production costs. Ohta, 23–26.

partly satiated with an interview with his wife.[86] Other crew members were also featured, including the mascot, a black Chow.[87] Even the Kaiser was momentarily eclipsed and mentioned just in the zeppelin's context: the *Asahi* carried a story of a Japanese expatriate who recalled watching Wilhelm observe an airship in 1909.[88]

The press also deployed substantial material resources to cover the zeppelin spectacle. The *Asahi*, the *Mainichi*, and the *Nichinichi* scrambled their company airplanes to intercept and photograph the approaching airship.[89] The *Kokumin* and the *Nichinichi* had the good luck of photographing the *Graf Zeppelin* above their offices, but the *Asahi* had to settle for a mail pouch dropped on its grounds.[90] Because successful newspapering means luring more readers, the papers churned out extras to announce new twists to the narrative. The *Nichinichi* issued one extra, the *Japan Times* two, and the *Asahi* three. Even the *Mainichi* in Osaka printed at least one. The *Kokumin* might not have commanded the readership to justify an extra, but it exceptionally, literally treated the zeppelin's landing as front page news, when the first page was reserved for advertisements. The *Kokumin* and the *Yomiuri* also featured the airship in their Sunday editions and youth sections. The papers were not merely witnesses and messengers. Instead, they cheered the zeppelin on, fretted when topography or weather threatened its progress, and welcomed it breathlessly. The *Nichinichi* and the *Asahi* ran a banner atop an inner page to greet the airship.[91] They were outdone by the *Yomiuri* and the *Kokumin*, which led with a bilingual Japanese-German column to salute the machine and men.[92] It mattered little that the crew might not see the messages, because they were meant for Japanese consumption to tout the papers' proximity to the subject. Other media outlets such as periodicals, movie theaters, and exhibition halls all offered information to enthusiasts who wanted to learn more about the dirigible.[93] Although Eckener embodied Germany by steering the *Graf Zeppelin* to Japan, it was the press that reduced the psychological distance between the two countries through saturation coverage of the airship and crew.

Beyond boosting newspaper sales, acclamation for the zeppelin created other marketing opportunities, especially for firms with at least tangential connections to the dirigible. Japan might even acquire the *Graf Zeppelin* for 6 million RM, or so claimed a sensationalist *Nichinichi* article, next to one denying the transaction, next to one on how such a hypothetical sale

[86] TN, August 16, 1929.   [87] TN, August 21, 1929.   [88] TA, August 17, 1929.
[89] TA, August 20, 1929, EE; OM, August 20, 1929; TN, August 19, 1929, extra edition.
[90] K, August 20, 1929; TN, August 20, 1929; TA, August 19, 1929, extra edition.
[91] TN, August 20, 1929; TA, August 21, 1929.
[92] Y, August 19, 1929; K, August 19, 1929.
[93] K, August 28, 1929; K, August 15, 1929, EE; Y, August 22, 1929.

would improve Japanese military aviation.[94] Certainly, Eckener was trying to open a market for zeppelins, but he could not just leave the only one available in the middle of its promotional tour. Bosch manufactured parts for the airship and hence could boast that "when the utmost reliability is desired, and the lives of men and the honor of nations are at stake, Bosch Ignition is chosen on land, in air and sea!"[95] The motor oil brand Veedol emphasized that its product was coursing through "the heart of the zeppelin's engine" and the sole American component trusted by "the same engineering genius that made the *Graf Zeppelin* ... designed by a German, made in Germany, built with German money, with German metal, fabric, motors."[96] Other companies claimed ties with the crew and passengers, such as Filmo, the brand of cameras used by reporters on board to capture the historic flight.[97] Union Beer crowed that its "authentic German-style king of beers" was fittingly served at the reception honoring the "masters of the skies."[98] Kikkoman implied that its soy sauce was to season meals during the Pacific crossing.[99]

Businesses that could not contrive a virtual endorsement by the zeppelin had to persuade readers to become customers. Goods made in Germany could point to their common place of origin as a sign of quality. The few Japanese who could afford to watch or record the airship might choose Zeiss binoculars or Agfa film, which like the *Graf Zeppelin* carried the mark of German craftsmanship.[100] More tenuously, a German brand of bath essence imprinted its name on a sketch of an airship as its sales pitch.[101] And a "rational, new cure" for sexual dysfunction and nervous breakdowns was promoted as "made in Germany."[102] Other manufacturers compared the performance of their wares to the zeppelin's speed and strength. A centrifuge maker pointed out that its product could spin a longer distance in a minute than the zeppelin could fly.[103] The car maker Marmon succinctly stated: "The *Graf Zeppelin* in the air, Marmon on land."[104] Goodyear even attempted to pass itself off as Zeppelin's peer by incorporating a drawing of the dirigible in its advertisement, but Goodyear made non-rigid blimps, not rigid airships.[105]

The unique, and uniquely German, occasion of the *Graf Zeppelin* visiting Japan afforded some Japanese an opportunity to extrapolate beyond marketing to advocate closer Japanese-German relations. The department store Matsuzakaya printed an advertisement entirely in

---

[94] TN, August 18, 1929, EE.   [95] JTM, August 23, 1929.
[96] TA, August 20, 1929; JTM, August 21, 1929.   [97] TA, August 21, 1929.
[98] Y, August 26, 1929, EE.   [99] JTM, August 20, 1929.
[100] JTM, August 19, 1929; TA, August 21, 1929.   [101] TA, August 27, 1929, EE.
[102] TN, August 21, 1929.   [103] TA, August 23, 1929.   [104] K, August 19, 1929.
[105] JTM, August 27, 1929.

German to congratulate Eckener and his men on bridging Japan and Germany through the air.[106] Yebisu Brewery bought a quarter-page in both the *Asahi* and the *Nichinichi* for a welcome message in German, adorned by the Japanese and German flags.[107] Newspapers took the lead in verbal diplomacy and exalted the national character behind the feat. Although few newsmen ever doubted Germany's regenerative power, Eckener and the zeppelin furnished indisputable imagery and vocabulary to describe German greatness – the man represented his folk and the machine its country. The *Nichinichi* spoke of the "great scientific prowess of Germany."[108] The *Japan Times* revered the zeppelin as the "materialization of the great German spirit unconquerable in the face of adversity and fired with imagination to accomplish the 'impossible' – determined through the mastery of technical detail and painstaking care to push back the veil of the unknown."[109] Such a milestone, the *Asahi* and the *Kokumin* concurred, surely signified Germany's rehabilitation as a full member of the peaceful community of nations.[110] The *Kokumin* lauded the zeppelin not just as a technical marvel but an instrument for "solidarity between German and Japanese cultures."[111] The *Yomiuri* echoed this sentiment and proclaimed that the dirigible symbolized and enhanced Japanese-German friendship.[112]

German ascent generally and the *Graf Zeppelin* specifically lifted the notion "Japanese-German rapprochement" from an allegation that met denials to a prospect to be anticipated. Eckener, once a reporter himself, pronounced that the airship came to Japan in order to consolidate bilateral relations.[113] Ambassador Ernst Arthur Voretzsch also credited the zeppelin for "firmly binding together the two nations" and expected that "Japan and Central Europe would soon be neighbors."[114] Japanese officials, too, publicly embraced the flight as a bonding moment and the *Graf Zeppelin* its agent. Tokyo's mayor welcomed the airship as a "flying envoy for Japanese-German goodwill."[115] The communications minister cheered its impact on bilateral convergence and cohosted with three other cabinet members a reception for Eckener and his crew.[116] The *Asahi* hailed the occasion as "profoundly significant Japanese-German fraternization around the behemoth in the sky."[117] Like the newsmen, the politicians interpreted the zeppelin as evidence of German strength. So the education minister admired "the German national character"

---

[106] K, August 19, 1929.   [107] TA, August 21, 1929; TN, August 20, 1929.
[108] TN, August 19, 1929.   [109] JTM, August 20, 1929.
[110] TA, August 20, 1929; K, August 20, 1929.   [111] K, August 19, 1929.
[112] Y, August 19, 1929.   [113] TN, August 20, 1929; TA, August 20, 1929.
[114] TN, August 20, 1929, EE; TA, August 20, 1929, EE.   [115] TN, August 19, 1929.
[116] Ibid.   [117] TA, August 21, 1929.

and "indomitable spirit and tireless research" for creating the zeppelin and as inspiration for Japanese aviation.[118] The navy minister declared "German science champion in the world" and that the airship's success stemmed from "the knowledge, bravery, perseverance, and excellent technology" that established Germany's awe-inspiring reputation in humanity.[119] The foreign minister praised the Germans' "genius, courage, innovation, and scientific civilization" that made the circumnavigation possible and as a force for international reconciliation.[120] And Prime Minister Hamaguchi Osachi applauded the feat as a "triumph of will and science."[121] The widespread respect for Germany did not escape Voretzsch, who reported to the Foreign Office that he would use the goodwill to foster a "clan of admirers and supporters in the ruling classes."[122]

Why did Japanese journalists and officials utter such effusive compliments and harbor such anticipation for Japanese-German linkage? The dirigible set sail as the last of three German mechanical juggernauts in summer 1929, after the first flight of a Dornier seaplane capable of carrying over 100 passengers and the maiden voyage of the state-of-the-art liner SS *Bremen*. The seaplane, liner, and airship formed a troika signifying German size, power, speed, endurance, and most important, the capacity to reach Japan.[123] After the zeppelin's circumnavigation, a string of scientific breakthroughs established more ties between Japan and Germany, and pushed the prospect of using technology to overcome distance closer to reality. In 1930, Tokyo and Berlin exchanged greetings via an experimental telephone, and radio owners in Tokyo heard music transmitted from Germany.[124] Plans were drawn for an airmail service.[125] In 1931, Eckener published a column in the *Japan Times* outlining his vision of a fleet of airships commuting between continents.[126]

In the early 1920s, Japan had to observe Germany from afar and take German ability on faith, but in 1929 the *Graf Zeppelin* delivered evidence of what Germany could mean concretely for Japan. Many Japanese saw Germans and heard German for the first time during the zeppelin's visit. Even those with no interest in Germany could not escape the saturation coverage in the press. Without a sense of feasibility grounded in the technological innovations in communications and transportation in the early 1930s, the phrase Japanese-German exchange, let alone

---

[118] TN, August 19, 1929.   [119] TA, August 20, 1929.   [120] TN, August 20, 1929.
[121] Ibid.   [122] PA AA, R 35845, Voretzsch to Foreign Office, January 16, 1930.
[123] K, August 25, 1929, supplement; TA, August 24, 1929, EE.
[124] TA, June 24, 1930; TN, September 25, 1930.   [125] K, September 7, 1930, EE.
[126] JTM, September 13, 1931.

rapprochement, would have rung hollow. Advancing science did not make the eventual alliance inevitable, but the Axis also could not have been forged without the feeling of connectedness. Unlike the Anglo-Japanese Alliance built on the British and Japanese Empires' physical expansion, any interwar Japanese-German bond had to be founded on technology and ideology, given the geopolitical reality in the 1930s. The zeppelin, telephone, and radio could not shrink the distance between Japan and Germany but reduced the time and effort needed for traffic and provided the wherewithal for collaboration. The last link in the chain, the political shifts, would be forged in the mid-1930s.

Warming to Hitler and Nazism

Just as excitement for the *Graf Zeppelin*'s circumnavigation rippled from New York, the Wall Street Crash in October 1929 sent tremors around the world. It crippled the economy in Germany and energized right-wing and left-wing extremisms that polarized and paralyzed politics by mid-1932. In Japan, too, many lost patience with democracy as it floundered in the "extraordinary times" (*hijōji*), a phrase that gained currency in the media from the 1930s. Although Japan was not battered by the financial storm nearly as violently as Germany, Japanese observers saw Germany either as a cautionary tale of what could happen or a testing ground for solutions. This realization drove the third peak of press attention, in the early and mid-1930s.

Unlike the previous spikes, when newspapers unanimously sympathized with postwar Germany and welcomed the zeppelin, the surge in the 1930s assumed a partisan tone. The dailies saw high stakes and took sides in distant ideological battles. The Communist organ *Sekki* was of course no stranger to channeling news through political filters. Starting in 1932, a year of many elections in Germany, *Sekki* began to comment on German politics frequently. It cheered when the Communist Party of Germany won over 5 million votes "for a proletariat dictatorship" and voiced solidarity against the "fascist dictatorship" of Chancellor Franz von Papen.[127] But the real fascist, Hitler, was dismissed as yet another reactionary stooge until he started jailing communists en masse in 1933.[128] When *Sekki* finally came around to excoriating Hitler, it lumped opposition to the Führer with hostility to the Japanese emperor.[129] By viewing Germany through ideological lenses, Japanese communists like their German comrades made the same error of misreading Nazism as an

---

[127] S, August 5, 1932; S, July 30, 1932.   [128] S, February 5, 1933.
[129] S, February 10, 1933; S, July 1, 1933.

unsustainable last gasp of capitalism and conservatism. But at least *Sekki* could claim distance and cultural differences as excuses.

While *Sekki* applied Marxist-Leninism to reach orthodox conclusions, the mainstream press did not do much better at the outset in analyzing Hitler and Nazism. Newsmen and readers alike needed a sharp memory to recall Hitler, who last made news around the putsch in 1923. But even those who could remember him might struggle to pinpoint the details. Not only had the dailies misrepresented him as a monarchist, for years they could not agree on the pronunciation of "Hitler," transliterated as "Hittoreru," "Hitora," "Hittorā," and finally "Hitorā." Nazism was described as "restorationist," "fascist," or simply "Nachisu." The press could afford to dismiss the fringe ideology until the early 1930s, but as the Nazi Party became the largest and Hitler forced Hindenburg into a runoff election in 1932, Nazism could no longer be ignored.

Newspapers instinctively assumed that Nazism's rise foreshadowed the Kaiserreich's resurrection. As talks of a Hitler cabinet swirled, the dailies anticipated a royalist revival. The former crown prince made news for expressing enthusiasm for Hitler, while conversely politicians received attention for supporting the monarchy's restoration.[130] The speculation intensified in December 1932 when Hindenburg lifted the ban on Wilhelm's return to Germany.[131] Some even alleged that Hindenburg would transfer the presidency to the crown prince.[132] Hitler's appointment as chancellor in January 1933 only encouraged more rumormongering.[133] Wilhelm's wife heading to Berlin, the raising of the old imperial flag across Prussia, and Germany's withdrawal from the League of Nations were all said to presage restoration.[134] The election in March that gave the Nazi-Nationalist coalition a majority unleashed more wishful thinking for a monarchist comeback, especially because the crown prince attended the new Reichstag session's opening.[135] Waseda University professor Gorai Kinzō, an expert on and sympathizer with fascism, conjectured in the *Kokumin* that the crown prince joining the Nazi Party paved the way for restoration.[136] The *Yomiuri* even reported that Hindenburg had handpicked the crown prince to become regent.[137] The last bout of hallucination broke out in August 1934 when Hindenburg's will revealed that he personally favored the monarchy's return.[138]

---

[130] TA, April 5, 1932; TA, June 11, 1932.   [131] TN, December 16, 1932.
[132] TA, December 18, 1932.   [133] Y, February 1, 1933.
[134] TA, February 20, 1933; TA, March 4, 1933; TA, March 13, 1933; K, October 17, 1933; K, October 18, 1933.
[135] TN, March 11, 1933; JTM, March 21, 1933.   [136] K, March 17, 1933.
[137] Y, August 30, 1933.   [138] JTM, August 16, 1934; Y, August 17, 1934, EE.

But by then only diehards fancied that Wilhelm still had any role to play. Most observers had come to accept that Hitler's Germany resembled nothing they had seen up to that point. Still, they could not refrain from measuring the Third Reich on the scale of the Second. Both the *Japan Times* and *Yomiuri* described the Enabling Act in 1933 that gave Hitler legislative authority as making the Führer "even more powerful than the Kaiser."[139] The *Asahi* commented in 1935 that Hitler celebrated his birthday "as if he were the emperor."[140] Even if the royals were no longer expected to be restored, their opinions were still deemed insightful. The *Yomiuri* relayed Wilhelm's prophesy in 1934 that Hitler could fall within the year and then the ex-Kaiser himself would return to Germany.[141] The *Japan Times* covered an exiled prince's speech in 1935 that attacked Nazism and predicted a military coup that would topple Hitler.[142]

Such unflattering portrayals belonged to broader criticisms of Nazi Germany during its early months. Two aspects of the Third Reich drew particular opprobrium: its external ambitions and internal violence. Hitler did not prioritize reacquisition of colonies, but because the journalists mistook him for a monarchist they also presumed that he sought imperialistic expansion. An irredentist Berlin would have unnerved Tokyo because Japan was holding onto Germany's former Oceanic colonies as League of Nations mandate. Japan's quitting the league in March 1933 cast doubt on the legitimacy of its continued control of the territory, a claim the press aggressively defended. When some German officials raised the issue with Japan, the *Nichinichi* mocked them for their "ludicrous demands" and "Chinese-style diplomacy."[143] The *Asahi* ran several cartoons to illustrate Japan's rightful ownership.[144] The *Yomiuri* argued that Japan had paid for the land through its sacrifice in the Great War.[145] The *Japan Times*, with its foreign readers in mind, translated several similar editorials from domestic dailies to demonstrate Japanese unity and determination to the world.[146] Japanese paranoia peaked in June when the Nationalist Economics Minister Alfred Hugenberg suggested that restoring Germany's colonies could help Germany pay down its debts and reparations.[147]

The newspapers also denounced the Nazi regime's domestic fury. They highlighted any mistreatment of Japanese nationals in Germany,

---

[139] JTM, April 10, 1933; Y, April 9, 1933, EE.   [140] TA, April 21, 1935.
[141] Y, June 24, 1934, EE.   [142] JTM, March 1, 1935.
[143] TN, March 26, 1933; TN, March 29, 1933.
[144] TA, March 26, 1933; TA, March 30, 1933; TA, June 18, 1933.
[145] Y, March 30, 1933.   [146] JTM, March 28, 1933; JTM, April 2, 1933.
[147] K, June 18, 1933, EE.

as when Nazi hooligans beat a girl or when the widow of a German veterinarian felt driven by the "heartless Nazi wind" to flee.[148] To the journalists' credit, they often transcended national self-interest and exposed Nazi savagery with no repercussions for Japan. Readers encountered headlines in 1933 on sensational deeds, such as a boycott of Jewish businesses, sterilization of individuals deemed "hereditarily ill," abolishment of most political parties, beheading as capital punishment, and imposition of the Nazi salute.[149] The dailies likewise responded to Nazi anti-Semitism with incomprehension or disapproval. The *Asahi* satirized it with a cartoon.[150] Its Berlin correspondent, Kuroda Reiji, lambasted Nazi racial "fastidiousness" and "medieval regressivism."[151] The plights of familiar personalities such as Albert Einstein and Fritz Haber not only enabled the press to humanize the victims but also congratulate itself on Japanese hospitality when some of them found refuge in Japan.[152]

The newsmen reserved the most outrage for the suppression of free expression under the increasingly dictatorial state. Papers from the liberal *Asahi* to the nationalistic *Kokumin* slammed Nazi press censorship.[153] The former diplomat, sitting parliamentarian, and new president of the *Japan Times* Ashida Hitoshi wrote that "under the censorship the German people will live in darkness ... Germany, by the sweep of a pen held by one who has gained power by the meanest tricks of propaganda and mob organization, is left stripped of the fundamental human right to read and reason."[154] The book-burning in May elicited another chorus of condemnations. The *Yomiuri* reacted especially energetically. It invited experts to detail the damage of Nazi anti-intellectualism and anti-Semitism to German culture and publicized protests by Japanese literati against Nazi "atrocities against human civilization."[155]

But the rejection of Nazi revisionism and despotism was overtaken by developments or tempered by the papers' politics by mid-1933. Reporters came to distinguish the rising Nazis from the declining Nationalists. Hugenberg, who had scandalized world opinion by calling for the return of colonies, was sacked by Hitler partly as a result of the fallout. The dailies gradually learned to handle German clamor for colonies as

---

[148] TN, October 20, 1933, EE; TN, November 7, 1933.
[149] Y, April 2, 1933; TA, July 27, 1933, EE; K, July 16, 1933, EE; Y, August 5, 1933; JTM, October 18, 1933.
[150] TA, May 21, 1933.   [151] TA, April 2–3, 1933.
[152] TA, September 9, 1933; Y, May 5, 1933; TN, June 25, 1933; TN, August 20, 1936; Meron Medzini, *Under the Shadow of the Rising Sun: Japan and the Jews during the Holocaust Era* (Boston: Academic Studies Press, 2016).
[153] TA, April 7, 1933; K, October 6, 1933, EE.   [154] JTM, March 11, 1933.
[155] Y, May 12, 1933; Y, May 13, 1933; Y, June 3, 1933.

negotiation postures rather than strategic goals. The international outcry against Nazi persecution, including Japanese voices, pressured the Nazi regime to curtail or cloak its violence with a legal façade. The boycott lasted only a day, while passages of discriminatory laws made less dramatic headlines than beatings or book-burnings. Moreover, not all papers reacted negatively to anti-Semitism. The *Kokumin* praised the boycott because the paper faulted Jewry's "evil hands" for Japan's isolation.[156] The *Japan Times* quoted an American anti-Semite approvingly.[157] The *Yomiuri*, perhaps in a bid to expand through sensationalism, warned readers that Jews were infiltrating Japan's financial and intellectual circles.[158] The acceptance and spread of anti-Semitism, an imported prejudice with no historical basis in Japan, indicates that Nazism was becoming transnational.

Also by mid-1933, the dailies and other businesses concluded that Nazism would dominate Germany for the foreseeable future and they could profit from Hitler and his movement's publicity. Even amid the negative press coverage in May, the beverage maker Calpis opened an exhibition on resurrected Germany to highlight its "stoic spirit, rational mindset, and ambitious temperament" as inspirations for Japan.[159] The same month, the *Nichinichi* carried an advertisement for Oraga Beer that invoked Nazi imagery and rhetoric (Figure 1.1).[160] A pharmaceutical company promoted its product in 1934 with a man holding a swastika and a comparison with Nazism's indispensability for Germany (Figure 1.2).[161] The press benefited most from turning curiosity into sales and shifted the spotlight from the Kaiser to the Führer. Every detail of Hitler became reportable. Like Hohenzollern, Hitler's birthday, marital status, health, and ancestry made news.[162] In this light, the speculations about restoration since the Hitler chancellorship in 1933 reveal not only a fixation on Wilhelm but also on Hitler's intentions. Newsmen hung onto his every word. The *Nichinichi* scored an interview shortly after his appointment as chancellor.[163] Kuroda, who so eloquently denounced Nazi anti-Semitism in 1933, glowingly recounted a 1935 audience with the Führer where he relayed a message of respect from the *Asahi*'s management.[164] The personality-driven style of the press seems almost purpose built to promote in Japan someone like Hitler and his personality-dominated movement.

---

[156] K, February 22, 1933, EE; K, February 23, 1933.   [157] JTM, September 25, 1933.
[158] Y, April 5, 1933.   [159] TA, May 20, 1933.   [160] TN, May 3, 1933.
[161] K, February 13, 1934, EE.
[162] JTM, May 21, 1934; TN, March 27, 1933; K, August 17, 1933, EE; TA, August 5, 1933.
[163] TN, February 4, 1933.   [164] TA, January 27, 1935, EE.

Figure 1.1 Full-page advertisement for Oraga Beer: "Oraga Beer. Absolutely strong. Absolutely splendid. Thirty million Oraga party members! A great beer nation's hero with a lion's roar!" The advertisement invokes Nazi rhetoric and imagery to compare the product and its consumers with Hitler and his followers. *Tōkyō nichinichi shinbun*, May 3, 1933.

Kuroda and the *Asahi*'s conversion from critics to admirers of the Third Reich, which took place within Japan's nationwide rightward lurch, exemplifies transnational Nazism. Kuroda's about-face was especially dramatic – "Kuroda Reiji" was born Okanoe Morimichi, a leftist active in the 1920s who chose his pen name to invoke Kropotkin and Lenin – but hardly unique.[165] A day before criticizing Nazi censorship, the *Japan Times* complimented the very same regime: "In Japan as in Germany, there are the forces of nationalism on the one hand and on the

---

[165] David G. Goodman and Masanori Miyazawa, *Jews in the Japanese Mind: The History and Use of a Cultural Stereotype* (Lanham: Lexington Books, 2000), 102.

Figure 1.2 Advertisement for a brand of skin lotion: "Nazism for Germany. Mussolini for Rome. Never forget our lotion for aftershave." The swastika in the man's hand is the reverse of the Nazi one, an indication that enthusiasm for Nazism did not necessarily translate into knowledge. *Kokumin shinbun*, February 13, 1934, evening edition.

other those of communism – the latter to a very less degree to be sure, yet still manifested, if not politically, at least in police activities. Hence it is with close attention that Japan witnesses the conflict of these divergent forces in Germany."[166] Even if the papers never endorsed Nazi excesses, in the face of existential threats such as communism or the encirclement of Japan, they could overlook Germany's boorishness and find common interests, especially after Germany cosmeticized its violence. The *Japan Times* had become so smitten with the Third Reich by mid-1934 that it published the supplement "Japan and Germany Linked in Friendship" to celebrate warming relations (Figure 1.3).[167] It stated:

The German people will contribute even more to the progress of mankind in the future than they have already done in the past. Their great gifts are acknowledged by all, even by their severest critics. Japan has been indebted to Germany in many ways – in the fields of science, culture and of jurisprudence. The nation which was long regarded as one of Japan's preceptors is now undergoing a most important crisis – a rebirth in which the Young Germany is discovering and developing new found powers. Japan too has undergone similar crises. Thus

[166] JTM, March 10, 1933.   [167] JTM, May 29, 1934, supplement.

Figure 1.3 The supplement "Japan and Germany Linked in Friendship." The inclusion of the Imperial German flag indicates a lingering interest in the Kaiserreich. The landscape scenes of Mount Fuji and the Rhine suggest a cultural bond between the two civilizations. *The Japan Times and Mail*, May 29, 1934.

the phenomenon of modern Germany calls for deep attention and sympathetic understanding.[168]

The next year it issued the "German-Japanese Friendship Number" to promote bilateral goodwill (Figure 1.4).[169] Even if it is unclear whether the paper was beholden to the government through subsidies, given the involvement of its president, Ashida Hitoshi, in diplomatic and

---

[168] JTM, May 30, 1934.   [169] JTM, July 5, 1935, supplement.

Figure 1.4 The supplement "German-Japanese Friendship Number."
Unlike the supplement in 1934, this one contains no symbols of the
Kaiserreich, only Nazi ones. The photographs of Hitler and Prime
Minister Okada Keisuke and sketches of the Brandenburg Gate and the
Japanese Diet hint at a political and diplomatic dimension of Japanese-
German rapprochement. *The Japan Times and Mail*, July 5, 1935.

parliamentary circles, its change of heart conceivably reflected evolving attitudes beyond the press and in the state.[170]

As in the zeppelin summer, advancing technology, now coinciding with converging ideological outlooks, concretized Japanese-German community and solidarity in the mid-1930s. Weimar Germany had joined the international criticism of Japan's seizure of Manchuria, but Nazi Germany saw an opportunity for collaboration from Japanese expansion and isolation. Japan's conquest resurrected some Japanese and Germans' dream of Japan acquiring a zeppelin. The Zeppelin company entered into negotiations in 1934 with a Japanese firm to establish air routes within and beyond the Japanese Empire.[171] The *Asahi* promoted the scheme by publishing a long essay by a zeppelin captain on how Japan could become an airship hub linking San Francisco and Batavia.[172] The *Asahi* reported in 1935 that in a year Japan would take possession of a dirigible twice as large as the *Graf Zeppelin* worth ¥10,000,000, to be paid for with Manchurian soybeans.[173] The *Kokumin*, too, detected strategic value in deploying zeppelins to tie Japan with Manchuria, its Pacific islands, and the Dutch East Indies.[174] German engineering thus promised not only to bond Japan with Germany but also with its perceived destiny and prosperity in Greater East Asia.

Ideological reorientation and scientific progress enabled newspapers to articulate Nazi Germany favorably. Whereas in 1929 the zeppelin awed mostly only Tokyoites, in the 1930s Germany gained an audience across Japan after more breakthroughs in long-distance communications. Tokyo and Berlin conversed via "wireless telephone" in October 1933 and in November executed a two-way radio broadcast, a feat the *Yomiuri* hailed "a Japanese-German handshake through the air."[175] Henceforth, German sounds constituted a part of regular and special programming on Japanese airwaves, including the live relay of Hindenburg's funeral and Hitler's eulogy. The concerted synchronization of the Japanese media with Germany plateaued in January 1935 during the plebiscite for the Saar Territory to choose to remain under League of Nations administration,

---

[170] The *Japan Times* was suspected of taking government subsidies from its founding in 1897. The Foreign Ministry explained to the German Embassy in 1931 that the paper was no longer an official organ and had stopped receiving financial support from 1929: see PA AA, R 85848, Voretzsch to Foreign Office, November 20, 1931; Hasegawa Shin'ichi, *Japan Taimuzu monogatari: Bunkyū gannen (1861) kara gendai made* (Tokyo: Japan Taimuzu, 1966), 70.

[171] TA, November 20, 1934; TA, December 11, 1934; Fox, 105.

[172] TA, December 22, 1934, EE.   [173] TA, January 19, 1935.

[174] K, January 19, 1935.

[175] TA, October 28, 1933; TA, November 15, 1933; Y, November 16, 1933.

join France, or reunify with Germany. The Third Reich invested the vote with national significance, but Japanese dailies discussed it intensely as if Japan had something at stake too. They speculated over the outcome before the election and afterward updated the tally as frequently as the medium allowed, but they were superseded by radio's live coverage of the ballot.[176] But because few Japanese households could afford to enjoy an audio Germany, the press had its revenge during the 1936 Olympics by using telephotography to deliver a visual Germany to many more doorsteps.[177] Japan never purchased a zeppelin, but the larger, faster *Hindenburg* still captivated Japan. The airship's appearance over the Berlin Olympic Stadium so impressed Japan that a similar flyover was planned for the 1940 Tokyo Games, with tickets already available for reservation in 1936.[178] The *Japan Times* similarly merged German engineering and Nazi ideology by juxtaposing photographs of the *Hindenburg* and Hitler at the stadium (Figure 1.5).[179]

Much of the press had adopted transnational Nazism by the time of the Saar plebiscite in January 1935. Newspapers transitioned from a predisposition for a rightist Germany to enthusiasm for Hitler and his regime. The *Kokumin* evolved most rapidly, from calling for a "second Bismarck" in September 1932 to crediting Hitler in June 1933 for fixing Germany's "habit of internecine squabbles."[180] The *Japan Times* followed in October with an editorial proclaiming:

On the whole there is in Japan an admiration for the Nazi spirit and regime. Strongly patriotic themselves and deeply imbued with the traditions of their own race, the Japanese respect the manifestation of a similar spirit on the part of other peoples. Thus the Fascism of Italy and the nationalism of Germany all strike a certain responsive chord in the hearts and minds of Japanese.[181]

The invocation of race, far more meaningful for the Nazis than the Japanese, indicates the internalization of Nazi rhetoric and ideology among Japanese transnational Nazis. The paper went on to excuse the anti-Semitic outbursts: because "the Germans were going through a period of great emotional stress and strain." It even dismissed the harassment of Japanese in Germany as "isolated incidents ... at moments of great national emotionalism" and declined to "make mountains out of such molehills." The *Nichinichi* voiced support for Nazi Germany prominently in a Tokutomi Sohō column and through a telephone conversation

---

[176] TN, January 14, 1935.   [177] TA, March 25, 1936, EE.
[178] TA, December 7, 1936; Sandra Collins, *The 1940 Tokyo Games: The Missing Olympics* (London: Routledge, 2008).
[179] JTM, August 31, 1936.   [180] K, September 20, 1932; K, June 30, 1933.
[181] JTM, October 22, 1933.

Hindenburg Takes In Games

The giant airship Hindenburg as it cruised over the Olympic Stadium at Berlin with a capacity load of passengers to take in the opening ceremony of the 11th Olympic Games on August 1.

Hitler At The Olympic Games

Reichsfuehrer Adolf Hitler as he entered the Olympic Stadium on August 1 before he formally opened the Olympic Games. In the foreground left of the khaki uniformed Reich leader is Count Henri Baillet-Latour, chairman of the International Olympic Committee, who visited Japan this spring and whose favorable report played a strong role in the I.O.C.'s selection of Tokyo as the venue for the 12th Olympiad.

Figure 1.5 Adjacent photographs of the airship *Hindenburg* and Hitler at the 1936 Olympics. Together they symbolize Nazi Germany's command of technology and ideology, both important elements for transnational Nazism and Japanese-German convergence. *The Japan Times and Mail*, August 31, 1936.

with Propaganda Minister Joseph Goebbels.[182] The *Asahi* tellingly published Kuroda's gushing interview with Hitler just days after Germany's overwhelming Saar victory. The ubiquitously positive coverage of the plebiscite won over many readers. The German diplomatic mission received congratulations from numerous Japanese; one confessed that he "can no longer read newspapers through sincere tears."[183] Thereafter, Germany's diplomatic coups in 1935 and 1936 – the reimplementation of conscription, establishment of an air force, expansion of the navy, remilitarization of the Rhineland, and Berlin Olympics – furnished ready-made narratives for the dailies, often in extras, to glorify a resurgent Germany dwarfing a moribund Europe or a defiant Hitler hurling bombshells at cowed adversaries. Rather than excoriating the violations of Versailles from a signatory's perspective, Japanese newspapers adopted Nazi Germany's position and reacted with admiration for the Führer's decisiveness or schadenfreude from British and French humiliation.

The press began to advocate political Japanese-German rapprochement from mid-1935, a reversal of its kneejerk rejection of such a prospect in the early postwar years. The *Kokumin* again led the metamorphosis. In August 1935, just after Germany began rearming openly, it published a column by the ex-diplomat Funakoshi Mitsunojō. He argued that Japanese-German partnership and restoration of Germany's right of self-defense and parity in armaments would safeguard world peace – the same rhetoric used by Hitler.[184] The leftist economist Sakisaka Itsurō followed in the *Yomiuri* in February 1936. Also echoing Hitler, he called for the redistribution of territory currently hoarded by Britain and France to the three "hero nations" of Japan, Germany, and Italy for the sake of world peace.[185] The English edition of the *Mainichi* and *Nichinichi* issued a "Japan-Germany Amity Special" in late July (Figure 1.6).[186] Then in September, the *Japan Times* reprinted an opinion piece from *Contemporary Japan*, a journal closely tied to the government. It employed similarly idealistic and altruistic language to justify Japanese-German collaboration:

As long as Bolshevism threatens world peace, the two nations must naturally sympathize with each other, and it is quite possible that they will endeavor hand in hand to check this menace, not only for their own sakes, but also for that of humanity at large . . . it can be safely asserted that Germany and Japan, similarly

---

[182] TN, March 20, 1935, EE; TN, March 14, 1935.
[183] PA AA, R 85850, Osaka–Kobe Consulate General to Foreign Office, January 29, 1935.
[184] K, August 22–23, 1935.   [185] Y, February 15, 1936.
[186] *The Osaka Mainichi & The Tokyo Nichi Nichi*, July 31, 1936, supplement.

Japan-Germany Amity Special

Nippon-Reich Relations Bound by Cultural And Scientific Ties

Figure 1.6 "Japan-Germany Amity Special: Nippon-Reich Relations Bound by Cultural and Scientific Ties." The slogans on the top read, "Bonds of culture are closer than those of materialistic origin," and "Friendship based on mutual respect stands time's test." The ocean liner in the background signifies technology's role in fostering Japanese-German connectedness and rapprochement. *The Osaka Mainichi & The Tokyo Nichi Nichi*, July 31, 1936.

inspired with deep patriotic sentiment, and a full recognition of their respective situations, will find it easy to come to understanding and cooperation with each other.[187]

Taking this cue, observant reporters began to track the movement of Ambassador Herbert von Dirksen, who returned from Germany to Japan the same month, said by both the *Asahi* and *Japan Times* to have orders to consummate a compact.[188] The *Nichinichi*, *Asahi*, and *Yomiuri* all covered Dirksen's meetings with Foreign Minister Arita Hachirō and Prime Minister Hirota Kōki in mid-November.[189] The *Yomiuri* captioned a photograph of the ambassador and foreign minister: "Firm Japanese-German Handshake!" On November 25, Tokyo and Berlin announced the conclusion of the Anti-Comintern Pact.

Transnational Nazism in Newspapers

Few officials or even attentive newspaper readers could have missed the signs pointing to an agreement with Germany in late 1936. But the *Japan Times* printed an editorial on October 29 by its president Ashida Hitoshi on a prospective Japanese-German pairing:

This time it is to be among Germany and Italy (a temporary expediency but a long-time impossibility) and this Empire of Japan ... The rumors of a secret German-Japanese military alliance were dealt with at some length in this column a few months ago and need not be reiterated here. Sufficient to say that they apply with even greater force to any three-Power grouping of which two of the three Powers are on the Continent of Europe. Unalterably opposed as Japan is to Communism and despite the existence of certain other interests which conflict with those of the Soviet Union, this Empire will never be so foolish as to enter into a formal agreement, secret or open, which would bind it to come to the material aid of a European ally in a purely European struggle.[190]

Even if the Anti-Comintern Pact did not involve Italy or stipulate military assistance, how could an insider like Ashida seemingly be caught so flat-footed within a month, especially since his own daily had been boosting Nazi Germany for years? Ashida had probably heard of the backchannel negotiations and was attempting to steer or slow them with the only instrument at his disposal – a newspaper. The pact was chiefly shepherded by Major General Ōshima Hiroshi. The military was encroaching upon the state and sidelining moderates such as Ashida, who would

[187] JTM, September 7, 1936.
[188] TA, September 20, 1936; JTM, September 22, 1936.
[189] TN, November 12, 1936; TA, November 12, 1936; Y, November 13, 1936, EE.
[190] JTM, October 29, 1936.

become prime minister only after 1945. By then, his admonition would have proven prophetic. The Tokyo–Berlin–Rome Axis was indeed temporarily expedient and eventually impossible. And Japan was foolish to form an alliance with Eurocentric partners.

Ashida was not alone in reacting with surprise to the pact. The bipolar responses of the *Japan Times*, trumpeting Nazism and Hitler, and acting shocked by the announcement of the compact, mirrored the contemporary political landscape. Vestiges of Taisho democracy were being swamped by Showa militarism. As a publication catering to the English-speaking world, particularly Americans, the *Japan Times* had reasons to maintain a liberal appearance and handle American concerns sensitively. Newspapers are also inherently incentivized to react to novel developments with astonishment and to sell daily revelations as news. But some journalists seemed genuinely taken aback. For them, it was one thing to advocate vague notions of Japanese-German solidarity, even one implicitly anticommunist. But it was quite another to see it take shape as an agreement targeting an organization headquartered in Moscow that had no meaningful activity in Japan or Germany. The transnational Nazi newsmen, officers, and politicians championing rapprochement allowed their own partisanship to lead them to believe that Japan could cozy up to Germany without antagonizing the liberal democracies or the Soviet Union. Moderates in the Japanese press and government scrambled to clarify that the arrangement did not have any state in its sights and render the pact's title with nuance as "defense from communism" (*bōkyō*) rather than "opposition to communism" (*hankyō*).

After the initial confusion, the press moved to rally around the pact. Within days, some businesses were already incorporating the Japanese-German entente in their advertisements, including the confectionary Morinaga, the theater Nihon Gekijō hosting the Jewish German jazz band Weintraub Syncopators, and various trading firms.[191] The dailies strove of their own volition to allay domestic and international worries. The *Nichinichi* mobilized Matsumoto Tokumei, a visiting professor at the University of Bonn, to counter critiques of the pact.[192] Perhaps to reassure itself and its readers, the *Asahi* cautioned the public not to confuse collaboration with Germany with the dawn of a fascist Japan.[193] The *Japan Times* entreated its foreign clients to "suspend judgment" of the pact, to which Britain and

---

[191] OM, November 27, 1936; Y, November 27, 1936, EE; JTM, December 11, 1936. That the Weintraub Syncopators were promoted through the news of Japanese-German convergence indicates that Nazi anti-Semitism had little purchase in Japan, despite the spread and acceptance of other National Socialist tenets.

[192] TN, December 24, 1936.   [193] TA, November 27, 1936.

France might yet accede, and understand that fascism was unwanted in Japan.[194] These papers supported Hitler and Nazism in Germany, but not necessarily Japan imitating the Third Reich.

The press could claim ignorance of the precise form or timing of the compact, but it could not plead innocent in the years of bilateral ideological resonance. Newspapermen did not dictate the conclusion of the agreement. But well before Tokyo and Berlin signed the pact, journalists had already used words to prepare its setting by propagating a positive attitude toward and depiction of Germany. Throughout the 1920s and 1930s, Germany was given chances to make news in Japan almost daily so that it never strayed far from the Japanese public consciousness. Casual and expert readers alike knew of momentous and mundane happenings in Germany. Individual Germans were familiar enough to the Japanese public that reporters could use them as humanizing agents to illustrate faraway and abstract developments. Sympathetic curiosity about Germany led to closer attention, which enabled a relatable stance that in turn contributed to a favorable view.

Beyond this background interest, Germany rode three peaks of heightened focus. The first, obsessing with the ex-Kaiser's fate in the early 1920s, primed reporters and readers to expect a resurrection of an authoritarian Germany at every turn. The personality-driven coverage and the specific personas discussed combined to create a virtual conspiracy of silence against German democracy as the press glided blithely from Hohenzollern to Hindenburg to Hitler. The Weimar Republic through no fault of its own lacked a long-lived celebrity to dazzle the journalists. To the extent German democracy was mentioned, it was usually in the context of when it would fall and by whose hands. The *Japan Times* had a point when it proclaimed in July 1932 that the "Kaiser's shadow is over German future," though only in the newsmen's minds as Wilhelm had become irrelevant long ago.[195]

The second, triggered by the *Graf Zeppelin* in 1929, materialized not only Germany and its attributes such as strength and precision but also reduced the psychological distance separating the two countries. One may even argue that the Axis was technically "made in Germany" because of the diversifying and increasingly sophisticated mechanical and electrical bridges built in the early 1930s between Japan and Germany. The zeppelin summer marked a turning point in perceptions, after which the notion of Japanese-German collaboration no longer needed to be ridiculed outright but instead sounded more and more feasible.

---

[194] JTM, November 28, 1936; JTM, December 6, 1936.   [195] JTM, July 19, 1932.

The third, instigated by Nazism's rise from the early 1930s, coincided with progress in engineering and a political reorientation within Japan – transnational Nazism – that brought Japan closer to Germany technologically and ideologically. The newspapers did not all portray the Third Reich or Hitler positively all the time, but their skepticism quickly gave way to enthusiasm and admiration. Early Nazi acts such as the suppression of Jewish Germans and press freedom, and the supposed revival of imperialism alarmed journalists, but these irritants soon became a new normal to which the press acclimated. Nazi anti-Semitism, or even racism against non-Aryans, affected far too few Japanese expatriates to exercise the whole nation. If anything, discrimination against Japanese Americans in the American West always elicited more outrage in the press.[196] The personality-driven narrative style of Japanese journalism perfectly suited someone such as Hitler, whose propaganda machine spun a Hitler myth that the newspapers could retail. Hitler's anticommunism and policy successes won over reporters of different political backgrounds. Germany did not need to be perfect in Japanese eyes, only good enough when the right circumstances emerged so that the government had the option to forge an alliance. Finally, because the press was the broadest and thus least engaged and invested level of the media, one must expect some voices of criticism and unease toward Hitler and Nazism. We will see in the following chapters that as knowledge of Germany became more refined, support for Hitler and Nazism also became more vociferous and uniform.

[196] Y, April 18, 1924; TA, April 20, 1924, EE.

A Japanese crew found itself idling in the Indian Ocean, halfway between India and Somalia, on the evening of December 8, 1920. Having set sail together on November 13 from London for Kobe on the mail ship *Kaga Maru*, the 19 passengers traveling first and second class constituted a club of knowledgeable gentlemen. They included a professor of medicine, the police commissioner of Kanagawa Prefecture, an Osaka city councilman, two painters, an embassy secretary, a Finance Ministry attaché returning from the International Financial Conference in Brussels, three navy officers, and two executives of the X-ray manufacturer Shimadzu. At least eight had graduated from university, including one in America. Two others had a doctorate. So the assembled talents resolved to make the most of their time on board and hold talks to entertain and educate one another. This seminar at sea began with a pharmacologist's lesson on poison gas warfare, followed by the embassy secretary Amō Eiji's on the Comintern in Europe, and the attaché Aoki Kazuo's on Germany's war indemnity. Others spoke on eclectic subjects, including venereal diseases, Japan–US trade relations, British labor problems, and X-ray technology. Three months after the voyage, the Shimadzu director published the talks at his own expense in *Lectures in the Indian Ocean.*

The collection's publication captured, dispersed, and preserved uttered sounds as printed words. Thus, Japanese not privileged enough to sail on the *Kaga Maru* – even on board only the first and second classes took part in the "course" – could benefit from the specialists' musings. This realization was on the ship captain's mind when he inaugurated the lecture series. He proclaimed that the Yamato race had earned a universal reputation for perseverance and self-improvement. Now that Japan ranked among the great powers, its citizens had a duty to comport themselves correspondingly by keeping abreast of developments in the world. This zeitgeist inspired the passengers to seize the dull moments at sea to teach and learn from one another. The captain envisioned a brighter future for the Yamato race if similar saloon classrooms opened on other Japanese vessels crisscrossing the oceans.[1] For the professionals on board, then, the presentations were far more than a diversion to kill time but a vehicle for potentially enlightening an entire nation.

After newspapers, lectures and pamphlets were the most convenient sources of information on Germany in interwar Japan. Like journalists, lecturers and pamphleteers were captivated by events in Germany and used their own media outlets to propagate knowledge and opinions to consumers. Unlike the press, speeches and booklets targeted specific social classes. Lecturers spoke to small, elite circles, while pamphleteers wrote for the vast reading masses. The two audiences' distinct interests and perspectives were reflected in different receptions of Germany and Nazism by lectures and pamphlets. These attitudes evolved in three phases. First, during the 1920s, objective and expert lecturers reacquainted listeners with Germany after war, revolution, democratization, and economic chaos. Then, from 1930, and coinciding with Hitler's ascent to power, transnational Nazism began to spread as writers and speakers became enthralled with the man, his ideology, and his actions. Populist pamphleteers emerged from obscurity and conservative lecturers abandoned previous reservations to advocate aspects of National Socialism and Japanese-German solidarity. Finally, between 1936 and 1937, as diplomacy caught up with the opinion makers' agitation for a Japanese-German entente, pamphleteers and lecturers converged to rally around officialdom and exploited the remaining latitude in speech and association to explain and trumpet the Anti-Comintern Pact.

Lectures and Pamphlets as Media and Sources

Although lectures and pamphlets are sometimes consulted as primary sources for pre-1945 Japanese history, historians rarely include them in examinations of mass media or analyze how their peculiarities affect their contents. The microcosm of the *Kaga Maru* demonstrates how information in Japan trickled down from the elites to the populace via words in their incarnation as lectures and reincarnation as pamphlets. As in *Lectures in the Indian Ocean*, the identical contents could assume spoken and printed forms. Both formats are ephemeral and not intended to preoccupy consumers' time or attention. Speech fades into the air and a talk lasts at most an hour or two. Booklets can survive longer, but their thin, pulpy sheets and flimsy binding make them vulnerable to the

[1] Nojiri Momoki, introduction to *Indoyō kōenshū*, edited by Shimazu Tsunesaburō (Kyoto: Shimazu Tsunesaburō, 1921), 1–3.

ravages of time. Their serial, periodical nature also favors discard over preservation. Individual lectures, and to an extent pamphlets, seldom appeared in self-standing pieces but instead belonged to collections containing works on disparate topics that competed for listeners' or readers' interest. A speech or an essay takes up no more than a few dozen pages and can be read in one sitting.

Lectures and pamphlets both purported to convey facts – not just any facts, but interesting, useful, and relevant facts. Newspapers could claim greater currency and frequency, but speeches and booklets explored subjects in more depth. Usually they did not delve into themes deemed overly abstruse because their consumers were not expected to command much, if any, expertise on the subject. On the *Kaga Maru*, the talks on venereal diseases and X-ray technology did not indulge in medical or technical arcana. Instead they sought to engage listeners by offering practical tidbits and insights that the attendees could use to improve their lives. Even the lessons on such impersonal matters as the Comintern, reparations, and Japan–US commerce were supposed to benefit the passengers by helping them understand and adapt to the postwar order. Because that knowledge might quickly lose applicability in the rapidly shifting world, the Shimadzu director likely thought it imperative to publish the speeches soon after the vessel docked. In a similar but more extreme case, the Japanese Associated Press rushed pamphlets to Japan on the latest intelligence on Germany's economy via the *Graf Zeppelin* in 1929.[2]

These commonalities aside, lectures and pamphlets each have their own peculiarities. Not all booklets originated as oral presentations. In fact, most talks did not find a second life in print. Most important for our purpose, each lecture mentioned in this chapter was preserved as a pamphlet because there was no mechanism for recording even a fraction of the lecture circuits prevalent in interwar Japan. Talks could also be held, often informally and spontaneously, whenever and wherever a group of interested individuals gathered. A glance at just a few lectures turned pamphlets reveals that they took place in venues as diverse as the saloon of a ship, Buddhist temples, private clubs, radio studios, and universities. One can only imagine the full variety of locales for the orations that left no trace on paper.

In general, lectures were aimed at select audiences because crowd sizes were limited by physical spaces and speech volumes, even if amplified by loudspeakers. Radio could potentially transmit sound throughout the country, but it remained out of reach for most Japanese during the

---

[2] "Introduction," in Tsukamoto Yoshitaka, *Saishin no Doitsu wo hōzu: Tsepperin hikōsen ni takushite* (Osaka: Shinbun Rengōsha Ōsaka Shisha, 1929), 1.

interwar era. Out of a population of 70 million, there were about 2.4 million registered radio owners by early 1936, mostly clustered in the Tokyo–Yokohama, Kyoto–Osaka–Kobe, and Nagoya metropolitan areas.[3] Receivers, pricy and bulky, resembled furniture rather than appliances. A Matsushita three-vacuum-tube radio cost ¥45 in 1931, equivalent to the monthly salary of an elementary school teacher.[4] Yet, for affluent urbanites, lessons over the airwaves offered a novel channel for informal education. From the outset of Japanese radio, speeches had been a pillar of the programming. A lecture, Beethoven, and traditional Japanese music made up part of the inaugural transmission in Japan by the Tokyo Broadcasting Bureau in March 1925.[5] Radio listeners could expect to hear talks regularly on various subjects by luminaries or public intellectuals by the early 1930s. Many more lectures were delivered in person by speakers to audiences in private social or professional associations. Members of the National Association for Education were invited to watch Ashida Hitoshi's presentation "Japan's Diplomacy in Emergency" in early 1933.[6] Those belonging to the Franco-Japanese Association in Tokyo could go to a lecture meeting in their club building.[7] Unaffiliated individuals might attend as guests, though they likely had to purchase tickets.

The Economic Club (Keizai Kurabu) was one of the most prestigious of such associations, founded in 1931 as a forum for highly placed gentlemen to exchange ideas, relax, and socialize. Though not quite an exclusionary fellowship, the club adopted stringent requirements for initiation that only the wealthy and well connected could meet. Prospective applicants had to be nominated by two current members and then approved by the standing committee. Upon joining the new member – all 218 founding members were men – paid a one-time fee of ¥30, enough to sustain a household of four for a month, and thereafter monthly dues of ¥3. A lecture customarily took place at the club's weekly luncheon or supper, on which members spent another yen or so per meal.[8]

The Economic Club was an unusually high-profile organization among countless others. Most catered to specific audiences, operated in particular regions, or focused on narrow interests. Some could call on

---

[3] Nihon Hōsō Kyōkai, ed., *Nihon Hōsō Kyōkai shi* (Tokyo: Nihon Hōsō Kyōkai, 1939), 312–315.

[4] Morinaga, 214, 398.

[5] "Explanatory Notes," in Tōkyō Hōsōkyoku, ed., *Rajio kōenshū 1* (Tokyo: Nihon Rajio Kyōkai, 1925), 1; Edward Seidensticker, *Tokyo from Edo to Showa 1867–1989: The Emergence of the World's Greatest City* (Rutland: Tuttle Publishing, 2010), 349.

[6] JTM, April 2, 1933.   [7] JTM, February 14, 1933.

[8] *Keizai Kurabu 50-nen* (Tokyo: Keizai Kurabu, 1981), 4–9.

the support of thousands of members, but others stayed relevant only through a few leaders' willpower. A handful, including the Economic Club, continued to thrive for decades into the present day. But many more appeared overnight and disappeared just as quickly. This chapter will introduce several of these groups.[9]

Because most Japanese could not splurge on a radio or an active associational life, lectures would have had very limited audiences and would have been lost to posterity had they not been printed and fossilized as pamphlets. Even the pioneers behind Japan's first radio broadcast recognized the timeless potential of spoken words captured on paper and saw themselves as fulfilling a civilizing mission in society by publishing the speeches.[10] Likewise, the Economic Club from its founding anthologized and distributed the lectures delivered at its weekly gatherings.[11] Priced respectively at ¥1.00 and ¥0.20, the collections of orations on radio and at the club were affordable even to poor readers. If expensive equipment or membership barred most of the populace from learning on air or on site, then booklets provided a cheap back door into this wonderland of knowledge.

Most pamphlets sold for even less, at ¥0.10 each or the cost of just a few days' newspapers. Whereas neither the Tokyo Broadcasting Bureau nor the Economic Club sought to sustain itself through selling speeches, pamphleteers made their living from selling as many copies as possible. Pamphlets could be found at newsstands across the country and any bookstore remotely matching that description. Readers could also subscribe to a series as they would a magazine. The Publisher of Current Issues (Kyō no Mondaisha) mailed three issues to customers' homes monthly. As the firm's name suggests, its pamphlets delved into current events of pertinence and import to the public. Germany made its way into speeches and booklets in Japan as one such developing situation worthy of exploration in the early interwar years.

Years of Acquaintance, 1919–1930

Historical narratives on Japanese-German relations often dismiss World War I as a detour in a long march toward convergence or even celebrate it as an episode of intercultural bonding because Japan treated German internees humanely. But the conflict imposed a real caesura in bilateral

---

[9] Ricky Law, "Between the State and the People: Civil Society Organizations in Interwar Japan," *History Compass* 12, no. 3 (2014): 217–225.

[10] "Explanatory Notes," in *Rajio kōenshū 1*, ed. Tōkyō Hōsōkyoku, 1.

[11] *Keizai Kurabu 50-nen*, 12.

ties and contact. War severed communications and transportation. Both countries, Germany more so than Japan, also underwent fundamental changes during and after the war that altered their interactions. The Germany after 1918 differed so much from that before 1914 in politics, society, economy, culture, demography, and territory that much of the knowledge of antebellum Germany that Japan had accumulated no longer applied. There was thus a need in the immediate postwar years to discover this new Germany, understand its transformations, and extract lessons for Japan.

As seen in the speeches on the *Kaga Maru* on the Comintern, poison gas, and reparations, World War I and its repercussions loomed large in Japanese discussions on Germany. Commentators sought to expound the causes for Germany's defeat soon after the Armistice in Europe. The Association for Promoting Domestic Manufacturing organized a summer lecture circuit to educate the public in August 1919.[12] Navy captain Hitaka Kinji lectured on the moral of Germany's failure for the future of Japan's defense. He reasoned that Germany lost the war because it could not replenish losses and foolishly brought unrest to its own population when it inserted radical revolutionaries into Russia.[13] Meanwhile, at a forum hosted by Honganji, army lieutenant Saitō Seijirō cited clumsy diplomacy and dwindling resources as factors leading to Germany's downfall. He also faulted the spread of extremism within the ranks of the German army for melting its will to fight.[14]

By "radical" or "extreme" thoughts, both officers were referring to communism. When they delivered their talks, not only was Germany gripped by revolutionary and counterrevolutionary turmoil, but Japan, too, experienced rising popular discontent, labor activism, and spreading subversive ideas. Japanese opinion makers and intellectuals, many of whom were aligned with or sympathetic to the establishment, saw Germany as a test case for the global ideological struggle between the left and the right. Correctly interpreting or even anticipating events in Germany was thus highly relevant and useful for Japan. So retrospective interest in debating the reasons for Germany's wartime failure quickly gave way to purposeful fact-finding of current developments on the ground.

---

[12] "Preface," in Kozai Sutetarō, ed., *Matsushima kōenshū* (Tokyo: Kokusan Shōreikai, 1919), 1.

[13] Hitaka Kinji, "Doitsu haisen no kyōkun to waga kokubō no shōrai," in ibid., 180–181.

[14] Saitō Seijirō, "Ōshū senran ni okeru Doitsu haisen no riyū," in *Fukyō kenkyūkai kōenshū* 9, ed. Honganji Kyōmubu (Kyoto: Honganji Kyōmubu, 1920), 203–204. Though unspecified, the venue was likely Nishi Honganji, known for its Buddhist nationalism: see William M. Osuga, "The Establishment of State Shintō and the Buddhist Opposition" (MA thesis, University of California, Berkeley, 1949).

Several speakers returned from Germany to relate the latest trends in politics, society, culture, and the economy throughout the 1920s and up to late 1930. The Enlightenment Society (Keimeikai) alone sponsored three talks on developments in Germany on separate occasions within a decade. The association attached such importance to understanding Germany that, of its 38 meetings between 1920 and 1930, Germany was the only topic discussed more than once. In April 1920, the club hosted a presentation by the scholar of religion Takakusu Junjirō about his tour in Europe the previous year. Like correspondents, Takakusu could enter and stay in Germany as a private individual before formal diplomatic relations were restored. He spoke of the misery of the "new poor" who used to be the middle class, including his host, a trade consultant who lacked fuel for heating water and could only "treat" his guest with a small slice of smoked fish.[15] From what he witnessed and experienced in Germany – shortages, a weak currency, treaty obligations, radicalism, and dearth of leadership – he speculated that it would take the nation at least 50 years before it could hope to mount any campaign of retribution.[16]

Other lecturers echoed Takakusu's worry about the threat of leftist ideologies in Germany stemming from economic hardship. On the *Kaga Maru*, Aoki Kazuo advised against burdening Germany with unreasonable reparations lest extremism gain a wider foothold.[17] Later, the bureaucrat-turned-newspaperman Oka Minoru voiced the same sentiment in a speech on Europe's economy at the Kobe Economic Association (Kōbe Keizaikai). He revealed that Germany had been reduced to printing money to meet its financial obligations. In turn, consumer goods disappeared with the collapse of the Reichsmark, further hurting the hard-pressed middle class, who, should it radicalize, would rapidly plunge Germany into critical condition.[18]

None of these orators had shown an inordinate interest in Germany so far in their careers. Only Takakusu had lived in the country. But in his speech he made sure to quash any appearance of preference for Germany. He stated that, although he had studied there, he was by no means smitten with the country and considered it responsible for its own

---

[15] Takakusu Junjirō, "Doitsu no kinkyō," in *Keimeikai kōenshū 2* (Tokyo: Keimeikai, 1920), 20–21, 23.

[16] Ibid., 40.

[17] Aoki Kazuo, "Doitsu no baishō mondai ni tsuite," in *Indoyō kōenshū*, ed. Shimazu Tsunesaburō, 69–70.

[18] Oka Minoru, "Saikin Ō-Bei keizaikai to waga kuni," in *Kōbe Keizaikai kōenshū 5* (Kobe: Kōbe Keizaikai, 1923), 1, 3–4. Oka became president of the *Ōsaka mainichi* in 1933.

current misery.[19] Why then did these lecturers suddenly care so much whether Germany succumbed to revolution? They were probably less concerned with Germany than the spread of communism worldwide. Not all was well in Japan at the time of these lectures. Although Japan's reputation, territory, and economy grew because of World War I, the Wilsonian and Leninist ideals shook Japanese complacency at home and abroad, notably through rising Chinese nationalism and a Korean independence campaign. Most worrisome for these elite speakers – officers, bureaucrats, businessmen, and academics – the Rice Riots in 1918 and the rise of organized labor organizations rocked Japan itself. After faulting radicalism for demoralizing the German military, the army lieutenant Saitō recommended vigilance against the same contagion within Japanese ranks.[20] Moreover, the stabilization of the Soviet Union pushed communism to East Asia and could exemplify and popularize the ideology throughout the continent. Japan fought to avert these prospects by sending troops to eastern Siberia during the Siberian Intervention, in an unintended partnership with right-wing German militiamen in Eastern Europe. Indeed, shared animosity toward the Soviet Union and communism would eventually serve as the basis of Japanese-German rapprochement and its first manifestation as the peculiar Anti-Comintern Pact.

But in the first interwar years, Japanese opinion makers did not express interest in any strategic alignment with Germany. Instead, they tried to learn more about the altered Germany through cultural interactions. Takakusu's prediction of a decades-long recovery did not quite bear out. The Weimar Republic had righted the ship of state by 1924 through floating a new currency, restructuring its reparations, and defeating putsch attempts. The return of a modicum of normalcy, coupled with the resumption of formal ties, created room for civil society to conduct Japanese-German exchanges. In particular, Fritz Haber and Wilhelm Solf proved pivotal in engendering Japanese goodwill toward Germany. Haber visited Japan in 1924 and was received warmly. Upon his return to Germany, he delivered remarks in Berlin to urge closer economic collaboration.[21] Five months later, the Industry and Politics Association translated and published the speech as a booklet in Japan.[22]

---

[19] Takakusu, 6–7.   [20] Saitō Seijirō, 204.

[21] Okada Kenzō, *Hakodate chūtō Doitsu Ryōji Hābā-shi sōnanki*, Hakodate sōsho 4 (Hakodate: Hakodate Hābā Kinenkai, 1924), 29.

[22] Fritz Haber, *Nichi-Doku keizai teikei no hitsuyōnaru yuen* (Tokyo: Kōseikai Shuppanbu, 1925). This speech was probably similar to the one he delivered at a conference of the German chemical industry. Fritz Haber, "Wirtschaftlicher Zusammenhang zwischen

Just as with the lectures in the Indian Ocean, words spoken abroad appeared in a pamphlet in Japan.

The normalization of relations finally lent dealings with Germany an aura of respectability and removed the stain of consorting with a former enemy. Solf and some like-minded Japanese such as Viscount Gotō Shinpei reconstituted the Japanese-German Cultural Society (Nichi-Doku Bunka Kyōkai) in mid-1927 to replace a predecessor that had folded because of the war. As another illustration of the influence lectures and pamphlets were perceived to exercise in society, the association chose these media outlets as its primary means of raising Germany's profile in Japan and facilitating mutual understanding.[23] Solf, a trained Sanskritist, held a lecture on Mahayana Buddhism at the inaugural meeting.[24]

But the organization's high profile might also have limited its effectiveness in carrying out its missions. Though the society's publication left no direct evidence detailing the makeup of or requirements for its membership, the barrier to entry could only have exceeded that to the Economic Club. Few Japanese could roam in social circles that featured Solf and Gotō. Even if neither Excellency was expected to attend meetings regularly, the association could still mobilize presenters of impeccable qualifications. Within the first few years of its inception, it managed to summon recognized leaders in philosophy, history, law, economics, literature, and science to lecture on their specialties. But the very eminence of these speakers might well have intimidated or deterred laypeople only casually curious about Germany. Moreover, the lectures took place at prestigious universities or clubhouses that the general public were unlikely to frequent. Worse yet, the talks often indulged in academic topics such as "the current state of Germany's intellectual world" or "characteristics of German literature" that could excite only rarefied audiences already knowledgeable about Germany.

The rest of the Japanese, to the extent that they paid attention to Germany, did so only when happenings there might affect them. As Germany stabilized politically and economically, Japanese observers turned their focus to these changes. They abandoned the earlier gloomy rhetoric and chattered expectantly of new opportunities. Takarada Tsūgen of the *Kokumin shinbun* spoke in 1926 on "resurgent Germany"

Deutschland und Japan" (lecture, Verein zur Wahrung der Interessen der chemischen Industrie Deutschlands e. V., Frankfurt a. Main, June 11, 1925).

[23] Gotō Shinpei, "Kaikai no ji," in *Nichi-Doku bunka kōenshū 1* (Tokyo: Nichi-Doku Bunka Kyōkai, 1927), 2.

[24] Wilhelm Solf, "Daijō Bukkyō no shimei," in ibid., 91.

at the Scholarly Lectures News Agency (Gakugei Kōen Tsūshinsha). He declared that witnessing Germany's rebirth from its nadir should inspire "divine awe" in the Japanese and shake them from their own malaise.[25]

In the same spirit, a small chorus of lecturers and pamphleteers emerged in the mid-1920s to marvel at Germany's regeneration. A private individual was so moved by what he encountered in Germany that he self-published a booklet in 1928 on the lessons in organization, meticulousness, and discipline that he learned there.[26] The economist Oikawa Shigenobu shared his insights at the Enlightenment Society on the latest events in Germany after living there for 23 years. He was convinced that Germany, should it manage to revise the Versailles Treaty, would surely regain its strength thanks to its hardworking, frugal, and earnest people.[27] At yet another talk on the German phoenix, the Enlightenment Society's director Tsurumi Sakio opened the meeting by reminding the audience that this story of rebirth from defeat might serve as a roadmap for Japan to break out of its present doldrums.[28] The confidence and optimism these commentators felt in Germany's near future even materialized as the first pamphlet in a series on business and industry expedited to Japan on the *Graf Zeppelin* in August 1929.[29]

Japanese public intellectuals maintained a persistent and growing interest in the new Germany throughout the 1920s. World War I had intensified Japanese curiosity by depriving Japan of information from Germany for four years. Then the breathtaking vicissitudes until 1924 captivated spectators in Japan. The Japanese listening and reading publics had much to catch up on, and they chose lectures and pamphlets as the vehicle for the outlets' combination of currency and depth. Speakers and writers in this period worked mostly to reacquaint Japan with the transformed Germany. None held a grudge against the former enemy. All articulated sympathy for its postwar hardship, but several also took pains to adopt a neutral tone and to dispel any appearance of undue bias for Germany. Many cheered on Germany's economic and diplomatic comeback, though this attitude did not amount to any inherent pro-German sentiment. At the time, Germany and Japanese-German

---

[25] Takarada Tsūgen, *Shinkō Doitsu no genjō*, Gakugei Kōen Tsūshinsha panfuretto 32 (Tokyo: Gakugei Kōen Tsūshinsha, 1926), front cover.

[26] Koide Jōyū, *Doitsu wa nani wo watakushi ni oshieshiya* (N.p.: Koide Jōyū, 1928), 2.

[27] Oikawa Shigenobu, "Doitsu no kinkyō," in *Keimeikai kōenshū 22* (Tokyo: Keimeikai, 1927), 54.

[28] Tsurumi Sakio, introduction to "Saikin no Doitsu," in *Keimeikai kōenshū 37*, by Nagaoka Harukazu (Tokyo: Keimeikai, 1930), 2. Nagaoka was the ambassador to Germany.

[29] Tsukamoto, 54.

relations did not yet divide Japanese public opinion into "for" or "against" camps. Few deviated from the consensus that Japan would gain from a strengthening Germany through trade, exchange, and principally learning from its suffering and rehabilitation. The creators of the speeches and booklets eagerly mined lessons from Germany's experiences in war, economic crisis, political upheaval, or cultural revival.

But this enthusiasm is also confounding – what could a nation that lost a world war, territories and colonies, the flower of its youth, its cumulative savings, and its system of government teach an ascending power? Japan arguably fared best among all combatants in World War I. It suffered few casualties and no physical devastation. It became more powerful, populous, and prosperous in the 1920s than ever. To be sure, the Rice Riots, Great Kanto Earthquake, and Showa Financial Panic of 1927 dampened any excessive self-congratulatory mood, but these events hardly legitimized the pundits harping on stagnation and decline, much less comparisons to the putsches, reparations, humiliation, hyperinflation, and foreign occupation burdening Germany. Such foreboding and dread may be dismissed as collective hypochondria, but if it was feverish enough it would amount to an ailment in its own right. All the lecturers mentioned so far belonged to society's elites and had reasons to fear any disruption to the system that benefited them.

Furthermore, the Japanese chattering class's worry may reflect a fear of the unknown rather than a response to any actual ill in the country. In some ways, the leaders of Meiji Japan confronting Western challenges in the late nineteenth century faced clear if painful choices: imitation or inundation. But Taisho Japan found itself in an unfamiliar world by the end of World War I. Europe lay exhausted. America retreated behind its oceans. Communism became a reality. The anchor of Japanese diplomacy for two decades, the Anglo-Japanese Alliance, was replaced by the untested League of Nations and multilateral instruments such as the Washington Treaties and Kellogg-Briand Pact, which supposedly made the world and Japan safer by limiting arms and outlawing war.[30] Meiji's formula for success, industrialization based on low wages and aggressive imperialism, was no longer accepted by disgruntled workers at home and the new international order abroad. Japan's way forward in the 1920s looked far less straightforward and caused anxiety and insecurity in society, especially among those with something to lose from changes to

---

[30] Daniel Gorman, *The Emergence of International Society in the 1920s* (New York: Cambridge University Press, 2012); Oona A. Hathaway and Scott J. Shapiro, *The Internationalists: How a Radical Plan to Outlaw War Remade the World* (New York: Simon & Schuster, 2017).

the status quo. So the experts called for learning from German ways to make Japan more competitive, such as its national character, rationalization of manufacturing, and scientific management, but not the means to liberalize society, such as the Weimar Constitution and democratic government by universal suffrage.

Years of Advocacy, 1930–1935

While the *Graf Zeppelin* sailed gracefully around the globe in 1929, the world economy was hurtling toward a precipice. Two months after the pamphlet on the "latest intelligence on Germany's industry and economy" arrived, it was rendered obsolete by the Wall Street Crash. Now that Japan and Germany faced the same crisis, the teachings from Germany assumed heightened urgency. The rhetoric in the media became shriller. Some new entrants into punditry felt less averse to upsetting the status quo to save Japan from the long-dreaded, now-actualized crisis.

The economy returned to the center of attention. Saitō Yoichirō, a physician, published a pamphlet in 1931 on the temperament of German students that somehow connected it to Germany's financial straits. He argued that Japan had much to learn from the heart the Germans exhibited in combating the depression.[31] Kobe Commerce University's Economics and Business Administration Research Institute hosted two lectures the same year just on Germany's indemnity, which had supposedly been made manageable in the 1920s but was now again a drag on the world economy.[32] Both speakers suggested lowering payments and debt forgiveness, a pragmatic compromise that could only come from a disinterested party, such as Japan. Even the stodgy Japanese-German Cultural Society, which tended to indulge in academic minutiae and shun politics, waded into the debate and sponsored two presentations on the reparations.[33]

German domestic politics also stirred heated discussions in Japan. While Nazis and communists fought street battles in Germany, their Japanese sympathizers clashed by proxy through words in orations and

---

[31] "Foreword," in Saitō Yoichirō, *Doitsu gakusei kishitsu*, Hakodate Toshokan sōsho 10 (Hakodate: Shiritsu Hakodate Toshokan, 1931), 2.

[32] Ikushima Hirojirō, "Doitsu baishōkin shiharai riron no kōsatsu," in *Shōgyō Kenkyūjo kōenshū 50* (Kobe: Kōbe Shōgyō Daigaku Shōgyō Kenkyūjo, 1931), 1–39; Masui Mitsuzō, "Doitsu no gaishi shunyū to baishō shiharai no shōrai," in *Shōgyō Kenkyūjo kōenshū 51* (Kobe: Kōbe Shōgyō Daigaku Shōgyō Kenkyūjo, 1931), 1–48.

[33] Ōtake Torao, "Taidoku baishō mondai ni tsuite," in *Nichi-Doku bunka kōenshū 7* (Tokyo: Nichi-Doku Bunka Kyōkai, 1931), 1–30; Karl Knorr, "Doitsu-gawa yori mitaru baishōkin mondai," in *Nichi-Doku bunka kōenshū 7* (Tokyo: Nichi-Doku Bunka Kyōkai, 1931), 31–52.

booklets. Events in distant Germany with no immediate, ostensible consequences for Japan elicited strong emotions as if the stakes involved not just Germany's soul but Japan's as well. Some of the first partisan commentaries surfaced in the early 1930s. Writing in Berlin in October 1930, just a month after the Nazi electoral breakout, the correspondent Suzuki Tōmin voiced his disapproval of the rise of "German fascism" in a series on social science. At the time, social science meant something akin to socialist science, and Weimar Germany provided a safe, liberal haven for Japanese leftists and anti-imperialists.[34] Though hostile to Nazism, Suzuki took the trouble to familiarize himself and his readers with the Nazi Party's 25-point program. But in his criticism he merely fell back upon Marxist-Leninist orthodoxy and lumped Nazism in with generic fascism. He predicted that the "inevitability of history" would expose Hitler's lie of representing workers and sweep Nazism aside as the last gasp of German capitalism.[35] In the same issue, Kōno Mitsu, a social democrat, likewise toed his party line and expressed concern for the proletariat in Germany amid radicalization of both the left and the right.[36]

From 1932, when the Nazi Party went from strength to strength at the polls, lectures and pamphlets began to articulate transnational Nazism. Not only were voters in Germany drawn to Hitler and Nazism, in Japan, too, speakers emerged to take advantage of the moment and claim the role of interpreters of Nazism. Gorai Kinzō, a scholar of fascism who also wrote for the *Kokumin*, returned to Japan in August to discuss at the Japanese Lectures Agency the tectonic shifts in politics he felt in Germany.[37] He witnessed during his eight-month stay three national elections in which the Nazis gained successively more adherents to become the largest party in the Reichstag. He credited Hitler with the organizational skill behind the success and conjectured that just as Napoleon took over France after the French Revolution, the Weimar Republic seemed ripe to meet a similar end through Hitler.[38] Gorai gave an expanded version of the talk a few months later at the Economic Club, where he

---

[34] Katō Tetsurō, *Waimāruki Berurin no Nihonjin: Yōkō chishikijin no hantei nettowāku* (Tokyo: Iwanami Shoten, 2008).

[35] Suzuki Tōmin, "Doitsu fasshisuten to sono undō," in *Shakai kagaku kōza 4* (Tokyo: Seibundō, 1931), 10–12.

[36] Kōno Mitsu, "Sekai kakkoku fukeiki taisaku 2," ibid., 24.

[37] Gorai Kinzō, *Hittorā to Mussorīni*, Nihon kōen tsūshin 158 (Tokyo: Nihon Kōen Tsūshinsha, 1932), back of front cover. The agency printed a few other lectures, no longer extant, on Germany; for example, no. 151 on Germany's emergency economic policies and no. 169 exploring Berlin's attitude toward Japan.

[38] Ibid., 36.

became even more effusive and marveled at the "godlike power" Hitler wielded over the masses through rousing orations.[39]

Gorai deserves attention because he embodies transnational Nazism. His attitudes toward Germany and Nazism evolved from interest to knowledge to politicization to action, a transformation that many of his intellectual peers – several even with leftist roots – underwent between 1932 and 1936. Gorai was not yet an unqualified admirer of the Führer in 1932, in part because he esteemed the Duce more highly. He thought Mussolini looked like a heroic leader while Hitler merely resembled a shopkeeper.[40] Still, Gorai's defense of Nazi violence as a last resort to overcome self-serving class divisions was a gross misrepresentation of German politics.[41] In his eyes, the bloodshed he must have seen in Berlin was justified by a patriotic cause. Thus, word by word, sound by sound, the wall separating expertise from partisanship, namely between objectivity and subjectivity, was being dismantled.

The installation of Hitler into power in January 1933 altered Japanese and German history through the voluntary conversion of several Japanese opinion makers from mere observers to fervid adherents, from sympathizing with Germany to sympathizing with Nazism. At the Third Reich's outset, curiosity about the Nazi movement did not translate into accurate information. Tabata Tamehiko, a prolific author on economics, boasted at the Japanese Lectures Agency that he had confidential knowledge of the Führer. But he could not even get the pronunciation of Hitler's name right and only repeated Nazi hagiography on Hitler's political epiphany.[42] But it did not take long for a more enthusiastic Japanese supporter of Hitler to ditch paraphrasing propaganda and to publish Hitler's own speeches as "an oratorical tour de force of resurgent Germany's hero."[43] Writing the introduction, Nakano Seigō, a Diet member and ardent advocate of fascism, could hardly contain his excitement for the Hitler regime and its exemplary potential for Japan. Nakano particularly admired the dictator's ruthlessness in bulldozing obstacles to his agenda and excoriated Japanese politicians for their dithering and incompetence:

Japan's current situation in the extraordinary times is very similar to that of resurgent Germany ... There is not another unleashed statesman like Hitler in Germany ... He boldly, personally saves Germany from its national crisis by

[39] Gorai Kinzō, "Ōshū seikyoku no zento to fasshizumu," in *Keizai Kurabu kōen 14* (Tokyo: Tōyō Keizai Shuppanbu, 1932), 50.

[40] Gorai, *Hittorā to Mussorīni*, 40.   [41] Ibid., 37.

[42] Tabata Tamehiko, *Hītorā no jinbutsu kaibō*, Nihon kōen tsūshin 170 (Tokyo: Nihon Kōen Tsūshinsha, 1932), 1.

[43] Adolf Hitler, *Hitorā no shishiku: Shinkō Doitsu no eiyū Adorufu Hitorā Shushō enzetsushū*, ed. Joseph Goebbels, trans. Taki Kiyoshi (Tokyo: Nihon Kōensha, 1933).

demolishing department stores, persecuting Jews, and burning books. Each of these policies has ignited controversy. Yet one cannot help but have absolute respect and sympathy for his passion, stamina, determination, courage, and confidence. Regrettably, comparing Hitler to the established politicians in Japan and their cowardice is like comparing clouds to dirt.[44]

For the rest of his life, Nakano remained the most zealous Japanese supporter of German Nazism. His antipathy toward corporations and Jews in the same context echoed Nazi ideology; though distinct from many other transnational Nazis, Nakano agitated for the Nazification of Japan. In 1943, the Japanese state that he so despised finally tired of his provocations and placed him under house arrest, during which he committed suicide. Nakano's career thus demonstrates that rapprochement with Germany had not always aligned with Japanese diplomacy but emerged in specific cultural and ideological contexts.

Moreover, Nakano, a journalist turned parliamentarian with ties to extragovernmental groups pursuing goals not in line with those of officialdom, personified and bridged the gulf between the regime and civil society organizations. Within civil society, too, attitudes toward Hitler and Nazism varied. Leftist voices such as Suzuki Tōmin denounced Nazi Germany, though they belonged to an overwhelmed minority under a government that abhorred left-wing ideologies. The main differences in opinion were among those who debated how much Japan should approach the Third Reich ideologically and diplomatically.

The more affluent, educated segment in Japan at first met National Socialism with some skepticism, chiefly because of the movement's early revolutionary rhetoric and unruly behavior. Although the Nazi Party had long abandoned its leftist aspirations, Keio University professor Kada Tetsuji still mentioned its socialist roots in his talk at the Economic Club in 1933.[45] Several lecturers continued to cite the party's 25-point platform as if it still mattered, even though it was adopted in 1920 and contained provisions forgotten or de-emphasized by the Nazis themselves.[46] Others discussed individuals in the left wing of the movement such as Gregor Strasser and Gottfried Feder, but they had been sidelined by Hitler in his bid to reassure industrialists and middle-class voters. The sources consulted by the speakers, such as the party's program or *Mein Kampf*, contributed to the skewed understanding of Nazism. But the responsibility of thinking critically still lay with the lecturers, several of

---

[44] Nakano Seigō, introduction to ibid., 1, 3–4.
[45] Kada Tetsuji, "Fasshizumu ni tsuite," in *Keizai Kurabu kōen 21* (Tokyo: Tōyō Keizai Shuppanbu, 1933), 5.
[46] Tabata translated the program in his lecture. Tabata, 33–36.

whom abdicated the task and functioned as passive conduits of the party's message. Besides populism, the elites were put off by Nazi boorishness. The literary critic Katsumoto Seiichirō, who witnessed the party's rise from September 1930 to early 1934, criticized the Nazis as uneducated and ignorant in a speech at the Economic Club.[47] In another talk at the venue, the constitutional expert and Tokyo Imperial University professor Minobe Tatsukichi described his confrontation with blue collar Nazis in a train carriage that almost came to blows because he did not greet a new rider with "Heil Hitler!"[48] Another constitutional scholar, Tokyo Imperial University professor Miyazawa Toshiyoshi, lamented the seepage of irrational Nazi mysticism into what should be logical legal theories.[49]

Despite the initial lukewarm reception by some elites, Nazism must still have aroused significant interest in their circles. Otherwise the literary and constitutional scholars would not have abandoned their areas of expertise to lecture on their impressions of Hitler's Germany. Club members wanted to hear the latest insights from those just returning from the Third Reich. As the Hitler regime consolidated, it also became an unavoidable topic for Japanese academics, businessmen, and bureaucrats. Once some speakers convinced themselves that Nazism had shed its socialist or rogue elements – that is, it had gained respectability – they became more amenable to the Führer and his regime. In a speech at the Economic Club in late 1933, the journalist and former parliamentarian Tagawa Daikichirō took Hitler at face value in maintaining that Germany was not preparing for war.[50] He adopted Berlin's perspective that Germany should enjoy equality in armaments with other nations, though he conceded that Hitler was "a little rash" in pulling Germany out of the League of Nations when the demand went unmet.[51] Tagawa believed, as did many German conservatives, that Hitler would moderate in order to win over the respectable classes.[52] Nothing in Tagawa's career up to that point indicated that he would favor Nazism. But like so many contemporary Germans who joined the Nazi movement under the regime's "coordination" (*Gleichschaltung*) campaign to co-opt society, Tagawa,

---

[47] Katsumoto Seiichirō, "Nachisu shihaika ni okeru Doitsu no genjō wo chūshin toshite," in *Keizai Kurabu kōen 52* (Tokyo: Tōyō Keizai Shuppanbu, 1934), 48–49.

[48] Minobe Tatsukichi, "Doitsu saikin no keizai jōsei," in *Keizai Kurabu kōen 69* (Tokyo: Tōyō Keizai Shuppanbu, 1934), 38–39.

[49] Miyazawa Toshiyoshi, *Doitsu kenpō no dokusaika* (Tokyo: Tōkyō Chūō Kōenkai, 1934), 67.

[50] Tagawa Daikichirō, "Doitsu no Kokusai Renmei dattai to sono kokusai seikyoku ni oyobosu eikyō," in *Keizai Kurabu kōen 41* (Tokyo: Tōyō Keizai Shuppanbu, 1933), 10.

[51] Ibid., 21–22.   [52] Ibid., 23–24.

too, added his voice to the chorus praising Hitler. What distinguished the Germans and those Japanese who chose to adhere to Nazism was that the former faced tangible pressure and gains, but the latter acted voluntarily and on purely ideological grounds.

Whereas lecturers speaking to refined circles such as the Economic Club still harbored reservations toward Nazism, pamphleteers catering to the reading masses showed no such restraint in rhetoric or content. Just a few months into the Nazi regime, Imasato Katsuo wrote a booklet on "Hitler's national revolution" with glowing passages lionizing the Führer for "charging like a tank" to realize 99 percent of his "all-or-nothing dictatorial ideal."[53] He advised the "astonished world" to take heed of this "ferocious tiger." A pamphlet by the Social Education Society called Hitler "a freak of nature" and "a star illuminating chaotic Germany."[54] Several publications reprinted the Nazi 25-point program in its entirety to explore its virtues.[55] The sentiment prevalent in these works may best be summed up in a pamphlet on Nazi youth groups by Count Futara Yoshinori, a cofounder of the Boy Scouts of Japan. He first visited Germany in mid-1931 and again in late 1933. On both occasions he pondered "Whither Germany?" – the first time in utmost despair, the second anticipating a bright future.[56]

The proliferation of pamphlets lauding Nazi Germany reveals a vibrancy in interwar Japanese civil society that is often obscured by scholarly debates over authoritarianism or fascism. The government in the mid-1930s was still willing to concede some freedoms of speech and association for public debates on topics deemed not particularly sensitive or subversive, such as reactions to developments in faraway Germany. Under these circumstances the Resurgent Germany Research Association (Shinkō Doitsu Kenkyūkai) was established in March 1934. Its expressed mission was to relate the latest topics from the new Germany through a biweekly pamphlet series, *Introduction to Resurgent Germany*, on the country's politics, economy, law, and culture.[57] Anyone could become a subscribing member for monthly dues of ¥2.

---

[53] Imasato Katsuo, *Hittorā no kokumin kakumei* (Tokyo: San'yōkaku, 1933), 25.

[54] Takakura Shinobu, "Hittora to sono ittō," in *Minshū bunko 76* (Tokyo: Shakai Kyōiku Kyōkai, 1933), 2.

[55] Matsunami Jirō, *Nachisu no ugoki* (Tokyo: Nōgeisha, 1934), 43–48; Akamatsu Kotora, "Hittorā undō wo kataru," in *Shakai kyōiku panfuretto 189* (Tokyo: Shakai Kyōiku Kyōkai, 1934), 5–9.

[56] "Introduction," in Futara Yoshinori, "Nachisu Doitsu no seishōnen undō," in *Minshū bunko 86* (Tokyo: Shakai Kyōiku Kyōkai, 1934), 1.

[57] Masumoto Yoshirō, ed., *Shinkō Doitsu no shōkai 2* (Koganei-mura: Shinkō Doitsu Kenkyūkai, 1934), back page.

Though authoritative sounding, the association was little more than a one man club. The soul, indeed the only soul, behind the organization was one Masumoto Yoshirō. Before founding the association, Masumoto seems not to have produced anything of note on Germany, as no book, essay, article, or lecture can be attributed to him. He did know German because the pamphlets consisted mostly of speeches and articles translated by Masumoto himself. Probably very few people paid to join the association, which operated out of Masumoto's residence in a suburban village outside Tokyo. The "single-handedness" of the organization manifested itself as a delay, caused by Masumoto's illness, of the seventh volume in the series, which never lived up to the promised frequency of two issues per month. He published only one more volume. Then at the end of 1934, he, the series, and the association disappeared altogether from historical records as abruptly as they emerged. Of course, Masumoto and his handiwork had no perceptible impact in improving Japanese familiarity with Germany or Japanese-German relations, but they illustrate the latitude an enterprising individual – even an amateur – enjoyed in promoting his pet causes in public discourse as long as they did not infringe on the regime's prerogatives.

Masumoto's association might yet have thrived despite its shortcomings had it been founded later. The year 1935 witnessed a spike in interest in Hitler and Nazi Germany among both elites and the public. Their vehicles of communication, respectively lectures and pamphlets, began to converge in accentuating transnational Nazism, though each in ways appropriate for their venues and audiences. Thus Kondō Harubumi, a bureaucrat in the Education Ministry, wrote a booklet for the Imperial Youth Organization to celebrate the Hitler Youth's exploits in Germany under Nazi leadership, with numerous quotes from propagandistic Nazi lyrics and pronouncements.[58]

The Economic Club hosted no fewer than seven lectures the same year on developments in Germany and their repercussions. In January alone, it invited three diplomats to speak at the club, an indication of convergence of the government's and society's attitudes toward Germany. The lecturers' tone remained cautious and their concern was mostly economic, but they also expressed optimism for the direction the country was taking. In discussing the reintegration of the Saar Territory into Germany, Ashida Hitoshi of the *Japan Times* concluded that the Germans' patriotism would enable them to overcome any material

---

[58] Kondō Harubumi, "Nachisu Doitsu chika ni okeru seishōnen undō toshite no Hittorā Yūgendo ni tsuite," in *Teikoku Shōnendan Kyōkai sōsho 4* (Tokyo: Teikoku Shōnendan Kyōkai, 1935), 11.

hardship.[59] Yanagisawa Ken, responsible for cultural diplomacy in the Foreign Ministry, warned that Japan would suffer the Kaiserreich's fate if it did not learn from Germany's current campaign to promote its culture abroad.[60] The club even landed Nagai Matsuzō, the most recent ambassador to Berlin, for a presentation on Germany under Nazism. Nagai explained that the Japanese asked him repeatedly about Hitler, whom he perceived to be sharp, smart, and focused on practical common sense.[61]

Audience curiosity about Hitler's personality likely led the club to invite one special guest, Nihon University professor Momo Minosuke. As far as can be ascertained, Momo enjoys distinction as the first Japanese person to have met Hitler. The interview took place in late September 1930, about two weeks after the Nazis' electoral breakthrough. Without knowing beforehand whether he would be received by the Führer, Momo made a pilgrimage to Munich just for a chance to pay his respects in person. After the Nazis took over Germany in 1933, Momo capitalized on his unique, marketable experience and embarked on a lecture circuit for various audiences on the sensational but little understood Hitler and Nazi phenomena. In his presentation at the Economic Club, he added to the Führer's mystique by dramatizing the difficulty in securing an audience – he had worried that Hitler would hold a grudge against Japan for fighting Germany in World War I. He dismissed charges against Hitler of draft-dodging in Austria as "social democratic demagoguery" and gossip about Hitler's rumored Jewish heritage based on his hair color: "Japanese have black hair, too, but are clearly not Jewish."[62] Instead, the combination of Hitler's "dark brown hair" and pale skin exuded an unworldly aura and "uniquely Germanic intelligence."[63]

Momo's effusive praise for Hitler at the exclusive club was matched by bombastic adulation of Nazism in popular print. A biographical booklet claimed that Hitler's "handsomeness" and "masculinity" attracted German women.[64] It justified Nazi anti-Semitism with claims that Jews had achieved their success through shamelessly exploiting productive members of society.[65] A *Mainichi* pamphlet applauded

[59] Ashida Hitoshi, "Zāru kizoku mondai to Ōshū seikyoku no zento," in *Keizai Kurabu kōen 79* (Tokyo: Tōyō Keizai Shuppanbu, 1935), 21.

[60] Yanagisawa Ken, "Bunka gaikō to kakkoku no bunka jigyō ni tsuite," ibid., 50.

[61] Nagai Matsuzō, "Nachisu seikenka ni okeru Doitsu no genjō to shōrai," ibid., 51–52.

[62] Momo Minosuke, "Hittorā to Nachisu wo kataru," in *Keizai Kurabu kōen 94* (Tokyo: Tōyō Keizai Shuppanbu, 1935), 14–15, 11–12.

[63] Ibid., 12.

[64] Nakagawa Shigeru, *Hittorā*, Ijin denki bunko 67 (Tokyo: Nihonsha, 1935), 17.

[65] Ibid., 14.

言宣彈爆のツ〔
と
戰慄の歐洲

特245

81   84

社聞新日每阪大
社聞新日京東

Figure 2.1 The *Mainichi* pamphlet *Germany's Bombshell Announcement and Shuddering Europe*. Its cover features a captivating photograph of Hitler to attract readers. But Hitler's name is not mentioned – or needed – because potential customers were expected to already recognize his face. There is a swastika in the lower left, but it is the reverse of the Nazi one. Original in color. National Diet Library.

Hitler's "bombshell announcement" to resume conscription as a "lightning unilateralist" move to destroy the Versailles Treaty (Figure 2.1).[66] It also maintained much confidence in Germany's "excellent mechanical civilization" in propelling its military to the world's greatest in a

[66] Ōsaka Mainichi Shinbunsha, ed., *Doitsu no bakudan sengen to senritsu no Ōshū* (Osaka: Ōsaka Mainichi Shinbunsha, 1935), 3–4.

year or two.[67] The pamphlet *The Memelland Problem and Führer Hitler* in late October went so far as to use Germany's agitation for recovering the Memelland from Lithuania as an excuse to cheer Nazism. Its author, Sugiyama Akira, declared that the Nazi dictatorship looked nothing like oppressive regimes in the feudal age, and that Hitler had an "elegant, humble" character.[68]

The pamphlet, predating the Anti-Comintern Pact by more than a year, stands out as one of the first publications to broach and rationalize the subject of Japanese-German cooperation. Besides the aforementioned title, the identical contents also appeared as the pamphlet *The Chance for a Japanese-German Alliance*.[69] Because very few Japanese knew of the Memelland, a thin strip of land northeast of East Prussia, why then would anyone in Japan write and hope to sell a pamphlet about it? The answer, as well as the key to any Japanese-German entente, was the Soviet Union. In the introduction, Major General Ōuchi Kazuta compared the situation in Europe in 1935 with that in 1903, when unrest in the Balkans kept Russia from focusing its attention on Manchuria before the outbreak of the Russo-Japanese War.[70] The current Nazi-Soviet tension over the Memelland could escalate to a war that might present an opportunity for Japan to check the spread of international communism that threatened both Japan and Germany.[71] That is, Tokyo and Berlin had a common enemy in Moscow.

For the pamphleteers, Japan's traditional diplomatic partners did not present any meaningful alternative to the country's isolation. Europe and America viewed any Japanese-German alliance with great suspicion.[72] Writers singled out Britain as the chief villain scheming to contain Japan. Sugiyama and Ōuchi collaborated on two more pamphlets to blame Britain or Jews for attempting to encircle Japan or financially infiltrating northern China.[73] The scapegoating of Jews for diplomatic or economic intrigues hints at Nazi influence on the writers' thinking. Another pamphleteer called for the "downfall of the crafty British Empire" and redistributing land in the world through Japanese-German-Italian

[67] Ibid., 62–63.
[68] Sugiyama Akira, *Mēmeru mondai to Hittorā Sōtō* (Tokyo: Kyōzaisha, 1935), 24–26.
[69] Sugiyama Akira, *Nichi-Doku dōmei no kiun* (Tokyo: Kyōzaisha, 1935).
[70] Ōuchi Kazuta, introduction to *Mēmeru mondai*, 1–2.
[71] Sugiyama, *Mēmeru mondai*, 50.   [72] Ibid., 48.
[73] Sugiyama Akira, *Kakudai suru hainichi no yōun: Kyokutō wo nerau Ei-Bei-So*, Kōtōkaku panfuretto 3 (Tokyo: Kōtōkaku, 1936); Sugiyama Akira, *Hokushi wo meguru Ei-Yudaya zaibatsu no inbō*, Jikyoku panfuretto 1 (Tokyo: Kōtsū Tenbōsha, 1937).

Figure 2.2 The pamphlet *Japan, Germany, Italy, and the League of Nations*. The cover places the flags of the three countries side by side. The "League of Nations" is in flames and tilting, seemingly on the verge of collapse. Original in color. National Diet Library.

solidarity.[74] He further urged readers to realize that Japan could save itself from self-destruction only through a tripartite community. Another booklet issued in the last week of 1935 warned Japan about "cunning Britain" and proposed that true world peace could only be achieved through a coalition of Japan, Germany, and Italy (Figure 2.2).[75]

[74] Sassa Kōkichi, *Rōkai Daiei Teikoku wo taose: Nichi-Doku-I no teikei ni yorite sekai ryōdo no saibunkatsu jitsugen wo kantetsu seyo* (Tokyo: Kokusai Jijō Kenkyūkai, 1935), 46.
[75] Ōtomo Shingo, *Nihon Doitsu Itaria to Kokusai Renmei* (Tokyo: Kokusai Jijō Kenkyūkai, 1935), 42–43.

The years from 1930 to 1935 thus saw the chorus of Japanese voices espousing transnational Nazism and bilateral partnership grow steadily louder, anticipating official diplomacy by at least a year. But differences in opinion on Nazism still divided the upper and the lower echelons of society. The business-friendly and established elements, as revealed in their musings at the Economic Club, treated Hitler and Nazism with measured approval and cautious optimism. Most welcomed his steadfast anticommunism and admired his miracle work in resuscitating Germany's economy. But they also expressed some reservations about Nazi socialism, rampant violence and illegality, and the inflationary pressure of rearmament. Meanwhile, sensationalist pamphleteers exhibited far less restraint in their enthusiasm for National Socialism, going so far as to advocate Japanese-German collaboration.

This schism in Japanese reactions approximates that in Germany itself. There, conservatives in the bureaucracy, military, and industry accepted Hitler in a pragmatic maneuver and as a lesser evil versus communism. The middle and lower classes embraced Nazism as an ideology with promises of improving their conditions. Because many Japanese already believed that Germany had much to teach Japan, it was merely a logical extension for some in the less privileged populations to call for approaching, perhaps even emulating, Nazi Germany to help Japan break out of its predicament in the extraordinary times. Moreover, Hitler and Nazism excited considerable curiosity among readers and generated a sizable demand for information that needed to be met. Pamphlets were primarily moneymaking vehicles for their writers and publishers. At ¥0.10 per issue, many copies needed to be sold for the producers to turn a profit. If favorable views on Nazi Germany were perceived to turn off potential customers, it seems unlikely that so many authors would have flocked to the topic. To catch busy commuters' glances, pamphlets often incorporated exaggerated graphics and provocative titles, such as *Down with the Crafty British Empire* or *The Chance for a Japanese-German Alliance*.

Years of Activism, 1935–1937

Not until November 1936 would that chance for an entente become reality with the signatures of Joachim von Ribbentrop and Mushakōji Kintomo on the Anti-Comintern Pact. During a return to Japan back in October 1935, Mushakōji, the plenipotentiary ambassador to Germany, spoke at the Economic Club. He gave no hint of the government even contemplating an arrangement with Berlin, much less trying to sell Japanese-German rapprochement. Instead, he politely praised Hitler as a teetotal bachelor dedicated single-mindedly to serving Germany. But he also identified threats to the Nazi regime such as liberals, Jews, and communists.[76] How then did official diplomacy come to march in lockstep with those pundits calling for bilateral cooperation in a year's time?

The populist, transnational Nazi pamphlets kept up their self-appointed activism to promote Hitler and Nazism, and to agitate for closer relations. One writer felt touched that at the Berlin Olympics Hitler personally congratulated Japanese swimmers and showed "a shared consciousness" between the two peoples. He even thought Hitler somehow "belonged" with or harbored sympathy for Japan.[77] Another marveled at Hitler's ability to intimidate Europe, which was forced to follow every sleight of his hand and tremble at every stomp of his foot.[78] Yet another cited papal support for Hitler's "declaration of war" on communism and argued that Japan should pay close attention should conflict break out between Germany and the Soviet Union.[79] Finally, another booklet titled *The Chance for a Japanese-German Alliance* warned readers against British, American, and Soviet designs in East Asia and attempts to isolate Japan. Its writer pointedly mentioned that a portion of the Japanese intelligentsia maintained favorable views on Nazism and predicted that a Japanese-German partnership would materialize in due time.[80]

The positive rhetoric on Nazi Germany in the pamphlets was just a continuation from the previous years of advocacy, but the real change in tone since 1936 took place among the elites and their lectures. More and more traditional conservatives reconciled themselves with the reality of Nazism. In a lecture at the Economic Club, Kajima Morinosuke, a diplomat turned industrialist, equated the Comintern's purported assault on Germany with an attack on Japan's military. He thereby treated the two countries as one unit with a common enemy.[81] He advised his fellow businessmen that Nazism could at least keep communism in check and that they should hope for a balance between

[76] Mushakōji Kintomo, "Hittorā seiken to Doitsu no kokujō," in *Keizai Kurabu kōen 101* (Tokyo: Tōyō Keizai Shuppanbu, 1935), 24–26.
[77] Katayama Takashi, *Dokusai sannin otoko: Sonogo no Hittorā Shōkaiseki Mussorīni* (Tokyo: Morita Shobō, 1936), 6.
[78] Kondō Keisuke, *Bakudan otoko Hittorā no zenbō: Zen Ōshū wasen no kagi* (Tokyo: Yūkōsha, 1936), 1–2.
[79] Miki Rin, *Doitsu wa danzen kyōsan shugi e sensensu: Hitorā Doitsu Sōtō netsuben Pio Rōma Hōō rikisetsu seien* (Tokyo: Tsūzoku Seidan Kenkyūkai, 1936), front leaf.
[80] Kuroki Shōma, *Nichi-Doku dōmei no kiun: Sono hitsuzensei no kentō* (Tokyo: Kyōzaisha, 1936), 27, 40.
[81] Kajima Morinosuke, "Doitsu no Rokaruno Jōyaku haiki to Ōshū no anzen hoshō mondai," in *Keizai Kurabu kōen 117* (Tokyo: Keizai Kurabu, 1936), 28.

liberalism and fascism.[82] Maita Minoru, a noted commentator on foreign affairs, linked the destinies of Japan and Germany through the Soviet Union. He argued that the improved Trans-Siberian Railway threatened Japan because it could expedite Soviet troop movements not only to Germany but also to Japanese-controlled Manchuria.[83] The erudite Japanese-German Cultural Society, too, ventured into politics and hosted a lecture on the Third Reich by Tomoeda Takahiko, the association's former head. He extolled the Nazi education system for instilling new weltanschauung toward life and nation and marveled at Hitler's vision to launch a "restorative revolution" through combining ancient symbols with a modern outlook on the world.[84] The industrialist Godō Takuo gave several presentations after returning from a tour of Nazi Germany. Godō was so impressed by what he witnessed that he brought a documentary film to his talk at the Japanese Economic Federation so that spectators could see the miracle with their own eyes.[85] He wanted to spread the Nazi gospel so fervently that he delivered the identical speech at two other venues, the Economic Club and the Japanese Lectures Agency.[86] Although Godō vaingloriously made sure his audiences knew that he had met the Führer in person, he also insightfully, if belatedly, stressed that monarchical restoration was an illusion. From his impression of Hitler, Godō assured listeners that the Führer's selflessness in making Germany great again would ultimately find success.[87] Japan could benefit by cozying up to the new master of Europe.

The synchronization of official diplomacy with the public exhortations in lectures and pamphlets for Japanese-German rapprochement through the Anti-Comintern Pact on November 25, 1936 unleashed a burst of civil activism to rally around government action. If some opinion makers had hesitated to reveal their support for closer ties with Germany, the pact freed them to speak their minds. Some in the media responded enthusiastically to the development. Before the year ended, no fewer than 13 speeches and booklets were published to extol the compact. Pamphleteers took the initiative in selling and interpreting the new

[82] Ibid., 30.

[83] Maita Minoru, *Echiopia no haisen ni tomonau Ōshū no seikyoku*, Nihon kōen tsūshin 317 (Tokyo: Nihon Kōen Tsūshinsha, 1936), 24.

[84] Tomoeda Takahiko, "Doitsu Daisan Kokka ni tsuite," in *Nichi-Doku bunka kōenshū 10* (Tokyo: Nichi-Doku Bunka Kyōkai, 1936), 28, 30.

[85] Godō Takuo, *Doitsu shisatsudan*, Keizai Renmei kōen 81 (Tokyo: Nihon Keizai Renmeikai, 1936), front leaf.

[86] Godō Takuo, "Doitsu shisatsudan," in *Keizai Kurabu kōen 121* (Tokyo: Tōyō Keizai Shuppanbu, 1936); Godō Takuo, *Doitsu wa doko e iku*, Nihon kōen tsūshin 318 (Tokyo: Nihon Kōen Tsūshinsha, 1936).

[87] Godō, "Doitsu shisatsudan," 38–39.

diplomatic order. Many bore provocative, sensationalist titles, such as *Why Did Japan and Germany Become Allies? A Joint Declaration of War on Communism*; *The Japanese-German Pact and Other Nations' Actions: Struggle against the Red Demon's Threat*; *Bombshell for Humanity's Enemy, the Communists: The Causes of the Japanese-German Anticommunist Pact*; *The Far Eastern Red Encirclement of Our Lifelines: Pros and Cons of the Japanese-German Pact*; *Weighing the Japanese-German Anticommunist Pact, Calling for the World's Attention: Does It Really Counter the Comintern's Activity?*; *Why the Japanese-German Anticommunist Agreement? Tense Soviet-German Relations and Imperial Japan's Attitude*; and *The Japanese-German Agreement and Japan's Leap of Progress* (Figure 2.3).[88]

These pamphlets largely conveyed predictable contents – vigilance against Soviet machinations and communism in China, with occasional parroted anti-Semitism borrowed from the Nazis – but the associations that published them still warrant attention. By December 1, a group of transnational Nazis had established the Japanese-German Comradeship Society (Nichi-Doku Dōshikai).[89] The founders counted the *Asahi* correspondent Kuroda Reiji, who converted from a leftist to a vocal admirer of Hitler and Nazism. Though far from a one man enterprise, the club still accomplished relatively little. It embarked on a lecture circuit across the country, but the outbreak of war against China in July 1937 eclipsed the importance of collaboration with Germany. Its planned series of pamphlets and brochures each seems to have only one issue.[90] Other publishers such as the Patriotic Newspaper Company (Aikoku Shinbunsha) or the International Ideas Research Association (Kokusai Shisō Kenkyūkai) fared little better, bursting with activity after the pact and then sinking into obscurity soon afterwards.

---

[88] Respectively, Mishima Yasuo, *Nichi-Doku wa naze dōmei shita ka: Kyōsan shugi e no kyōdō sensen* (Tokyo: Kyō no Mondaisha, 1936); Suzuki Hidesuke, *Nichi-Doku kyōtei to kakkoku no dōkō: Sekima no kyōi ni kōsō* (Tokyo: Morita Shobō, 1936); Nagata Kenzō, *Sekai jinrui no teki kyōsantōin e bakudan – Nichi-Doku Bōkyō Kyōtei no yurai* (Tokyo: Aikoku Shinbunsha Shuppanbu, 1936); Kawasaki Minotarō, *Waga seimeisen wo obiyakasu sekka no Kyokutō hōijin: Nichi-Doku kyōtei ze ka hi ka* (Tokyo: Rakutensha, 1937); Kuroki Shōma, *Nichi-Doku Bōkyō Kyōtei no kentō: Sekai no kanshin no yobu hatashite Kominterun no katsudō wo fusegu ka* (Tokyo: Kyōzaisha, 1936); Takeo Hajime, *Naniyue no Nichi-Doku Bōkyō Kyōtei ka: Kinpaku jōtai no So-Doku kankei to Kōkoku Nihon no tachiba*, Kōtōkaku panfuretto 4 (Tokyo: Kōtōkaku, 1936); Shibata Yoshihisa, *Nichi-Doku kyōtei to Nihon no yakushin* (Tokyo: Nihon Jiji Tsūshinsha, 1936).

[89] Iwamura, 195–221.

[90] Kuroda Reiji, *Nichi-Doku dōmeiron: Bōkyō Kyōtei wo sarani ippo mae e!* Nichi-Doku Dōshikai panfuretto 1 (Tokyo: Nichi-Doku Dōshikai, 1936); Kuroda Reiji, *Nichi-Doku Bōkyō Kyōtei no igi*, Nichi-Doku Dōshikai shōsasshi 1 (Tokyo: Nichi-Doku Dōshikai, 1937).

Figure 2.3 The pamphlet *The Japanese-German Agreement and Japan's Leap of Progress*. The signatories are represented by their flags and two uniformed men side by side. Original in color. National Diet Library.

Still, pamphleteers took advantage of the remaining latitude in print and association to press their point.

The final phase of the convergence between mass media and official-dom saw several current or former politicians and bureaucrats take to the pamphlet-sphere to drum up support for the new direction in Japanese diplomacy. The Foreign Ministry, too, deigned to publish a brochure on the Anti-Comintern Pact.[91] Ida Iwakusu, an army officer turned parliamentarian, emphasized the inevitability of the alliance.[92] Another Diet

---

[91] *Nichi-Doku Bōkyō Kyōtei ni tsuite* (Tokyo: Gaimushō Jōhōbu, 1937).
[92] Ida Iwakusu, *Nichi-Doku Bōkyō Kyōtei ze ka hi ka* (Tokyo: Kokusai Shisō Kenkyūkai Jimushitsu, 1936).

member, Funada Naka, wrote a tract to urge Japan to imitate resurgent Germany.[93] Matsuoka Yōsuke, a diplomat whose handiwork included Japan's melodramatic withdrawal from the League of Nations in 1933, composed a speech and a booklet to explain the Anti-Comintern Pact to the populace from an insider's perspective.[94] His choice to communicate through a lecture and a pamphlet neatly embodies the agreement of public opinion and state policy.

Transnational Nazism in Lectures and Pamphlets

The Anti-Comintern Pact, the moment of validation for those pundits who so adroitly manipulated the power of words as sound and in print to agitate for rapprochement with Germany, also marks the end of their influence. The formalization of collaboration with Germany eliminated the very latitude that the lecturers and pamphleteers had used to express their enthusiasm for Nazism and Hitler. The pact resulted from the metamorphosis of relations with Germany from the fantasy of a few individuals to the prerogative of diplomacy to be executed solely by the government. From now on, the state had to maintain an appropriate level of esteem for its ally and counterparty, but the adulation of Nazi Germany voiced by some writers would have to be tempered lest it be mistaken for obsequiousness.[95] Moreover, the escalation of the war in China led Japan into a "valley of darkness" with more intensive censorship, regimentation of society, and unbridled expansion.[96] Perhaps not coincidentally, Amō Eiji and Aoki Kazuo, the embassy secretary and the attaché who lectured in the saloon on the *Kaga Maru*, rose with the extraordinary times from the 1930s. Amō as chief of the Information Division in the Foreign Ministry proclaimed Japan's "Asian Monroe Doctrine" on his own initiative in 1934. Aoki became the inaugural Minister of Greater East Asia in 1942. The next time Amō and Aoki found themselves confined together in a small place was 1945, when both were charged and detained as Class A war criminals.

Interwar Japan's attitudes toward Germany, as reflected in lectures and pamphlets, evolved through three stages. Immediately after World

---

[93] Funada Naka, *Tazan no ishi: Haisen Doitsu kara Daisan Teikoku kensetsu e*, Kokusei isshin ronsō 21 (Tokyo: Kokusei Isshinkai, 1937).

[94] Matsuoka Yōsuke, *Nichi-Doku Bōkyō Kyōtei no igi to waga gaikō no kaiko*, Man'ichi sōsho 7 (Dairen: Manshū Nichinichi Shinbunsha, 1937); Matsuoka Yōsuke, *Nichi-Doku Bōkyō Kyōtei no igi*, Daiichi Shuppan jikyoku sōsho 1 (Tokyo: Daiichi Shuppansha, 1937).

[95] Ida, 26–27.

[96] Thomas R. H. Havens, *Valley of Darkness: The Japanese People and World War II* (New York: W. W. Norton, 1978).

War I, lectures – mostly lectures because pamphlets were a later phe-nomenon – aimed to reacquaint Japan with a much transformed Ger-many. In this phase, lasting until the early 1930s, knowledge of this new Germany was largely in the care of a few handfuls of genuine experts with experience in the country. They maintained a serious, neutral tone when describing Germany and focused their presentations on fact-finding, always with an eye for extracting applicable lessons for Japan in its perceived predicaments.

Then beginning in around 1931, developments in both countries altered Japanese public perceptions of Germany. The popularization of pamphlets vis-à-vis closed speaking engagements as a channel of mass communications swelled the ranks of opinion makers and enlarged potential audiences. Those pontificating on Germany in print no longer had or needed the qualifications associated with the lecturers in the 1920s. Most pamphleteers commanded little firsthand knowledge of Germany and relied heavily on sources such as *Mein Kampf*, speeches, or the Nazi Party's 25-point program of 1920, so they often relayed to readers little more than Nazi propaganda. While the Economic Club never needed to sell a printed lecture to stay solvent, the thin profit margins of each pamphlet and intense competition among publishers privileged inflammatory opinions over uninspiring facts. The scholars, officials, and businessmen in their lectures always maintained some skepticism toward Nazism, but the rabble-rousing pamphleteers embraced National Socialism wholeheartedly, both for its intrinsic populist appeal and its potential to sell copies.

On an ideological level, the weltanschauung offered by Nazism chal-lenged Japanese of all stripes to question the existing social, economic, and political arrangements in their own country. The world economic crisis and the two nations' shared but independently achieved diplomatic isolation seemed to offer a legitimate basis for comparison and collabor-ation. Generally, in Germany as in Japan, the establishment lived up to its conservative reputation. High bureaucrats, industrialists, academics, and others with much to lose in any upheaval reacted to Nazism with caution. They approved of its anticommunism, economic nationalism, and authoritarian government but abhorred its socialist heritage and indiscriminate violence. Meanwhile, those in the lower and lower middle classes with little to risk found the National Socialist rhetoric of classless equality, shared benefits and sacrifice, and ruthless determination in solving the nation's existential crises most appealing. A few leftist intel-lectuals raised objections in social science pamphlets, but these publica-tions were intended for a small, committed readership and did not resonate with the wider public.

The convergence of the traditional conservatives and populist nationalists around 1936 marks the third stage. Some elites, impressed by Hitler's international and domestic successes, joined ranks with the pamphleteers to call for rapprochement with Germany. Without the support or at least acquiescence of the well positioned in Japanese society, the Anti-Comintern Pact might well have not materialized. To be sure, the media alone did not make the accord. Instead, they contributed to the discourses in Japanese business, academic, and government circles that made the entente imaginable. In short, years before diplomats signed the pact in late 1936, there had already been a lively conversation within Japanese civil society in which determined individuals used what freedom of speech and association was available to plant pro-German, then pro-Nazi ideas.

Japanese-German collaboration would not have come to pass but for the unpredictable rise of Hitler and Nazism. How did such an arrogant, chauvinist ideology gain converts in Japan without the Nazis even trying to propagate it overseas? The party's 25-point program so often reproduced in pamphlets and lectures embodied the particular brand of Nazism that became transnational and known in Japan. It was not the narrowly anti-Semitic, xenophobic, and racist version that offended so many in the Western, especially Anglo-American, world. Rather, it was the broadly populist, egalitarian, nationalist, and agrarian iteration that could cross borders. Only two points explicitly warned of Jews, who meant little to the vast majority of Japanese despite some scaremongers' attempts to turn anti-Semitism into a call to arms. Other points that were understood to infer the Jews would have lost their subtlety and context when translated literally into Japanese. Anti-Semitism struck most Japanese as a curious, if crude, white on white struggle that did not touch Japan. Still, that some opinion makers parroted anti-Semitism shows that transnational Nazism attracted adherents in Japan. Nor did Nazi prejudice against non-Aryans in general catch that much attention because there was not a meaningful Japanese minority in Germany to be mistreated or even for Japanese back home to experience such persecution vicariously, unlike in America. Japanese readers or listeners encountering the Nazi program would have put themselves in the shoes of Germans and not identified with "fellow victims" of Nazism such as Jews. Under this light, aggrieved Japanese in the lower classes could readily agree with tenets in the Nazi program such as freedom from interest slavery, equal rights and responsibilities for all citizens, accessible higher education, and profit sharing by major industries. Not only did the Nazi utopian mirage appeal to Germans of similar social stations, it also seduced enough Japanese opinion makers to generate a positive image that carried transnational consequences.

Although the lecturers and pamphleteers, single-handedly or collectively, did not father the alliance, their spoken and printed words at least played the part of midwives for the idea of bilateral collaboration. As the speeches and booklets demonstrate, the history of interwar Japanese-German relations is also the history of Japan. Even if not all lecturers and few pamphleteers had exhaustive knowledge of Germany, unlike the book authors and translators to be examined next, developments in Germany still provoked a soul-searching struggle over the direction Japan should take in the 1930s. For experts who knew a great deal more about Germany, Hitler, and Nazism, the battle only escalated.

3   Germany in Nonfiction

The week of February 20, 1936 was a consequential one for Japan, bracketed as it was by an election for the Diet's lower house and the insurrection by army officers on February 26. It was also singularly fateful for one particular household. The start of the seven-day span brought Kita Reikichi his first victory in a contest for a seat in the House of Representatives. The end saw his older brother Kita Ikki implicated in the attempted coup as the alleged spiritual leader of the mutineers. That is, just when Reikichi sought to enter the legislature through ballots, men radicalized by Ikki's teachings strove to overthrow the same governing system through bullets. To be sure, the brothers personified the clashing weltanschauungs only imperfectly. Reikichi the parliamentarian joined the comparatively reformist Constitutional Democratic Party (Minseitō), but he also embraced illiberal ideas such as expansion, charismatic leadership, concentrated authority, and even fascism.[1] Ikki, though often condemned in posterity as a vanguard of Japanese fascism, actually expounded populism before he turned rightward and inspired the anti-establishment revolt. But because the siblings espoused ideologies competing for dominance, the Kita family feud may stand in as a microcosm of the political milieu in interwar Japan.[2]

As seen in lectures and pamphlets, the world economic crisis, Japan's domestic and diplomatic impasses, and the metamorphosis of the Weimar Republic into the Third Reich triggered a soul-searching crisis in Japan over its own future directions. The Kita brothers, too, contributed to the debate through their publications. Ikki did not study Germany closely, but he was a Japanese national socialist before National

---

[1] Christopher W. A. Szpilman, "Fascist and Quasi-Fascist Ideas in Interwar Japan, 1918–1941," in *Japan in the Fascist Era*, 73–106; Christopher W. A. Szpilman, "'Misunderstood Asianism' and 'The Great Mission of Our Country,' 1917," in *Pan-Asianism: A Documentary History, Volume 1: 1850–1920*, eds. Sven Saaler and Christopher W. A. Szpilman (Lanham: Rowman & Littlefield, 2011), 297–303.

[2] Inabe Kojirō, *Ikki to Reikichi: Kita kyōdai no sōkoku* (Niigata: Niigata Nippō Jigyōsha, 2002).

Socialism came into existence in Germany. He completed his main treatise, *Fundamental Principles for the Reorganization of Japan*, in 1919, just before the Nazi Party's program. It articulated comparable tenets on land ownership, access to education, and caps on corporate profits.[3] Reikichi wrote *Germany in Another Revolution* in 1933 to reflect on the unrest that the country experienced at the beginning and end of the Weimar Republic. He witnessed the aftermath of the general strike that defeated the Kapp Putsch and thus saved the republic in 1920. Then in 1933, he departed Germany just days before Hitler became chancellor. He believed that the Germans, a stubbornly dogmatic people who lacked pragmatism, were doomed to build an incomplete nation-state that would continue to plague Europe and pose a danger to the world, much as the Goths once threatened Rome. A Germany undergoing a second revolution, this time by the Nazis, would only make Germany even more German and so likelier to cause trouble for the world.[4] Just as the brothers' ideological outlooks diverged, their published views on national socialism also differed.

Beyond newspapers, lectures, and pamphlets, nonfiction was the most authoritative source of knowledge of Germany in 1920s and 1930s Japan. At first glance, surveying interwar Japanese books on Germany, or even just the extant subset (numbering over 1,000 at the National Diet Library), appears an insurmountable feat. I make the task manageable by setting aside literary works by Japanese writers and fiction translated from German.[5] I also exclude factual books too arcane for the populace or far removed from current events, such as *An Overview of the Confederation of Youth Hostels in Germany* or *The History of Slavery in Medieval Germany*.[6] Works on the German language and learning German will be discussed in the next chapter.

Moreover, this chapter does not scrutinize individually nonfiction translated from German without commentary, such as law codes, trade practices, or technical manuals. These publications each conveyed little beyond its own subject, but together they constituted the main channel of knowledge transfer from Germany to Japan and thus reflected

---

[3] Brij Tankha, *Kita Ikki and the Making of Modern Japan: A Vision of Empire* (Folkestone: Global Oriental, 2006), 161–229.

[4] "Introduction," in Kita Reikichi, *Saikakumei no Doitsu*, Sekai no ima asu sōsho 8 (Tokyo: Heibonsha, 1933), 1–2.

[5] Lee M. Roberts, *Literary Nationalism in German and Japanese Germanistik* (New York: Peter Lang, 2010).

[6] Kokusai Kankōkyoku, ed., *Doitsu seinen shukuhakujo renmei gaikan* (Tokyo: Kokusai Kankōkyoku, 1931); Uchiyama Toshio, *Chūsei Doitsu doreishi*, Shakai mondai sōsho 5 (Tokyo: Fukunaga Shoten, 1920).

Japan's perception of Germany. What a people invests in the human resources, time, and money to render from a foreign language says a lot about what it prioritizes as worthwhile from another nation. So the aggregate of translated works is one civilization's evaluation of another. Seen from this perspective, interwar Japan esteemed Germany highly and broadly. It even imported works on obscure topics such as procedures for transporting corpses by rail or regulations governing horseracing.[7] Where appropriate, this chapter analyzes translated volumes collectively as a gauge of what information from Germany piqued Japanese interest.

The chapter concentrates primarily on the few score books on current affairs, politics, culture, economy, and contemporary history. Their genres include monographs, biographies, travelogues, memoirs, and encyclopedic anthologies. Like pamphlets and lectures, these works purported to relay facts. Unlike speeches and booklets, nonfiction did not operate within such thin profit margins or tight publication schedules. The quick turnaround of pamphlets enabled, even demanded, responses to breaking news, such as the commentaries chiming in within days of the Anti-Comintern Pact. But book authors and editors could use the extra time and pages to incorporate in-depth analyses and wider contexts. The more generous profit and time margins also allowed books to indulge in themes deemed less pressing or practical than those in pamphlets. Information in books was meant to last far longer, like the paper it was printed on. Hardcovers were sold with a sturdy sheath for preserving the volume inside for years and even decades. Book writers should have felt less pressure than pamphleteers to sensationalize issues because their readers were probably more educated and committed in time and money than consumers of pulpy booklets. Whereas many pamphlets were adorned with graphics and slogans to boost sales, most books, especially hardcovers with a brown cardboard shell, were designed to be judged not by their covers but their contents.

The depictions of Germany in interwar Japanese nonfiction fall into two phases. In the first, spanning the 1920s, authors and translators explored a wide range of topics that reflected the relatively open, liberal Weimar and Taisho zeitgeists. Early publications dwelling on the postwar gloom soon gave way to those that marveled at Germany's recovery in the mid-decade, though opinion makers could not agree what a resurgent Germany should look like. But just as the revival was accepted as a

---

[7] Tetsudōshō Un'yukyoku Kokusaika, ed., *Doitsu shin tetsudō unsō kitei* (Tokyo: Tetsudō Un'yukyoku, 1928); Teikoku Keiba Kyōkai, ed., *Doitsukoku keiba shikō kitei* (Tokyo: Teikoku Keiba Kyōkai, 1929).

fixture, the world economic crisis altered Germany so fundamentally that it forced commentators to reassess the country. The second stage, from the early 1930s, marks the ascent of transnational Nazism in Japan. The once-diverse interests in Germany rapidly narrowed down to politics, specifically interpretations of and reactions to Hitler and Nazism. Although many writers fixated on the Führer and his deeds, their discussions were often superficial and indulged in personality tidbits or reciting Nazi propaganda. Still, the charismatic leader elicited such enthusiasm in Japan that publishers responded extraordinarily with multiple biographies and graphic covers. Well before the Anti-Comintern Pact was signed, authors and editors had already formed a chorus extolling the virtues of Nazism and rapprochement with Germany.

Defining Postwar Germany

The repercussions of World War I dominated Japanese nonfiction on Germany in the early interwar years. Commentators were captivated by Germany's transformations during and after the war. Forces at play in Europe, especially the Wilsonian vision of democracy and self-determination, and the Leninist one of internationalism and dictatorship of the proletariat, threatened the Japanese Empire's legitimacy at home and abroad. But the speed and scale of the postwar turmoil left authors with little leisure to revisit the war or to squeeze the last profits from remnant wartime paranoia about Germany.[8] In any case, the war's outcome presented no great mystery for writers to pore over, so retrospective dissections of the war soon became the confines of military enthusiasts.[9] One book that critiqued German military and foreign policies reached a conclusion that was probably widely shared in Japan. Namely, Germany generally prevailed over the Allies on the battlefield. But the same prowess led its leaders to be complacent and arrogant, and to rely too heavily on force at the expense of diplomacy to break out of "Anglo-Saxon encirclement."[10]

---

[8] There was a market in Japan for fearmongering about Germany. A novel about Germany invading Japan through Siberia sold well enough to warrant at least 12 printings: see Higuchi Reiyō, *Doitsu no Nihon shinnyū* (Tokyo: Dokuritsu Shuppansha, 1918). The same work appeared under a different title after the war: see Higuchi Reiyō, *Shiberia yori Tōkyō e* (Tokyo: Dokuritsu Shuppansha, 1920).

[9] Ernst von Hoeppner, *Ōshū taisen ni okeru Doitsu kūgun no katsuyaku*, trans. Rikugun Kōkūbu (Tokyo: Fuji Shoin, 1923); Hirose Hikota, *Doitsu sensuikan no daikatsuyaku: Emono wo motomete* (Tokyo: Kaigun Kenkyūsha, 1928).

[10] Setsudō, *Sekaisen ni okeru Doitsu no sakusen oyobi gaikō hihan* (Tokyo: Miyamoto Burindō, 1919), 3–4.

Diagnosing the evolving conditions in revolutionary and then republican Germany attracted far more attention. The Foreign Ministry took the lead in trying to make sense of the new landscape. It published in March 1919 the prematurely titled *Political Conditions in Post-Revolutionary Germany*. But dependable intelligence was so scarce that even the government analysts who composed the study resorted to using stereotypes to explain the crisis that just would not subside. They had anticipated that unrest would settle down quickly because "the Germans are an organized people, with education and culture." Instead, unemployment and food shortages unexpectedly fueled the turmoil for five months "after the revolution" and seemed to push the country to the brink of disintegration and devolving into "a second Russia."[11]

Japanese nonfiction in the early 1920s reflected the chaos in Germany, with revolutions, counterrevolutionary putsches, strikes, assassinations, foreign occupation, and border clashes. Perhaps too much was unfolding too quickly for writers and translators to commit themselves to following any one development. Very few would have wanted to write or translate a tract, only to see the next upheaval invalidate its contents. Thus, no one in Japan seems to have written an entire book on the fleeting Bavarian Soviet Republic in 1919 or Hitler's failed Beer Hall Putsch in 1923. Even the Foreign Ministry, despite its expertise and resources, was taken aback by the duration of disorder. Because it took months for Japan to reopen diplomatic representation throughout Germany, private individuals such as Kita Reikichi were often better positioned to document the situation on the ground.

Experiences in Germany and with Germans allowed these first postwar Japanese observers to portray German misery concretely and compassionately. Tagawa Daikichirō, a Christian activist and journalist, admitted in *A Survey of Reforming Europe and America* that his hatred for the Germans collectively had intensified during a tour of the devastated Western Front. But when he met German prisoners of war in France and Belgium toiling to rebuild what they themselves had destroyed, he underwent a change of heart and began to perceive them as innocent individuals caught in events beyond their control.[12] Writing in November 1919, the *Asahi* correspondent Nagura Mon'ichi lamented in *Republican Germany* the shortages he encountered: even the luxurious Hotel

[11] Gaimushō Rinji Chōsabu, ed., *Kakumeigo no Doitsu seijō* (Tokyo: Gaimushō Rinji Chōsabu, 1919), 75.
[12] Tagawa Daikichirō, *Kaizō tojō no Ō-Bei shakai kenbutsu* (Tokyo: Nihon Hyōronsha Shuppanbu, 1920), 298–300.

Kaiserhof had to serve coffee without sugar, and horse-drawn carriages had replaced automobiles in Berlin.[13] The journalist and travel writer Yamada Kiichi described in 1919 conditions in Germany that he overheard reported in Switzerland in *A Chronicle of Wandering in Postwar Europe and America*: a citizenry exhausted by war and privation, pretty women reduced to wearing rough clothes, shoes so worn they exposed the wood inside, and faces telling tales of hunger and malnutrition.[14] He had originally planned to venture inside Germany but gave up upon discovering a months-long waiting period for an entry permit.

Meanwhile, another traveler, the pharmacologist Kimura Hikoemon, boasted in *Sampling Defeated Germany* to have spent "a record two hours" to acquire an entry permit because he worked as a purchasing agent of pharmaceuticals.[15] Though given to exaggeration, he probably did not stray far from the truth in commenting that Germany had been reduced to a land of tears.[16] The book was particularly powerful because it included photographs of civilians picking edible morsels from garbage heaps. The pity that these authors felt was enhanced by friendly interactions with Germans, several of whom asked the visitors in bewilderment why Japan had warred with Germany despite their once-close ties.[17] Reminiscing in 1933 and approaching from a political angle, Kita Reikichi pitied the pervasive fear and anxiety among the populace he sensed after the Kapp Putsch. He especially rued the "mechanical fashion" in which the old order continued to operate and the dearth of bold leaders with the drive and determination to consummate the revolution.[18]

Of course, Reikichi enjoyed the benefit of hindsight in knowing how German democracy would fare. But even before the fledgling Weimar Republic managed to stabilize and repel threats from the far left and right, Japanese opinion makers had already reached a consensus that German recovery was only a question of when and how, not if. As early as 1919, a general work concluded that the blows dealt to Germany, though painful, did not cause a fatal wound, and that given time Germany would surely regain its prewar stature.[19] Even those writers who so

---

[13] Nagura Mon'ichi, *Kyōwakoku Doitsu* (Tokyo: Ōsaka Yagō Shoten, 1922), 159–160. Many of the essays had first appeared in the opinion section of the *Tōkyō asahi*.

[14] Yamada Kiichi, *Sengo no Ō-Bei man'yūki* (Nishisugamo-machi: Hōten Gijuku, 1920), 131.

[15] Kimura Hikoemon, *Senpai no Doitsu wo rekiyū shite* (Osaka: Suzuya Shoten, 1921), 10.

[16] Ibid., 10–11.   [17] Yamada Kiichi, 130; "Introduction," in Kimura, 1–2.

[18] Kita, 6.

[19] Inahara Katsuji, *Saikin no Doitsu*, Tsūzoku kokusai bunko 1 (Tokyo: Gaikō Jihōsha Shuppanbu, 1919), 4–5.

dramatically depicted Germany's travails never lost faith that the country would rise again. Nagura, perhaps the least sanguine of the Germany watchers, conceded that the implementation of republicanism saved Germany as a nation and could lead to a positive outcome.[20] Kimura the pharmacologist ended his book with a confident prediction that Germany would undoubtedly recuperate within 20 years.[21] The travel writer Yamada blamed the Kaiser for plunging Germany into its catastrophe and took comfort that Wilhelm had since been exiled while Germany's administrative and social structure remained largely intact. Much as the German nation rebounded after its defeat by Napoleon and then redeemed itself through the Franco-Prussian War, he added, so could Germany overcome the present hardship and once again hold its head high.[22] That is, whereas Reikichi faulted the failure to uproot the old regime as the republic's original sin, Yamada credited the preservation of core elements of the old system as the key to German salvation.

Three trends marking the portrayals of Germany were starting to emerge already in these uncertain years. First, Japanese travelers to Germany, Europe, and the West were interested in deriving lessons from abroad for Japan. All the authors mentioned thus far journeyed far for either commerce or study, by definition the acquisition of unfamiliar goods or knowledge. Reikichi traveled to Germany to research philosophy. Kimura was touring Germany to purchase medical technology. The duties of the correspondent Nagura and the travel writer Yamada also involved watching Europe for the latest developments and their implications for Japan. Ozaki Yukio and Tokutomi Sohō, luminaries contributing forewords to some of these books, both stressed the need for Japan to learn from and about the postwar world, and praised the authors for working toward this goal.[23] Even the titles of these books convey nuances of gaining new experiences and insights through traveling.[24]

Second, Japanese opinion makers mostly maintained the conviction that Germany and its people would rebound, even though what they themselves witnessed and experienced there, particularly in the immediate postwar years, hardly justified such optimism. Even in the face of the Versailles Treaty and heavy reparations, designed precisely to burden

---

[20] Nagura, 25–26.   [21] Kimura, 148.   [22] Yamada Kiichi, 133, 135.

[23] Ozaki Yukio, foreword to *Kaizō tojō*, 4; Tokutomi Sohō, foreword to *Sengo no Ō-Bei*, 3–4.

[24] *Rekiyū* in Kimura's book comprises two elements: *reki* refers to an experience and *yū* to wandering. *Kenbutsu* in Tagawa's title also implies more than its common translation as "sightseeing" and means something closer to "surveying," especially since the term is placed in the context of "reforming Europe and America."

Germany for decades, none of the authors believed that Germany could be kept under a yoke for long. Rather, their belief resembled faith or intuition – they just knew that the Germans would soon enough regroup. Some writers pointed to the precedent of Germany's resurgence after Napoleon.[25] But more often, they put stock in the Germans' unquantifiable national character or the "German soul" (*Doitsu-damashii*). This intangible German spirit, though deemed critical to the nation's survival and success, was never described in detail. Instead, it evolved with the times and the needs of the observers commenting on Germany. In the postwar context, this spirit became loosely associated with stereotypical traits such as chivalry, perseverance, discipline, hard work, and self-sacrifice.

Third, and related to the ambiguity and malleability of this German essence, a budding disagreement arose over what exactly would constitute a reborn Germany. In a sense, the war created a tabula rasa for Japanese intellectuals to reconceptualize an ideal Germany. Some saw in the disaster a repudiation of the old regime and hoped the revolution would run its course. Others were relieved that the revolution did not live up to its name and that familiar faces remained in positions of authority, wealth, and influence. These views indicate not only contrasting visions of Germany but also a fundamental level of concern for the country that enabled such a difference of opinion to exist. Moreover, Germany provided a battleground for ideologies that attracted observers of various political persuasions. Unlike Soviet Russia or Fascist Italy, where extreme movements established dictatorial control, republican Germany in its first, turbulent years played host to struggles between the left and the right that were more or less evenly matched. Thus, Japanese commentators partial to either side could take heart in the successive coups and countercoups. Postwar Germany's uncertain fate furnished invested Japanese authors with drama and creative space to imagine the triumph of their preferred worldview. Because conditions in Germany remained in flux for a few years, the opinion makers had to learn about all developments in the dynamic country.

Beyond the Postwar Shadow

Through a coincidence of a jolt in Earth's crust, the capacity of money presses, and one man's hubris, the Great Kanto Earthquake, the peaking of Germany's hyperinflation, and the Hitler Putsch all took place within a

---

[25] Toyosaki Zennosuke, *Fu-Futsu Sensō igo no Doitsu keizai* (Tokyo: Kōgyō no Nihonsha, 1920).

couple of months. Japan and Germany were each picking up pieces of either a flattened metropolis or a shattered economy by the end of 1923. At the same time, both countries entered a more liberal, democratic phase. In Japan, political parties were given opportunities to form cabinets with parliamentary majorities. In Germany, the republic fended off the last violent challenge to its legitimacy and could focus on implementing a new system of governance. The extreme left and extreme right, neither able to vanquish the other, committed themselves to pursuing power through mostly legal channels. Their activity and the similar factors affecting Taisho Japan and Weimar Germany meant that Japanese commentators had yet more reasons to keep a close watch on Germany. The relative openness in both countries also enabled Japanese intellectuals to discuss more aspects of Germany in more diverse types of publications.

The number, contents, and variety of volumes rendered from German into Japanese attest the applicability of Germany's situation that the Japanese discerned for their own nation. Beginning in 1922, when one could reasonably conclude that the Weimar Republic would survive and remain relevant, several works on public administration were translated into Japanese. Because democratization meant a reorganization of the legal regime, the republic passed new laws and enacted reforms. The Japanese Ministry of Justice translated a host of German laws and commentaries from 1922 to 1926 on matters ranging from juvenile courts to regulation of the economy.[26] Certainly, Japan did not unthinkingly swallow any German law whole, but the Japanese thought it worthwhile to take the trouble – and much trouble it must have been to decipher German legalese – to translate the laws into Japanese exactly. Because a society's corpus of laws is built on its beliefs, traditions, and precedents, none of which Japan shares with Germany, Japan's effort to make sense of Germany's new laws demonstrates Japan's high esteem for German jurisprudence. Even if Japan could not internalize the spirit of German laws, it was at least interested in the letter.

Other institutions sought lessons from a Germany renewing itself in multiple areas. The City of Tokyo and the Interior Ministry's Reconstruction Bureau, charged with rebuilding and redesigning the capital, translated several German reports on urban planning.[27] Some in the

---

[26] Gustav Radbruch, *Doitsukoku shōnen saibanshohō*, trans. Shihōshō Chōsaka, Shihō shiryō 31 (Tokyo: Shihōshō Chōsaka, 1923); Arthur Nussbaum, *Doitsu shin keizaihō*, trans. Shihōshō Chōsaka, Shihō shiryō 33 (Tokyo: Shihōshō Chōsaka, 1923).

[27] Fukkōkyoku, ed., *Toshi keikaku ni kansuru Doitsu hōsei oyobi gyōsei* (Tokyo: Fukkōkyoku Keikakuka, 1924); Tōkyō Shisei Chōsakai Shiryōka, ed., *Doitsu ni okeru tochi kukaku seiri no jitsurei* (Tokyo: Tōkyō Shisei Chōsakai, 1924).

media talked of doing away with the winding streets of Edo and making
the unconventionally wide Showa Avenue Tokyo' s answer to Berlin's
tree-lined Unter den Linden.[28] Losses from the earthquake and the fire
afterward likely prompted Japan to explore ways to manage the risk of the
next disaster. The Postal Insurance Bureau imported several volumes on
Germany's insurance system, including poignantly three on fire insurance and one on using insurance funds to finance public housing.[29]
The appreciation for Germany's inspiration in rebuilding Tokyo ran so
deep that in 1934 Tokyo's mayor sent a commemorative copy of *The
Reconstruction of Tokyo* to Hitler as a token of thanks.[30] Other institutions
such as the Bank of Japan, South Manchuria Railway, and office of the
Governor General of Korea also translated German publications relevant
to their purview.[31] Whatever the German spirit stood for theoretically,
many in official and semi-official circles in Japan found much practical
value in picking the German mind.

As broadly as the Japanese establishment introduced German laws
and regulations, the Weimar Constitution, as far as can be ascertained,
appears not to have been translated whole or published by the Japanese
government. The omission could not have resulted from neglect because
Japan imported works from the minute, such as the protocol for operating a ship's lamps, to the monumental, such as the Versailles Treaty.[32]
Neither length nor linguistic complexity should have deterred translators
because the short constitution was written in clear prose. Nor should
doubts about a work's applicability for Japan have played a role. The
Foreign Ministry translated German election laws that implemented

---

[28] Seidensticker, 312.

[29] Karl Domizlaff and Eugen Friedrich Wolfgang Freiherr von Liebig, *Ippan kasai hoken
yakkan*, trans. Kan'i Hokenkyoku (Tokyo: Kan'i Hokenkyoku, 1925); Eugen Friedrich
Wolfgang Freiherr von Liebig, *Doitsu ni okeru kasai hoken seido*, trans. Kan'i Hokenkyoku
(Tokyo: Kan'i Hokenkyoku, 1925); Heinrich Wessels, *Doitsu kōei kasai hoken seido*, ed.
and trans. Kan'i Hokenkyoku (Tokyo: Kan'i Hokenkyoku, 1925); Kan'i Hokenkyoku,
ed., *Berurin ni okeru kōeki jūtaku kenchiku jigyō*, Tsumitatekin un'yō shiryō 7 (Tokyo:
Kan'i Hokenkyoku, 1926).

[30] BArch, R 43II/1454, Japanese Embassy's *note verbale* to Foreign Office, January
25, 1934.

[31] *Senzen oyobi sengo ni okeru waga taidoku bōeki jōkyō narabini Doitsu sangyō fukkō no waga
kuni ni oyobosubeki eikyō* (Tokyo: Nihon Ginkō Chōsakyoku, 1925); Minami Manshū
Tetsudō Kabushiki Kaisha Shomubu Chōsaka, ed., *Doitsu gyōshōnin seido no kenkyū to
Doitsu bōeki no shinkō ni kōkenseru chōya no shokikan*, trans. Ōta Sankō and Nakamura
Hisashi (Dairen: Minami Manshū Tetsudō Shomubu Chōsaka, 1923); Chōsen
Sōtokufu, ed., *Kyū Doku-ryō Pōrando tōchi gaikan 1*, Chōsa shiryō 9 (Keijō: Chōsen
Sōtokufu, 1924).

[32] Teishinshō Kansenkyoku Sen'yōhin Kensajo, ed., *1906-nen Doitsu sentō shaken kisoku
shōyaku*, Kenkyū shiryō 3 (Tokyo: Teishinshō Kansenkyoku, 1921); *Dōmei oyobi
Rengōkoku to Doitsukoku no heiwa jōyaku narabini giteisho* (Tokyo: Chōyōkai, 1920).

female suffrage, which Japan would not adopt until 1945.[33] The main factor that disqualified the constitution from official rendition into Japanese thus seems to have been its liberal and, for the Japanese imperial government, subversive elements. Article One proclaimed that "state authority derives from the people." Amid the riots and protests just after World War I, censors in Japan might have thought it prudent to deprive the restive populace of easy access to a blueprint for an alternative arrangement of power between the governing and the governed.

If so, the authorities overestimated the people's familiarity with political happenings in Germany. Consumers did not need much investigation to read from the constitution, just not a version translated by the government. Nagura Mon'ichi discussed several provisions of the document in *Republican Germany*. Other authors published the document with annotations in the early 1920s.[34] But Nagura erred in predicting that Article One would raise controversies over whether Germany should be a federal or centralized state.[35] The article in fact said nothing about federalism; the republic kept the Kaiserreich's decentralized structure. He also crafted a fanciful explanation for Article Three that made black, red, and gold the republic's colors.[36] He claimed that the hues symbolized the parties upholding the government: black represented monks' robes and the Catholic Center Party, red the Socialists, and gold the propertied Democratic Party and its Jewish members. But the tricolor flag predated all three parties and even Germany as a nation-state, with a tradition stretching back to the Napoleonic Wars.

As the Weimar Republic entered the "golden" mid-1920s, the Japanese writing of their experiences in Germany drifted from political and economic topics to social and cultural ones. Although up until 1925 readers in Japan could still find publications on Germany's reparations, postwar fiscal policies, and socialism, the research for these works had been completed before mid-1923. Such books were becoming scarce by 1925, as Japanese popular interest in Germany shifted from weighty problems to more lighthearted affairs.

Berlin Night Tales, published in 1925, unintentionally captures this change in sentiment. Its author, Koizumi Eiichi, had not set out to compose a watershed opus but stated humbly that it would please him

---

[33] *Doitsukoku senkyohō yakubun*, Ōshū seijō kenkyū shiryō 22 (Tokyo: Gaimushō Ōbeikyoku Dainika, 1924).
[34] Yamada Junjirō, *Doitsu shin kenpō ni arawaretaru shakaiteki shisō* (Tokyo: Ganshōdō Shoten, 1923); Fujii Shin'ichi, *Shin Doitsu kenpō seiji* (Tokyo: Yūhikaku, 1929).
[35] Nagura, 8.   [36] Ibid., 7–8.

just to amuse readers with leisurely stories about Berlin.[37] Even if he was simply being modest, the use of furigana, a reading aid for deciphering difficult words, throughout shows that the book was meant for the lay population. The book would have lived up to his intention but for the events described within. His stay coincided with a turning point in German history. He resided there for a year starting in April 1923 and saw "Germany at its nadir and on the road to recovery."[38] The book's contents are correspondingly arranged to reflect the different experiences. The first part, "Germany's Year of Misery," was in a way the last major Japanese account on German politics and economy in the 1920s. The second, "From the Streets of Berlin" and "Travelogue," was the first exposition on culture and society. Koizumi was definitely qualified to interpret state affairs – his career would lead to a judgeship on the supreme court – but he devoted more attention to the relaxed second half.

In hindsight, Koizumi should have written more for the first part. He seems to be the first Japanese observer to describe in book form the hyperinflation and the Hitler Putsch. The hyperinflation, which he encountered through astronomical exchange rates and prices of merchandise skyrocketing by the minute, made gripping reading material. The putsch lasted not quite a day and would have been consigned to a footnote in history but for later developments. Koizumi lived in Berlin at the time and did not witness the coup in Munich; but he evidently paid enough attention to the incident to reconstruct it vividly and criticize "thoughtless" Hitler for the "ill-conceived coup."[39] The jurist was also drawn to details of the subsequent trial such as Hitler's "lengthy tirade" and the prosecutor's disputation. Koizumi pointed out specifically that Hitler received the minimal five-year jail term but was freed after serving just 13 months.[40] Even if Koizumi could not have fully known in 1924 the significance of the events he described, he observed shrewdly that the "Hitler faction" actually benefited from the failed coup and captured seats in the Reichstag for the first time. He predicted that upon leaving prison Hitler would further affect politics.[41]

Of course, in 1925 few Japanese knew of Hitler or had reason to. Writers' and readers' interests moved from matters of the state to diversion, beginning with the rest of Koizumi's book. Of 458 pages of text, only the first 103 dealt with the hyperinflation and putsch. The remainder wandered across German restaurants, museums, parks, and theaters,

---

[37] "Introduction," in Koizumi Eiichi, *Berurin yawa* (Tokyo: Waseda Daigaku Shuppanbu, 1925), 2.
[38] Ibid., 1.   [39] Koizumi, 96.   [40] Ibid., 100–101.   [41] Ibid., 102.

from Berlin to the Rhine. Indeed, books by Japanese visitors to Germany published after *Berlin Night Tales* tended to steer away from the political economy. This new outlook emerged not only in Kitahara Toshiko's *Europe from a Child's Eyes*, about a girl's trip to the continent, but also *A Chronicle of Wandering in Europe and America* by Takatori Junsaku, a Diet member attending a meeting of the Inter-Parliamentary Union.[42] The schoolgirl wrote of her pleasant time visiting the Berlin Zoo. The parliamentarian, too, described leisurely tours of the Reichstag and University of Berlin. Both ate at a Japanese restaurant during their stay. Then, in 1928, the *Mainichi* organized a tour group of 120 Japanese to support their national team at the Amsterdam Olympics and to sightsee along the way. The newspaper published their travelogues collectively as *A Chronicle of Sightseeing in Europe*. The tourists stayed in Germany for a little over a week and all recalled fond experiences visiting the country.[43] Meanwhile, the journalist-turned-parliamentarian Matsumoto Kunpei detoured from his official duty to represent Japan at the Geneva Naval Conference in 1927 for a personal visit to Germany and a private audience with the ex-Kaiser in the Netherlands.[44] This playful era is capped by *Erotic German Ladies*, a mishmash of tales and factual observations by the storywriter Hata Toyokichi during his time in Berlin as a Mitsubishi employee.[45] Hata also translated Erich Maria Remarque's *All Quiet on the Western Front* into Japanese.[46]

What a reversal of mood from the austere to the libertine in a few years. In 1920, an author pitied German women for having to wear rough clothes. In 1928, another celebrated German women for not wearing any. One agent of change was the popularization of tourism for affluent individuals – the price of a grand tour of the West dropped from about ¥6,000 to ¥3,500 for the *Mainichi* tour, then to ¥1,500 in 1929.[47] The authors in the early 1920s all traveled to Europe either for work or study, but several of those in the mid-decade visited the continent for pleasure. None illustrates this phenomenon better than the child

---

[42] Kitahara Toshiko, *Kodomo no mita Yōroppa* (Tokyo: Hōbunkan, 1926); Takatori Junsaku, *Ō-Bei man'yūki: Bankoku Giin Kaigi sanretsu* (Tokyo: Takatori Jimusho, 1926).

[43] Ōsaka Mainichi Shinbunsha, ed., *Ōshū kankōki* (Osaka: Ōsaka Mainichi Shinbunsha, 1928).

[44] Matsumoto Kunpei, *Kaizaru Kōtei to kaiken: Ikin to suru Ōshū wo mite* (Tokyo: Seinen Kyōdan, 1928).

[45] Hata Toyokichi, *Kōshoku Doitsu onna* (Tokyo: Bungei Shunjū Shuppanbu, 1928).

[46] Erich Maria Remarque, *Seibu Sensen ijō nashi*, trans. Hata Toyokichi (Tokyo: Chūō Kōronsha, 1929).

[47] Ōsaka Mainichi Shinbunsha, ed., *Ōshū kankōki*, 3; Takimoto Jirō, *1500-en sankagetsukan Ō-Bei kenbutsu annai* (Tokyo: Ō-Bei Ryokō Annaisha, 1929), 1.

Kitahara, who did not go to Germany for business or school. And the
Mainichi tour is one of the earliest instances of Japanese tourist
groups abroad.

The first peaceful postwar decade coincided with and facilitated the
spread of intercontinental tourism worldwide. Whereas in the early
1920s Japanese travelers to Europe had to journey by sea, in 1927 the
faster and cheaper Trans-Siberian Railway resumed regular international
operation.[48] The Diet member Takatori returned to Japan from the
Inter-Parliamentary Union meeting by train through Russia. The *Mainichi*
group traveled to Europe by rail and returned by sea. The envoy to
Geneva Matsumoto rode trains for both his outbound and inbound
legs. But the railway did not provide travelers with just another mode
of transportation. It also colored their impressions of Germany. The
Soviet Union in the 1920s was hardly a land of abundance. For Japanese
passengers to Europe, entering Germany after traversing Russia would
have felt like reentering modern civilization. Or for those heading homeward from Europe, their experience in resurgent Germany would have
served as the standard against which communist Russia was judged.
So the *Mainichi* editors commented on Muscovites' dirty clothes and
beggars in the streets.[49] Takatori also mentioned panhandlers swarming
visitors arriving at Moscow's train stations.[50]

The books also capture a real shift in perception from gloomy to
hopeful among Japanese observers of Germany in the mid-1920s, when
authors declared Germany beyond "postwar." Whereas the titles of the
earlier books contained phrases such as "after the war," "defeated," and
"post-revolutionary," the ones in the mid-decade no longer mentioned
the Great War. As the Weimar Republic stabilized and Germany's
economic woes faded from headlines, Japanese visitors noticed the
tangible material recovery and edgy cultural blossoming. Having heard
stories of Germany's loss of millions of men and reparations payments
of hundreds of millions of Reichsmark, the *Mainichi* tour guides had
expected to see a ruined landscape. Instead, they were surprised by
bustling cities with numerous shops and cars zooming to and fro.[51]
Matsumoto Kunpei was also struck by the unanticipated vitality he
encountered in both the countryside and Berlin.[52] So the titles of
travelogues from this period featured more-pleasant words such as
"wandering" or "sightseeing." And their authors, including those

---

[48] Tetsudōshō Un'yukyoku, ed., *Shiberia keiyu Ōshū ryokō annai* (Tokyo: Tetsudōshō
Un'yukyoku, 1929), 1.
[49] Ōsaka Mainichi Shinbunsha, ed., *Ōshū kankōki*, 18.   [50] Takatori, 134.
[51] Ōsaka Mainichi Shinbunsha, ed., *Ōshū kankōki*, 23.   [52] Matsumoto Kunpei, 34.

posted to Europe for business such as Hata Toyokichi, wrote relatively little about work and more on their extracurricular activities.

This shift in emphasis from the political and economic to the social and cultural appeared in another genre of nonfiction. Like the travel writers moving away from dwelling on the physical repercussions of the war and hyperinflation to reveling in life in Weimar Germany, some scholars changed their focus from the concrete to the intangible. Or more precisely, they derived the intangible from the concrete as they presented Germany's material recovery as both an illustration of the German national character's spiritual strength and justification for their pontification thereon.

Experts in literature spearheaded this drive from the materialist to the spiritual. As early as 1922, the philologist Yamagishi Mitsunobu completed the two-part *Contemporary German Opera*. He argued that because a nation's literature served as the clearest lens into a people's character, literature was the key to comprehending the German race's rebirth or demise.[53] Three works in 1924 alone attempted to extrapolate Germany's national character from its literature and explain Germany's recovery. In *On Contemporary German Literature*, the lexicographer Katayama Masao felt so confident in Germany's inherent strength that he declared that its culture had actually emerged more brilliant from the war and now indisputably led the world.[54] Another critic, Kyoto Imperial University professor Naruse Mukyoku, expressed virtually the same opinion in *The Latest German Literary Thoughts*. He believed that the German "sentiment of yearning, stubborn persistence, deep meditation, and thorough intellect" that permeated German culture would give rise to a new literature from the "redemptive fire" of the present ordeal.[55] Tokyo Imperial University professor Aoki Shōkichi devoted an entire book, *Germany's Literature and National Thought*, to dissect the German national character. From his overview of historical literature, he concluded that the Germans were a warlike, thorough, persevering, and hardworking folk.[56]

Though signs of German recovery abounded in the mid-1920s, these literary specialists preferred distant lore over accessible evidence in telling the story of Germany's rebound. Katayama, Naruse, and Aoki's

---

[53] "Introduction," in Yamagishi Mitsunobu, *Gendai no Doitsu gikyoku 1* (Tokyo: Ōmura Shoten, 1920), 6.

[54] "Foreword," in Katayama Masao, *Gendai Doitsu bungakukan* (Tokyo: Bunken Shoin, 1924), 1.

[55] "Introduction," in Naruse Mukyoku, *Saikin Doitsu bungaku shichō* (Tokyo: Hyōgensha, 1924), 1–2.

[56] Aoki Shōkichi, *Doitsu bungaku to sono kokumin shisō* (Tokyo: Shun'yōdō, 1924).

narratives all follow a template: the Thirty Years War left the German lands devastated, but Prussia eventually arose from the ruins. Then Napoleon humiliated the German peoples, who through willpower and perseverance returned to defeat France and to establish the Kaiserreich that rivaled even the British Empire.[57] The scholars thus viewed Germany's current trial as just another chapter in the nation's saga of epic rises and falls. Indeed, they favored ephemeral traditions so heavily that they downplayed tangible facts. Both Katayama and Aoki feared that Germany's physical revival might corrupt their beloved German soul. Aoki warned that too heavy an emphasis on material enrichment at the expense of spiritual refinement would lead Germany astray, much as anticipated conquests had tempted the country into World War I.[58] Katayama, too, lamented Berlin's transformation into a sleepless hub of nightlife and popular entertainment with crowded theaters, restaurants, and cafés as proof of moral decay.[59] Whereas in the early postwar years some observers who were served sugarless coffee counted on the German national character to resuscitate the country, by the mid-1920s others saw the material recovery as a threat to the very same spirit. In short, while most Japanese commentators in postwar Germany witnessed much hardship but maintained their faith in the German character, others in Japan in the mid-1920s read about physical recovery but worried about the state of the German mindset. What contributed to the contrasting interpretations?

Those writing immediately after the war and those writing in the mid-Weimar years had different professions and dissimilar interests. The early writers – journalists, travel writers, and merchants – were more inclined to describe Germany's physical state. The tourists in the mid-decade were also impressed by the recovery that they heard in busy streets, smelled from billowing chimneys, and tasted in sweetened coffee. Meanwhile, the literary critics were more drawn to the mental and spiritual by profession. They were writing in Japan and had to imagine Weimar Germany's latest developments, which deviated from the ones in the Kaiserreich that the academics intimately knew and admired. So some of them equated the focus on physical recovery with materialism or socialism. Katayama feared that the urge to acquire more goods would reward profiteers and the nouveau riche, stratify German society further, and hasten its moral decay.[60] Naruse likewise fretted that the emphasis on wealth harbingered a rise of social democracy in literature.[61]

---

[57] For example, Katayama, *Gendai*, 39.   [58] Aoki, *Doitsu bungaku*, 280.
[59] Katayama, *Gendai*, 39–40.   [60] Ibid., 41.   [61] Naruse, 177.

The Weimar Republic became at the end of the 1920s the subject of a final category of nonfiction – encyclopedic overviews designed to give readers a broad but shallow understanding of the country. At least three series with a volume on Germany were published: *World Geography for Youngsters* and *An Overview of the Current World* in 1930, and *A Compendium of World Geography and Custom* in 1931.[62] Although only one of these works mentioned a specific readership, all targeted lay readers because furigana ran next to the texts throughout. With minor differences in style, the three volumes presented their contents following a general pattern. All featured ample maps, photographs, and illustrations. All discussed aspects such as geography, demographics, history, culture, economy, politics, and military.

It is probably no coincidence that the three volumes appeared within a year of one another. Such works required a level of expected stability and certainty in a subject, which in Germany's case did not become apparent until the mid-decade. Such anthologies could not have been published in the turbulent early 1920s. At that time, even a seemingly timeless topic such as geography was fraught with ambiguity because postwar Germany's borders remained in flux for a few years. If one could not define what land was German, how could one speak with any confidence about its population or institutions? In addition, the two edited works, *Overview* and *Compendium*, mobilized several knowledgeable writers. The editors and authors would not have found such compilations sensible had they foreseen major changes in Germany. As in any collaborative project involving multiple contributors, edited volumes usually need more time. This fact shows that the anthologists anticipated a stable German republic and explains the tardiness, in the early 1930s, when the works were published.

In sum, the coinciding eras of relative democracy in both countries spawned a range of Japanese nonfiction on Germany, including literal translations, casual travelogues, literary commentaries, and overarching surveys. Two related phenomena in the mid-1920s enabled the diversification from the single-mindedly gloomy accounts right after the war. The upheavals and reforms Germany experienced fascinated writers with an interest in the outside world. Furthermore, the defeat of the Hitler Putsch and the taming of hyperinflation created breathing space for the republic to develop as well as assurance for its Japanese observers to study it in some detail without fear of quickly

---

[62] Nishiki Masao, *Shōnen sekai chiri bunko 7* (Tokyo: Kōseikaku Shoten, 1930); Satō Yoshisuke, ed., *Sekai genjō taikan 2* (Tokyo: Shinchōsha, 1930); Nakama Teruhisa, ed., *Sekai chiri fūzoku taikei 11* (Tokyo: Shinkōsha, 1931).

becoming outdated. This liberal era is the golden age of interwar Japanese publications on Germany.

The three trends identified in books from the immediate postwar years hold firm in the later works. First, writers and translators continued to mine German knowhow for Japan and acknowledge their intellectual debts to Germany. The numerous and diverse works rendered from German into Japanese show that Japan voraciously imported expertise from Germany. The general compendiums, too, carried the implicit mission of learning and intellectual enrichment through explaining Germany's achievements in multiple areas of endeavor. *World Geography for Youngsters* declared that "everyone agrees that 'Germany is great'" and that Japan did and could learn much from Germany.[63] Yamagishi Mitsunobu also explained that the Japanese needed urgently to study a people whose destruction was widely reported but who somehow turned their fortune around to overtake the victorious powers.[64] Even the tourists in the *Mainichi* group kept an eye out for lessons for Japan. Several expressed admiration for Germany's order and apparent prosperity. At least one mentioned specifically that Japan should emulate the nationwide exertion toward revival that he witnessed in Germany.[65]

Second, Germany's recovery gave Japan a reason to study the country and validated the authors' faith in the German national character. A *Mainichi* tour participant wrote lucidly that of all the European countries he liked Germany best because of the spirit the German people exhibited in rebuilding their country.[66] Although the translators did not stray from their duties by editorializing on the German soul, the act of translation articulated fundamental admiration for the thought processes and sentiments behind the original works. Meanwhile, the literary scholars made careers out of commenting on the ethereal and wrote books to distill the German spirit from its literature. These academics all overlooked current factors contributing to Germany's revival. They dismissed the very real material recovery and credited instead Teutonic traditions stretching back at least to the Thirty Years War for Germany's resurgence in the mid-1920s. Even if the scholars were simply plying their trade, only a genuine belief in the power of the German soul explains its inclusion in the encyclopedic compendiums as a legitimate feature of the country. These supposed compilers of facts and figures did not shirk from something as intangible and unquantifiable as national

---

[63] Nishiki, 3, 6.

[64] "Introduction," in Yamagishi Mitsunobu, *Doitsu bunka gairon* (Tokyo: Kanasashi Hōryūdō, 1927), 1.

[65] Ōsaka Mainichi Shinbunsha, ed., *Ōshū kankōki*, 123.   [66] Ibid., 125.

character. They even outdid the literary critics and traced the German spirit to prehistoric landscape and climate. One contributor wrote that harsh natural conditions hammered the Teutonic folk into one impervious to hardship.[67]

Third, those writing on Germany could not agree on what an ideal, rehabilitated Germany should look like and what its lessons for Japan might be. Travelers to Germany were taken in by the recovery in prosperity, but those pontificating from afar in Japan emphasized the spiritual aspect. These conflicting imaginations of a physically grounded Germany versus one metaphysically oriented mirror debates among Romantic literati in the German lands in the nineteenth century over the essence of the nation-to-be. Although Japanese authors were almost uniformly impressed with Germany, they found different aspects impressive. While the literary scholars fantasized about a historical Germany, the translators, tourists, and encyclopedists mostly looked forward to a modern country. One member of the *Mainichi* group wrote longingly of the freedom of expression in the Weimar Republic. Another admired the leaders who led Germany out of its ruins.[68] Most visitors remarked on the orderliness and cleanliness of Berlin and the German countryside.[69] All lamented Japan's perceived deficiency vis-à-vis their particular objects of admiration in Germany, whether freedom, leadership, or infrastructure. But not everyone liked what they saw. At least one traveler warned his fellow Japanese against a shallow worshipping of Europe and advocated instead looking inward for inspiration.[70] Discussing Germany was thus not just about Germany but often about Japan.

The Return of Politics

Against the expectations of the compendiums' contributors, events in Germany and the world soon made their publications obsolete. Almost as soon as the books were published, the world economic crisis and the consequent breakdown of Germany's political system invalidated essays on Germany's growing economy or stable government. Germany played host to problems writ large that also plagued Japan, such as unemployment, social tension, political impasse, and limits on international trade. Once again Germany became an object of intense studies for the Japanese seeking inspiration to help Japan out of the extraordinary times.

---

[67] Satō Yoshisuke, ed., 5; Nakama, 97.
[68] Ōsaka Mainichi Shinbunsha, ed., *Ōshū kankōki*, 206, 237.   [69] Ibid., 216.
[70] Ibid., 224.

As in previous crises, translators pioneered bringing German ideas to Japan. Whereas German legislation and policies attracted attention in the mid-1920s, works on the economy were the mainstay in the early 1930s. Because Germany suffered from and attempted to tackle severe unemployment, Japan could benefit from works on the topic. Two editions of Germany's labor insurance laws were published. The translator compiled an additional work comparing Germany's unemployment benefits with those of other countries.[71] Other legislation on protection of workers was also translated into Japanese.[72] An industry group translated the entire emergency law on managing the economy, while a work on the German mortgage system was imported.[73] The Ministry of Justice, too, introduced a report on simplifying and cutting the costs of legal procedures. The protocols were adopted in Germany in 1921, but Japan did not import them until 1932 when circumstances made them acutely relevant. The translating team unambiguously pointed out that Japan could learn from the austerity measures that Germany had used a decade before.[74]

Individuals joined the search for applicable German lessons. If the unrest in Japan after World War I had already convinced observers to look to Germany for solutions, the more severe downturns in the 1930s made an even more pressing case for looking harder. A cluster of monographs emerged in the early 1930s with the mission of enlightening Japan with German wisdom, exemplified by *The Rising German Spirit* in 1930. The book was received so enthusiastically that it went through five editions in two weeks. Part of its popularity must be attributed to its author, Ikeda Ringi, a prolific writer and proponent of eugenics, but the idea of contrasting a resurgent Germany to stagnant Japan likely caught readers' imagination. Ikeda told readers that they should indeed view his ample compliments for Germany as criticisms of Japan.[75] At first glance, any talk of a strengthening Germany in 1930 bordered on the absurd, but

---

[71] *Doitsu rōdō hokenhō*, trans. Okada Kashinosuke (Shinagawa-chō: Kawaguchi Insatsujo Shuppanbu, 1930); Okada Kashinosuke, *Doitsu oyobi sonota shokoku shitsugyō hoken oyobi shitsugyō kyūsai* (Shinagawa-chō: Kawaguchi Insatsujo Shuppanbu, 1930).

[72] Shakai Rōdōbu, ed., *Doitsu rōdō hogo hōan narabini riyūsho*, Rōdō hogo shiryō 34 (Tokyo: Shakaikyoku Rōdōbu, 1932).

[73] *Doitsu no keizai kokka kanri ni kansuru kinkyū hōki 1–2*, Sangyō keizai shiryō 7–8 (Tokyo: Zenkoku Sangyō Dantai Rengōkai Jimukyoku, 1932); Arthur Nussbaum, *Doitsu teitō seidoron*, trans. Miyazaki Kazuo (Tokyo: Shimizu Shoten, 1932).

[74] "Foreword," in *Shihō jimu no keihi setsugen kan'ika oyobi sokushin: Doitsu saibansho shoki dōmei no kaikakuan*, trans. Shihōshō Chōsaka, Shihō shiryō 169 (Tokyo: Shihōshō Chōsaka, 1932), 1.

[75] "Foreword," in Ikeda Ringi, *Shinkō Doitsu-damashii* (Tokyo: Banrikaku Shobō, 1930), 3.

as in nonfiction in the immediate postwar years, difficult conditions on the ground never diminished Japanese faith in the German spirit, which was worshipped fervently precisely in the contexts of hardship and struggle. The German national character could not be invalidated by reality – in bad times one should believe in its potential, and good times proved its impact.

The book dealt not with the present crisis but the 1920s, when Germany did regain a modicum of prosperity and stability. Ikeda especially admired Germans' ability to rally around the fatherland and tap into the strength of its national character.[76] Several other books – four in 1931 alone – also commented on current Japan through the recent German past. *The Tale of the Demise of Germany's Currency* by the economist Oikawa Shigenobu focused on the hyperinflation. An old Germany hand, Oikawa wrote the book to warn his countrymen of the danger of a weakening currency, a reference perhaps to the Japanese government's decision to abandon the gold standard.[77] The philosopher Kanokogi Kazunobu in *The Japanese Mind and the German Spirit* excoriated the Japanese state for pursuing materialistic hedonism, couched in terms of seeking peace. He excused Germany's "mechanical technology" as not a tool for improving physical livelihood but rather as a manifestation of the "indomitable Gothic heroic spirit."[78] The *Asahi* correspondent and pamphleteer Kuroda Reiji published *Before and After the Kaiser's Deposition*. Writing on contemporary German history, he denounced the dictatorships of both militarism and democracy, which approximated the tension in Japan between those who partook in parliamentarianism such as Kita Reikichi and the mutineers inspired by Kita Ikki.[79] Finally, the pedagogue Osada Arata dedicated his *Tidings from Germany: A Second Journey* to combating the narrow-minded, inward-looking nationalism taking hold in Japan, which he compared with the detrimental effects of a self-pollinating flower.[80] Whereas Ikeda the eugenicist praised Germany for searching within itself for salvation, Osada the educator cited Germany to urge Japan to explore beyond itself. While one expert detected monetary lessons in Germany for Japan, another idealized the very same

---

[76] Ibid., 309.
[77] "Introduction," in Oikawa Shigenobu, *Doitsu kahei botsuraku monogatari* (Tokyo: Banrikaku, 1931), 1.
[78] Kanokogi Kazunobu, *Yamato kokoro to Doitsu seishin* (Tokyo: Min'yūsha, 1931), 140–141, 149–150.
[79] Kuroda Reiji, *Haitei zengo* (Tokyo: Chūō Kōronsha, 1931).
[80] "Introduction," in Osada Arata, *Doitsu dayori: Saiyūki* (Tokyo: Meguro Shoten, 1931), 2–3.

country as a paragon of mind over matter. All the while, Kuroda the wavering leftist was torn between governments by the many or the few.

These questions over searching outward or inward, the physical against the spiritual, looking forward to the future or harking back to the past, and liberalism versus authoritarianism stemmed from the fundamental, ideological struggle in Germany and to an extent Japan. Generally, writers associated the left with internationalism, concern with material possessions, a vision to construct a utopia to come, and majority rule, at least in principle. By contrast, the right evoked nationalism, belief in willpower, a tendency to romanticize former greatness, and hierarchical leadership. But a dichotomy does not mean an even split. The ideation of Germany in Japanese nonfiction, with a historical narrative of the country recovering from catastrophes through its national character, was much closer to that of the traditionalists. For those Japanese sympathetic to a conservative Germany, in the early 1930s the German far right received a powerful spokesman whose words elicited excitement even in faraway Japan.

Thus far Hitler had attracted scant coverage in Japanese nonfiction. Only *Berlin Night Tales* discussed his failed putsch in any detail. Other Japanese visitors' works ignored the man and his movement altogether. This neglect changed in 1931 with the appearance of the first Hitler biography in Japan. Its publication is remarkable because only a handful of Germans were honored with the genre in interwar Japan. Not Friedrich Ebert, who rose from humble origins to become the first republican president. Not Fritz Haber, the Nobel chemist who revolutionized agriculture but also pioneered poison gas warfare. Thus, by the strokes of a writer's pen Hitler was elevated to the ranks of biography-worthy personalities such as Wilhelm, Hindenburg, Goethe, and Luther. But when Izeki Takao, an economics professor, wrote *Hitler: The Giant of Rising Germany* in 1931, Hitler held no official position, headed only the second largest party, and was not even a German citizen (Figure 3.1). What propelled Hitler from being mentioned only in passing to becoming the subject of an entire book?

Foremost, Hitler and the Nazis made news in Japan. As seen in newspapers, lectures, and pamphlets, the media covered Hitler and Nazism extensively. Some Japanese thirsted to know more about Hitler, so authors and publishers responded to consumer demand. The biography was evidently put together hastily just to enter the market first. Izeki does not seem to command much expertise on Germany. He did not write another work on either the country or the person before or after *Hitler*. The book also contained little original material and was mostly derived from the highly favorable biography *Hitler* by the Englishman

Figure 3.1 *Hitler: The Giant of Rising Germany*, the first Japanese biography of Hitler. The use of colorful graphics on the cover makes the book stand out from most publications at the time and hints at the influence of pamphlets' visual style on nonfiction. Original in color.

Wyndham Lewis.[81] But the work's main selling point was the transcript of Momo Minosuke's 1930 interview with Hitler, the first by a Japanese. For Japanese interested in learning more about the man and his ideology that appeared increasingly frequently and urgently in the media, the biography offered a rare book-length treatment of the subject, though a biased one. The work even blended elements of pamphlets and books because its cover featured Hitler's portrait and signature. This visual

---

[81] "Introduction," in Izeki Takao, *Hittorā: Shinkō Doitsu no kyojin* (Tokyo: Senshinsha, 1931), 4. Izeki was so unfamiliar with the subject that "Lewis" was transliterated into Japanese as if it were a German name.

element set the biography apart from most other publications in plain brown covers or cardboard sheaths.

Moreover, the biography marks the emergence of transnational Nazism in Japanese nonfiction. It inaugurated a trend of positive coverage of Hitler and Nazism by authors and translators. The year after the biography saw the first full Japanese translation of *Mein Kampf*. The translator, the educator Sakai Takaji, made a show of striking an impartial tone and described the translation as a fact-finding middle path between critique and adulation of Nazism. But he also conceded that one must respect the Hitler movement for overcoming official repression and media attacks, and persevering for over ten years before achieving its current successes.[82] In a similar vein, Kinoshita Kōtarō in *Hitler and the German Fascist Movement* adopted a supposedly balanced approach and ended the book with a chapter on criticisms of Nazism. Yet he then proceeded to rebut the critique point by point; and this last section hardly balanced the rest of the book, in which he praised Hitler as "not merely a politician but the incomparable leader of a million National Socialists."[83] The nationalistic pundit Murobuse Kōshin eschewed the pretense of dispassionate observation altogether in *Hitler and the Hitler Movement*. He marveled at the amateur statesman's progress in winning over the German populace and proclaimed, "Hitler is the future."[84] Those words proved prescient, not least for Murobuse, who in 1940 would lend his name as the translator of the bestselling Japanese edition of *Mein Kampf*, with a print run of at least 219,000 copies.[85]

Even in the early 1930s, one did not need to be an enthusiastic fan of the Führer to sense that Nazism was a phenomenon to be reckoned with. The Nazi Party was the largest in Germany by the end of 1932 and Hitler forced the venerable Hindenburg to a run-off election for the presidency. As long as the Nazis stayed out of government, there was creative space for Japanese observers to project their imagination of Nazism in publications. Though the Nazi movement never prioritized restoring the monarchy, Momo still asked Hitler about the possibility of elevating Wilhelm's fourth son, a party member, to the throne if the Nazis obtained power. Hitler unsurprisingly replied that the prince was just one National Socialist comrade like everyone else, and that he

---

[82] Sakai Takaji, translator's introduction to Adolf Hitler, *Yono tōsō: Doitsu Kokumin Shakai Shugi undō* (Tokyo: Naigaisha, 1932), 2.

[83] Kinoshita Kōtarō, *Hittorā to Doitsu Fashizumu undō* (Tokyo: Naigaisha, 1932), 26.

[84] "Introduction," in Murobuse Kōshin, *Hittorā to Hittorā undō* (Tokyo: Heibonsha, 1932), 1–2.

[85] Adolf Hitler, *Waga tōsō*, trans. Murobuse Kōshin (Tokyo: Daiichi Shobō, 1940).

intended to establish a dictatorship.[86] Adding to the ambiguity from the party's lack of a track record, the Nazi movement masterfully manipulated its own image through propaganda and selectively emphasized priorities to different audiences. So Japanese books on Hitler often repeated the myth of the Führer launching his political career as the seventh member of the tiny German Workers' Party. They also relied on Hitler's own romanticized account of his previous incarnation as a drifter retroactively invested with significance for his later political epiphany.

Even if the publications on the Führer showed much curiosity about the life of a celebrity, attention to Hitler's personality was not simplistic star-struck obsession. The primacy of politics returned to discussions on Germany in Japanese nonfiction from the 1930s. And discussions of German politics increasingly revolved around Nazism and Hitler. It is not just a coincidence that the books on Nazism mentioned so far all used "Hitler" in their titles. Even the one book-length criticism of the ideology was labeled *Hitlerism*, written by an American and translated into Japanese.[87] Hitler's rhetoric and autobiographical tales of overcoming failure, heroic struggles, and unswerving belief in an ultimate triumph of the will neatly personified the storyline of Germany at large so prevalent in the books. When Hitler burst onto the national political scene, several authors trained their attention to one individual as a proxy for the whole country, a familiar narrative arch used also by journalists and pamphleteers. The diversity of interests and topics in nonfiction in the 1920s narrowed down to difference in political opinion in the early 1930s. Because talks of the vaunted German spirit and national tradition of recovering from catastrophes already predisposed commentators to sympathize with the rightist vision of Germany, Hitler and Nazism soon found more eager Japanese adherents.

Books for Hitler and Nazism

When the Führer greeted his followers from the Chancellery on January 30, 1933, Nazism began to crystallize from theory into reality. The Weimar Republic was never violently overthrown. Instead, German democracy died a legal death through constitutionally permitted moves such as the Reichstag Fire Decree and the Enabling Act. Once the Nazis held the levers of authority, they took steps to consolidate power through legislative and administrative acts. Much as the Weimar Republic's innovations had

---

[86] Izeki, 33–34.
[87] Louis Leo Snyder [Nordicus, pseud.], *Hittorā shugi*, trans. Kizaki Masaru (Tokyo: Kaizōsha, 1932). The original title was *Hitlerism: The Iron Fist in Germany*.

attracted attention a decade earlier, the Third Reich's reorganization of society triggered a similar response in Japan in the mid-1930s.

Translators as usual took the lead in introducing knowledge of this new Germany. Although Japan suffered less severely during the economic crisis, other countries' protective trade barriers hurt Japan's export industries and led to job losses. Because Germany had shed the most jobs proportionally but seemed on its way to recovery, it made sense for Japan to seek lessons there. The Tokyo prefectural government translated a series of works on the system and legal basis of the Nazi National Labor Service.[88] A think tank translated a publication on the economic role of public corporations, and later in the decade another research institute imported information on the Four-Year Plan.[89]

The Nazi regime also broke ground in using the law as an instrument for controlling society. The Ministry of Justice translated several legislations by the Third Reich, including the new penal law code that criminalized behaviors deemed harmful to the national community such as miscegenation with Jews, even if its applicability in Japan was limited.[90] The ministry also translated the Nazi Party's legal theory, even though it was not an official German government document.[91] Then in 1937, the ministry produced a summary report on preemptive arrest by the police, a favorite tactic of the Nazi regime against its opponents.[92]

The de jure and de facto establishment of dictatorship in Germany and Nazi lawless violence in the mid-1930s finally aroused voices of opposition among Japanese intellectuals, much as in the press. Kita Reikichi, completing his book in July 1933, warned that Germany under Nazism would loom threateningly over Europe like a low pressure weather system.[93] In *Nazi Laws*, Tokyo Imperial University law professor Wagatsuma Sakae elaborated some of the most eloquent liberal attacks on Nazi

---

[88] Helmut Stellrecht, *Doitsu rōdō hōshi seido*, trans. Tōkyō Chihō Shitsugyō Bōshi Iinkai and Tōkyō-fu Gakumubu Shakaika, Shitsugyō taisaku shiryō 3 (Tokyo: Tōkyō Chihō Shitsugyō Bōshi Iinkai, 1934); Erich Gräf, *Rōdō hōshi seido no hōritsu genri*, trans. Tōkyō-fu Gakumubu Shakaika, Shitsugyō taisaku shiryō 6 (Tokyo: Tōkyō-fu Gakumubu Shakaika, 1934).

[89] Tōa Keizai Chōsakyoku, ed., *Doitsu ni okeru kōdantai no keizaiteki katsudō*, Tōa shōsatsu 13 (Tokyo: Tōa Keizai Chōsakyoku, 1933); *Doitsu shin yonkanen keikaku kenkyū shiryō 1* (Tokyo: Nichi-Man Zaisei Keizai Kenkyūkai, 1937).

[90] *Nachisu no keihō*, trans. Shihōshō Chōsaka, Shihō shiryō 184 (Tokyo: Shihōshō Chōsaka, 1934).

[91] Hans Frank, ed., *Nachisu no hōsei oyobi rippō kōyō keihō oyobi keiji soshōhō*, trans. Shinotsuka Haruyo, Shihō shiryō 211 (Tokyo: Shihōshō Chōsaka, 1936).

[92] Sakakibara Yoshio, *Doitsu ni okeru yobōteki keisatsu kōryū seido*, Shihō kenkyū hōkokusho 21 (12). Tokyo: Shihōshō Chōsaka, 1937.

[93] Kita, 186–187.

lawmaking and abuse of power.[94] He methodically refuted the Nazi legal views on race relations, the preference for the "Germanic legal spirit" at the expense of the Roman legal tradition, and the reliance on rhetoric invoking German comradeship as a substitution for arbitration of labor disputes. Wagatsuma was not hostile to Germany itself. He had devoted his entire career to studying German laws on property and personal rights, and was dismayed to see the Nazi dismantling of the German state of law (*Rechtsstaat*).

Leftist commentators also reacted to Nazism with hostility. The sociologist Shinomiya Kyōji was studying in Germany during the Nazi "seizure of power" and the early years of the Third Reich. He was incensed by the politicization of higher learning and research. He labeled the expulsion of racially undesirable professors and burning of books disapproved by the movement "the crucifixion of universities." He even compared Hitler with the tyrannical first emperor of China who also purged scholars and torched books.[95] Suzuki Tōmin, a leftist correspondent in Berlin from 1926 to 1934, launched the most vociferous critique of Nazi Germany. Suzuki had already published a pamphlet to excoriate "German fascism" in 1931. Upon returning to Japan, he wrote *Looking at the Nazi Country* to sum up his experiences, thoughts, and outrage at the punishments meted out by the regime to such enemies as communists and socialists. He suspected foul play behind the Reichstag Fire that gave the Nazis a convenient pretext to grab emergency power. He went as far as to attend the trial of the accused arsonists at the high court in Leipzig, where a crowd outside jeered him with shouts of "Jap."[96] Reflecting on what he witnessed in Nazi Germany and dreading more to come, he lamented, "An age of terror began on the night of January 30, 1933."[97]

The most comprehensive, extensive critique of the Third Reich, *An Exposé of the Hitler Regime*, appeared in 1936. It comprised transcripts of an interview with three correspondents posted to Germany. The conversation covered topics ranging from international relations to unflattering gossip about Hitler. The newsmen's mastery of details enhanced their accounts with concreteness and closeness. Rather than denouncing Nazi anti-Semitism by invoking nuances and ideals of individual rights, they illustrated the plight of Jewish Germans familiar to the Japanese public such as Albert Einstein and Fritz Haber. Besides describing the Nazi

[94] Wagatsuma Sakae, *Nachisu no hōritsu* (Tokyo: Nihon Hyōronsha, 1934), 155–157.
[95] Shinomiya Kyōji, *Nachisu* (Kyoto: Seikei Shoin, 1934), 40–41.
[96] Suzuki Tōmin, *Nachisu no kuni wo miru* (Tokyo: Fukuda Shobō, 1934), 29.
[97] Ibid., 163.

dictatorship in legislative and administrative terms, the journalists also discussed the bloody Night of the Long Knives in gory detail, including the executions of some of Hitler's closest associates. Looking to the futures of Germany and Japan, one of the reporters was relieved that Japanese democracy still had time to ponder its own path and relations with fascism or Nazism, and to stop short of approaching extremism.[98]

Unfortunately for these critics, his optimism could last only hours. The manuscript went to printing presses in Tokyo on November 25. Eight time zones away on the same day, the Anti-Comintern Pact was signed in Berlin. Japan might not have turned fascist or Nazi, but it became a partner of the Hitler regime that these newsmen so abhorred. The editor of *Exposé* could only put on a brave face and suggest in the foreword that the agreement made it imperative for Japan to discover the real Germany and that the book helped balance the overwhelmingly fawning coverage of Hitler and Nazism.[99] He certainly realized that the few voices disapproving of Nazism were being drowned out by the chorus of compliments for Hitler and his ideology. Accounts such as *Exposé* did not hinder Japanese-German rapprochement, but they show the remaining, and still significant, freedom of expression on the subject on the eve of the pact.

Indeed, critical publications such as *Exposé* were countering not only Japanese-German convergence but also the propagation of transnational Nazism in popular Japanese nonfiction. Three more Japanese biographies of the Führer appeared in the years between Hitler's appointment and the Anti-Comintern Pact. Ikeda Ringi published *Hitler* in 1933. The book contained little more than excerpted propaganda speeches and Hitler's self-aggrandizing tales in *Mein Kampf*, including the obligatory myth of him as the seventh party member. Reiterating his themes in *The Rising German Spirit*, Ikeda specifically admired Hitler's boldness in clearing a path through the uncertain times and argued that Japan needed a similar bugler to lead the public forward.[100] The prolific biographer Sawada Ken articulated a similar sentiment in *Hitler* in 1934. That is, now that Japan found itself in the existential emergency of being squeezed on all sides, the nation needed a hero of Hitler's caliber to lead it out of the crisis.[101] Kuroda Reiji had completed his ideological conversion from a critic to convinced follower of Hitler and National Socialism

[98] Iizawa Shōji, ed., *Hittorā seiken no hyōri* (Tokyo: Teikoku Shuppan Kyōkai, 1936), 410–411.
[99] Ibid., "Editor's foreword," 1–2.
[100] "Introduction," in Ikeda Ringi, *Hittorā* (Tokyo: Taiyōsha, 1933), 1–2.
[101] "Introduction," in Sawada Ken, *Hittorā den* (Tokyo: Dai Nihon Yūbenkai Kōdansha, 1934), 1–6.

獨裁王
ヒットラァ

著二禮田黑

Figure 3.2 The cardboard case of Kuroda Reiji's *Hitler the Dictatorial King* features a photograph of Hitler posing in full uniform. This photograph of Hitler was widely reproduced in Japanese books. Most book sheaths at the time were plain brown.
Courtesy of SHINCHOSHA.

by 1936. In *Hitler the Dictatorial King*, Kuroda claimed he set out to write an "annotated biography" to examine the topic dispassionately, but he also admitted that he considered Hitler a hero (Figure 3.2).[102] In fact, Kuroda's portrayal of Hitler so impressed the German Embassy that it forwarded a copy to the Chancellery.[103] So much for dispassion.

Beyond obsessing with Hitler the person, publications capitalized on the interest in Germany to praise Nazi ideology. In 1933, Hata Toyokichi, who just a few years before had celebrated erotic German

[102] "Introduction," in Kuroda Reiji, *Dokusaiō Hittorā* (Tokyo: Shinchōsha, 1936), 3.
[103] BArch, R 43II/1456, Noebel to Foreign Office, May 20, 1936.

Figure 3.3 The dust jacket of *The Truth of the Nazis*. The book's subtitle is "Baptism by Blood and Bullets." The photograph of Hitler and the Nazi swastika evoke the personality and ideology that were central to transnational Nazism's appeal. The publisher, ARS, became a press specializing in books on Nazi Germany in the 1940s. Original in color.

women and translated *All Quiet on the Western Front*, now defended the Third Reich's illiberal policies. In *Berlin-Tokyo*, he attempted to normalize Nazi repression as understandable actions with which Japanese could sympathize. He even dismissed the burning of books deemed pornographic or unpatriotic as merely a staged act for public consumption with little concrete significance, not unlike, he claimed, the frequent anti-Japanese demonstrations in Shanghai.[104] He excused also the persecution of Jews as a legitimate response to the usurpation of one's homeland by foreigners.[105] Hata is yet another example of a former leftist who succumbed to transnational Nazism. The army officer Adachi Kenzō wrote *The Truth of the Nazis* the same year to share his excitement at hearing Hitler's speeches in person (Figure 3.3).[106] Another author, Kitagami Ken, lionized Hitler for having "a revolutionary's blood in his veins" and the audacity to burn books and even have his former

---

[104] Hata Toyokichi, *Berurin Tōkyō* (Tokyo: Okakura Shobō, 1933), 261–262.
[105] Ibid., 278.   [106] Adachi Kenzō, *Nachisu no shinsō* (Tokyo: Arusu, 1933), 1–3.

獨逸大観

Deutschland
ein
Ueberblick

1936

Figure 3.4 The cover of *An Overview of Germany, 1936* features the Nazi swastika prominently. Original in color.

comrades executed to consolidate power.[107] Ōtsuka Torao, the *Nichinichi*'s Berlin correspondent, figuratively sanctified the Führer in 1936 by declaring the ascendancy of "holy Hitler."[108]

The affirmation of the Nazi regime in Japanese nonfiction materialized as the encyclopedic *An Overview of Germany, 1936* (Figure 3.4). Like the anthologies on late Weimar Germany, the work embodied the implicit expectation that Nazi Germany would endure for some time. This assumption was explicitly reinforced by the title's inclusion of the year of publication, meant to lead readers to expect similar books for years to

[107] Kitagami Ken, *Nachisu Doitsu* (Tokyo: Gakuji Shoin, 1935), 44.
[108] Ōtsuka Torao, *Nachi Doitsu wo yuku* (Tokyo: Ari Shoten, 1936), 1.

come. It had taken the Weimar Republic more than a decade to earn acknowledgment by such a genre in Japan, but the Third Reich needed only three years. The publisher, a communications and advertisement agency, explained the anthology's purpose:

Just as Fascism is certainly unique to Italy, so must Germany's National Socialism be understood through the Germans' special character and history. All great national movements arise from the unique internal inevitability within a nation. Because such inevitability varies from people to people, one cannot simply transpose a nation's movement onto another. But it may not be denied that we can derive beneficial lessons from resurgent Germany's experiments in various fields. Thus this book is devoted entirely to describing the many aspects of this new Germany.[109]

This statement concisely summarizes the essence of transnational Nazism in Japan – admiration for Nazi Germany without necessarily advocating the Nazification of Japan. The publication was received so enthusiastically that it went through five editions in 20 days. The publisher also made plans to compile a sister compendium, *An Overview of Japan*, for German readers.[110] The next year, after the conclusion of the Anti-Comintern Pact, the 1937 edition was published (Figure 3.5). Mitsunaga Hoshirō, the company's founder and president, reflected on the alliance and its relations to the anthology series:

We published *An Overview of Germany* last summer to provide our society with useful suggestions and systematically introduce the resurgence and construction that embodied the German national movement. We hope the 1937–1938 edition will exceed mere inspirations but perform an enlightening role as well. One cannot help but enthusiastically cheer the Anti-Comintern Pact the previous autumn as the basis for consolidating Japanese-German rapprochement. Moreover, one cannot deny that the pact becomes more and more crucial in view of the new situations in Europe and East Asia. We hope and pray with all our hearts that the agreement will form the linchpin of bilateral collaboration and fulfill its historic mission.[111]

In fact, the publishing industry had already taken steps to realize civil society Japanese-German collaboration. The parent company of the *Japan Times* published *Converging Japan and Germany* in October 1935 to celebrate and encourage Japanese-German solidarity, just as the newspaper did through special supplements.[112] The editors reasoned

---

[109] "Preface," in Nihon Denpō Tsūshinsha, ed., *Doitsu taikan 1936* (Tokyo: Nihon Denpō Tsūshinsha, 1936), 1.

[110] Ibid., 2.

[111] Mitsunaga Hoshirō, preface to *Doitsu taikan 1937–38*, ed. Nihon Denpō Tsūshinsha (Tokyo: Nihon Denpō Tsūshinsha, 1937).

[112] "Editors' foreword," in *Sekkin suru Nihon to Doitsu* (Tokyo: Taimusu Tsūshinsha, 1935), 2–3.

Figure 3.5 The cover of *An Overview of Germany, 1937–38* features an eagle clutching the Nazi swastika. These covers make no distinction between Germany and Nazism – party and country were one, just as the Nazis proclaimed. Original in color.

that because the two newcomer nations faced similar threats and challenges in the extraordinary times, Japan and Germany should cooperate more closely in cultural and economic activities. The publication not only preached but also practiced bilateral collaboration. It comprised essays from comparable numbers of Japanese and German contributors. That is, months before the Anti-Comintern Pact's conclusion, writers and publishers were already binding Japan and Germany together between book covers by producing works with reciprocal counterparts such as *Overview* or working with German partners on *Converging Japan and Germany*.

Transnational Nazi nonfiction extolling Hitler and his ideology had for a few years been setting the ideological and cultural background for the diplomatic alliance. At first glance, National Socialism had little to offer Japan in the 1930s. Japan had entered and exited the world economic crisis early on. Its unemployment never reached disastrous levels. The largely homogeneous nation lacked a visible, overrepresented minority to scapegoat. Nor did the other boogeyman, communism, pose a realistic menace. And the Nazi emphasis on Aryan superiority and discrimination against other races should have antagonized the Japanese. But many more writers and readers were captivated than repulsed by Nazism. Unusual among books in the interwar era, several publications espousing favorable opinions of Nazi Germany and Hitler featured sharp, colorful graphics, such as the cover of the first Hitler biography. The cardboard case of Kuroda Reiji's Hitler biography also showed a photograph of the Führer in full uniform. The *Overviews of Germany*, too, bore the Nazi swastika on their covers. *The Truth of the Nazis* most clearly showcased this shallow fascination with Nazi imagery. Its cover combined both the symbols and colors of the movement with photographs of Hitler. Echoing the earlier misreading of the Weimar Republic's black–red–gold colors, the author noted with satisfaction that the Nazi flag, with a red background punctuated by a white circle, exactly mirrored Japan's. He added that because the swastika symbolized the ancient Germanic valor that resembled Japan's Bushido, the Germans were definitely not a warlike people.[113] It seems to matter little that Hitler spoke longingly, excitedly of wars past, and combat played an indispensable role in Nazi views on racial health and foreign policy. The writers believed what they wanted to believe.

Such misinterpretations of Hitler and Nazism, willful or otherwise, occurred frequently. Many books contained little original research and merely relayed various Hitler myths. Some even circulated unfounded rumors of Hitler having worked as a journalist or dentist. The authors exhibited a similarly superficial grasp of Nazism, as many publications simply reprinted the party program or speeches by Nazi leaders in lieu of meaningful analysis of the movement's actual deeds. The books' simplicity and their targeted audiences' susceptibility may be gauged by the use of furigana – all the Hitler biographies employed the reading aid, but the works critical of Nazism did not. With their graphic covers and easy language, pro-Nazi nonfiction resembled sensationalist pamphlets visually, linguistically, and politically. Without the Nazis quite trying, several

---

[113] "Introduction," in Adachi, 1.

Japanese authors became adherents of Hitler and his ideology. Their transnational Nazism not only foreshadowed diplomacy but also left its mark in Japanese publishing.

The allure of Hitler's charisma in Japan should not be understated. The Hitler myth of an underdog ne'er-do-well inspired by patriotism to overcome obstacles through willpower and ambition, and triumphing in the end resonated in Japanese culture and history. It is not entirely surprising that in the interwar era more Japanese biographies were written about Hitler than any other German – the story was compelling. The Führer was seen as more than a mere politician like the squabbling ones he displaced but rather the leader of a national rebirth and revival. In short, Hitler was not just a person but a personality. This perception justified the curiosity about trivialities, such as his mustache, hair color, relations with women, and daily routine. The Hitler regime also enjoyed real foreign and domestic successes, such as achieving full employment, repudiating the reparations, and remilitarizing Germany in the first few years. Transnational Nazi authors and readers alike had much to look forward to from Hitler.

Transnational Nazism in Nonfiction

On a Sunday afternoon in July 1922, the art critic Abe Jirō took a stroll in Berlin's western outskirts. He was not prepared for what he experienced. A man with a beer belly walked past him and yelled, "Japp'an!" Another man walking his dog called out, "Jap, Jap!" Three young women spotted him from afar, approached him, and shouted in unison, "Japanese!" Abe reflected in his diary that none of these encounters could have taken place in central Berlin, where he usually moved in circles that treated Japanese guests with respect and politeness. Still, he philosophically gave thanks for these run-ins with the lay population as a teaching moment. He cautioned readers that the exclusive interactions that Japanese had with cosmopolitan Germany skewed their perceptions of the overall German attitude toward Japan. Such misunderstanding could become quite dangerous.[114]

His countrymen would have done well to heed his advice. Although Abe published his account in 1933, more than a decade after the unpleasant encounters, he might still have acted prematurely. Many Japanese authors were becoming adherents of Hitler in the mid-1930s and fostering the intellectual atmosphere that made eventual Japanese-German

---

[114] Abe Jirō, *Yūō zakki: Doitsu no maki* (Tokyo: Kaizōsha, 1933), 71–72.

rapprochement imaginable and sensible. The Anti-Comintern Pact thrilled Japanese boosters of Hitler and Nazism, and generated even more interest in the subjects. At least two Hitler biographies for young readers appeared.[115] Sawada Ken's 1934 biography of Hitler reached its thirty-seventh edition in 1939. Murobuse Kōshin's 1940 translation of *Mein Kampf* was a bestseller. ARS, the publisher of the colorful *The Truth of the Nazis*, even became a specialist press of books on Nazi Germany, with more than two dozen titles by 1941. Translators, too, joined the frenzy with renditions into Japanese of harangues by Hitler and Goebbels, and works on the Nazi martial spirit and the financing of Germany's war effort. Institutional translators began talking about war in the late 1930s when they imported several tracts on Germany's wartime economy and propaganda during World War I.[116] Then in World War II, their attention shifted to technical and specialized areas such as the production of ball bearings or Germany's aviation industry, knowledge that Japan desperately needed to stave off defeat. But Japanese interpreters of Germany, translators and authors alike, did not fully appreciate Hitler's intentions and goals.

The production of interwar Japanese nonfiction on Germany falls into two phases. In the first, overlapping the relatively open 1920s, Japanese writers conducted broad inquiries into Germany from its political economy to literature. Throughout the gyrations and vicissitudes of the decade, three beliefs held firm – that Japan had much to learn from Germany, the German spirit would eventually reinvigorate the country, and German recovery should be defined according to one's ideology. In the second, inaugurated by the emergence of Hitler from obscurity, interests in Germany rapidly narrowed to political reactions to Hitler and Nazism. The evidential or experiential investigations of Germany in the 1920s were crowded out by books featuring eye-catching graphics or bombastic rhetoric lifted wholesale from Nazi hagiography or a fixation with minutiae concerning Hitler. Those writing about Germany in the 1920s had usually already earned expertise on the country. But some who pontificated in the 1930s joined discussions on Germany just to praise and profit from Hitler and Nazism. The three trends from the previous decade continued, though in distorted forms. Writers still saw Germany as a laboratory for Japan. Enthusiasts for Nazism pointed to its

[115] Iida Toyoji, *Shōnen Hittorā den* (Tokyo: Kōa Shobō, 1939); Ikeda Nobumasa, *Hittorā* (Tokyo: Kaiseisha, 1941).

[116] *Taisen tōsho Doitsu no torero senji zaisei keizai hōsaku: Doitsu Teikoku kōbunsho yōyaku,* Chōsa shiryō 11 (Tokyo: Shūgiin Chōsabu, 1938); Walter Nikolai, *Taisenkan Doitsu no chōhō oyobi senden,* trans. Sanbō Honbu (Tokyo: Naikaku Jōhōbu, 1938).

achievements and their potential benefits for Japan, while opponents excoriated the same deeds and attempted to steer Japan away from imitation thereof. The German spirit gained more accolades, and in the 1930s it became increasingly amalgamated with the will power much trumpeted by the Nazis. Although few disputed that Germany was recovering in the mid-1930s, not all Japanese observers agreed that the country was transforming into the wonderland the Nazis promised, or if it was, whether that was a good thing.

One may be tempted in hindsight to lionize the few vocal Japanese critics of Nazism such as Wagatsuma Sakae or Suzuki Tōmin. But their distaste for the ideology also affected their appreciation of the Nazi regime's staying power and stability. Both Wagatsuma and Suzuki thought that rampant violence was undermining state institutions in the Third Reich. Instead, the state institutionalized the violence, first in Germany and then throughout Europe. In the short term, they might have been confounded by the regime's durability, but in the long run they were of course proven right.

4   Germany in Language Textbooks

Every evening from five to eight o'clock in 1938, a group of dedicated individuals in Tokyo attended Seminar Germania, a language course targeted at Japanese speakers taught by native German instructors. A poster promoting the class featured an eye-catching eagle emblazoned with the Nazi swastika (Figure 4.1).[1] It also enticed applicants with the chance to learn "German from the Germans!!!" Despite the colorful graphic and catchy pitch, it was unlikely that many participants took the nightly three-hour course out of whim or curiosity alone. What, then, drove ordinary Japanese to study this foreign language at Seminar Germania and other, sometimes tuition-charging, night schools?[2]

Before long, those Japanese trying to learn more about or from Germany would bump up against an inflexible ceiling. The hundreds of Japanese nonfiction works on Germany and translations from German published during the interwar years were vastly outnumbered by works about Germany in German and thus inaccessible to uninitiated readers. For non-expert Japanese to become self-sufficient in their pursuit of German knowledge, they first had to learn from an indispensable group of cultural intermediaries: linguists and instructors of German.

This chapter investigates German learning in Japan and language textbooks' depictions of Germany as factors in Japanese-German relations. Unlike the transient media formats examined so far, foreign language acquisition demands much more time than the minutes, hours, or days that newspapers, lectures, or books need. Especially for adult learners, achieving and maintaining proficiency may require sustained investments in time, money, and effort. The repetitive, accumulative nature of language studies ensures that students are exposed to new concepts and ways of thinking in the forms of vocabulary and grammar. Wilhelm von Humboldt asserted, "Language is, so to speak,

---

[1] BArch, Plak 003-008-022/F. Greil, 1938.   [2] TA, July 25, 1936.

134

Figure 4.1 A poster advertising Seminar Germania showcases an eagle with the Nazi swastika. It contains information about the course and offers students the chance to learn "German from the Germans!!!" Original in color. Bundesarchiv, Plak 003-008-022/F. Greil, 1938.

the manifestation of a nation's spirit. Its language is its spirit and its spirit its language. One can never think of them as identical enough."[3] This idea that language dictates thought was formulated in the twentieth century as the theory of linguistic relativity or Sapir–Whorf Hypothesis.[4] Even if one rejects such determinism, one cannot deny that language is integral to a people's identity and that studying a

---

[3] Quoted in Yamada Kōzaburō, *Doitsugo hattatsushi* (Tokyo: Daigaku Shorin, 1935), 1.
[4] For an overview: see John J. Gumperz and Stephen C. Levinson, eds., *Rethinking Linguistic Relativity* (Cambridge: Cambridge University Press, 1996).

foreign tongue leads to familiarity with facets of the countries where it is spoken such as culture, politics, and society. Because most of the commentators discussed in the previous chapters learned some German, analyzing the impact of their teachers and German studies can illuminate their interests and biases. Language instructors are incomparably influential in international image formation through their function as "key opinion leaders."[5] They direct a knowledge field by training practitioners and producing materials such as textbooks and reference works consulted by other experts. Linguists and teachers of German in interwar Japan educated the journalists, lecturers, authors, and translators who in turn spoke to the government and reading masses. Language learning also makes possible some of the most intense intercultural experiences, such as travel, study abroad, commerce, religious conversion, and marriage. In the 1920s and 1930s, many elite, cosmopolitan Japanese interpreters of Germany toured Germany and Europe. Several studied, and a handful even taught, overseas. Others did business with or for German companies. Some converted to Christianity.[6] A few, women and men alike, married Germans.[7]

Although language textbooks attracted far fewer readers than newspapers, pamphlets, or nonfiction, that German studies had an audience in Japan after World War I attests the Japanese' enduring appreciation for German civilization. Still, because of linguistic differences between Japanese and German, interwar German's peculiarities, and limitations in instruction methods, German suffered in Japan from its notoriety as being difficult and boring. But German was considered so useful and passing a German proficiency test promised such rewards that many Japanese still attempted to teach themselves the language. Germanists responded to the demand by churning out numerous, diverse publications, each purporting to be the key to overcoming the German problem. Moreover, these linguists used their control of the quality and contents of German lessons to express their political preference for a monarchist,

---

[5] "Key opinion leaders" often applies to prominent, pioneering physicians who affect how their colleagues practice medicine. Jeffrey J. Meffert, "Key Opinion Leaders: Where They Come from and How That Affects the Drugs You Prescribe," *Dermatological Therapy* 22, no. 3 (2009): 262–268.

[6] Most Jesuit missionaries sent to pre-1945 Japan were German. Hans Martin Krämer, *Unterdrückung oder Integration? Die staatliche Behandlung der katholischen Kirche in Japan, 1932 bis 1945* (Marburg: Förderverein Marburger Japan-Reihe, 2002).

[7] An example of a Japanese woman with a German husband was Kunze Haruko. She wrote a cookbook to introduce German cuisine to Japan: see *Nihonjin muki no Doitsu katei ryōri* (Nagoya: Ichiryūsha, 1934). The philosopher Kanokogi Kazunobu married Cornelia Zielinski. The couple eventually divorced, but Cornelia kept her adopted surname and stayed in Tokyo as a German teacher.

nationalistic, and martial Germany. Once Hitler rose to power, more and more language teachers enthusiastically incorporated Nazi phrases, images, and concepts in language textbooks. Indeed, across the entire media linguists manifested transnational Nazism most pronouncedly and thoroughly through their voluntary *Gleichschaltung* to become advocates of Hitler and his ideology in Japan.

German the Difficult

Because Japanese and German are unrelated languages with different vocabularies, grammars, and sounds, German can strike even educated Japanese as quite strange. Certainly, most foreign tongues can appear alien from the perspective of Japanese, a "language isolate" with tenuous ties to other languages, but some features of interwar German made it particularly challenging for Japanese students vis-à-vis other European languages.[8] One such trait was blackletter or Fraktur (broken typeface), in use in Germany alongside roman type (Antiqua) since the fifteenth century.[9] Many Germans elevated blackletter to the national German type during the nineteenth century, in opposition to the roman one favored by France and the rest of Europe. Otto von Bismarck reportedly refused to read German books printed in a roman typeface.[10] The Reichstag waded into this "Antiqua-Fraktur Controversy" in 1911 but failed to reach a resolution. So German, unique among major European languages in the twentieth century, retained blackletter along with roman type. Newspapers printed columns in different typefaces depending on contexts, for example, business news in roman and literature in Fraktur. But blackletter was not tied to an ideological outlook. The Communist Party organ *Rote Fahne* used Fraktur in its masthead, while that of the Nazi organ *Völkischer Beobachter* appeared in roman. In fact, although blackletter is often associated with the Third Reich, Nazi attitudes toward the typeface were inconsistent. The Nazi regime blanketed Germany with posters and banners with slogans in Fraktur, but Hitler both privately and publicly denigrated "Gothic" type as a provincial relic unsuitable for the modern, German-led Europe he envisioned.[11] And

---

[8] J. Marshall Unger, *The Role of Contact in the Origins of the Japanese and Korean Languages* (Honolulu: University of Hawai'i Press, 2008).

[9] Fraktur can refer to blackletter in general or to a specific category or font.

[10] Peter Bain and Paul Shaw, eds., *Blackletter: Type and National Identity* (New York: The Cooper Union and Princeton Architectural Press, 1998).

[11] Hitler, *Monologe*, 124 (November 2–3, 1941).

yet the *Völkischer Beobachter* printed the Führer's proclamation that "being German means being clear" in blackletter.[12]

This parallel use of typefaces made German harder for Japanese readers. Beginning learners definitely already knew the Latin alphabet in roman type from their experiences with English or romanized Japanese, rōmaji (literally, Roman letters).[13] Many language textbooks thus took advantage of students' familiarity with English and pointed out that German has the same basic 26 letters.[14] But unlike English, German also uses umlauted vowels (ä, ö, ü) and the sharp s (ß). In Fraktur, several letters and combinations of letters in both upper and lower cases look very similar and can be easily confused by those new to the typeface. So textbooks had to highlight their differences and advise students to pay attention to these groups of letters.[15] Tyros especially would be frustrated by nearly indistinguishable letters because they need to identify the first letter of a word to look up its meaning in a dictionary. That German nouns are capitalized only made the problem worse.[16]

Readers also had to master various forms of German handwriting. All had to learn the traditional German cursive, Kurrent. Another style, Sütterlin, rose in popularity in the 1920s.[17] Sütterlin was taught as the official script to pupils in Germany's schools from 1935, but then in 1941 it was abolished by the same mercurial Nazi government. Though designed for relative simplicity, Sütterlin can appear quite illegible to those familiar only with Kurrent. The combined effects of the differences between blackletter and roman types, and Kurrent and Sütterlin, meant that in practice Japanese students had to learn to read and write the German alphabet repeatedly. So almost all textbooks began with lessons on the alphabet in different forms, often illustrated with tables to demonstrate the variations. Several texts also mixed passages in different typefaces to help readers practice deciphering Fraktur.[18] But switching between typefaces could also confuse students already struggling with grammar and vocabulary.

---

[12] *Völkischer Beobachter: Kampfblatt der nationalsozialistischen Bewegung Großdeutschlands* (hereafter: VB), September 6, 1934, Munich edition (hereafter: ME).

[13] "Introduction," in Tsuzumi Tsuneyoshi, *Shōkai Doitsu bunten* (Tokyo: Ōkura Shoten, 1921), 1.

[14] Okada Shun'ichi, *Okada Doitsugo kōza* (Tokyo: Heigensha, 1937), 5.

[15] Uchida Eizō and Tada Motoi, *Doitsugo seibatsu* (Tokyo: Ōkura Kōbundō, 1932), 56.

[16] Tsuzumi Tsuneyoshi, *Katsuyō Doitsu bunpō* (Tokyo: Daigaku Shorin, 1934), 4.

[17] Ludwig Sütterlin designed the handwriting style for the Prussian Ministry of Culture and Education in 1911.

[18] "Explanatory notes," in Akimoto Kikuo, *Shōkai shin Doitsu gogaku* (Tokyo: Kōgakukan Shoten, 1926), 2–3.

German's peculiar and bewildering use of multiple scripts prompted textbook authors to offer explanations to customers, including from two of Japan's most insightful Germanists. Hosei University professor Seki-guchi Tsugio agreed with German advocates of blackletter that Fraktur was elegantly suited for the efficient production or consumption of German, just like kanji's function in Japanese.[19] The sociologist Gonda Yasunosuke informed readers that blackletter and roman types served distinct purposes: Fraktur mostly for newspapers and literature, Antiqua for scientific and other works intended for international readership.[20]

Linguists also attributed to the German mindset Germany's retention of Fraktur long after the rest of Europe had abandoned it. Gonda saw "the Germans' love of argument" in sustaining the controversy between the two typefaces, and urged students to be proficient in both.[21] He acknowledged that Fraktur was tied to the German nation's essence, but he also labeled it a parochial remnant, to be inevitably displaced by Antiqua.[22] One textbook contrasted the "round, circuitous" roman type preferred by the British with the "formal, earnest" blackletter stubbornly preserved by the Germans.[23] Another argued that as blackletter was not specifically German in origin, the Germans were just blindly following tradition in continuing to use Fraktur.[24] The literary critic Yamagishi Mitsunobu, too, called the Germans "obdurate" for keeping their own style of writing.[25] Sekiguchi traced blackletter's seeming ubiquity in early 1930s Germany to rising nationalism.[26] As late as 1940, one book still credited the Nazi regime with reviving Fraktur.[27] But this interpretation was soon invalidated because in 1941 Hitler condemned Fraktur as "Jewish letters" and banned its official use–in a decree with a letterhead in blackletter.[28]

---

[19] Sekiguchi Tsugio, *Doitsugo daikōza 1* (Tokyo: Gaikokugo Kenkyūsha, 1934), 9. On Sekiguchi: see Araki Shigeo, Manabe Ryōichi, and Fujita Sakae, eds., *Sekiguchi Tsugio no shōgai to gyōseki* (Tokyo: Sanshūsha, 1967); Ikeuchi Osamu, *Kotoba no tetsugaku: Sekiguchi Tsugio no koto* (Tokyo: Seidosha, 2010).

[20] Gonda Yasunosuke, *Saishin Doitsugo kōza 1* (Tokyo: Yūhōdō Shoten, 1931), 3.

[21] Ibid., 4.

[22] Gonda Yasunosuke, *Kijun Doitsu bunpō* (Tokyo: Yūhōdō Shoten, 1931), 2.

[23] A. Hahn and Sawai Yōichi, *Seiongaku hon'i Dokubun shinkai* (Tokyo: Nichi-Doku Shoin, 1924), 63–64.

[24] Matsuoka Binkō, *Sōyō Doitsu bunten* (Tokyo: Shōbundō, 1932), 101.

[25] Yamagishi Mitsunobu, ed., *Shin Doitsugo kōza 1* (Tokyo: Doitsugo Kenkyūsha, 1934), 15.

[26] Sekiguchi, *Doitsugo daikōza 1*, 9.

[27] Shō Naokazu, *Jishū Doitsu bunpō shōkai* (Tokyo: Taiyōdō Shoten, 1940), 3.

[28] BArch, NS 6/334, *circulaire* by Martin Bormann, January 3, 1941; Stanley Morison, *Politics and Script: Aspects of Authority and Freedom in the Development of Graeco-Latin Script from the Sixth Century B.C. to the Twentieth Century A.D.* (Oxford: Clarendon Press, 1972), 323.

German pronunciation was also troublesome, even though Japanese and German share some sounds. The fundamental problem was that no book could teach pronunciation adequately, a futile task that one expert compared to trying to swim on tatami mats.[29] Technology offered a privileged few a novel solution. Households in Tokyo with a radio could tune in for German lessons by the Japan Broadcasting Corporation from the late 1920s.[30] Listeners who had purchased the accompanying course text could read passages aloud after the instructor and learn the correct pronunciation from an expert or even a native speaker.[31] For affluent Japanese urbanites, the radio could bring them closest to hearing native German spoken live until the popularization in the 1930s of foreign "talkie" films, many with their own companion books for understanding the dialog.[32]

But because most learners lacked access to such luxury, writers had to use printed words to convey uttered sounds. Their main tools were hiragana and katakana, the syllabaries for Japanese and transliterated foreign words, respectively. Many language books thus used katakana to convert German into Japanese sounds even though it is a poor instrument for replicating spoken German accurately. The linguists mostly recognized katakana's inadequacies, but for a lack of alternatives many still shoehorned the syllabary into the unintended role. Sekiguchi crafted sample sentences such as "Deutschland lehrt Japan" (Germany teaches Japan), phonetically marked as "Doichulanto lēruto Yāpan," or "Japan lernt von Deutschland" (Japan learns from Germany) as "Yāpan lerunto fon Doichulanto."[33] He thoughtfully attempted to improve katakana by adding a diacritical mark to the Japanese "r" spelling to indicate that it represented the "l" pronunciation instead. He also mixed hiragana and katakana graphemes to make finer distinctions that katakana by itself cannot accommodate. Still, the resultant transliteration was imprecise and could not account for subtle differences in pronunciation, such as those between the identically spelled "ch" and "r" sounds in Japanese and German.

---

[29] Ishikawa Renji, *Doitsugo hatsuon kenkyū*, Daigaku Shorin bunko 14 (Tokyo: Daigaku Shorin, 1938), 17–18.

[30] Nihon Hōsō Kyōkai Kantō Shibu, ed., *Rajio Doitsugo kōza* (Tokyo: Tōkyō Chūō Hōsōkyoku, 1927).

[31] Sekiguchi cohosted a radio program of German lessons with Rolf Henkl in 1938. *Rajio tekisuto sokusei Doitsugo: Kaki* (Tokyo: Nihon Hōsō Kyōkai, 1938).

[32] For example, the book for the film *Hitlerjunge Quex*: see Karl Aloys Schenzinger, *Heigensha tōkī shirīzu A(12): Hittorā seinen Doku-Wa taiyaku* (Tokyo: Heigensha, 1934).

[33] Sekiguchi Tsugio, *Hyōjun shotō Doitsugo kōza I* (Tokyo: Tachibana Shoten, 1933), 63.

A minority of textbook authors rejected the katakana shortcut and tried to teach spoken German with the International Phonetic Alphabet (IPA). Whereas foreknowledge of English helped students to learn the German alphabet, for pronunciation some teachers saw it as a liability. Sekiguchi stated specifically that he chose to use the syllabaries rather than the IPA because most Japanese who learned the IPA did so from studying English, and he did not want to double the burden on the system.[34] Several writers deemed familiarity with English so detrimental to learning German that they cautioned readers not to confuse the two languages' pronunciations.[35] A few books specializing in German phonetics even included anatomical diagrams to show the proper positions of the tongue, teeth, and lips for any sound.[36] But there were only a few such innovative works.

Like German's problematic typefaces and handwriting scripts, spoken German's peculiarities frustrated teachers and students, and added to the language's notoriety in Japan. The philologist Yamada Kōzaburō alerted readers that even native Germans enunciated "r" differently depending on locales and dialects.[37] Sekiguchi half-jokingly celebrated the stereotypically Japanese tendency to confuse the "l" and "r" sounds as a national icon that gained worldwide recognition like Mount Fuji and Bushido.[38] The economist Tada Motoi called the umlauted vowels the hardest sounds in German partly because they cannot be straightforwardly transliterated into Japanese.[39] Some Japanese believed that spoken German, in contrast to English or French, demonstrated obstinate boorishness.[40] To some Japanese, German was a rugged, harsh language that sounded like windows shattering. To others, it resembled angry curses by stable hands. Yet others joked that God spoke German when he irately banished Adam and Eve from Eden.[41] Also invoking God, the folklorist Saigō Keizō compared learning German progressively to God's accretive creation of the universe.[42] Another linguist comforted readers that with hard work they, too, could

---

[34] Sekiguchi Tsugio, *Doitsugo daikōza 1*, 7. His concern was unfounded because the IPA is designed to function across languages.
[35] Saigō Keizō, *Shin Doitsugo yonshūkan* (Tokyo: Shōbundō, 1930), 10.
[36] Momonoi Tsuruo, *Doitsugo hatsuon no kenkyū* (Tokyo: Taiyōdō Shoten, 1936).
[37] Yamada Kōzaburō, *Jishū shin Doitsugo* (Tokyo: Taiyōdō Shoten, 1930), 32.
[38] Sekiguchi, *Doitsugo daikōza 1*, 19.
[39] Tada Motoi, *Hyōjun Doitsugo daiippo* (Tokyo: Gakushūdō, 1934), 12.
[40] Michibe Jun, *Dokushūsha no Doitsugo: Ei-Doku taishō hatsuon yakudoku bunpō shōkai* (Tokyo: Ikubundō Shoten, 1926), 11.
[41] Gonda, *Saishin Doitsugo kōza 1*, 7.   [42] Saigō Keizō, 93–94.

hope to master German, because even God himself must have sweated and toiled before he became omnipotent.[43]

Jests and fables aside, overcoming German's myriad hurdles was a serious struggle for learners. In addition to the alien scripts and sounds, students had to wrestle with German grammatical subtleties absent in Japanese. Articles and declension of noun phrases confounded and deterred numerous aspirants.[44] Several Germanists conceded that inherent noun gender just made no sense to the Japanese.[45] Gonda diagnosed a "sex problem" for novices, while Sekiguchi wrote a funny skit to help students make peace with arbitrary noun genders.[46] Sekiguchi even went so far as to credit relative pronouns for enabling the white race to grasp complex ideas and act as the vanguard in spiritual affairs. He lamented that the Japanese language lacks such logical ways of thought and expression so that even a simple relative clause in German can seem difficult to the Japanese.[47] On a more advanced level, idioms and the subjunctive mood presented formidable roadblocks.[48] Understanding idioms requires knowledge beyond linguistic proficiency. The subjunctive mood was called the hardest topic in German because it overturns grammatical rules that students memorized at the outset of their studies.[49] Keio University lecturer Komura Minoru promised readers that once they mastered the subjunctive, the road ahead would be flat and easy.[50]

Perhaps worse than the actual difficulties German presented was the reputation for difficulty that German suffered in Japan. It was a widely shared view attributed to the differences between the two languages.[51] German was also believed to be much harder than English or French.[52] Its grammar was often associated with boredom, intricacy, and adversity. These impressions were exacerbated by the method of study, rote

---

[43] "Introduction," in Okamoto Shūsuke, *Gendai Doitsu bunpō kōwa: Hinshiron* (Tokyo: Sanseidō, 1937), 1.

[44] "Foreword," in Iwamoto Tsunemaru, *Doitsu bunpō yōketsu: Sankō jishū* (Tokyo: Daigaku Shorin, 1930), 1. Whole books were written on articles: see Yamada Kōzaburō, *Doitsugo kanshi no kenkyū* (Tokyo: Daigaku Shorin, 1937).

[45] Saigō Keizō, 25.

[46] Gonda, *Saishin Doitsugo kōza 2*, 24; "Postscript," in Sekiguchi, *Doitsugo daikōza 6*, 1.

[47] Sekiguchi, *Doitsugo daikōza 1*, 261, 263.

[48] "Introduction," in Kagawa Tetsuo, *Hoshū Doitsu ibun kaishakuhō* (Tokyo: Nanzandō Shoten, 1930), i.

[49] "Introduction," in Sakurai Waichi, *Doitsugo wahō no kenkyū* (Tokyo: Daigaku Shorin, 1934), 1; Hashimoto Tadao, *Doitsugo no shūjiteki kōsei* (Tokyo: Nankōdō Shoten, 1933), 4.

[50] Komura Minoru, *Shin Doitsu bunpō: 24-jikan seiri* (Tokyo: Taiyōdō Shoten, 1933), 86.

[51] "Preface," in Tanaka Mitsuharu, *Yoku wakaru shonensei no Doitsu bunpō* (Tokyo: Taiyōdō Shoten, 1939), 1–2.

[52] "Introduction," in Ōshima Muneharu, *Doitsugo dokushū* (Tokyo: Doitsugo Gakkai, 1919), 1.

memorization of rules and vocabulary.[53] The idea "German is difficult" was evidently so ingrained among the Japanese that many linguists found it necessary to debunk the preconception and to assure readers that their own language textbooks provided the solution.

In the face of German's formidable reputation, language teachers devised strategies to entice students. The most common, apparently most appealing, sales pitches described a book as instructing German in a "new" way. Other works attempted to assuage students' fear by invoking prominent Germanists such as Gonda or Katayama Masao as a guarantee of quality.[54] Some linguists chose encouraging book titles such as *Introductory German as Hobby*, *German Is Fun*, *Easy to Understand Beginning German Grammar*, and *Practical German-Japanese Conversations*.[55] A few, notably Sekiguchi, mixed humor with earnest grammar instruction effectively.

In contrast to these positive messages, several linguists took to mobilizing readers with warlike exhortations to gain command of German. The great novelist Uchida Eizō, who had once taught German at the Army Academy, explained that he had wanted to title his book *The Hell of German*, but the publisher thought it too intimidating to potential customers, so he renamed it the more motivational *Conquering German*.[56] Saigō, too, compared learning German to a military campaign. He argued that just as commanders need to understand the limit of their abilities and consolidate captured territories, so should students not attempt to learn German in a hurry but take time to review past lessons. Learners should mind their figurative supplies of ammunition and food by managing the knowledge they already acquired.[57] One textbook advertised itself as the "new weapon" in subduing German.[58] Another called the mastery of German linguistics a "spiritual weapon" for Japanese-German translation.[59] Its author admonished readers that as a

---

[53] "Introduction," in Kasuya Mahiro, *Kasuya Doitsu jishū bunten* (Tokyo: Kōbundō Shoten, 1922), 1; Ōshima Shun'ichirō, *Jitsuyō Doitsu shōgyō tsūshinbun* (Tokyo: Ōkura Shoten, 1929), 2.

[54] "Advertisements," in Gonda Yasunosuke, *Doitsu shinbun kenkyū*, Doku-Wa taiyaku shōbin bunko 2 (Tokyo: Yūhōdō Shoten, 1929).

[55] Respectively, Oyanagi Tokuji, *Shumi no Dokugo nyūmon* (Tokyo: Nichi-Doku Shoin, 1929); Tomita Kumao, *Doitsugo wa tanoshimi da* (Tokyo: Seikōsha Shoten, 1941); Tanaka Mitsuharu; Yamaguchi Miki and Okakura Ichirō, *Jitsuyō Doku-Wa kaiwa hen* (Kobe: Kawase Nisshindō Shoten, 1926).

[56] "Introduction," in Uchida and Tada, 1. Uchida is better known under his pen name Uchida Hyakken.

[57] Saigō Keizō, 95–96.

[58] "Introduction," in Obara Shizuto, *Doitsugo henka zenpyō* (Tokyo: Daigaku Shorin, 1935), 1.

[59] Miura Kichibee, ed., *Kōdō Doitsugo kōza 1* (Tokyo: Daigaku Shorin, 1931), 151.

country's defense should not consist solely of artillery, cavalry, or poison gas, so should students of translation not neglect other aspects of German studies.[60] German tests on university entrance examinations struck such fear in students that Gonda tried to inspire them with a Chinese parable about a king who had lost a battle and his kingdom but eventually defeated his enemy by persevering and subjecting himself to humiliation and hardship.[61] The frequent use of military imagery and rhetoric may seem hyperbolic, but for many Japanese students of German, mastering the language was unambiguously important and serious. That many Japanese decided to tackle German despite its complexity and notoriety indicates their anticipation of tangible spoils once they vanquished the language.

German the Useful

Besides the inherent linguistic difficulties, German learning in interwar Japan faced challenges specific to its time and place. Most ordinary Japanese had little use for German because they did not expect to meet Germans or visit Germany. The educated elites studied classical Chinese and English before they would consider a third non-native language such as German or French. The precedence of English over all other Western tongues in Japan was such that the Germanists used it to teach the German alphabet or reminded students not to confuse German with English sounds.[62] For Japanese aiming to venture abroad, German did not recommend itself as the obvious foreign language of choice. Those with ambitions in continental Asia likely armed themselves with knowledge of modern Chinese, Russian, or Korean. Those casting their dreams farther afield could focus on Spanish or Portuguese for emigrating to South America, French for Europe in general, and above all English for the entire world. Even Esperanto, created to foster international understanding, might seem a more suitable choice after the horrors of the Great War. Moreover, when Germany relinquished its Asian-Oceanic possessions after World War I, German lost its official presence near Japan. The conflict also imposed a caesura in Japan's exposure to German. Soon after Japan entered hostilities in 1914, the government banned all German newspapers to snuff out enemy propaganda. Combat severed commerce, including the importation of German books. Most Germans in the Japanese Empire, many of whom had been

---

[60] Ibid., 152.
[61] Gonda Yasunosuke, *Kijun Dokubun Wayakuhō* (Tokyo: Yūhōdō Shoten, 1933), 37.
[62] Gonda, *Saishin Doitsugo kōza 2*, 61.

working as language instructors, were expelled or interned as enemy aliens. For Japanese students of German, particularly those who had been learning from teachers or texts from Germany, World War I was detrimental to their progress.[63]

Although the war reduced German's visibility and availability for over four years, German learning reemerged in postwar Japan in a robust position. The numerous textbooks claiming to be new seemed to proclaim a fresh start. German expatriates and internees rejoined Japanese society and reprised their roles as language instructors and cultural intermediaries.[64] The Japanese appetite for German stayed strong, so publishers furnished the supply to satisfy this demand. Of the 1,100-odd Japanese nonfiction works on Germany published between 1919 and 1937 preserved at the National Diet Library, nearly a quarter deal with its language. Despite the repercussions of World War I, German acquisition remained a major component of interwar Japanese-German cultural relations.[65]

Echoing the opinion makers discussed previously, linguists credited German civilization for German's ability to maintain a presence in Japan and the world disproportionally greater than Germany's own. Much like the literary critics, they turned Germany's travails around into an argument for studying the country. They were confident that the German national character, as revealed in the language, would make Germany great and worth knowing again. An advertisement for a German-Japanese dictionary in 1929 declared that understanding the Germans' indomitable spirit behind their politics, economy, and scholarship was vital for the Japanese.[66] A book on German for dentistry proclaimed that those who despised foreign languages would have a hand in the downfall of their own country and people.[67] Saigō Keizō concluded in 1930 that because the Germans' "thoroughness and expansiveness" underpinned their culture and its contribution to world civilization, the Japanese would do well to emulate these German qualities.[68] He added that although over four years of war and the Versailles Treaty seemingly doomed Germany the way Pompeii or Sodom were damned, thanks to its unique culture the country

---

[63] Even the Great Kanto Earthquake in 1923 dealt a blow to German learning. It destroyed the draft prints of Katayama's German-Japanese dictionary, slated to come out that year. It did not appear until 1927. Katayama Masao, *Sōkai Doku-Wa daijiten* (Tokyo: Nankōdō Shoten, 1927).

[64] TN, July 8, 1919.

[65] Miyanaga Takashi, *Nichi-Doku bunka jinbutsu kōryūshi* (Tokyo: Sanshūsha, 1993).

[66] "Advertisements," in Ōshima Shun'ichirō.

[67] "Preface," in Shimada Masami and Kokubu Shirō, *Shika Doitsugo dokushūsho* (Tokyo: Kanehara Shoten, 1929), 1.

[68] Saigō Keizō, 20.

was making a furious comeback that was bound to sweep over the world. So readers should not treat German studies lightly but as the key to unlocking this culture's secrets.[69] The authoritative Yamagishi Mitsunobu held the same opinion:

Although news of Germany's demise was propagated immediately after the world war, everyone now knows that Germany has turned its fortune around and is superseding the victorious powers. Studying such cultural potential of Germany is thus essential for breaking the impasse in which our country currently finds itself. To study German culture, one must use correct knowledge of German as the foundation and proceed steadily, gradually by consulting original works.[70]

According to Yamagishi and many of his colleagues – as seen in Sekiguchi's "Japan learns from Germany" pronunciation exercises – learning German and by extension learning from Germany were a matter of Japan's national welfare. In 1942, during another world war, the leftist economist Kobayashi Ryōsei argued that Germany rebounded from its nadir to become a world power thanks to Nazi reforms. Because German underwent changes under Nazism such as the outlawing of Fraktur and Sütterlin, Japanese students who sought to understand the New Germany must also familiarize themselves with the New German.[71]

Beyond imparting lessons from the national character it embodied, German brought concrete benefits for Japanese students. In interwar Japan, indeed throughout the world, German served as the lingua franca in several professional and academic fields. Proficiency in German guarded the gates to many Japanese institutions of higher learning. Most universities required applicants to pass a foreign language test as part of the entrance examination. The prestigious imperial universities specific-ally mandated one for German.[72] It mattered little what prospective enrollees intended to study. The schools of economics, law, medicine, philosophy, engineering, physics, pharmacy, agriculture, and chemistry all administered a German test.[73] Outside academia, civil servants and army cadets could brighten their prospects for advancement by proving German proficiency.[74] The high stakes involved, university admission or

---

[69] Ibid., "Introduction," 1.
[70] "Introduction," in Yamagishi Mitsunobu, *Shotō Doitsu bunten* (Tokyo: Kashiwaba Shobō, 1929), 1.
[71] "Foreword," in Kobayashi Ryōsei, ed., *Shin Doitsu seiji keizai goi* (Tokyo: Nikkō Shoin, 1942), 1–2.
[72] Baba Hisayoshi, *Teikoku daigaku juken jūyō hissu Doitsugo tangoshū 5000-go* (Tokyo: Nichi-Doku Shoin, 1930).
[73] Nichi-Doku Shoin, ed., *Zenkoku teidai nyūgaku shiken Doitsugo mondai to sono kaitō: Jukensha no tame ni 1932* (Tokyo: Nichi-Doku Shoin, 1932).
[74] Nichi-Doku Shoin, ed., *Shiken mondai Doitsugo shōkai* (Tokyo: Nichi-Doku Shoin, 1925).

career promotion, spawned a cottage industry of guidebooks to help aspirants overcome the institutionalized hurdle of German examinations. For test takers, German looked nothing like a living language but appeared only on paper as texts to be translated from and into Japanese within a set amount of time.

German's all-important, institutional status in Japan's higher education and professions commercialized the language. Students realized that mastering German could reap them sizable benefits, but they also knew that such a valuable skill could only be earned through expenditures in time, effort, and certainly money. That is, one could move upward socially by conquering German, but one also had to pay an entrance fee just for the opportunity. Although interwar Japan was a hierarchical society in which people born into privilege enjoyed advantages, it also abounded with anecdotes of individuals of lowly births who made their own fortune with sheer will and talent. Sekiguchi, Gonda, the literary critic Aoki Shōkichi, and many other Germanists rose from humble backgrounds to become respected scholars and professors.[75]

As sincerely as these linguists wished to share their passion and admiration for German, they also wanted to profit from their own exertion through selling products and services. German's prized position in segments of Japanese society meant that knowledge of the language was bought and sold like other goods. Besides examination guidebooks, pronunciation exercises for radio lessons, and companions to talkies, Germanists published school textbooks, grammar manuals, collections of quotations and idioms, conversation booklets, vocabulary flashcards, handwriting templates, declension and conjugation charts, and dictionaries. Moreover, they translated German works into Japanese, including not only timeless classics by Goethe and Schiller but also the timely and political *Wage-Labor and Capital* by Karl Marx and the Nazi Party program.[76]

The linguists also profited from publishing or serializing the lessons that they taught at higher schools or universities. Yamagishi Mitsunobu was the general editor of *Short University German Course*, an anthology of lectures by eminent professors. Others edited periodicals on learning German. Gonda Yasunosuke launched *German Studies* in 1929. Sekiguchi Tsugio steered the monthly *Elementary German*. Aoki Shōkichi

---

[75] Kamimura Naoki, *Kindai Nihon no Doitsugo gakusha* (Suwa: Chōeisha, 2008).

[76] Karl Heinrich Marx, *Chinrōdō to shihon*, trans. Hirono Toshikama, Doitsu shōronbun taiyaku 2 (Tokyo: Daigaku Shorin, 1933); Gottfried Feder, *Nachisu kōryō*, trans. Kido Hiroo, Doitsu shōronbun taiyaku 5 (Tokyo: Daigaku Shorin, 1934).

oversaw the monthly *The German Language*.[77] These magazines competed with older ones founded in the late nineteenth century, including *Journal of the German Studies Association*, *Journal for Self-Studying German*, and *New Journal of Accelerated German Studies*. Some smaller publications fell as casualties during World War I, but the Society for the Journal of German Studies continued its flagship periodical into the early postwar years. Its textbooks, first published in the late Meiji period and approved for schools by the Ministry of Education, remained in print well into the 1920s. But under the altered state of German learning in interwar Japan, the society, too, withered as a new generation of specialists emerged to compete for market share.

German lessons were economically significant for their producers and consumers as a commercial good. Some publishers concentrated on books on German as an essential component of their product lines. Ikubundō Shoten, then as now, led German teaching in Japan with its textbooks and grammar manuals. Others included Nankōdō Shoten, Nichi-Doku Shoin, and Daigaku Shorin. Most language texts in the interwar era cost between ¥0.80 and ¥2.50, with some inflation. Reference works such as German for chemistry or medicine usually sold for ¥3.50. Comprehensive lexicons set the reader back at least ¥5.00, with the priciest specimen going for ¥12 in 1937. Of course, students from low income families could hardly build a collection of such books, though many seem to have saved up enough to purchase at least a teach-yourself German text and a dictionary, of paramount importance for textual translation, as evidenced by their multiple editions. Readers could also access textbooks in libraries, but these communally available copies often suffered from missing or scribbled pages.[78] Learning German was costly enough that most students could not dabble in it out of curiosity or admiration for some vague German national traits, despite what many Germanists wanted to believe. Rather, most learners studied German with expectations of tangible returns for their investment. Teaching German was good business and learning German was serious business.

The pressure in mastering German, compounded by the all-or-nothing tests used to gauge proficiency, deformed the German being taught and learned to resemble a dead language more than a living tongue. Because the examinations comprised two-way translation questions only, teachers

---

[77] "Advertisements," in Gonda, *Doitsu shinbun kenkyū*, 1; "Advertisements," in Matsuoka Binkō, *Shōkei Dokubun shoho* (Tokyo: Shōbundō, 1933), 1; "Advertisements," in Uchida Mitsugi, *Doitsu shin bunten* (Tokyo: Ikubundō Shoten, 1930), 1.

[78] Some users who encountered stolen pages vented their frustration by cursing the thieves: see the National Diet Library's copy of Gonda, *Saishin Doitsugo kōza 1*, 89; Ōshima Muneharu, 7.

and students targeted that narrow task. Readers learned grammar and vocabulary by rote memorization, honed by endless translation drills. The emphasis on replication rather than comprehension also led to reliance on katakana to approximate German sounds in lieu of a proper understanding of phonetics. A few topical works offered conversation lessons, but most texts did not discuss pronunciation at all.[79]

Appreciating that many readers merely wanted to survive the proficiency test and not to master German, some linguists tailored their merchandise or advertisements to lure desperate customers. Many works proclaimed themselves "new" when in fact no new method of instruction was introduced. Several labeled themselves "interesting," but the translation exercises therein made them anything but fun. Some sold themselves as "practical," even though after the test students would hardly find value in translating German word for word. Some verged on false advertising in promising readers that they could teach themselves German with no external help, as many titles featured the phrase "self-study" (*dokushū* or *jishū*). The most outrageous specimens even offered to teach students German in four weeks or to improve their grammar in 24 hours.[80] Students who resorted to such quick fixes were not seeking a lifelong bond with German but only steeling themselves to suffer through the hell of German as a means to further ends.

Far from diminishing the regard for Germany in Japan, this utilitarianism illustrates German's role as the de facto working language of some professional or academic communities. One such field was physical and life sciences, in which German chemists and physicists achieved transformative breakthroughs in the early twentieth century. Names of Nobel laureates such as Röntgen, Bosch, Planck, and especially Einstein and Haber, resonated among educated and lay Japanese. As a German for chemistry book put it, "Germany is a country of chemistry. In scholarship, it reigns over the world's academic community with its top knowledge. In practice, its newest technology pushes the frontier of civilization."[81] It added that the development of Japan's knowhow in medicine and pharmacology, as well as all areas of chemistry, owed much to Germany, so knowledge of German was a sine qua non for the studies of chemistry in Japan. An advertisement for another German for chemistry book concurred, and declared that for chemists German was the most

[79] Komura Minoru, *Beruringo* (Tokyo: Daigaku Shorin, 1935); Watanabe Kakuji, *Tei-Doitsugo kenkyū* (Tokyo: Daigaku Shorin, 1943).

[80] Mori Toshio, *Doitsugo yonshūkan* (Tokyo: Kashiwaba Shobō, 1929); Komura, *Shin Doitsu bunpō: 24-jikan seiri*.

[81] Takagi Seiji, introduction to *Kagaku Doitsugo kenkyū*, by Nakayama Hisashi (Tokyo: Mokuseisha Shoin, 1930), 1.

essential language. If one could not read German, one's studies in chemistry would become mired in difficulty.[82] Even when an author believed that chemistry in Japan had caught up with that in the West, he still emphasized the importance of learning European languages for accessing Western knowledge.[83]

Indeed, German underlay the Japanese nomenclature in chemistry and physics. Many Japanese scientific terms, notably chemical elements and compounds, have Germanic roots. Mercury in Japanese, *suigin* (watery silver), approximates the German *Quecksilber* (quicksilver). Nitrogen in both Japanese, *chisso*, and German, *Stickstoff*, means "suffocating material." Titanium, potassium, and uranium in Japanese are *chitan*, *karium*, and *uran*, transliterations of *Titan*, *Kalium*, and *Uran*.[84] Malic acid is labeled in Japanese as *ringosan* (apple acid), corresponding to the German *Apfelsäure*. Succinic acid is *kohakusan* in Japanese and *Bernsteinsäure* in German, both meaning "amber acid."[85] Pigment in both Japanese (*shikiso*) and German (*Farbstoff*) is expressed as a compound word consisting of "color" and "material."[86] Although the names of some basic chemical elements arrived via Dutch to Japan before its "opening" in the nineteenth century, by the interwar era the Japanese were studying German, not Dutch, for science. The differences between the English and the German terms for the same chemicals, and the correlation between the German and the Japanese ones, demonstrate the influence of German in scientific knowledge in Japan. As an advertisement for a book on German for engineering proclaimed, "The era of English omnipotence has passed. The rise in fortune of German studies is all but a matter of certainty."[87]

German also dictated the way Japanese researchers and practitioners of dentistry, pharmacology, and medicine articulated their knowledge. Many Japanese believed that medical students could not study medicine without German.[88] Experts freely acknowledged that Japan had

---

[82] "Advertisements," in Enomoto Tsunetarō and Kurotsuka Juichi, *Doitsugo ronbun sakuhō kenkyū* (Tokyo: Taiyōdō Shoten, 1932), 1.

[83] "Introduction," in Hashimoto Kichirō, *Kagaku yōgo shin jiten* (Tokyo: Taiyōdō Shoten, 1927), 1.

[84] Nakayama Hisashi, ed., *Nichi-Doku Shoin Doitsugo zensho 1: Butsuri to kagaku* (Tokyo: Nichi-Doku Shoin, 1934).

[85] Isobe Kōichi, *Rika Doitsu gohō kyōtei* (Tokyo: Kanehara Shoten, 1933), 13.

[86] "Introduction," in Ōno Yūji, *Senryō seizō kagaku: Kagaku kōgyō*, Doitsu bunko (Tokyo: Shōbundō, 1932), 2.

[87] "Advertisements," in Enomoto and Kurotsuka, 1.

[88] "Advertisements," in Isobe Kōichi, *Doitsu ibun no kakikata* (Tokyo: Daigaku Shorin, 1932), 1; Satō Sankichi, introduction to *Igaku Doitsugo kenkyū: Kiso iga hen*, by Takizawa Yuzuru (Tokyo: Mokuseisha Shoin, 1931), 1; "Introduction," in Hamada Saburō and

Germany to thank for its advancement in these fields.[89] Satō Sankichi, a famous surgeon, wrote that Japan felt gratitude and awe for the "colleague, nay, mentor" that was Germany, which surpassed by far other countries in medical expertise.[90] Germany had been especially instrumental in the development of modern medicine in Japan from the Meiji period.[91] The studies of German and medicine remained inextricably intertwined in the interwar era. Not only did all Japanese physicians trained in Western medicine have to know German, but several Germanists first came into contact with the language through their professional aspirations in medicine. Many Germans taught their native tongue in Japanese medical schools. The link between German and medicine even manifested itself in the publishing world, as publishers of German texts such as Nanzandō, Nankōdō, and Kanehara Shoten also specialized in medical reference works.

As in chemistry, German terminology permeated Japanese medical and biological nomenclature. Protein translates into German as *Eiweißkörper* and Japanese as *tanpakushitsu*, both for "egg white substance." Cerebrum and cerebellum are *Großhirn* and *Kleinhirn* in German and *dainō* and *shōnō* in Japanese: "big brain" and "small brain."[92] A suspected bone fracture was not diagnosed by X-ray but *rentogensen* (Röntgen rays) instead. German was so internalized that some Japanese physicians could practice in German, while many more spoke a type of hybrid language intelligible only among themselves.[93] No monolingual Japanese or German can make out the meanings of "Neugeborene wa gesund desu ka" (Is the newborn healthy?) or "Magenkrebs to kimatte Operation wo suru" (When I diagnose stomach cancer, I perform an operation).[94] The German words substituted in these bilingual sentences all have functional, untransliterated native counterparts. That Japanese doctors mixed Japanese and German showcases the ingrained training they received and the entrenched position of German in Japanese medicine.

Takahashi Toshio, *Doku-Wa taiyaku: Shinsatsu mondō* (Tokyo: Nichi-Doku Shoin, 1936), 1.

[89] "Advertisements," in Takizawa Yuzuru, *Igaku Doitsugo kenkyū: Kiso iga hen* (Tokyo: Mokuseisha Shoin, 1931), 1.

[90] Satō Sankichi, 1.

[91] Hoi-eun Kim, *Doctors of Empire: Medical and Cultural Encounters between Imperial Germany and Meiji Japan* (Toronto: University of Toronto Press, 2014).

[92] Takizawa, 56.

[93] JTM, July 9, 1933; Naitō Hachirō, *Iyō gaikokugo nyūmon: Doitsugo Ratengo yomikata* (Nagoya: Nagoya-shi Ishikai Fuzoku Kango Fusanba Gakkō, 1933), 23; Paul Glynn, *A Song for Nagasaki: The Story of Takashi Nagai—Scientist, Convert, and Survivor of the Atomic Bomb* (San Francisco: Ignatius Press, 2009), 76.

[94] Naitō, 24.

German the Political

In addition to its static dominance in Japanese chemistry and medicine, as well as law, engineering, aviation, economics, and classical music, German was a dynamic phenomenon.[95] German was static in that it maintained its significance in these fields before and after World War I, as Japanese continued learning the language to access valuable knowledge. What made German dynamic in the 1920s and 1930s was that Germany innovated in politics. The Weimar Republic provided an open arena for various, contrasting ideologies, each with its own jargon and worldview. Then the Third Reich introduced a host of unfamiliar ideas and institutions that aroused curiosity and required analysis and translation in Japan. Particularly to those Japanese who saw their country floundering in the extraordinary times, Germany's experience seemed to offer lessons and give them an urgent incentive for studying political German.

The Germanists generally harbored a positive view of Germany and projected it in their works. They admired the language and its speakers and country enough to devote their lives to its studies. Although Japan and Germany fought on opposing sides in World War I, language texts published immediately after the war exhibited no ill will or bitterness toward Germany. Nor did Japanese students pick the language with any intention of deploying it for military or intelligence purposes against its country. Despite the political upheavals in the early Weimar years, language texts in Japan were largely free of editorial comments, and German learning occupied an apolitical role.

But this absence of explicit commentary on current events does not mean that the linguists lacked political opinions on Germany. Rather, and perhaps subconsciously, they sketched a particular picture of the country in their works. At first glance, lessons on the alphabet, pronunciation, or grammar may not leave much leeway for value judgment, but many writers found enough room to use German as a proxy tool for interpreting Germany. Many Germanists concluded that the peculiarities of German typography revealed not only the uprightness but also

---

[95] For law, Mitsuma Shinzō, *Doitsu hōritsu ruigo idōben* (Tokyo: Yūhikaku, 1935); for mechanical engineering, Tsuboi Michizō and Okabe Noboru, *Kikai Doitsugo kaishaku kenkyū* (Tokyo: Taiyōdō Shoten, 1935); for aviation, Kobayashi Yasutarō, *Hikōki kikai no chishiki*, Doitsugo bunko (Tokyo: Shōbundō, 1936); for economics, Haruta Ikuzō, *Doitsugo nyūmon sōsho 3: Seiji keizai Doitsugo nyūmon* (Tokyo: Hakusuisha, 1935); for music, Satō Tsunehisa, ed., *Doitsugo kyōhon ongaku gakkōyō* (Tokyo: Musashino Ongaku Gakkō, 1941).

obstinacy and inflexibility of the German people. German sounds evoked the image of a virile, tough, and disciplined people. German's clearly demarcated tenses seemed to indicate a quintessentially German and precise observance of time.[96] Some saw grammatical rules such as inherent noun gender and the subjunctive mood as products of a dogmatic, arbitrary national character. Sekiguchi Tsugio outdid all others in extrapolation by singling out relative pronouns as a key for the success of the whole white race.[97]

Under this light, the martial exhortations to students and comparisons between military campaigns and German acquisition no longer appear so random or incongruous. War loomed large in the minds of the linguists and their works. Writing in 1926 in the latest edition of the bestselling textbook since the Meiji era, one Germanist reminisced that he and his coauthors had labored on the first edition during the Sino-Japanese War.[98] The conflict left a legacy in the form of sample sentences such as, "The enemy has fled," "The enemy will have vacated the field," and "The officer was captured alongside the soldiers."[99]

In the 1920s and 1930s, when the world lived in memory or fear of a great military conflagration, references to combat and weapons shadowed the depiction of Germany in language books.[100] Not every book mentioned war in lessons on German. Those that did, did not do so on every page. But war appeared far too frequently to be accidental. Throughout the interwar era, Japanese students of German were taught military-related words of limited general applicability in life or in tests, including armored cruiser, field hospital, heavy artillery, and high treason.[101] Sample sentences and homework exercises also show writers'

---

[96] Mugikura Tatsuo, *Nichi-Doku ryōminzoku no jikankan: Toki no hyōgen ni miru gengo jijitsu wo fumaete* (Okayama: Daigaku Kyōiku Shuppan, 2001).

[97] German was not alone as a language with a reputation. A book on German for dentistry argued that people who studied French or Russian could become susceptible to communism or nihilism: see "Preface," in Shimada and Kokubu, 1.

[98] "Introduction," in Ōmura Jintarō, Yamaguchi Kotarō, and Taniguchi Hidetarō, *Doitsu bunpō kyōkasho 1* (Tokyo: Nichi-Doku Shoin, 1927), 1. Only Taniguchi was still alive in 1927, but the textbook, first sold in 1894, remained a bestseller into the 1920s, reaching more than 70 editions.

[99] Ibid., 50, 52, 165.

[100] Paul K. Saint-Amour, *Tense Future: Modernism, Total War, Encyclopedic Form* (New York: Oxford University Press, 2015).

[101] Yamaguchi Miki, *Doitsugo kaitei* (Tokyo: Kanasashi Hōryūdō, 1931); Hayakawa Bun'ya, *Kan'yō Doitsu bunten* (Tokyo: Nanzandō Shoten, 1927); Tsuzumi Tsuneyoshi, *Kihon Doitsu bunpō* (Tokyo: Daigaku Shorin, 1933); Kamei Tōtarō, *Jitsuyō Doitsu bunpō kōgi* (Tokyo: Kanasashi Hōryūdō, 1931).

bias for military German. A question on the past tense had readers translate into German the incongruous and impractical sentence "The barbed-wire fence hindered the enemy's assault."[102] Others included "The German soldiers fought extremely bravely at the Battle of Verdun," "If the enemies confront us, our aircraft will come and help us from above, and in the end we will prevail as usual," and "The deeds of those who liberated our fatherland from the enemy's hands are immortal."[103] Moreover, linguists selected passages for reading comprehension with martial or nationalistic themes. So students read stories such as "I Do Not Need to Know More!" It described a soldier who lost both eyes and both legs at the Battle of the Nations in 1813 but cared only about the battle's outcome. When assured that "Germany" had defeated Napoleon, he passed away in peace and satisfaction.[104] Other passages featured the conquests of Frederick the Great, Wilhelm's musings on the Great War, and field posts by fallen German soldiers. War might not have been a predominant topic in all texts, but many authors and presumably their readers saw warfare and German fitting enough that talk of war served as a vehicle for teaching German.

Much as journalists' fixation on Kaiser Wilhelm distorted newspapers' coverage of Germany, so the linguists' focus on him skewed the teaching of German. Indeed, language books mentioned Hohenzollern and used him as a conduit for illustrating German grammar more than any other personality. Students learning the four noun cases in German frequently saw their application to the phrase "the Kaiser Wilhelm."[105] A few works complicated the grammar by adding the suffix "the Second" to the name.[106] Countless sample sentences and homework questions mentioned the Kaiser. The one statement that students encountered in almost every language textbook was a version of "Long live the Kaiser!" Readers could learn at least eight different ways in German to wish the Kaiser well, such as "God save the Kaiser!," "May the Kaiser live long!," "God look after our merciful Kaiser!," and "May God shield the Kaiser!"[107] Despite the self-proclaimed mission of many linguists to

---

[102] Aoki Shōkichi, *Shokyū shō Dokubunten* (Tokyo: Nanzandō Shoten, 1937), 15–16.

[103] Yamagishi, *Shotō Doitsu bunten*, 72; Sekiguchi, *Hyōjun shotō Doitsugo kōza II*, 41; Aoki Ichirō, *Sūgaku butsurigaku kagaku wo manabu hito no Doitsugo kontei* (Tokyo: Tōkyō Butsuri Gakkō Dōsōkai, 1935), 141.

[104] Aoki Ichirō, *Shin Doitsu shō-dokuhon* (Tokyo: Nanzandō Shoten, 1943), 26.

[105] Matsuoka Binkō, *Sōyō Doitsu bunten*, 36.

[106] Aoki Ichirō, *Meikai Dokubunten* (Tokyo: Nanzandō Shoten, 1936), 179; Iwamoto, 189–190.

[107] One may assume that these exclamations for an emperor's health are the German equivalent of the Japanese cheer *banzai*, but there are subtle differences. *Banzai* by itself does not connote the spirit of wishing the emperor long life. Unless preceded by

teach practical, everyday German, their obsession with German royalty belies their claim. Unless Japanese students planned to converse solely with diehard East Prussian monarchists, they would find cheers invoking the Kaiser distinctly useless in the Weimar Republic and all the more so in the Third Reich.

As in the other media formats, the gratuitously military and royalist images of Germany and German provoked leftists to counter their right-leaning colleagues and teach a different version of the language. They viewed the German in mainstream books, with references to war, nation, and the Kaiser, as merely a subdivision – German for militarism or nationalism – not much different from German for chemistry or medicine. So they produced or reproduced works that reflected a vision of Germany not found in popular German textbooks. The Communist Party organ *Sekki* encouraged proletarians to learn foreign languages to grasp imported ideological terminology.[108] Leftist presses translated communist treatises to remind readers that Germany produced not only Wilhelm, Bismarck, and Hindenburg, but also Marx, Luxemburg, and Liebknecht.

Leftist linguists took to teaching socialist German so that readers could understand and appreciate German socialism. One edited a book on German for social science that featured passages and excerpts by prominent socialists on topics such as the Soviet Union's first Five-Year Plan, materialism, and the world economic crisis.[109] Another compiled a dictionary for social science that drew heavily from socialist vocabulary.[110] The leftist economist Ikumi Takuichi published a whole book on German for the proletariat in 1932. Like his fellow Germanists who believed that learning German and from Germany provided Japan a way out of its predicament, Ikumi stated that language studies could serve as a weapon and solution for the Japanese proletariat, who suffered from insularity and lack of international networking.[111] Passion for communism and hostility to anything to its right, with particular venom reserved for social democrats, permeated Ikumi's book. *Kaiser* was still used as an example of a word with two syllables, though followed by another

"His Majesty the Tennō," *banzai* is simply a celebratory cheer, similar to "hurrah" or "bravo." A few books translated "Tennō" as "Kaiser," but the vast majority used "Kaiser" to refer to any emperor and not specifically the Japanese one.

[108] S, August 5, 1931.

[109] Katsuya Arito, ed., *Shakai kagaku Doitsugo kenkyū* (Tokyo: Ryūshōkaku, 1933).

[110] Kinoshita Hanji, ed., *Shakai kagaku tangoshū: Nichi-Doku-Futsu-Ei-Ro taishō* (Tokyo: Daigaku Shorin, 1934).

[111] "Foreword," in Ikumi Takuichi, *Puroretaria gogaku sōsho 1: Doitsugo hen* (Tokyo: Nanboku Shoin, 1932), 1.

two-syllable word, *sterben* (to die). The book's vocabulary included ideo-logically loaded terms such as class enemy, comrade, and expropriator. To those who trumpeted a nationalist Germany, Ikumi countered with a quotation by Marx: "Proletarians have no fatherland."[112] Whereas most Japanese learned noun cases from the example of "the Kaiser Wilhelm," Ikumi's readers mastered declension with Liebknecht and Marx.[113] Rather than repeating chants wishing the Kaiser long life and health, Ikumi's intended students of workers had their own slogans: "Workers of the world, unite!," "Long live the International!," and "Long live the international unity of workers against the chauvinism and patriotism of the bourgeoisie of the world!"[114] The book ended with reading exercises from the communist canon by Marx and Engels, as well as works by Lenin, Nikolai Bukharin, and Eleanor Marx translated into German.

Even when the linguists did not inject their own politics into language lessons, German still arrived in Japan with a preexisting ideological subtext. This phenomenon can be seen in the depictions of Jews in German in Japan. Japanese linguists had no grounds to espouse anti-Semitism, but Jews in language texts sometimes appeared in a deroga-tory light by dint of German's latent bias, even in dictionaries where there should be little room for spin. Readers in 1919 could find in an authoritative lexicon the word *jüdeln*, defined as "to haggle like a Jew, to cheat other people."[115] In another popular dictionary in 1929, users again encountered *jüdeln*, meaning "to act like a Jew, to become a Jew, to figuratively practice usury, or to speak with a Jewish accent."[116] *Jude* (Jew) carried the rhetorical burden of "usurer, greedy or dishonest merchant." *Jüdisch* (Jewish) was synonymous with "niggardly, urban, voracious, or vulgar." Jews were said to have their own type of face (*Judengesicht*) and beard (*Judenbart*). A collection of German idioms included "to give the kiss of Judas" and "to pay Judas blood money," both referring to traitorous, treacherous behaviors.[117] Reading about such a maligned race, Japanese students might well begin to sympathize with those Germans who warned of a menacing *Judenfrage* (Jewish question). After the most rabid among these fearmongers, Hitler, built a movement (*Hitlerbewegung*) that took control of Germany, Gonda

---

[112] Ibid., 19.   [113] Ibid., 42.   [114] Ibid., 85, 191.

[115] Tobari Chikufū, ed., *Shinshiki Doku-Wa daijiten*, 32nd ed. (Tokyo: Ōkura Shoten, 1919), 1117.

[116] Katayama Masao, *Sōkai Doku-Wa daijiten*, 6th ed. (Tōkyō: Nankōdō Shoten, 1929), 1073 1073.

[117] Kanokogi Koruneria and Koide Naosaburō, *Doitsugo kan'yōku 2000* (Tokyo: Taimusu Shuppansha, 1939), 126.

Yasunosuke included the term in his German-Japanese dictionary.[118] Nazi jargon had infiltrated German so thoroughly that Gonda also incorporated terms such as the Hitler salute, NSDAP (Nationalsozialistische Deutsche Arbeiterpartei), and SA (Sturmabteilung).[119] One dictionary advertised itself in 1933 as holding the key to Japanese-German cultural convergence when Hitler was "wielding his strong arms."[120]

As elsewhere in the media, linguists responded to Nazism much as German society did. A few on the left fought back, with books on proletarian German, but were soon overwhelmed. The majority, generally law-abiding and supportive of the military and nation, accepted the Hitler regime as a fait accompli and stayed away from overt politicking in their works. Some, the transnational Nazis, multiplied in number after January 1933 and enthusiastically echoed the ideology and welcomed its implementation. Upon receiving power, the Nazis immediately set about to Nazify all facets of life in Germany and to establish totalitarian rule through *Gleichschaltung*. The campaign was usually dictated by fiat from above, but often the populace conformed of its own volition. Within a short time, *Gleichschaltung* penetrated Germany and German so thoroughly that it concocted a Nazi-speak that differentiated Germans on racial grounds ("quarter Jews" or "non-Aryans"), regulated interpersonal greeting (*Heil Hitler!*), and subsumed concepts such as "leadership principle" (*Führerprinzip*) and "national community" (*Volksgemeinschaft*) into the people's consciousness.[121]

Faced with the wholesale Nazification of German, more and more Japanese Germanists aligned themselves with Nazism and propagated it in their works – in the clearest manifestation of transnational Nazism and one of very few instances of voluntary *Gleichschaltung* by non-Germans. A few books introduced the Hitler salute and Nazi greeting to Japanese readers.[122] Language books' interest in German political developments from the late 1920s began with works to help readers understand German newspapers. To some linguists, Germany seemed a pioneer in politics and society, so Japan could benefit by learning from its innovations, much as in chemistry and medicine. Gonda wrote that it was

---

[118] Gonda Yasunosuke, ed., *Gonda Doku-Wa shin jiten* (Tokyo: Yūhōdō, 1937), 578.
[119] "Introduction," ibid., 2, 4.   [120] TN, June 2, 1933.
[121] Christopher M. Hutton, *Linguistics and the Third Reich: Mother-Tongue Fascism, Race and the Science of Language* (London: Routledge, 1999); Thomas Pegelow Kaplan, *The Language of Nazi Genocide: Linguistic Violence and the Struggle of Germans of Jewish Ancestry* (New York: Cambridge University Press, 2009); Horst Dieter Schlosser, *Sprache unterm Hakenkreuz: Eine andere Geschichte des Nationalsozialismus* (Cologne: Böhlau Verlag, 2013).
[122] Iinuma Hajime, *Denki kiso Doitsugo* (Tokyo: Rajio Kagakusha, 1940), 48; Komura Minoru, *Ikeru Doitsugo kaiwa* (Tokyo: Taiyōdō Shoten, 1937), 116.

essential for Japanese students to keep up with the "new German" arising in the new Germany through reading newspapers.[123] Another author saw the press as a microcosm of society, so perusing German newspapers could help Japanese make sense of current events in Germany.[124] A 1935 handbook on vocabulary in politics and economics showcased only passages by Nazi leaders such as Hitler and Alfred Rosenberg.[125] A later text on newspapers likewise contained solely articles on Nazi policies such as punishment for racial defilement or the wartime prohibition on dancing.[126] Readers, too, had Nazism in mind when they studied German – someone scribbled "Heil Hitler" on the title page of the National Diet Library's copy of a work on newspaper German.[127]

The linguists also used their editorial license to promote Nazism. Within a year of the Nazis coming to power, Sekiguchi Tsugio crafted a homework question on the Hitler chancellorship and its dominance over Germany. He also had students translate the statement "The solution of the Nazis, that is, National Socialists, for elevating the nation in 1933 was 'Germany, awake! Judas, go to hell!'"[128] A 1935 grammar textbook featured the sample sentence "Right now all Germans support the Hitler regime."[129] The prolific Germanist Hashimoto Fumio asked readers to translate into German "Hitler says, 'Jewishness is un-German and only Germanness is sacred.'"[130] For students who found Nazism overly aggressive and violent, Hashimoto rejoined that "The Nazis are all patriots. They are not always militarists."[131] In case any reader still harbored faith in liberal democracy, the philosopher Takakuwa Sumio countered, "Democracy again? Who still thinks of it as a spiritual factor today? The era of National Socialism is now marching forth in Germany!"[132]

The linguists' voluntary *Gleichschaltung* intensified from the mid-1930s. They replaced the extant conservatism in language texts with transnational Nazism. Momo Minosuke, who had been capitalizing on his 1930 audience with Hitler, boasted in a letter to the Führer in 1934 that his own works enjoyed great success in German textbooks for

[123] "Foreword," in Gonda, *Doitsu shinbun kenkyū*, 1.
[124] "Introduction and Foreword," in Uenishi Hanzaburō, *Mottomo jissaitekina shinbun Doitsugo no yomikata* (Tokyo: Taimusu Shuppansha, 1932).
[125] Haruta, 26–27, 32–34.
[126] Aoki Shigetaka, *Doitsu shinbun no yomikata* (Tokyo: Daigaku Shorin, 1941), 67, 93.
[127] Dokubun Sekai Shichō Henshūbu, ed., *Doitsu shinbun no yakkai* (Tokyo: Tachibana Shoten, 1933).
[128] Sekiguchi Tsugio, *Hyōjun Doitsu bunpō* (Tokyo: Shōbundō, 1933), 35, 109.
[129] Tanaka Kōichi, *Doitsu bunpō kyōkasho* (Tokyo: Hakusuisha, 1935), 86.
[130] Hashimoto Fumio, *Shin Doitsu bunpō* (Tokyo: Shōbundō, 1936), 52.   [131] Ibid., 29.
[132] Takakuwa Sumio, *Teiyō Doitsu shōbunten* (Tokyo: Nanzandō Shoten, 1936), 42.

military academies, several universities, and language institutes.[133] He added that a chapter on "Germany's commitment to peace" had the best reputation. Even before Italy joined the Anti-Comintern Pact in November 1937, a book published in April already used Tokyo, Berlin, and Rome to demonstrate noun cases.[134] Moreover, the Führer displaced the Kaiser as the dominant personality. So readers learned to distinguish the different pronunciations of the spelling "er" in *Hitler* and *vergessen* (to forget).[135] Students could practice expressing dates in German with sentences such as "After President Hindenburg's death, Hitler was elected Führer in a referendum on August 19, 1934" and "Adolf Hitler, Führer of the German nation, was born on April 20, 1898 [*sic*] in Braunau am Inn as the son of the Austrian customs official Alois Hitler."[136] Many textbooks elevated Hitler's writings and other Nazi publications to the status of great works that deserved to be studied thoroughly, alongside or even in lieu of literary classics. Linguists replaced the Romantic patriotism in earlier works with combative nationalism in the 1930s. Instead of reading nineteenth-century works such as "My Fatherland" and "The Watch on the Rhine," students encountered *Mein Kampf* and the Nazi anthem *Horst Wessel Song*.[137] To mark the complete transformation of Germany under Nazism, a text informed readers that "before the world war Germany was an empire and after the war a republic, but now it is a Führer state."[138] Even the normally dull examination guidebooks became tainted by ideology, as terms such as "racial hygiene" seeped into proficiency tests.[139]

Finally, transnational Nazism even affected the visual appearance of German. At least a handful of authors stated their reasonable but mistaken belief that the Nazi regime favored Fraktur, which led to their choice to print in blackletter.[140] A Germanist decorated the pages between the table of contents and lessons on the alphabet with photographs of Hitler with his admirers and a gathering of Nazis.[141] Another placed an image of Hitler and Mussolini on the front page.[142] A book

---

[133] BArch, R 43II/1454, Momo to Hitler, April 25, 1934.   [134] Okamoto, 89.

[135] Komura, *Ikeru Doitsugo kaiwa*, 28–29.

[136] Aoki Ichirō, *Meikai Dokubunten*, 150, 162. Hitler was born in 1889.

[137] Akimoto, 236, 240. For excerpts of *Mein Kampf*, Aoki Ichirō, *Shin Doitsu bunpō-dokuhon* (Tokyo: Nanzandō Shoten, 1941), 109; of Horst-Wessel-Lied, Sakuma Masakazu, *Doitsugo shin kyōten* (Tokyo: Ikubundō Shoten, 1940), 173.

[138] Tenri Daini Chūgakkō Doitsugoka, ed., *Chūtō Doitsu-dokuhon 1* (Tanbaichi-chō: Tenri Daini Chūgakkō Doitsugoka, 1940), 76.

[139] Sakurada Tsunehisa, *Doitsugo nyūshi mondai kaitō* (Tokyo: Shōbundō, 1937), 9.

[140] "Preface," in Tanaka Mitsuharu, 4–5; Shō, 3.   [141] Okada, front plates.

[142] Aoki Ichirō, *Shin Doitsu bunpō-dokuhon*, front leaf.

on spoken German juxtaposed a photograph of a Nazi rally next to a sample conversation.[143] The covers of several books featured the Nazi symbol of an eagle clutching a swastika.[144] During World War II, photographs of the triumphant German military became a common feature in language books.[145]

Transnational Nazism in Language Textbooks

"How to learn German?" Just like any other endeavor, acquiring a language takes intense enthusiasm ... If one is committed, then time should not pose any problem. The transition from secondary school to higher education may consume so much time that many people cannot find the leisure to learn a language, but if one really has the will, one should be able to gain command of a language in one year. But intermittent bursts of dedication for language studies will not bear fruit. When one is learning a language, one should invest in the subject the same fanaticism Germany is displaying in its headlong assaults on Leningrad.[146]

So the introductory text *The ABC German Course* advised its readers when it was published in December 1941. Drunk with German victory, its editors urged students to imitate the German way of war in language studies. But for the readers, "conquering" German resembled the Leningrad campaign in an unintended way: they could go no further. No amount of willpower could help them overcome the immutable distance between them and their destination. Within a few years, the war, diplomatic alliance, Führer, and Nazi ideology that they supported brought about the wholesale destruction of their handiwork, the propagation of German learning in Japan. Despite their impressive talent and exertion, the Germanists left no lasting legacy in modern Japan. Few Japanese doctors and fewer chemists need to know German today. The language lingers mostly in the memory of older generations of academics and professionals in enclaves such as classical music and philosophy or as individual words long since absorbed into Japanese.

But in the interwar era German enjoyed a high profile and commanded the energy and attention of a crucial segment of Japanese society.

---

[143] Komura, *Ikeru Doitsugo kaiwa*, 28–29.

[144] Uchida Mitsugi, *Tōkei ni motozuku hyōjun tango 6000* (Tokyo: Ikubundō Shoten, 1938); Nihon Bunka Kenkyūkai Doitsugobu, ed., *Doitsugo-dokuhon 5* (Tanbaichi-chō: Tenri Jihōsha, 1941); Yūki Shintarō, *Sokushū Doitsugo kōza 3* (Tokyo: Taiyōdō Shoten, 1942).

[145] Aoki Ichirō, *Shin Doitsu shō-dokuhon*; Sekiguchi Tsugio, *Nyūmon kagakusha no Doitsugo 1* (Tokyo: Sanshūsha, 1943); Sumi Hidesuke, *Shokyū Doitsugo-dokuhon* (Tokyo: Nanzandō Shoten, 1942).

[146] Heigensha, ed., *Doitsugo ABC kōza* (Tokyo: Heigensha, 1941), 1.

Though hobbled by World War I and evoking specters of suffering in the minds of many, German studies regained dominance in the 1920s and thrived in the 1930s at the hands of capable Germanists such as Sekiguchi and Gonda. They created all the tools that students used to learn enough German to advance their studies and careers. Except for a very few interested individuals, German was merely the means toward further goals. The two most common types of texts quintessentially embody aspects of German learning in Japan. Self-study books represent students' dream of learning German rapidly, affordably, and independently. Bilingual dictionaries were crucial to the singular task of textual translation that test takers had to master. German held such key, sometimes unassailable, positions in chemistry, medicine, and several other professional fields that most Japanese seeking higher education had to study the language and prove their proficiency in an examination. Few Japanese could aspire to become engineers or physicists, much less chemists or physicians, without first learning some German and thereby Germany. Knowledge of German brought upward social mobility in Japan through a better career or larger income. Once the students broke through the language ceiling, they had unfettered access to all the information that Germany had to offer. The more extroverted learners could even venture to Yokohama or Kobe to try their luck in encountering Germans and put their book-learning to practical use.

But the impact of German studies in Japan had limits because German was secondary to English throughout the interwar era. At least twice as many native speakers of English as of German resided in Japan at any point between 1919 and 1937.[147] Far more Japanese traveled to English-speaking lands than anywhere else outside Asia. Not only did more Japanese study English than German, they also studied English before they would consider German. Many institutions of higher learning required a German test, but all required students to demonstrate English proficiency. Although enrollment records are scattered among schools and do not account for the many self-learners, some statistics can still be illuminating. To prepare for university entrance, pupils in higher schools had to study English and German, with the choice of either as the primary foreign language. About 65 percent of the 11,687 enrollees in Japan's 20 higher schools in 1921 prioritized English over German.[148] Even in scientific fields where German publications held sway, German

---

[147] Naikaku Tōkeikyoku, ed.
[148] PA AA, R 85846, Renner to Foreign Office, August 11, 1922.

diplomats in Japan still noted nervously that English stalked not far behind.[149] German was dominant, but English was predominant.

Just as the popularity of English studies did not keep Japan from plunging into war against America and Britain, the prevalence of German did not single-handedly bring about the rapprochement with Germany. Although most students in higher education had to learn German, most Japanese could not aspire to attend university or master the language on their own. That is, even the mere opportunity to acquire German to open other doors was a privilege. The increasing difficulty and requirements in money, time, and dedication as one delved into language studies whittled down the student population further. German was as highly priced as it was prized. That despite major drawbacks German still attracted much attention attests the language's influence and stature, but it touched the lives of only a modest number of Japanese.

Still, this thin layer of the demographic, the elites, affected politics, culture, society, and the economy. The language teachers functioned as key opinion leaders when their students went on to become media commentators, diplomats, officers, scientists, academics, and business-men. What they learned of Germany and from the linguists must have shaped their imagination of the country and its people, as in the imported attitude of anti-Semitism. Most Japanese in the interwar period did not know a Jew, but many knew of the Jews. Germans of Jewish ancestry like Einstein and Haber commanded much goodwill in Japan. Their Jewish heritage did not attract attention until the Nazis made it a cause for persecution. Even then, Japanese society reacted with remarkable sympathy. But Jews collectively as an abstraction suffered from the same stereotypes that circulated in Germany. A small but loud group of Japanese pundits parroted Western anti-Semitism in their works. So consumers of newspapers, pamphlets, nonfiction, and language texts came into contact with the so-called Jewish question. Of course, one cannot prove with certainty that any Japanese turned anti-Semitic through exposure to bigoted German phrases. But in an absence of firsthand familiarity with individual Jews, some readers conceivably internalized suspicion or even loathing of the Jews.[150]

Likewise, the image of Germany went through filters, some deliberately installed by language teachers, in textbooks. Students read a lot about war, nation, and the Kaiser in the 1920s. Then from the mid-1930s they

---

[149] PA AA, R 85978, Trautmann to Foreign Office, March 28, 1922; PA AA, R 85978, Voretzsch to Foreign Office, March 4, 1933.

[150] Cf. Christopher R. Browning, *Ordinary Men: Reserve Police Battalion 101 and the Final Solution in Poland*, rev. ed. (New York: Harper Perennial, 2017), 182.

read even more about war, Nazism, and the Führer. This seamless "upgrade" from the Second to the Third Reich in the books toed closely the line that the Nazis were pushing to the German people and the world. The politicization of German learning lowered the lessons' quality through the inclusion of incongruous sample sentences and passages, and impractical vocabularies and expressions such as the many forms of hailing the Kaiser. Though impossible to prove absolutely, the linguists' reverence for Wilhelm may explain the journalists', lecturers', and authors' fixation on the ex-Kaiser. As elsewhere in the media, language textbooks hatched a conspiracy of silence against German liberal democracy and marginalized the Weimar Republic. Readers seldom learned of the republic's achievements or had a chance to sample works by Bertolt Brecht, Thomas Mann, or Franz Kafka. One moment, they learned German from Romantic nationalists. The next, they studied the language of the National Socialists. The linguists' focus jumped from Wilhelm to Hitler, from nineteenth-century patriotism to twentieth-century fascism. Virtually no Germanist celebrated the foundation of a new Germany in 1918, but many enthusiastically endorsed the establishment of another "New Germany" in 1933. If few Germans defended the republic in its hour of need, even fewer Japanese mourned its demise. Only the far left attempted to resist through proletarian German.

The sharpness of the right-left ideological divide among language texts should not obscure its unevenness. The nationalistic, martial, and personality-driven imagination of Germany overshadowed the internationalist, peaceful, and democratic one, so much so that the former ruled as the mainstream norm familiar to the Japanese. But this simplistic portrayal misrepresented politics in Weimar Germany, where the Marxist parties enjoyed substantial popular support. To those Germanists whose formative, impressionable years coincided with the apex of the Kaiserreich, the wobbly, freewheeling republic could seem like a mere interregnum. So they kept teaching salutations for the Kaiser's health as if the phrases would be usable again. Japanese cultural intermediaries projected their own vision of Germany even though it deviated from reality.

When a rightist movement took over Germany, numerous linguists jumped at the chance to accommodate the regime and align themselves and their publications with Nazism and Hitler. Though totalitarian, the Third Reich did not dictate how Japanese should learn German or pressure Japanese Germanists to incorporate Nazism in textbooks. Rather, many language teachers became transnational Nazis when they voluntarily glorified Nazi ideology and Hitler. Just when the Nazi state "coordinated" German society and equated Germany with Nazism, transnational Nazi Germanists in Japan, failing or unwilling to differentiate the regime from the nation, simultaneously but independently collaborated with *Gleichschaltung* and introduced Nazi jargon, rituals, and concepts to students. Because some Japanese already believed that Japan could learn from Germany through its language, it did not take much of a leap for them to rationalize that Japan could gain from approaching the resurgent New Germany. By propagating favorable views of Nazi Germany in Japan, the linguists helped prepare the ideological and cultural contexts for Japanese-German rapprochement.

Part II

Transnational Nazism in Germany

5   Japan in Newspapers

> Farther south in Friedrichstadt there are a few imposing buildings, old
> fortresses of the intellect, renovated and expanded, inviting with their
> wide windows, threatening with their stone balustrades. Enticing yet
> defensive; beautiful, dangerous buildings. They belong to legendary
> kings and royal families, known as Ullstein, Mosse, and Scherl. When
> our last little revolution broke out, like the other kings, the newspaper
> kings were also driven from their castles ... But the newspaper kings
> returned much more quickly than the other monarchs. Once again their
> chariots stand in their courtyards, full of paper ammunition, and their
> ladies-in-waiting tiptoe through the editorial rooms, fleet-footed
> secretaries and typewriter girls.[1]   – Franz Hessel, *Walking in Berlin*, 1929

Hessel vividly depicted the presence and influence attributed to the press
as an elite power base in late Weimar Berlin. Just as in Japan, newspapers
were the predominant media format for spreading knowledge and opinions in interwar Germany. The Weimar Constitution guaranteed freedom of expression in print. This openness, alongside social, cultural, and
regional fissures that splintered the German populace, provided fertile
ground for a diverse press landscape. Germany had over 4,700 newspapers by 1932, more than America, or Britain, France, and Italy
together.[2] This fractured landscape stunted the development of nationally significant publications but also incubated myriad local dailies.
Berlin in particular saw an impressive growth in the number of newspapers, as Germans of various convictions sought a voice within and
around the newly democratic government. Party organs and other explicitly political dailies of the "ideological press" already accounted for half
of all newspapers in 1913.[3] The rest, the "commercial press," appeared
in the 1880s as general advertisers that relied on advertisements more

---

[1] Franz Hessel, *Walking in Berlin: A Flaneur in the Capital*, trans. Amanda DeMarco
(Cambridge: The MIT Press, 2017), 249.
[2] Bernhard Fulda, *Press and Politics in the Weimar Republic* (New York: Oxford University
Press, 2009), 13; Noakes and Pridham, 196.
[3] Fulda, 14–15.

than subscriptions for revenues. Tabloids thriving on circulation via street sales emerged as the third category after World War I.[4] The large publishing houses Ullstein, Mosse, and Scherl each churned out multiple titles in all three categories.

As Bernhard Fulda demonstrates, the press was deemed to hold great sway in molding public opinion and effecting outcomes in the Weimar Republic through its capacity to funnel and filter information for millions of readers and potential voters every day.[5] Many public and private institutions maintained archives of press clippings.[6] Some businesses even specialized in monitoring clients' reputation by gathering relevant news articles.[7] Political groups regularly used columns on newsprint to mobilize columns of marchers. Thus when violence traced to verbal incitement broke out, the republic would try to limit freedom of the press. The Berlin Police periodically banned Communist and Nazi dailies and rallies in the late Weimar years. As chancellor, Hitler certainly seized upon the potential of the press: "I have tried, since I came into power, to bring the whole of the German press into line. To do so, I have not hesitated, when necessary, to take radical measures. It was evident to my eyes that a State which had at its disposal an inspired press and journalists devoted to its cause possessed therein the greatest power that one could possibly imagine."[8] Indeed, David Dennis points out that the Hitler regime used the *Völkischer Beobachter* as an instrument for recasting Western culture under a Nazi light.[9]

But newspapers faced varied receptions individually. Of the three types, tabloids and advertisers sold best, trailed by some distance by the ideological press. This categorization relaxed during the 1920s, as tabloids sensationalized politics while the political papers incorporated popular features such as sports, illustrations, diversions, and advertisements.[10] Even the Communist organ carried department stores' promotions, for Christmas sales no less. Still, the ideological dailies suffered from anemic subscriptions and would have collapsed but for financial injections from their sponsoring political parties. That they kept disseminating and interpreting news shows their perceived power and position

---

[4] Ibid., 38.   [5] Ibid., 203–211.   [6] Ibid., 79.

[7] Patrick Rössler, *The Bauhaus and Public Relations: Communication in a Permanent State of Crisis* (New York: Routledge, 2014), 161–165.

[8] *Hitler's Table Talk 1941–1944: His Private Conversations*, trans. Norman Cameron and R. H. Stevens (New York: Enigma Books, 2000), 479–480.

[9] David B. Dennis, *Inhumanities: Nazi Interpretations of Western Culture* (New York: Cambridge University Press, 2012).

[10] Fulda, 30.

in German politics and culture. Both liberal Ullstein and conservative Scherl diverted profits from advertisers and tabloids to prop up loss-making but prestigious partisan standard bearers. Though mostly written by and for the elites, these publications were still accessibly priced for laypeople, who moreover could read or share copies in public places. Content in the political flagships also trickled down to other dailies when their commentators contributed to affiliated advertisers and tabloids.

Despite some limitations, newspapers, specifically the ideological ones, stood out in the days before widespread radio ownership as the primary channel for experts to discuss and non-experts to learn about Japan. The regionalism and economics of Germany's publishing milieu that confined tabloids and advertisers to provincial outlooks and markets also freed the ideological press to adopt a *world*-view and express partisan opinions unencumbered by financial considerations. This chapter applies some of Fulda's and Dennis's findings to examine newspapers' portrayals and discussions of Japan and German-Japanese relations. The interwar press across the political spectrum depicted Japan as a modern, Westernized great power deserving of German attention and respect. Coverage of Japan's participation in international diplomacy, commerce, culture, and sports placed it on a comparable footing with Germany in different sections of a newspaper. In the 1920s, mostly centrist dailies competently explained Japan without arousing ideological passion. The apolitical calm was shattered in September 1931 when Japan seized Manchuria from China. This violent challenge to the Versailles–Washington system catapulted Japan to the front page, where the papers analyzed Japan from their particular vantage points and urged readers to take actions. The Nazi dictatorship suppressed the press and its cacophonous opinions of Japan in 1933. The party organ, now predominant, promoted transnational Nazism's enshrinement of Japan's strength, physicality, and above all victories. These traits enabled the Nazis to accommodate Japan in their ideology and establish ties with Japanese transnational Nazis.

Japan as Fine Print

Notwithstanding its mosaic nature, the interwar German press portrayed some facets of Japan consistently. Newspapers spanning the ideological spectrum discussed Japan intensively at some point, though the complexity and consistency of analysis differed greatly. Beyond Berlin-based titles, newspapers elsewhere in Germany, too, mentioned Japan periodically, as can be gleaned from the clippings amassed by the Foreign

Office, the National Federation of German Colleges, and the Agricultural League.[11] Yet perhaps besides a few dailies in Frankfurt and Hamburg, these snippets of the regional press actually highlight the capital papers' indispensability to generating German knowledge of Japan because several of their contributing writers worked mainly for the ideological flagships. In addition to the spread across politics and geography, Japan could be found in a newspaper's morning, evening, weekly, or overseas edition, as well as topical or photographic supplements. Within a morning or evening issue, it might be depicted in the section on international and domestic news, finance, culture, or sports. Readers could gain basic familiarity with Japan through reading newspapers without having to search for it deliberately.

Though notable for a nation that no longer had Asian-Oceanic territories, this coverage was far from comprehensive. Happenings in Japan never seem to have been treated as breaking news deserving of extras – neither the Great Kanto Earthquake nor the conquest of Manchuria. Japan was rarely featured to any extent in advertisements, even in the *Berliner Tageblatt und Handels-Zeitung*, Mosse's bestselling general advertiser and daily. Japan's few appearances there reflect Germany's sizable trade surplus vis-à-vis Japan in the 1920s and 1930s.[12] Travelers heading to East Asia sometimes offered to represent German exporters during the journey.[13] Readers might notice promotions by trading firms, such as that of an Oriental art dealer offering "porcelain, bronze, tea accessories … Buddhas, sculptures, etc., etc.," or that of an importer selling Chinese tea with an illustration of a kimono-clad woman.[14] Individual Japanese companies were virtually invisible, except the steamship firm Nippon Yūsen Kaisha. Still, because most Germans had no plans for overseas travel, they might well have skipped the entire shipping section and the advertisements for "NYK" therein.[15] For German consumers, in both their newspapers and shops the notion "made in Japan" evoked images of generic handicrafts rather than merchandise with well-known brand names.

This impersonal, anonymizing style of describing Japan prevailed elsewhere in the press, but with exceptions depending on the publications' ideology or the particular occasion. Visiting Japanese luminaries were

---

[11] BArch, R 901/60323, Auswärtiges Amt, 1937; BArch, R 8088/901, Reichsverband der Deutschen Hochschulen, 1921–1928; BArch, R 8034II/5526, Reichslandbund/ Pressearchiv, 1907–1944.

[12] BArch, R 43I/1099, Memorandum to Treaty of Commerce and Navigation, 1927.

[13] *Berliner Tageblatt und Handels-Zeitung* (hereafter: BTH), August 18, 1926; BTH, September 16, 1923.

[14] BTH, April 22, 1925; BTH, November 27, 1921.   [15] BTH, February 24, 1928.

accorded due recognition. Many were diplomats, usually new ambassadors presenting their credentials in ceremonial garb.[16] The envoy Matsuoka Yōsuke was hosted for tea in Berlin in 1933 by the Mosse tabloid *8-Uhr-Abendblatt* to create a sensationalist scoop after his histrionic walkout at the League of Nations.[17] Artists touring Germany also attracted personal interest, as when Shigyō Masatoshi danced before Berlin spectators, Konoe Hidemaro conducted the Berlin Philharmonic, or Kiwa Teiko sang in the title role of *Madama Butterfly* at the German Opera House.[18] Some notables in Japan, including the two interwar emperors and some prime ministers, were also introduced in some detail.[19] But these personalities stood out precisely for the distinction they enjoyed because most leading Japanese did not receive comparable attention. Instead, the Japanese were habitually treated as a national entity under headlines such as "Manners and Mores in Japan," "Japanese Poetry," and "New Year in Japan."[20]

Despite shortcomings inherent in any generalization, these overarching accounts on Japan provided an affordable, expert source of knowledge for readers in Berlin. Josef Plaut, a Japan hand, wrote the article on Japanese New Year rituals in the *Vossische Zeitung*, Ullstein's leading liberal, learned, and cosmopolitan daily.[21] Andreas Eckardt, a Catholic missionary with over two decades of work in Korea, crafted the exposition on Japanese poems in the Catholic Center Party organ *Germania*. Karl Haushofer, a proponent of geopolitics and rapprochement with Japan influential in Nazi circles, composed the piece on Japanese custom in the *Völkischer Beobachter*. As a Munich-born paper that became a national publication, the different regional editions of the *Völkischer Beobachter* reveal the disparity in information on Japan available to Germans. Berliners without a ticket for one of Konoe's performances could tune in on their radios.[22] Those without access to a receiver could

---

[16] BTH, October 17, 1926, supplement; VB, April 9–10, 1933, North German edition (hereafter: NGE).

[17] *8-Uhr-Abendblatt*, March 6, 1933.

[18] *Vossische Zeitung: Berlinische Zeitung von Staats- und gelehrten Sachen* (hereafter: VZ), February 27, 1932, EE; *Neue Preußische (Kreuz)-Zeitung* (hereafter: NPK), October 3, 1933; VB, February 24–25, 1935, NGE. *Madama Butterfly* is an opera by Giacomo Puccini, first performed in 1904.

[19] VZ, January 27, 1927; VZ, May 10, 1921; VZ, December 20, 1921, EE.

[20] VB, January 15–16, 1933, NGE; *Germania: Zeitung für das deutsche Volk* (hereafter: G), March 3, 1932; VZ, February 20, 1921.

[21] The *Vossische Zeitung* issued supplements in foreign languages in the mid-1920s. It might even qualify as a national paper because it was sold in all bookstores in railway stations, and its weekly edition was shipped across the world. VZ, November 5, 1921; VZ, May 14, 1921, supplement.

[22] VB, December 12, 1933, NGE.

read previews or reviews of the concert in at least five dailies.[23] Likewise, Berlin residents could benefit from the active associational life in the capital. They could attend lectures on "Japan's heroic theater" at the German-Japanese Association and on Bushido at the Japan Institute, or at least read summaries thereof in the city section of the *Völkischer Beobachter*.[24] Germans elsewhere did not have the luxury of experiencing a similar array of events or even vicarious exposure via the airwaves or newsprint. Perhaps to compensate Munich's deficit, Alfred Rosenberg, the *Völkischer Beobachter*'s editor-in-chief, arranged for intellectuals to philosophize on Central and East Asia in the paper in the early 1930s. These treatises likely flattered Rosenberg, the self-appointed theorist of Nazism, but also bored many readers. At least one, Hitler, grumbled that neither he nor any woman he knew could make sense of them.[25]

Beyond the sporadic coverage revolving around famous individuals, Japan typically appeared in conjunction with or comparison to major Western powers, especially in foreign affairs. Newspapers throughout the interwar years diligently followed international diplomacy, often involving Japan. One of the most eye-catching headlines on Japan in the *Vossische Zeitung* splashed across its front page in 1919 to announce Japan's decision at Versailles to participate as one of four permanent council members in the proposed League of Nations.[26] Germany had an existential stake in the peace talks and so needed to concern itself with every new twist, but even when Germany played no role in designing the postwar world, the dailies still observed the developments closely. Japan received particularly heavy press in late 1921 amid the diplomatic man-euvers preceding the Washington Treaties. Headlines frequently situated Japan alongside the West, including "England and Japan's Conditional Agreement" and "Climax of the American-Japanese Antithesis."[27] Two correspondents for the *Vossische Zeitung*, Erich von Salzmann in San Francisco and Josef Plaut in Tokyo, each wrote a column around the same time on the negotiations, respectively titled "America and Japan" and "Japan and America."[28] By contrast, the newsroom in Berlin was reduced to speculating wishfully whether Germany might be summoned to join the powers gathering in Washington.[29]

---

[23] *Deutsche Allgemeine Zeitung* (hereafter: DAZ), September 29, 1933; NPK, October 3, 1933; *Berliner Lokal-Anzeiger: Zentral-Organ für die Reichshauptstadt* (hereafter: BLA), October 4, 1933; VZ, October 4, 1933; VB, October 5, 1933, NGE.

[24] VB, December 20, 1934, Berlin edition; VB, February 24–25, 1935, NGE.

[25] Hitler, *Table Talk*, 648–649; Hitler, *Monologe*, 356–357 (August 21, 1942).

[26] VZ, June 13, 1919, EE.   [27] BTH, November 16, 1921; BTH, November 20, 1921.

[28] VZ, April 20, 1921, EE; VZ, May 21, 1921, EE.   [29] VZ, November 26, 1921, EE.

After the compacts in the early 1920s that built the Versailles–
Washington system, the powers next engaged in similar multilateral
activities a decade later with rounds of talks on the global economy,
Japan's conquest of Manchuria, and arms limitation. Although Germany
had by then regained some diplomatic standing, as a debtor, European,
and disarmed nation it had to watch much of the great-power politics
from the sidelines. The loss of status chafed many Germans but also
elevated Germany in their eyes to a perch of moral purity and noncom-
plicity from which to critique the postwar order. Germany played a
passive or belated role in the Versailles Treaty, League of Nations,
Washington Treaties, and reparations regime, and so could not be
blamed when the international system began to fail. The press again
portrayed Japan as a member in the club of leading nations alongside
Western ones. But this time Japan's unilateralism and the political polarization in Germany led the papers to draw opposite conclusions. The
moderate *Vossische Zeitung* and *Germania* fretted that pressure on Tokyo
to rein in its military might unravel the international order and compel
Japan to lead an Asian organization to challenge the League of Nations.[30]
On the left, the Social Democratic Party organ *Vorwärts* and the Communist organ *Rote Fahne* attacked the league as merely a Western enabler
of fellow imperialist and militarist Japan.[31] On the right, the traditionally
conservative, nationalistic *Neue Preußische (Kreuz)-Zeitung* and the Nazi
organ *Völkischer Beobachter* not only relished the league's humiliation by
Japan with schadenfreude but even measured the status of German
armament through comparisons with other "great powers" such as
Japan.[32] The newspapers clashed over Germany's proper relations with
Japan, but they at least agreed that Japan, like Germany, belonged to the
clique of the world's most advanced countries.

The press also took notice of Japan as a significant participant in the
world economy, even though bilateral commerce with Japan only
accounted for a few percent of Germany's trade volume.[33] The respect
for Japan's economic prowess took two forms. On the one hand, Japan
was seen as an export powerhouse that competed against the West. The
Vossische Zeitung devoted a page-long article on "Japan's advance on the
world market" in 1934.[34] The *Völkischer Beobachter* spoke of Japan's
"export offensive" worldwide.[35] The dailies applied martial phrases to

[30] VZ, March 11, 1933; G, July 28, 1933.
[31] *Vorwärts: Berliner Volksblatt, Zentralorgan der Sozialdemokratischen Partei Deutschlands*
(hereafter: V), July 2, 1932; RF, October 22, 1932.
[32] NPK, December 7, 1931; VB, February 20, 1935, NGE.
[33] BArch, R 43I/1099, Memorandum to Treaty of Commerce and Navigation, 1927.
[34] VZ, January 6, 1934.   [35] VB, January 5, 1934, NGE.

describe Japanese commercial expansion into European colonies. The *Vossische Zeitung* wrote of Japanese rayon's "battle for the Indian market," Japan "conquering India" thanks to anti-British boycotts, and Japan's "thrust toward the Dutch East Indies."[36] The *Völkischer Beobachter*, too, depicted "Japan's march" on India.[37] Closer to Europe, Japanese steamers were said to be operating off West Africa.[38] The *Völkischer Beobachter* raised the specter of an "economic war" around the Red Sea between Japan and the West, including Germany.[39] Rather alarming for Germany, German beer had to contend with Japanese brands for world market share in the mid-1930s.[40]

On the other hand, an economically vibrant Japan presented Germany with business opportunities. Any relief from the postwar isolation in the early 1920s or the world economic crisis in the early 1930s warranted press coverage. The *Vossische Zeitung* announced the opening of a German porcelain factory in Osaka in 1921 and plans for a trade show in Tokyo by German industries.[41] Spiking demands for iron and grain in 1933 as a result of the fighting between Japan and China made welcome headlines, with Japan emerging as an important buyer of iron ore.[42] Yet this silver lining paled against the optimism in the mid-1920s for what German-Japanese commerce might have achieved. The *Berliner Tageblatt* already articulated visions of connecting Germany and Japan with airships in 1925.[43] The dream came true in 1929 with the flight of the *Graf Zeppelin* but was soon dashed by the world economic crisis.

Japan next appeared in connection to the West in the culture section. Certainly, Japanese civilization in and of itself attracted interest, as seen in the articles by Plaut, Eckardt, and Haushofer. But more often Japanese culture was discussed in one of two Western contexts. The first was Japan as imagined. Performance art portraying Japan drew audiences in Germany. Newspapers advertised their showings, such as the musical comedy *The Geisha*, a film adaptation of *Madama Butterfly*, and the movie *Port Arthur*.[44] The dailies also carried fictional works on or set in Japan, though ideology dictated their literary tastes. The *Berliner Tageblatt* and the *Vossische Zeitung* preferred lighthearted tales on traditional

---

[36] VZ, January 11, 1934; VZ, September 18, 1931, postal edition; VZ, November 2, 1933.
[37] VB, January 6–7, 1934, ME.   [38] VZ, December 31, 1933; VZ, February 22, 1934.
[39] VB, August 31, 1934, NGE.
[40] VZ, December 19, 1933; VB, February 6, 1935, ME.
[41] VZ, April 16, 1921, supplement; VZ, May 14, 1921, supplement.
[42] VZ, January 5, 1933; VZ, April 2, 1933; VZ, February 2, 1933, EE; VZ, March 30, 1933, EE.
[43] BTH, May 10, 1925; BTH, July 14, 1925, EE.
[44] VZ, March 29, 1919; VZ, September 3, 1933; VB, December 25–27, 1936, ME.

Japan featuring geisha, pleasure quarters, and sake.[45] *Vorwärts* and the *Rote Fahne* opted for politically poignant skits on workers on strike or Japanese conscript soldiers in China.[46] The *Völkischer Beobachter* translated a version of the historical story of the 47 ronin samurai who gave up their lives for loyalty and honor.[47]

The second aspect revolved around the propagation of Western civilization. Japanese pupils of Western art, such as the dancer Shigyō, conductor Konoe, and soprano Kiwa, drew attention when they performed in Germany. But they were celebrated not for being Japanese but being Westernized. Shigyō and Konoe both trained in Germany. Kiwa was the stage name of Laetitia Klingen, born to Dutch and Japanese parents.[48] Regardless of ideology, the papers approvingly reported the spread of Western learning in Japan. *Germania* highlighted the Jesuit-founded Sophia University as "the German university in Japan."[49] The *Kreuz-Zeitung* and *Vossische Zeitung* both suggested that Japan might follow Turkey in replacing its native script with the Latin alphabet.[50] *Vorwärts* and the *Vossische Zeitung* both remarked on the esteem for German music in Japan.[51] A *Berliner Tageblatt* correspondent wondered at the prevalence of European movies in Japanese cinemas.[52] The *Kreuz-Zeitung* boasted that German printing presses helped power the great Japanese dailies.[53] Writing at length, Plaut proudly assured readers of the *Vossische Zeitung* that German science and language remained strong in Japanese academia despite "the world war and various malicious postwar measures undertaken by the 'Allies.'"[54] Even if Japan could not be a Western nation, it had definitely Westernized enough to deserve Germany's praise and respect.

The sports pages were the last venue where Japan stood on a par with the West. Again Japan was credited for learning from Europe. The *Völkischer Beobachter* cheered that German horsemanship was being taught in Japan and when a Japanese official toured a German sports facility.[55] Self-congratulations aside, the dailies genuinely admired Japanese sports accomplishments. Japanese athletes visiting Germany were afforded individual attention, often even with the distinction of photographs in the

---

[45] BTH, September 9, 1923, supplement; VZ, August 3, 1919; VZ, April 18, 1933, EE.
[46] V, October 5, 1932; RF, April 6, 1932.   [47] VB, June 7, 1936, ME.
[48] William M. Balsamo, "Japan's Contribution to the World of Opera," *Kenmei Joshi Gakuin Tanki Daigaku kenkyū kiyō: Beacon* 37 (2002): 20–21.
[49] G, February 12, 1930.   [50] NPK, June 23, 1933; VZ, September 1, 1933, EE.
[51] V, July 9, 1932; VZ, May 5, 1926; VZ, March 20, 1934.   [52] BTH, October 15, 1926.
[53] NPK, April 12, 1933.   [54] VZ, September 5, 1923.
[55] VB, March 8, 1934, NGE; VB, October 4, 1934, NGE.

1930s. International sports competitions such as the Olympics, track and field meets, and aquatics provided frequent occasions for Japanese and Westerners to be seen together. When Japan played Germany in the Davis Cup competition, *Germania* linked the two countries with a punctuation mark in the headline "Japan – Germany 4:1."[56] Japanese swimmers' ability to overtake the dominant Americans especially impressed the press. The *Berliner Tageblatt* declared Japan "the coming great power in sports."[57] The *Vossische Zeitung* reported matter-of-factly on Japanese swimmers triumphing over Americans.[58] The *Völkischer Beobachter* exclaimed in 1933, "Eleven world records! Japan has the fastest swimmers."[59] The papers also welcomed the popularization of Japanese martial arts in Germany, though their reactions were colored by their worldviews. The scholarly *Vossische Zeitung* appreciated the chance to study "real Japanese jiu-jitsu" at a demonstration organized by the German-Japanese Association.[60] The *Rote Fahne* looked forward to "the first contest between Japanese masters and German worker athletes."[61] The *Völkischer Beobachter* justified practicing a foreign martial art with an instructor's claim that "our German Jiu-Jitsu" descended from medieval Germanic wrestling and differed from the Japanese kind.[62] Though seemingly dismissive of Japan, such verbal jiu-jitsu that the chauvinists had to perform to avoid admitting that Germany appropriated a Japanese sport is in fact high praise.

The structural peculiarities of the German press and the topics for which Japan made news combined to generate a skewed but overall positive image of Japan. The dailies' worldviews generated formulas for relating or interpreting developments overseas. The papers functioned both as mouthpieces and earpieces written by and for political insiders, who invested the words therein with power and significance. Hitler, too, perused the *Völkischer Beobachter* even though he could dictate its contents. Outside the ideological tribes, government officials monitored and sought to manage the press. Many of the newspaper clippings collected by the Foreign Office were underlined or commented on in the margins, and sometimes prompted internal discussions and responses. After Erich von Salzmann published an article in the Ullstein tabloid *B.Z. am Mittag* deemed unflattering to the Japanese emperor, the Foreign Office asked its envoys in Tokyo and Beijing to convince him to

---

[56] G, June 13, 1933.   [57] BTH, December 16, 1926.   [58] VZ, September 3, 1931.
[59] VB, December 29, 1933, NGE.   [60] VZ, November 9, 1931, EE.
[61] RF, October 1, 1932.   [62] VB, November 21–22, 1934, NGE.

be less critical in the future so as "not to damage the flourishing German-Japanese relations."[63] Conversely, diplomats tried to use newspapers to bolster bilateral ties. Embassy counselor Oskar Trautmann notified the Foreign Office in 1924 that he had placed an announcement in German dailies on the establishment in Japan of a "Union of Pro-German Japanese," with the hope that the Japanese press might notice the news and in turn publicize the obscure group.[64]

The inward orientation of the ideological press prepared it for domestic political activism but not global news analysis. So when Japan received attention, it did so from a Western angle. That is, Japan mattered to the papers mostly when it concerned Germany. Still, Japan was not only able to clear the hurdle of Eurocentrism to qualify as news, it was even regarded as a great power. The habitual inclusion of Japan in Western-dominated diplomacy, commerce, culture, and sports elevated Japan in the German journalistic mindset to one of the few modern, powerful states that could be discussed in the same breath as Germany without eliciting ridicule. Indeed, the idea of German-Japanese comparability was not only received as common knowledge but even conveyed prestige and exclusivity. The carmaker Buick advertised its new model to affluent customers in 1928 with the sales pitch: "From Berlin to Tokyo – most leading men in the whole world choose Buick."[65] The dailies rarely depicted Japan as superior or equal to Germany, but Japan did not have to be a mirror image to earn Germany's compliments, even if grudging and back-handed. After attending Kiwa's performance, Joseph Goebbels commented in his diary: "The Japanese sang stirringly. Her voice sometimes unsophisticated and off, but a great impression nonetheless."[66] Japan only needed to be good enough, and it was unanimously and consistently portrayed by the press as a Westernized great power that could face the West across negotiating tables or tennis nets.

Culture and Commerce

Against the backdrop of Japan as a great power, three phases mark the chronological coverage of Japan in the German press. The first and longest stretched from the Armistice in 1918 until the Japanese conquest of Manchuria in 1931. At the outset, Germany had just lost a world war

---

[63] *B.Z. am Mittag*, June 7, 1921; PA AA, R 85315, Arthur Schmidt-Elskop to German Embassy in Tokyo, June 24, 1921.

[64] PA AA, R 85968, Trautmann to Foreign Office, March 13, 1924.

[65] BTH, February 22, 1928.

[66] Joseph Goebbels, *Die Tagebücher von Joseph Goebbels: Teil I, band 3/I*, ed. Elke Fröhlich (Munich: K. G. Saur, 2005), 211 (April 3, 1935).

and, until mid-1919, remained blockaded. Even had readers clamored for information from Japan, newspapers were scarcely in a position to deliver it. Communications and transportation links had to be rebuilt, and trade and diplomatic relations repaired. The ideological papers were intrinsically far more invested in the fluid domestic political struggle. Whatever attention and resources the press could spare for events beyond Germany's borders – themselves shifting and making headlines – were devoted to Germany's immediate surroundings, especially Eastern Europe, and peace talks with the Allies.

These limitations meant that, to the extent Japan caught the attention of German newsmen and readers in the 1920s, only the papers with the financial wherewithal and interests beyond partisanship could discuss Japan meaningfully. In Berlin, the *Vossische Zeitung* and to a lesser extent the *Berliner Tageblatt* mostly bore the responsibility of relating tidings from Japan. But even with Ullstein's and Mosse's backing, the papers still struggled to provide timely and in-depth accounts. Particularly in the initial postwar months, articles tended to be brief and were invariably datelined somewhere other than Japan, usually London, Paris, or even New York. So news arrived late, by at least one day, and by way of foreign newspapers or agencies so that "German" reporting on Japan amounted to little more than tardy translations of excerpts from British, French, or American dailies. Once German correspondents returned overseas, the quality and quantity of news improved markedly, though stories were not wired directly from East Asia until the late 1920s. The European sourcing and technological constraints contributed to a portrayal of Japan in a Western context and prioritized items deemed important to Germany, such as great-power diplomacy or trade.

Meanwhile, the papers supplemented the snippets with essays by contributors familiar with East Asia. Although they had to write from Germany at first, their prognoses were still insightful. An admiral predicted in 1919 that the disposition of Germany's concessions in China would drive a wedge between Japan and the Allies.[67] Erich von Salzmann foresaw that the Allies' haughtiness would embitter Japan.[68] As international traffic resumed, the *Vossische Zeitung* dispatched Salzmann to Beijing and employed Josef Plaut in Tokyo. Both were qualified for their postings. Salzmann had toured and published books on China, but Plaut stood out for his engagement with Japan. Plaut had been exposed to Japanese civilization from childhood because his father taught Japanese at the Oriental Seminar at Berlin and wrote a language textbook.

[67] VZ, May 22, 1919.   [68] VZ, May 7, 1919, EE.

From 1909, Plaut taught at universities in Japan, where his three children were born.[69] The *Berliner Tageblatt* hired its own correspondent, Theodor Sternberg, who first arrived in Japan before World War I to teach law at Tokyo Imperial University.[70]

Plaut and Sternberg furnished readers with frequent, detailed analyses of Japan for most of the 1920s. But even with such well-connected newsmen, the physical transfer of knowledge of Japan still had to overcome an obstacle course to reach Germany. At least two of Plaut's manuscripts vanished during intercontinental transit in 1921 and had to be resent. When they were finally published, six months after completion, the editor had to assure readers that the contents still applied.[71] Even under normal circumstances, a submission could take up to two months to arrive. Salzmann's and Plaut's columns in 1921 on Japan and America, though datelined almost simultaneously, arrived a month apart. The time lag meant that such articles did not dwell on single events but addressed their ramifications or longer trends because news would long since have broken. So Plaut wrote widely on Japan, including its New Year celebration, fledgling democracy, fleet-building program, and rural discontent.[72] Sternberg commented more on its political economy, such as struggling farmers, class division, and the Diet after the adoption of universal male suffrage in 1925.[73]

As broadly as the papers discussed Japan, they did so without political passion, even in the partisan atmosphere of Weimar. To be sure, the dailies each put their own imprint on their reporting. The *Vossische Zeitung* was drawn to state affairs and culture. The *Berliner Tageblatt* preferred the economy and trade. *Germania* viewed the world through religion, so it highlighted police raids on "godless groups" and eulogized Prime Minister Hamaguchi Osachi as a peacemaker.[74] Yet these different approaches hardly rose to controversies in which the various papers took positions against one another. The coverage of the Great Kanto Earthquake best illustrates the apolitical consensus. As news of the catastrophe trickled in, the dailies were united in expressing their sympathy. Both the *Vossische Zeitung* and *Berliner Tageblatt* devoted days of front page headlines to the tragedy. The papers were also joined by uncertainty because the

---

[69] Kamimura Naoki, "Meijimatsu no Gokō no Doitsugo kyōshitachi," in *Kyūshū no Nichi-Doku bunka kōryū jinbutsushi* (Kumamoto: Kumamoto Daigaku, 2005), 102–103.

[70] Anna Bartels-Ishikawa, *Theodor Sternberg: Einer der Begründer des Freirechts in Deutschland und Japan* (Berlin: Duncker & Humblot, 1998).

[71] VZ, May 12, 1921, EE; VZ, November 5, 1921, EE.

[72] VZ, June 6, 1921, EE; VZ, January 9, 1927; VZ, September 2, 1926.

[73] BTH, December 23, 1926; BTH, August 8, 1926; BTH, April 18, 1929, EE.

[74] G, September 8, 1931; G, September 6, 1931.

earthquake disrupted communications and delayed updates, still relayed through third countries, and the fates of their correspondents remained unknown. After the initial shock, the press resumed its habit of portraying Japan under a Western light, just with ideological overtones. On the human toll, *Germania* mourned the losses suffered by Catholic missions, while the *Vossische Zeitung* expressed relief that the embassy and consulate staffs had been rescued.[75] On humanitarian aid, the *Vossische Zeitung* described a multinational campaign to help Japan, but the *Rote Fahne* specifically mentioned the Soviet contribution.[76] On diplomacy, the newspapers agreed that geology might have shifted geopolitics. The *Berliner Tageblatt* pointed out that the earthquake altered Japan's "place in the world" because it destroyed the country's political and economic centers.[77] *Germania* wondered if "Japan as a great power" had been damaged.[78] The *Vossische Zeitung* equated Japan's loss with America's gain.[79] The *Völkischer Beobachter* interpreted the natural disaster in Darwinian terms and suggested that the powers circling Japan might prey on the wounded nation. It also compared the ruin and reconstruction in 1923 to the Russo-Japanese War, from which Japan emerged exhausted and could not retain conquests it had won on battlefields.[80]

Because Japan's great-power status was widely accepted, it made sense for the press to support Germany building beneficial relations with such a significant counterparty, especially one untainted by bitter association with the victorious Allies and Versailles. Some commentators wrote wistfully in the early postwar years of Germany's former colonies now under Japanese control, but any lament for distant Pacific islands was overwhelmed by polemics against the occupation of the Rhineland or the loss of pieces of Germany itself.[81] The dailies showed no lingering resentment toward Japan. In fact, the fragmented press left plenty of room for pundits to push for maverick foreign-policy ideas. Paul Ostwald, a scholar of geopolitics, published essays in the *Kreuz-Zeitung* and other rightist papers in the 1920s to advocate an alliance consisting of Berlin, Tokyo, and Moscow.[82] Such sensational schemes might have attracted attention, but they were rejected by officials and observers with experience in Japan. After the Foreign Office forwarded to its Tokyo Embassy one of Ostwald's columns in 1924 faulting German diplomats for not doing enough to cultivate Japan, Oskar Trautmann retorted that

---

[75] G, September 30, 1923; VZ, September 6, 1923, EE.
[76] VZ, September 6, 1923; RF, September 14, 1923.   [77] BTH, September 5, 1923.
[78] G, September 7, 1923.   [79] VZ, September 5, 1923, EE.
[80] VB, September 15, 1923.   [81] DAZ, March 29, 1922; VZ, April 16, 1921.
[82] NPK, April 30, 1923; *Königsberger Allgemeine Zeitung* (hereafter: KAZ), August 23, 1929.

Germany had no leverage except patience and Ostwald appeared to be "a man who learned everything from newspapers but lacked contact with reality."[83] Plaut, too, dismissed advocates of a German-Soviet-Japanese pact as "dreamers" in 1926.[84]

Instead of a strategic alignment, from the mid-1920s Germany and Japan were heading toward closer cultural and commercial ties, a direction facilitated by the press through its control of information and publicity. News began to be transmitted directly from Japan in the late 1920s. Although Plaut left for China in 1928 to work for the German Legation, the *Vossische Zeitung* made up for the absence with contributions from Asia by Richard Katz and Colin Ross, two of the most popular travel writers in interwar Germany.[85] Then in 1929, Gustaf Kauder, an Ullstein correspondent, flew on the *Graf Zeppelin* to Japan alongside two other German newsmen and wired back Japan's "national excitement" for the zeppelin and commander Hugo Eckener's pronouncement of the airship as an envoy for friendship.[86] Kauder shared with the *Vossische Zeitung*'s readers the relevance of German culture in Japan. He noted with approval that local newspapers were plastered with greetings in German and that German music was played at the reception banquet. Even the dinner menu, also in German, was adorned with the colors black, red, and gold.[87] At the end of the circumnavigation, the *Vossische Zeitung* reported that some in business circles were planning regular airship traffic to Japan.[88] Indeed, the selling of German culture went hand in hand with attempts to grow sales of German goods. The pro-industry *Deutsche Allgemeine Zeitung* was already calling for a new trade agreement in 1922.[89] The *Berliner Tageblatt* converted an entire weekly edition in 1924 and 1925 to an "East Asian Special Number" to promote economic activities between Germany and Japan. The 1924 issue featured an interview with Chancellor Wilhelm Marx. He stated explicitly that Germany and Japan should interact through culture and commerce. While he was pleased that German scientists and artists were welcomed in Japan, he hoped that German exports might soon receive a similar treatment, and that Germany and Japan would trade at prewar levels again through signing an economic agreement.[90] Marx regretted that Japan was not yet prepared to formalize terms.

[83] PA AA, R 85847, Trautmann to Foreign Office, July 2, 1924.
[84] VZ, February 20, 1926.
[85] Sabine Richter, "Einblick in ein kunstpädagogisches Skizzenbuch. Leben und Werk von Eva Eyquem" (PhD diss., University of Erlangen-Nuremberg, 2016), 22.
[86] VZ, August 12, 1929, EE; VZ, August 19, 1929, EE.   [87] VZ, August 21, 1929.
[88] VZ, August 30, 1929, EE.   [89] DAZ, August 10, 1922.
[90] BTH, January 31, 1924, weekly edition.

It was not until December 1926 that Sternberg could send word that a treaty would soon be secured.[91]

The mid-1920s mark two milestones along the trajectory of non-partisan German-Japanese relations. After visiting Japan, Fritz Haber led a group of German intellectuals to launch the Japan Institute in December 1926, a civil society association dedicated to cultural exchange.[92] The *Berliner Tageblatt* publicized the occasion with not just an article but also a photograph, a rare honor.[93] Months earlier, the paper published a manifesto by Haber tasking German science and culture with the duty of helping Germany recover. He cited Prussia after the Seven Years War and Japan after the earthquake as inspiration for postwar Germany to innovate its way out of hardship.[94] Berlin and Tokyo officially concluded the German-Japanese Commerce and Navigation Treaty granting each other most favored nation status in July 1927.[95] The *Vossische Zeitung* credited "two years of arduous negotiations" and the trust Ambassador Wilhelm Solf cultivated among Japanese leaders for the deal.[96] It considered the treaty a triumph for Germany in view of Japan's "extreme protectionism" and trade deficit vis-à-vis Germany. But the Japan Institute and the treaty have not received the credit they deserve. The ideological press hardly treated culture or economics as front-page news at the time. Then events in the 1930s overshadowed these achievements by German liberal democracy and civil society, and tilted historiography to favor politics and war. The Third Reich was not the only Germany capable of rapprochement with Japan. Ten years before the Anti-Comintern Pact, Weimar Germany and Taisho Japan had already established bilateral links, links that benefited the two countries far more than the Axis ever did.

From Manchuria to the Streets of Berlin

Rarely can one pinpoint turning points in cultural history to specific times and locations. The depiction of Japan in the German press underwent one such change on September 18, 1931 when a cabal of Japanese officers detonated a small bomb along the South Manchuria Railway and derailed Germany's apolitical posture toward Japan. The Japanese Kwantung Army accused Chinese troops of sabotage and attacked Chinese garrisons across Manchuria. China appealed to the League of Nations for intervention, but by March 1932 Japan had conquered the

[91] BTH, December 2, 1926.   [92] BTH, July 1, 1926, EE.
[93] BTH, December 5, 1926; BTH, December 12, 1926.
[94] BTH, June 4, 1925, weekly edition.   [95] BTH, July 20, 1927, EE.
[96] VZ, July 20, 1927, EE.

entire region and proclaimed a new state, Manchukuo, under the last Chinese emperor, Puyi. The controversy the Manchurian conflict unleashed in Germany marks the most transformative stage of Japan's image in German newspapers.

Japan metamorphosed overnight from a topic that made uncontentious news to a controversy that pitted Germans against one another. The dailies took an immediate and intense interest in the struggle. Many newspapers had their own news wired from East Asia within a day of occurrence by September 1931. Photographs now took only a few weeks to appear, a vast improvement over the early 1920s when scenes from the earthquake needed months to reach Germany. Though wars generally grabbed headlines, the essence of this particular confrontation, in which a great power violently challenged the Versailles–Washington system, was irresistible to the press because the same system aroused strong, negative emotions in Germany. The *Vossische Zeitung* anticipated a battle of words over the Sino-Japanese struggle and pleaded for neutrality in its first article on the war: "While the German public is only indirectly affected by a further reduction of the hard-won trade ... by any political crisis in the Far East, our currently most amicable relations with the two states in question should not be jeopardized by rash partisanship in the public."[97]

But the continuation of the fighting soon wore out the patience even of the centrist papers. The *Vossische Zeitung* tried to maintain balance between the belligerents in the first days, likely because some readers of the moderate dailies belonged to the few Germans benefiting from the commerce and did not wish to alienate either combatant. The paper used its resources to transmit news from both Japan and China. It reasoned that Japan naturally wanted to protect its substantial investment in Manchuria while China just as instinctively needed to preserve its integrity and sovereignty.[98] The *Vossische Zeitung* and *Germania* also pinned their hopes on international instruments to resolve the conflict, so they closely followed developments at the League of Nations in Geneva.[99] Yet as combat intensified while diplomats speechified, the centrist papers too had to choose sides. Three weeks after the outbreak, when the *Berliner Tageblatt* could publish the first photographs, it had entrenched its position: "'War in the Far East!' Geneva and Washington send notes. China protests. Japan promises a withdrawal and peace. Still the war, once unleashed, rages."[100] It also used a picture of a Chinese civilian

---

[97] VZ, September 19, 1931, EE.   [98] Ibid.; VZ, September 20, 1931.
[99] G, September 23, 1931; VZ, September 22, 1931, EE.
[100] BTH, October 11, 1931, supplement.

being searched by Japanese troops as a metaphor for China, "which asked only for peace and the world's sympathy." It again voiced disapproval of the war two weeks later with the headline "China Is Bleeding" over the image of a wounded man.[101] Then in January 1932, it captioned a photograph of a cheering soldier, "Japanese troops win but the yen tanks."[102] The *Vossische Zeitung* abandoned its measured tone. Richard Katz denounced the war as "horror in the East" and criticized Japan's "independent military" for running amok in Manchuria.[103] After fighting spread to Shanghai in 1932, the paper could but lament that now "only cannons talk."[104] In contrast to the center left publications, *Germania* detected advantages of Japanese dominance in East Asia. It praised Japanese troops for enforcing order after a French mission in Manchuria was plundered by "Chinese bandits," a phrase often used by the Kwantung Army.[105] It reported in 1933 that with Japanese blessing Catholic missionaries were running the Red Cross and halting communism in Manchuria.[106]

Whereas the centrist dailies at first resisted politicking, the leftist and rightist mouthpieces never showed such restraint. Merely days into the fighting, *Vorwärts* decried the conflict as an "imperialistic power struggle" in which Japan was motivated by "imperialistic power politics rather than any racial feelings."[107] The paper pledged "full sympathy for China" against "Japan the disruptor of peace."[108] The *Rote Fahne* had to remain silent for the first month of the war because it was coincidentally suspended for supporting mutinying British sailors.[109] Berlin police chief Albert Grzesinski cited it for "interfering with the friendly relations between Germany and England, and thus threatening public security in Germany."[110] The organ made up for lost time and joined the fray on the first day it resumed publication, with the cry "Down with Japanese Imperialism!"[111] Like *Vorwärts*, it characterized the war as a "Japanese raid for plunder" and professed "solidarity with the working Chinese."[112]

The rightist dailies cared less about the righteousness of the confrontation than its nature and outcome. The *Kreuz-Zeitung* seemed more interested in Japan's modern weaponry and in speculating whether Manchuria would become a monarchy than in the purpose of the war, which it

[101] BTH, November 1, 1931, supplement.   [102] BTH, January 10, 1932, supplement.
[103] VZ, October 31, 1931, EE; VZ, September 24, 1931.
[104] VZ, February 20, 1932, EE.   [105] G, October 7, 1931.   [106] G, February 2, 1933.
[107] V, September 22, 1931.   [108] V, September 24, 1931; V, September 27, 1931.
[109] RF, September 17, 1931.   [110] RF, September 18, 1931.
[111] RF, October 16, 1931.   [112] RF, October 18, 1931; RF, October 24, 1931.

labeled blandly as a "martial conflict," "incident," "clash," or "imbroglio."[113] Although it accepted as self-evident that "overpopulated Japan needed colonial territories for living space (*Lebensraum*)," its amorality meant that it was not beyond satirizing Puyi as "the leader of 'independent' Manchuria."[114] It added that, even if Germany had little at stake, Asia's large population and "sphinx face demand our awareness, for it is always better to be prepared for than surprised by exigencies." The *Völkischer Beobachter*, consistent with its worldview, defined the conflict as a natural struggle for survival between two peoples, without right or wrong, only weak and strong.[115] But this cynicism was not indifference, because the paper admired Japan for ruthlessly pursuing its goals regardless of international norms or reactions. Just days after the outbreak, it proclaimed:

It is war in the East. Not just the incessant commotion of the Chinese civil war familiar to us, but open war as the means to win by force the struggle for living space. Japan has established a firm foothold in China by seizing the opportunity of its especially helpless state thanks to the disunity among its political and military leaders. Once again the "Far East" is showing old Europe how wars are waged. Japan is accordingly held back by as little scruple today as in 1904, when it opened hostilities against Russia and sank three warships in Port Arthur without first declaring war. Needless to say, nowadays Japan cares little for the League of Nations' pretty statutes, but as a member it will certainly not neglect to justify its military actions for the sake of appearance.[116]

That is, Germany should pay attention to Manchuria because conditions such as internal squabbles and the league's inaction applied not just to Japan and China but to Germany as well.

Physically remote Manchuria sparked so much debate because the press managed to project the war into contexts relevant to Germany. That the distant conflict affected German interests minimally only liberated the dailies to be at their ideologically purest. The failure of the postwar order to respond to Japanese aggression drew universal condemnation. Despite the disagreement in interpretation about the seizure of Manchuria, the press across the political spectrum was united by animosity toward the League of Nations as a proxy for the Versailles–Washington system. The centrist dailies grew frustrated by the league's inability to restore peace. As the conflict dragged on, the leftist organs began to suspect foul play and interpret the inability as unwillingness, and direct their vitriol toward the organization as an accomplice.

---

[113] NPK, November 30, 1931; NPK, April 12, 1932; NPK, May 18, 1932; NPK, November 27, 1931; NPK, September 19, 1931; NPK, September 20, 1931; NPK, October 14, 1931; NPK, October 1, 1931.

[114] NPK, March 6, 1932.   [115] VB, February 9 1932, ME.

[116] VB, September 23, 1931, ME.

Achtung – Kindesraub!

Völker, aufgepaßt! Wieder sind die Kindesräuber am Werk!

Figure 5.1 Cartoon in *Vorwärts*, "Watch out – baby snatching!" It warns, "Beware, nations! The baby snatchers are at work again!" The baby, "Peace," is about to be nabbed by Japanese soldiers while the mother, "League of Nations," sleeps. Two of the soldiers hold a dagger between their teeth, like ninjas. *Vorwärts*, May 19, 1932. Friedrich-Ebert-Stiftung.

Vorwärts alleged that the league remained passive because "the great powers leading it actually wanted it to be so."[117] The *Rote Fahne* deployed typically acerbic rhetoric and blasted Geneva as the den of "imperialistic banditry."[118] The rightist papers attacked the same inability as weakness toward a real aggressor while Germany, no longer a threat to peace, still had to live under its yoke. The *Kreuz-Zeitung* mocked the league for being "helpless" and "powerless."[119] The *Völkischer Beobachter* also derided the "helpless" league and its "capitulation before Japan."[120] The league was so loathed that the Social Democratic and Nazi organs joined in skewering it with caricatures (Figures 5.1, 5.2).[121]

The dailies used Manchuria to comment on issues in Germany as well. A war triggered by a violent plot in a corner of the globe contested by the great powers reminded the *Vossische Zeitung* of Europe in 1914. Richard Katz called Manchuria "the Balkans" of East Asia.[122] Another journalist

---

[117] V, February 7, 1932.   [118] RF, October 18, 1931; RF, October 20, 1931.
[119] NPK, September 24, 1931; NPK, September 29, 1931.
[120] VB, October 15, 1931, ME; VB, September 27–28, 1931, ME.
[121] V, May 19, 1932; VB, January 6, 1933, NGE.   [122] VZ, September 20, 1931, EE.

Figure 5.2 Cartoon in the *Völkischer Beobachter,* "Nothing Learned."
As the Chinese city Shanhaikwan burns in the background, a Chinese
man attempts to stop a Japanese bayonet thrust: "Wait! I am going to
tell the League of Nations!!" The cartoon does not pass moral judgment
but only mocks the league and those who put their faith in it. *Völkischer
Beobachter,* January 6, 1933.

saw it as the Eastern "Belgium," both evocative places for Germans.[123]
The more partisan papers of course milked supposed lessons for Germany. When border disputes in eastern Germany erupted in 1932, the
Völkischer Beobachter nimbly juxtaposed Europe and Asia and warned
that East Prussia might be usurped from its fatherland as a "German
Manchuria."[124] It applied the same epithet in 1933 to ridicule Austria as
an underling of the great powers because it was disarmed.[125] It argued
that Manchuria showcased why a nation should never count on diplomats, but only weapons, for self-defense. It assured readers that "Germany, too, would be reduced to a plaything of foreign interests like China
had not Hitler risen in the nick of time to lead the country away from the
'system.'"[126] On the left, *Vorwärts* invoked World War I by comparing
the establishment of puppet Chinese regimes under Japan to the Kaiserreich's strategy in Eastern Europe against Russia.[127] The *Rote Fahne*
asserted that after Manchuria the Soviet Union would be invaded next

[123] VZ, November 15, 1931.   [124] VB, March 3, 1932, ME.
[125] VB, January 20, 1933, NGE.
[126] VB, December 31, 1931, ME; VB, March 19–21, 1932, ME.
[127] V, September 30, 1931.

and that "millions of German workers will defend with their blood the land of socialist foundation."[128] In such a stark worldview, those who should be but were deemed insufficiently committed to defending Marxism received much of the Communist organ's fury. Not only did it denounce Japanese social democrats for not spiking the war machine, but it even accused *Vorwärts* of having been bought off by Japan.[129] When it sensationally revealed that German factories were selling arms to Japan, it eviscerated the Social Democratic Party for complicity by not calling for strikes with headlines such as "Social Democracy Murdering Chinese People" and "Social Democracy for Japan's War of Plunder."[130] For newspapers infused with ideology, Manchuria was not just in Asia but in Germany too.

With the stakes so high, fighting words soon concretized into fighting acts, so much so that Berlin became a microcosm of Manchuria. Violence first broke out between Japanese and Chinese expatriates, while the German authorities attempted to mediate. *Germania* mentioned a "Japan-China war in Berlin" that required police presence when Chinese students protested outside the Japanese embassy.[131] *Vorwärts* also reported a "war in a Chinese restaurant" where Japanese and Chinese came to a "tumultuous altercation" over an attempted ban of Japanese customers that had to be settled by the political police.[132] The spread of the war to highly visible Shanghai galvanized Chinese and leftist German opposition to Japan. The *Berliner Tageblatt* identified with the Chinese in Berlin when it exclaimed, "Shanghai is here."[133] Socialist labor unions staged demonstrations and issued several declarations demanding punitive measures including an arms embargo and economic sanctions.[134] The communists also organized mass rallies against Japanese imperialism.[135] Police chief Grzesinski, a Social Democrat, prohibited one such gathering and was promptly scorned by the *Rote Fahne* as a Japanese lackey (Figure 5.3).[136] Several acts of vandalism targeted Japanese diplomatic offices, businesses, and residences in mid-1932.[137] Most were committed anonymously, but in June gun-wielding communists stormed a social club, an incident widely reported in the press.[138] The Foreign

[128] RF, November 1, 1931.   [129] RF, October 28, 1931; RF, October 21, 1931.
[130] RF, February 9, 1932; RF, April 30, 1932.   [131] G, September 25, 1931.
[132] V, September 26, 1931.   [133] BTH, February 28, 1932, supplement.
[134] V, February 7, 1932; V, March 2, 1932; V, March 4, 1932.
[135] RF, February 3, 1932; RF, March 2, 1932.   [136] RF, February 5, 1932.
[137] PA AA, R 85848, Japanese Embassy to Foreign Office, June 16, 1932; BTH, April 6, 1932.
[138] VZ, June 15, 1932; NPK, June 16, 1932; BLA, June 15, 1932; DAZ, June 15, 1932; RF, June 15, 1932.

Japan: Bravo! Herr Grzesinski!

Figure 5.3 Cartoon in the *Rote Fahne*. A Japanese soldier thanks
Grzesinski for forbidding a demonstration against Japanese imperialism.
The Communist organ accuses the Social Democratic police chief of
siding with Japan. The seizure of Manchuria inflamed ideological
passion in Germany and pitted Germans against one another. *Die Rote
Fahne*, February 5, 1932. Staatsbibliothek zu Berlin.

Office asked for police protection for all Japanese establishments, but the
Prussian Interior Ministry rejected the request as impractical. On July 15,
the Foreign Office responded that "for months communist newspapers
have been recklessly agitating against Japan over the East Asian conflict,
and that the string of attacks resulted directly from such press baiting led
by the *Rote Fahne*."[139] It added that "because the systematic assaults
endangered German-Japanese relations, the newspapers in question
should at least be sternly warned and punished for any further outrageous anti-Japanese baiting." On July 17, the *Rote Fahne* published an
essay with a section on Japan's "bestial provocations in Manchuria."[140]
On July 20, police raided the headquarters of the Communist Party and
shut down its press organ for a week.[141] Thus, within a year of the
conquest of Manchuria, Germans were fighting one another over the
proper reactions to Japan.

How did faraway Japan elicit such strong responses from Germans?
Technology and ideology brought Japan to German readers. They

---

[139] PA AA, R 85848, Carl Severing to Foreign Office, June 27, 1932; PA AA, R 85848,
Bernhard Wilhelm von Bülow to Severing, July 15, 1932.
[140] RF, July 17, 1932.   [141] RF, July 28, 1932.

empowered but also entrapped the newspapers, each of which had its own subset of knowledge and interpretations. The dailies' creators and customers lived in parallel universes with disparate vocabularies and logics. Leftists talked about "imperialism" and "plunder." Rightists spoke of "living space" and "overpopulation." The proliferation of news sources from Japan diminished the centrality of centrist voices both quantitatively and qualitatively, as the moderate dailies no longer dominated direct reporting from Japan and had to compete and converse with the fringes. More important than technical advancement in inflaming opinions, the conflict coincided with a volatile period in Germany when news of elections and urban clashes filled front pages in 1932.[142] The foreign war fused with the domestic political struggle in which Nazis, socialists, and communists bludgeoned one another verbally and physically, so that Manchuria stretched to the streets of Berlin. That the dailies could use Japan for their own partisan purposes attests a fundamental familiarity with Japan. Technology transmitted news from Japan to Germany, where ideology provided ready analysis.

The once near-unanimity in the German press regarding Japan had shattered along political fault lines by mid-1932. Before the seizure of Manchuria, maintaining friendly interactions with Japan was a matter of course. But afterward Japan became a question in which Germans took "for" or "against" positions with moral implications. Generally, those on the right sided with or at least expressed understanding for Japan. *Germania* contextualized Japanese militarism within the struggle against communism and applauded Japan in 1933 for "its campaign against domestic social unrest."[143] The *Völkischer Beobachter* not only sympathized with the quest for living space but even lauded Japan for its willingness to trample international norms. The Nazis acquired such a pro-Japanese reputation that a left-liberal paper reported that Japan was recruiting Nazis to fight in Manchuria, an allegation the Japanese Embassy strenuously denied.[144] Those on the left disapproved of the aggression and disruption of peace. Although Fritz Haber nonchalantly compared the recoveries of Prussia and Japan, describing Japan as "Prussia of the East" did not always convey a compliment. When Richard Katz toured Korea, he remarked, "The Japanese are called the 'Prussians of the East' and that is an apt phrase because . . . the orderly and self-assured Japanese treat the Koreans as the Prussians treated the Alsatians, perhaps even more unpleasantly so."[145] After insurrectional officers assassinated

---

[142] Fulda, 184–190.   [143] G, March 26, 1933.
[144] PA AA, R 85848, notes by Referat IV Japan for Foreign Office, May 11, 1932.
[145] VZ, February 23, 1930.

Figure 5.4 Cartoon in *Vorwärts*, "The 'Prussians of the East.'"
Insubordinate soldiers threaten the war minister: "The army demands
the war minister's resignation. That is great European fashion now!"
Equating Japan with the West was not always positive. *Vorwärts*, May
18, 1932. Friedrich-Ebert-Stiftung.

Prime Minister Inukai Tsuyoshi in 1932, *Vorwärts* published a cartoon to
mock the Japanese as the "Prussians of the East" for having mastered
European militarism (Figure 5.4).[146] Much as events later in the 1930s
skewed historiographical attention toward political and military affairs
more than cultural and economic ones, the rightward march in both
countries also obscured the antipathy harbored by a potential, left-of-
center Germany toward Japan over the conquest of Manchuria.

Press Diplomacy

Hitler's appointment as chancellor in 1933 ended any prospect for such
an alternative Germany. Although by 1933 the Sino-Japanese conflict
had subsided to skirmishes that were fading from front pages, Japan and
newspaper coverage of it could not simply return to the status quo ante.
The Manchurian crisis pushed Japanese politics rightward. The populace
cheered the conquest, and the attempted coup and assassination of
Inukai in February 1932 ended party cabinets. Japan also transformed

---

[146] V, May 18, 1932.

from a pillar upholding the Versailles–Washington system to its most powerful challenger, even announcing its withdrawal from the League of Nations in 1933. Meanwhile, the Third Reich replaced the Weimar Republic. The concurrent rightward marches of Germany and Japan mark the third phase of Japan in German newspapers.

The imposition of Nazi control gutted the press and altered the portrayal of Japan. Entire publications disappeared, not only the leftist flagship organs but also their affiliated tabloids and regional papers. The *Vossische Zeitung* eked out an existence until early 1934, when the Jewish Ullsteins were coerced to sell their company cheaply.[147] *Germania* and the *Kreuz-Zeitung* were rendered shells of their former selves. The *Berliner Tageblatt* was allowed to survive after the Jewish Mosses and its chief editor went into exile. Indeed, to paraphrase Heinrich Heine on burning books and humans, where one banished newspapers, one also banished people. Of the 33 Germans whose citizenship was stripped by the Nazi regime in August 1933, ten worked primarily as newsmen – including the editors-in-chief of the *Vossische Zeitung*, *Vorwärts*, and the *Rote Fahne* – and a few as periodic contributors. Fifteen were of Jewish ancestry.[148] The Nazi proscription not only hollowed out the press but also the creation of German knowledge of Japan through newsprint and apolitical German-Japanese relations. Wilhelm Solf, who shepherded the commerce treaty, was sidelined as a critic of Nazism. Fritz Haber, who founded the Japan Institute, left Germany after trying futilely to intercede for colleagues of Jewish ancestry; he himself was Jewish. Richard Katz, also Jewish, emigrated to Switzerland. Josef Plaut, also Jewish, disappeared from written records after a detailed analysis of the Manchurian conflict.[149] Theodor Sternberg, also Jewish, found refuge in Japan with help from his former law students.

After the regime decimated the press, the *Völkischer Beobachter* as the nationally predominant daily propagated transnational Nazism through accommodating Japan in its worldview. It wielded more power than any newspaper ever had in Germany because of its closeness to the party and regime, financial strength, and regional editions. In a sense, the depiction of Japan returned to its condition before Manchuria, namely the primacy of a single source of information. Compared with the centrist papers, the *Völkischer Beobachter* covered Japan differently, in two ways

---

[147] George Bailey, *Germans: The Biography of an Obsession* (New York: The Free Press, 1991), 227–228.

[148] Michael Hepp, ed., *Die Ausbürgerung deutscher Staatsangehöriger 1933–45 nach den im Reichsanzeiger veröffentlichten Listen: Band I* (Munich K. G. Saur, 1985), 3–4.

[149] BArch, N 2311/10, confidential report by Plaut, October 24, 1931.

that foreshadowed German-Japanese rapprochement. It devoted less attention to the economy and fictional tales, and much more to sports, international politics, and military affairs. And it practiced a kind of "press diplomacy" through personal bonds. It highlighted Japanese individuals and deployed its own journalists overseas, including Roland Strunk, a roaming correspondent, and Professor Don Gato. From 1931, Gato published several glowing articles on Japan in the *Völkischer Beobachter* and other rightist dailies. He wrote approvingly that "the army, completely built on the Prussian model, is well organized. A fighting spirit lives in every Japanese ... Japan is undisputedly a country of the future."[150] He mentioned seeing portraits of Mussolini and Hitler in a school classroom, and remarked that Japan's "phenomenal military victory, progress in all technical and industrial fields, and cultural activity demand high esteem even from quiet observers."[151] Japan was beginning to be respected – by the Nazi organ no less – not only for emulating the West but even matching or outmatching it.

The expanded coverage of sports served as an arena for Japan to be visualized as a modern nation competing with the West on its own terms and turfs. Athletes belonged to the exclusive club of Germans and Japanese with the privilege of international travel. After German athletes ventured to Japan for a track meet in 1929 sponsored by the newspaper *Hōchi shinbun*, the *Völkischer Beobachter* talked expectantly of a rematch planned for 1934.[152] More often, Japanese athletes visited Germany to participate in competitions. Just before Berlin held a track meet in 1934, a headline declared that Japan now had "its own [Max] Syring," a renowned German runner.[153] Later, when some Japanese swimmers were invited on a European tour, the paper reported eagerly that they would compete with German swimmers, who after much training "were not far from parity with the Americans and the Japanese."[154] Japan took part in a five-nation contest in Germany alongside four European countries in 1935.[155] Then during the 1936 Olympics, Japan was given prominent coverage in the press and on the radio when it won the bid to host the next Olympiad and gold medals in aquatics and athletics, including the marathon.[156] For added effects, the paper generously carried photographs of Japanese athletes. So the Japanese often appeared visually as fit, young, and male bodies on Nazi newsprint.

---

[150] VB, October 29, 1931, ME.   [151] VB, November 25, 1931, ME.
[152] VZ, August 21, 1929, EE; VZ, August 30, 1929; VB, October 19, 1933, NGE.
[153] VB, May 9, 1934, NGE.   [154] VB, November 29, 1934, NGE.
[155] VB, August 28, 1935, NGE.
[156] Ricky W. Law, "Runner-Up: Japan in the German Mass Media during the 1936 Olympic Games," *Southeast Review of Asian Studies* 31 (2009): 164–180.

Certainly, the paper lavished attention on sports partly to distract the populace, but physical activities played a crucial ideological role in Nazi Germany. In fact, the *Rote Fahne* and the *Völkischer Beobachter* shared the view that sports were not merely games but imbued with political significance.[157] Almost all Nazi organizations, from the Hitler Youth to the SA to the SS, emphasized sports as part of their training regimen or camaraderie building.[158] Some groups such as the Nazi League for Physical Exercise, Strength through Joy, and German Labor Front, were founded on the belief that communal physical exertion nurtured a stronger, more cohesive nation. The *Völkischer Beobachter* proclaimed, in an article on physical education, "Strong youth – strong nation."[159] The paper reminded readers in 1936 that just as the National Socialist spirit powered Germany's success at the Olympics, "through physically and mentally strengthening the nation, our stamina will never again be so drained as when we had to submit to the shameful Versailles Treaty."[160] The organ gave so much thought to sports news that it highlighted the New York Athletic Club for being "without non-Aryans" and carefully distinguished between the "German fistfight" and, attempting English, the American "pricefight [*sic*]."[161]

In this light, the transnational Nazi admiration for Japanese athleticism conveyed progress by a people rather than just appreciation of performances by individuals. That the sportspeople played for and represented their nation made it easy for the newspaper to extrapolate and analyze Japan as a whole through the prism of physical exercise. Although by now the notion of "Japan the rising great power in sports" was broadly accepted, the speed and degree of Japan's ascent still astounded and prompted commentators to offer explanations. Werner Storz, a sprinter who traveled in 1929 with the German team to Japan, wrote: "Japan had joined the great powers in sports at the same tempo as it did in politics and the economy . . . one must ask what enabled the success."[162] Echoing the regime's view on sports, Storz was awed by the mental fortitude of the Japanese, whose "fighting spirit should be recognized as a model . . . With a particular asceticism the Japanese lives for only one goal, victory." Another correspondent concurred that "the Japanese concept of sports

[157] RF, February 28, 1932; VB, December 19, 1934, ME.
[158] VB, September 4, 1935, NGE.
[159] VB, October 24, 1936, ME; cf. William M. Tsutsui and Michael Baskett, eds., *The East Asian Olympiads, 1934–2008: Building Bodies and Nations in Japan, Korea, and China* (Leiden: Brill, 2011).
[160] VB, October 4, 1936, ME.
[161] VB, November 8, 1934, NGE; VB, October 28, 1936, ME. The headline used Fraktur for "fistfight" (*Faustkampf*) and roman for "pricefight" to typographically distinguish the two.
[162] VB, October 31, 1935, NGE.

is purely a concept of victory. The Japanese trains tenaciously for victory for his country."[163] Moreover, Storz reasoned that Japanese runners and jumpers outperformed German ones because their feet grew naturally without being confined by shoes with heels. Likewise, a journalist attributed Japanese successes in aquatics to "their slight physique in relation to strong muscles ... and highly developed leg and hip muscles."[164] Japan had achieved such a status that even on the racially critical topic of sports the *Völkischer Beobachter* could acknowledge Japanese superiority in some fields.

The Nazi emphasis on military affairs and foreign relations in the *Völkischer Beobachter* also enhanced the perception of Japan as a part of or counterpart to the West. It ran a series in 1933 titled "This Is 'Disarmament'" to belittle ongoing talks on arms control. Japanese actions and words, including the walkout from the League of Nations and demands for arms parity, furnished ready material for the newspaper. Japan was said to have held a naval exercise to parade its strength and determination.[165] It was reported to be insisting on an "unalterable fleet-building program," forming four new divisions, and protesting that Soviet bombers threatened Tokyo.[166] Germany also withdrew from the league and the arms limitation conference in October. Japan abrogated the Washington Naval Treaty in 1934. The attention to military affairs gave Japan opportunities to appear as a strong nation. Likely because Germany lacked a large navy, the *Völkischer Beobachter* described several maneuvers by the Japanese fleet.[167] After witnessing an air raid drill in Tokyo in 1934, a special correspondent concluded that "the earnestness and discipline with which the highly prepared Japanese handle the life-and-death problems of air defense can serve as a model worthy of imitation for the German people, whose cities are almost defenselessly exposed to enemy air attacks."[168] Even the *Völkischer Beobachter* conceded that Germany could learn from Japan in matters such as naval and aerial warfare.

In real combat, too, the paper showcased a Japan in control of its own fate as an assertive leader in its sphere of influence willing to stand up against communist penetration. Though Manchuria had faded into the background, simmering clashes in north China kept a martial Japan in the news. More important than periodicity, Japan appeared a habitual winner – an especially crucial quality for the Nazis, who greeted one

---

[163] VB, April 5, 1934, NGE.   [164] VB, August 31, 1935, NGE.
[165] VB, August 27–28, 1933, NGE.
[166] VB, September 19, 1933, NGE; VB, September 24–25, 1933, NGE; VB, October 3, 1933, NGE.
[167] VB, May 17, 1933, NGE; VB, December 19, 1934, ME; VB, December 5, 1936, NGE.
[168] VB, October 5, 1934, NGE.

another by invoking victory with "Sieg Heil!" Japan seemed unstoppable in the *Völkischer Beobachter* in the mid-1930s, as article after article detailed Japanese territorial encroachments or ambition, including marching on Beijing, pushing into Mongolia, or creating a client regime in north China.[169] Meanwhile, China received little sympathy – the Nazis were not a sympathetic bunch and saw a world where might trumped right. The *Völkischer Beobachter* interpreted the Sino-Japanese conflict from the outset as an anticommunist struggle, the very rhetoric and justification used by Japan.[170] It repeatedly depicted a China plagued by pirates and bandits that needed Japan as a stabilizing force lest communism spread further.[171] In the Nazi weltanschauung, Japan fighting China was just a proxy war between anticommunism and communism.

Away from battlefields in China, Japan appeared consistently as a power capable of defending its interests through diplomacy. When Italy prepared to invade Abyssinia in 1935, the *Völkischer Beobachter* published Tokyo's protests to Rome to safeguard its prerogatives in East Africa.[172] But far more frequently and prominently, Japan was portrayed as an opponent of the Soviet Union. Numerous articles throughout the 1930s underlined the tension between the two countries. A front page headline in 1936 announced that the homeward bound Japanese Olympic team was victimized by "Soviet officials as train robbers" in "an unprecedented outrage."[173] The daily ran a series in 1935 on the power relations around the Pacific because "everything that happens today in the Pacific realm has direct influence on Europe."[174] Two lengthy essays analyzed Soviet-Japanese interactions, with the conclusion that "Russia is a continent with all the prerequisites for building a powerful economic bloc from the potentials of its own boundlessly wide country. Japan, an industrialized nation without its own raw materials, an overpopulated country without obvious emigration destinations, must first secure for itself additional resources and markets" – words that the Nazis also applied to Germany.[175] After the Comintern's seventh congress called for popular fronts to combat the right, the *Völkischer Beobachter* reported that both Tokyo and Berlin protested vigorously to Moscow.[176]

---

[169] VB, May 23, 1933, NGE; VB, July 20, 1935, NGE; VB, December 24, 1935, NGE.
[170] VB, March 19–21, 1932, ME.
[171] VB, November 29, 1933, NGE; VB, June 25, 1936, ME; VB, April 2, 1936, ME.
[172] VB, August 23, 1935, NGE; VB, September 15, 1935, NGE.
[173] VB, September 4, 1936, ME.   [174] VB, May 28, 1935, NGE.
[175] VB, June 12, 1935, NGE; VB, June 14, 1935, NGE.
[176] VB, August 27, 1935, NGE; VB, September 12, 1935, NGE.

The *Völkischer Beobachter* even accommodated Japan in its racialized language to propagate transnational Nazism. The country and its people were most often referred to distinctly and specifically as "Japan" and "the Japanese." When Japan was mentioned as a member of a group, it was usually as one of the "great powers" or part of "the East." At the time, "the East" as a geographical idea covered a broad swath and could describe anywhere from eastern Germany to East Asia.[177] Headlines reported the Manchurian conflict as "war in the East." This amalgamative conceptualization, in addition to Nazi ideology, may explain the habit of the *Völkischer Beobachter* of mentioning Russia in discussions of Japan, as in the Great Kanto Earthquake's aftermath. Far more tellingly, the Japanese were almost never lumped in with other Asians under the label "Asiatics" (*Asiaten*). The main exception was the set phrase "Asia for the Asians," but even in this context the *Völkischer Beobachter* distinguished Japan, "the Asian colonial power," from its subjects, "Asiatics."[178] The distinction may seem trivial, but the Nazi regime fastidiously categorized peoples as acceptable and unacceptable, such as "Aryans" and "non-Aryans," German fist-fighters and American prizefighters, and "German workers" and "proletariat."[179] In this light, the question of whom the Nazis called "Asiatics" is especially revealing. Rather than the Japanese, the *Völkischer Beobachter* applied the slur to some of its most despised enemies. After the Nazis came to power, Albert Grzesinski and his deputy Bernhard Weiss, who had incurred the Nazis' wrath for attempting to curb left-right street violence in the last Weimar months, fled Germany and were among the first Germans to have their citizenship revoked.[180] Weiss, Jewish, was derided as "Isidor," and Grzesinski, gentile, was still savaged as a "Jew bastard."[181] Grzesinski and Weiss signed a contract in December 1933 with the Chinese government to reform its police.[182] They did not end up working in China, but the *Völkischer Beobachter* reacted as if they did – "Two Asiatics Heading to Asia: Grzesinski and Weiss in Shanghai."[183] For the Nazis and particularly the propagandists at their organ, words were ammunition.

In addition to depicting Japan as a physically, militarily, and diplomatically strong and victorious nation, the *Völkischer Beobachter* conducted transnational Nazi press diplomacy outside formal channels. It sent

---

[177] BTH, October 17, 1926.　[178] VB, July 20, 1935, NGE; VB, April 16, 1935, NGE.
[179] VB, May 1, 1935, NGE.　[180] Hepp, ed., 3–4.
[181] VB, December 7, 1933, NGE; Peter J. Fliess, *Freedom of the Press in the German Republic, 1918–1933* (Baton Rouge: Louisiana State University Press, 1955), 89.
[182] Astrid Freyeisen, *Shanghai und die Politik des Dritten Reiches* (Würzburg: Königshausen und Neumann Verlag, 2000), 79–80.
[183] VB, May 1, 1935, NGE.

emissaries to and won allies in Japan. Some individuals and publications were already using newsprint to influence foreign affairs even before 1933. A newspaper in East Prussia published an interview with Momo Minosuke in 1932 as proof that not just Germans but Japanese also abhorred the "unnatural Polish Corridor."[184] Also in 1932, after the press attributed to Hitler statements partial to Japan in the Manchurian conflict, 113 Japanese in Osaka signed a letter of thanks and support to Germany over border disputes around East Prussia.[185] When Professor Don Gato encountered the portraits of Hitler and Mussolini in Japan, he was not working just as a contributing writer but as a speaker introducing Nazism to Japan.

Although the line between news reporting and policy advocacy had long been blurred in the ideological press, the Nazi Party and the *Völkischer Beobachter* actively blended the two and used their assets to build unofficial connections with Japan. After the appointment of Hitler as chancellor, Gato intensified his media blitz to promote Hitler to Japanese audiences, including speaking on radio.[186] He also met with right-wing activists but lamented that Japanese fascism lacked a leader like Hitler.[187] But Gato was not just an overzealous partisan newsman. In fact, he was not a professor. He was not even Don Gato. Instead, he was a Nazi agent named Zander, one of a few shadowy figures operating in Japan.[188] Their tendency to inflate their credentials and attacks on Jews and official diplomats alienated German expatriates, but they were eagerly received by Japanese extremists such as the transnational Nazi Momo and members of the Black Dragon Society.[189] Zander and his ilk did not have an appreciable impact on German-Japanese convergence, but they illustrate transnational Nazism's capacity to accommodate and identify with the Japanese and the resources the Nazi Party could bring to bear in pursuit of its agenda.

The *Völkischer Beobachter* established its own personal links to Japan. It departed from the prevailing practice of discussing the Japanese collectively and instead profiled Japanese individuals. The organ conducted numerous interviews with Japanese personalities between 1933 and

---

[184] KAZ, February 29, 1932.
[185] PA AA, R 85848, Voretzsch to Foreign Office, January 11, 1932.
[186] VB, March 31, 1933, NGE.   [187] *Rheinisch-Westfälische Zeitung*, May 6, 1934.
[188] Malcolm D. Kennedy, *The Estrangement of Great Britain and Japan, 1917–35* (Berkeley: University of California Press, 1969), 228, 276–277; *Jewish Daily Bulletin*, July 30, 1933.
[189] PA AA, R 85961, Dirksen to Foreign Office, April 24, 1934; BArch, R 43II/1454, Momo to Hitler, April 25, 1934.

1936, from factory workers to industrialists to the puppet emperor Puyi.[190] The two successive ambassadors to Germany each had his own conversation with the paper – a treatment not granted to envoys from other countries – with the last published just ten days before the Anti-Comintern Pact.[191] Its correspondent in Japan interviewed several cabinet members, all of whom professed admiration for Nazism and German-Japanese solidarity. Education Minister Matsuda Genji told his interviewer that "all Japan followed Germany under Hitler with sympathy."[192] Army Minister Hayashi Senjūrō compared the national unity he had witnessed in Germany at the outbreak of World War I to what he was hearing about in the Third Reich.[193] Navy Minister Ōsumi Mineo grasped the correspondent's hands and assured him that the opposition around Japan only made the country stronger and "that is true for you Germans, too."[194] Even inaccessible Japanese received attention. The correspondent Roland Strunk dedicated a series in 1935 to "the last samurai" Nogi Maresuke, the general who defeated the Russian army in the Russo-Japanese War. Strunk variously called Nogi "Japan's Clausewitz" and "the Hindenburg of the Japanese people."[195] By a coincidence, readers of the Munich edition saw Nogi's victory in Manchuria in February 1905 commemorated across the page from Hindenburg's victory in East Prussia in February 1915: Japan and Germany fighting the same enemy, separated only by time (Figure 5.5).[196] The paper also revered the emperor as a bulwark against "family-destroying communism" and "parliamentary capitalism."[197] Nazism, too, saw itself as a cure to both these modern ailments, and the columnist stated that this "imperial ideology . . . can give new stimulation to the governing philosophy of Western nations." These interpersonal connections served not only to humanize Japan but to portray Germans and Japanese as two peoples combating the same foe.

The *Völkischer Beobachter*'s command of technology and ideology enabled the organ's last acts of press diplomacy. The paper reported on the growing technical connections between the two countries from late 1933, including a "German-Japanese friendship radio hour" in November and the first telephone conversation between Munich and Tokyo in

[190] VB, November 5, 1935, NGE; VB, October 19, 1935, NGE; VB, April 28, 1933, NGE.
[191] VB, April 9–10, 1933, NGE; VB, November 14, 1936, ME.
[192] VB, February 1, 1935, NGE.   [193] VB, December 4, 1934, NGE.
[194] VB, October 18, 1934, NGE.
[195] VB, February 8, 1935, NGE; VB, February 7, 1935, ME.
[196] VB, February 9, 1935, ME.
[197] VB, February 20, 1935, NGE; VB, February 21, 1935, NGE.

Figure 5.5 The *Völkischer Beobachter* commemorates side by side Japanese and German victories over Russia. The article on the left celebrates "Nogi, the last samurai, the Japanese hero of Port Arthur" during the Russo-Japanese War. The one on the right relives Hindenburg's exploits at the Winter Battle of the Masurian Lakes in 1915. *Völkischer Beobachter*, February 9, 1935.

early 1935.[198] The opening of "wireless telephone" service between Berlin and Tokyo in March was touted by the *Völkischer Beobachter* as "a new instrument of peace and bond from nation to nation."[199] The paper did not merely observe the engineering breakthrough but played an active role: the first conversation between Berlin and Tokyo was held by its newsmen in the capitals. The press was so influential in bilateral relations that Communications Minister Tokonami Takejirō spoke with the *Völkischer Beobachter* while Goebbels conversed with the *Nichinichi*.[200] Of course, technical advancement alone did not bring about the political rapprochement, but Alfred Rosenberg infused ideological significance in the technological moment:

The National Socialist movement is of the belief that from the outset faraway Japan understood and appreciated the endeavors of Germany's revival, and we hope that Japanese culture, willfully standing in our current lifetime but

[198] VB, November 17, 1933, NGE; VB, January 16, 1935, ME.
[199] VB, March 13, 1935, NGE.   [200] VB, March 14, 1935, NGE.

also firmly rooted in its millennia of ancient character, will also blossom anew out of the great spiritual struggles. In this spirit, old-young Germany greets old-young Japan.[201]

Then, in late 1936, the *Völkischer Beobachter* pulled off its most spectacular coup in press diplomacy. It collaborated with the *Nichinichi* to cohost an international game of Go. The match began in early October, with the German and the Japanese player each remaining in his homeland and communicating his moves via telegraph.[202] The *Völkischer Beobachter* covered the progress of the game almost daily for the next eight weeks. When it reported the last moves that ended with the Japanese master's expected victory, it declared:

Go players of the world fixated their eyes on Germany and Japan, while the attention of the many non-players was steered through the match to these two countries. The international match thus became a success not only in the game but also a unique accomplishment in cultural politics with an effect on the growing mutual understanding between Japan and Germany. News of that nature has already been widely reported yesterday.[203]

The Anti-Comintern Pact was signed the day before.

Transnational Nazism in Newspapers

Thus on November 26, the *Völkischer Beobachter* reported the Anti-Comintern Pact on its front page and on the fourth page the cultural and political connections established by the Go match in which a German and a Japanese sat virtually face to face. The paper promoted the pact over the next few days. It published columns by Goebbels, Rosenberg, and Deputy Führer Rudolf Hess.[204] Although the newspaper had not argued for a diplomatic compact with Japan, much less an anti-Comintern agreement, it just played a different role in German-Japanese rapprochement, or more precisely Nazi-Showa rapprochement. The daily saw its role as educating rather than winning over the populace.[205] The regime had neither the need nor incentive to seek the people's approval of its stance vis-à-vis Japan. Foreign policies were usually carried out, and then the people were "consulted" for their input via referenda, as when Germany withdrew from the League of Nations in 1933, remilitarized the Rhineland in 1936, and "reunified" with Austria in 1938. The *Völkischer*

---

[201] VB, March 13, 1935, NGE.   [202] VB, October 3, 1936, NGE.
[203] VB, November 26, 1936, NGE.
[204] VB, November 27, 1936, NGE; VB, November 28, 1936, NGE; VB, November 30, 1936, NGE.
[205] VB, November 12, 1936, ME.

Beobachter as an official organ was the last place one should expect leaks or speculations. Moreover, the Anti-Comintern Pact was concocted by amateurish "diplomats" led by Joachim von Ribbentrop, who was competing with Rosenberg to become the Nazi foreign minister.[206] That the Ribbentrop Office and the *Völkischer Beobachter* each pursued its own version of rapprochement only demonstrates the goodwill toward Japan within different corners of the Nazi polycratic jungle.[207]

In a sense, the political alliance in 1936 represents just one of at least three possible realities in German-Japanese relations. For an agreement of mutual assistance to be viable, each state had to be able to see the other as capable of rendering help. Japan appeared in the German press as a great power worthy of being mentioned alongside the West in diplomacy, commerce, culture, and sports throughout the interwar years. Germany and Japan interacted with each other as economically and culturally vibrant counterparties for over a decade. Technological and financial limitations barred all but the best equipped publications such as the *Vossische Zeitung* and the *Berliner Tageblatt* from reporting directly from Japan. These cosmopolitan dailies dominated the portrayals of Japan, which did not generate controversial news or fuel partisan rancor. The high points of Weimar-Taisho collaboration, the Japan Institute and the commerce treaty, reflected the cultural and economic interests of the centrist press. This trajectory of German-Japanese interaction did not survive the crises of the 1930s, but it resumed after 1945.

One of the crises, the conquest of Manchuria in 1931, inaugurated the second phase of Japan in the press. Japan transformed overnight into a heated political topic in a highly, sometimes violently, partisan Germany. Enabled by technology and ideology, the newspapers reported and commented on Japan almost daily. Japan's unpunished aggression against China betrayed the centrists' trust of postwar institutions, confirmed the leftists' suspicion of imperialist collusion, and strengthened the rightists' hatred of the League of Nations. The broad criticism of Japan, from the center to the far left, showcases another possible reality in bilateral relations in which a rightward marching Japan presented a mismatch to a Germany still adhering to international norms. In one of its last diplomatic acts, the Weimar Republic contributed to the league's Lytton Commission Report that reproved Japan's conduct.

---

[206] Rosenberg maintained his contacts in Japan into the 1940s. Jürgen Matthäus and Frank Bajohr, *The Political Diary of Alfred Rosenberg and the Onset of the Holocaust* (Lanham: Rowman & Littlefield, 2015), 269–270 (December 14, 1941).

[207] The label "polycratic" was made popular by Peter Hüttenberger, "Nationalsozialistische Polykratie," *Geschichte und Gesellschaft: Zeitschrift für Historische Sozialwissenschaft* 4 (1976): 417–442.

The third phase began in 1933 with the Nazi assumption of power and the consequent synchronization with Japan in a rightward turn and amputation of the left half of the press. The *Vossische Zeitung* retained its cosmopolitan learnedness until its very end. In its final issue, it fittingly published a Japanese short story translated by Komakichi Nohara, a writer of German and Japanese parentage.[208] Both such tales and people were to disappear from a press dominated by the *Völkischer Beobachter*, whose pro-Japanese transnational Nazi alternative reality was no longer challenged by leftist voices. Why did Nazism view Japan so favorably? Factors that concerned the centrist press such as Japanese economic hegemony in Asia did not preoccupy the Nazis as much: why worry about importing Manchurian soybeans when the Thousand Year Reich was to control fertile Eastern Europe? Moreover, visions of an old Japan with a warrior culture appealed to the Nazis. One of the very few fictional works on Japan in the *Völkischer Beobachter* revolved around the 47 loyal samurai. Articles on Japanese soldiers and athletes often invoked Bushido. Still, many places had an ancient warrior culture and Japan had a martial tradition well before the 1930s, so the Nazi fascination with samurai cannot completely explain the regime's alliance with Japan in 1936. Rather, as articulated by Rosenberg, Japan was an "old-young" nation like Germany in the process of rejuvenation. Its ancient pedigree enchanted the Nazis sentimentally. Its powerful modern state earned their pragmatic respect. Japan occupied such a special niche in the Nazi worldview that its people were acknowledged to enjoy some physiological advantages and were conceptualized apart from the "Asiatics." The transnational Nazi accommodation of Japan eased any ideological discomfort or hypocrisy from working with an East Asian nation.

The *Völkischer Beobachter* stood out as the channel most identified with the regime within the interwar German media. The day-to-day news reporting created the most presentist portrayal of a modern Japan. Although Nazism expertly exploited ancient imagery and prejudices, the ideology and certainly German-Japanese convergence were fundamentally modern phenomena, made possible by advances in technology and ideology. Other forms of the media were not as closely tied to the regime and faced less time pressure to publish, and so had more room to mobilize varied arguments to depict Japan as a potential ally.

---

[208] VZ, March 31, 1934. Nohara wrote under the name Wilhelm Komakichi von Nohara.

6   Japan in Films

> I knew that . . . the Orient is a movie . . . I was sitting in the third row in
> front of the green velvet curtain. Suddenly the hall darkened, the curtain
> slowly parted, and a mysterious light that could not have been created
> by God, and that nature couldn't manage in a thousand years, ran in
> soft rivulets over the silvery walls of the hall and down the front of the
> stage . . . This illumination was compounded of dawn light and evening
> red, of empyrean clarity and infernal haze, of big-city air and sylvan
> green, of moonshine and midnight sun. Things that nature can only
> accomplish separately or in succession, were here encompassed in the
> one hall and in one minute.[1]   – Joseph Roth, *Frankfurter Zeitung*,
>   November 19, 1925

Like many writers before and since, Roth compared his first encounter
with film in a cinema to supernatural phenomena: understandably so.
Though interwar German motion pictures were silent in the 1920s and
mostly black and white, they enchanted countless viewers. Sequestered
in a *Kino* away from the hubbub outside, seated at close quarters with
strangers in the dark, and immersed in the director's vision, cinemagoers
experienced film not merely as entertainment but also an opportunity to
broaden their horizons and gain insights about the world beyond their
environs.

Alongside newspapers, magazines, and, gradually, radio, cinema functioned as one of the more accessible and popular conduits of knowledge
in 1920s and 1930s Germany. For those Germans interested in learning
more about Japan than what they could glean from words and photographs on newsprint, the silver screen with its graphics, animation, and
sound recommended itself as a bright, alluring alternative. But because
motion pictures were screened only at specific times and in venues that
required tickets, fewer Germans could vicariously explore Japan in
cinema than through the press. Film watching often took hours and

---

[1] Joseph Roth, *What I Saw: Reports from Berlin 1920–1933*, trans. Michael Hofmann (New
York: W. W. Norton, 2003), 167–168.

demanded more commitment in time than the seconds or minutes for a newspaper cartoon or article. The lack of video replay made film a fleeting experience, like lectures, because spectators had little chance to revisit a motion picture once its theatrical run ended. The higher thresholds in cost, time, and technology meant that film was a more exclusive but also more powerful means than newspapers for opinion makers to mold Japan's image.

German national cinema is the subject of a vast scholarly literature, including analyses of the appearance of various nationalities and ethnicities.[2] Tobias Nagl in particular demonstrates the salience of race and racism in Weimar film.[3] Despite Japan's significance for Germany, its filmic portrayal has been largely neglected, aside from the attention lavished on the movie *The Samurai's Daughter*.[4] This chapter joins and expands the current scholarship by examining Japan's role in newsreels, documentaries, and movies. Weimar motion pictures of all three genres inherited stereotypical tropes from earlier arts. Filmmakers articulated Japan through "the familiar of the unfamiliar" – an oft-used catalogue of clichés of exotic Japan well known to viewers such as geisha, cherry blossoms, temples, and traditional storylines. Late Weimar films began to appreciate Japanese modernity but also condemned Japan's militarism and aggression against China. Just then the Third Reich imposed new values and priorities. On the one hand, its films propagated transnational Nazism. They sided with Japan's position and depicted Japan as a strong, willful great power with a capable military. On the other hand, Third Reich cinema exemplifies transnational Nazism's inherent tension and paradox, as motion pictures continued to apply orientalist rhetoric and imagery to Japan. Film contributed to German-Japanese convergence by

---

[2] Sabine Hake, *German National Cinema*, 2nd ed. (New York: Routledge, 2008); Stephen Brockmann, *A Critical History of German Film* (Rochester: Camden House, 2010); Réka Gulyás, *Von der Puszta will ich träumen...: Das Ungarn-Bild im deutschen Spielfilm 1929–1939* (Innsbruck: Inst. für Sprachwiss., 2000); Siegbert Salomon Prawer, *Between Two Worlds: The Jewish Presence in German and Austrian Film, 1910–1933* (New York: Berghahn Books, 2005).

[3] Tobias Nagl, *Die unheimliche Maschine: Rasse und Repräsentation im Weimarer Kino* (Munich: edition text + kritik, 2009).

[4] Janine Hansen, *Arnold Fancks* Die Tochter des Samurai: *Nationalsozialistische Propaganda und japanische Filmpolitik* (Wiesbaden: Harrassowitz, 1997); Janine Hansen, "Celluloid Competition: German-Japanese Film Relations, 1929–45," in *Cinema and the Swastika: The International Expansion of Third Reich Cinema*, eds. Roel Vande Winkel and David Welch (New York: Palgrave Macmillan, 2007), 187–197; Michael Baskett, *The Attractive Empire: Transnational Film Culture in Imperial Japan* (Honolulu: University of Hawai'i Press, 2008), 116–129; Valerie Weinstein, "Reflecting Chiral Modernities: The Function of Genre in Arnold Fanck's Transnational *Bergfilm, The Samurai's Daughter* (1936–37)," in *Beyond Alterity: German Encounters with Modern East Asia*, eds. Qinna Shen and Martin Rosenstock (New York: Berghahn Books, 2014), 34–51.

providing a stage for transnational Nazi filmmakers to imagine Japan as ideologically acceptable and for the two countries to collaborate on joint projects.

Films as Media and Sources

By the end of World War I, commercial cinema had been developing for a quarter century in Germany and was no longer a novelty for many Germans. Even those who had never set foot inside a movie theater knew of its existence and purpose. The war spurred the growth of domestic production by cutting off foreign imports and providing occasion for mass mobilization through film propaganda. The War Ministry in conjunction with several companies founded the production firm Universum Film AG (Ufa) in 1917. Ufa soon became Germany's dominant, most recognized film studio.

Germany's postwar "peace dividend" materialized not as political stability, social harmony, or economic growth but as cultural frenzy. Defeat, revolution, and democratization removed most censorship on film and unleashed pent-up energy in the industry. Creative trends in performance and visual arts, literature, music, and design predating the war blossomed in the "Golden Twenties." German Expressionism left its imprint on avant-garde works such as Robert Wiene's *The Cabinet of Dr. Caligari* (1920) and Fritz Lang's *Metropolis* (1927), modern classics and bookends of the age of Expressionist silent film.

Yet *Metropolis* also ended Ufa as an independent entity. The beautiful but costly movie ruined the company's finances. In truth, Germans encountered motion pictures far more frequently as mass entertainment than highbrow art. Studios produced films mostly to turn a profit at the box office rather than to revolutionize the medium. Distributors and cinema owners catered to spectators' tastes and focused on popular staples such as crime thrillers, musical comedies, Westerns, erotic flicks, and, above all, Hollywood imports. Ufa already had to accept assistance from its American competitors to shore up its balance sheet in 1925. It again found itself in financial difficulties after *Metropolis* and had to join the conservative mogul Alfred Hugenberg's media empire. The newfound backing enabled the studio to expand its distribution network overseas, construct cinemas across Germany, adopt audio technology, and weather the world economic crisis.

In spite, or even because, of the ongoing economic, political, and social turmoil, ever more German urbanites flocked to cinemas for entertainment, enlightenment, or escape. The headcount of moviegoers leaped from 276 to 624 million between 1925 and 1939, while

Germany's population grew only by a tenth.[5] The increase in the number of movie houses, from roughly 2,800 in 1919 to around 6,900 in 1939, provided more outlets for motion pictures to convert the populace into regular moviegoers. A ticket cost on average less than a Reichsmark, well within even the budget of unskilled laborers, who earned just over 1 RM per hour in the late 1920s.[6]

For such an affordable price, cinemagoers received a full dose of audiovisual stimulation. A typical visit to a cinema comprised three components: a newsreel, a short documentary, and the feature film, in that order. Cinemas employed musicians to fill the auditory void before the incorporation of sound. The Ufa Palace in Berlin had a 75-member orchestra to entertain over 2,000 spectators.[7] Altogether the process of "film watching" involved much more than watching just a film and could consume the better part of an evening. Because other amusement options such as theater or opera cost decidedly more than movies, more and more Germans opted to spend what leisure time and money they could spare on film.

Although the number of moviegoers and cinemas multiplied, the annual output of feature films peaked at 510 in 1920 and declined steadily afterward. Only 100 titles were released in 1938. Ufa's resources limited its productivity. Hugenberg's managers focused on reliably profitable musicals, escapist comedies, and nationalistic melodramas to cut costs and grow revenues.[8] So Ufa, a creature of the War Ministry and not necessarily a force for liberalism to begin with, turned less innovative and more conservative. Other studios produced movies with leftist messages or imported works from the Soviet Union. But even under the Weimar Republic, motion pictures deemed sympathetic to the left faced a greater chance of censorship or outright suppression.

The Third Reich imposed much stricter control and purged political suspects from the industry en masse. Nazi leaders recognized film's propaganda potential. To harness this power, the regime bought out Hugenberg's share in Ufa in 1937. The state commissioned full-length

[5] The population of Germany grew organically from 62.4 to 68.5 million during that period, excluding that in the Saar territory, Austria, and the Sudetenland: see Dietmar Petzina, Werner Abelshauser, and Anselm Faust, eds., *Sozialgeschichtliches Arbeitsbuch Band III: Materialien zur Statistik des Deutschen Reiches 1914–1945* (Munich: C. H. Beck, 1978); Wladimir S. Woytinsky, *Zehn Jahre neues Deutschland: Ein Gesamtüberblick in Zahlen* (Berlin: Rudolf Mosse Buchverlag, 1929). For the statistics on motion pictures, cinemas, and moviegoers: see Hans Helmut Prinzler, *Chronik des deutschen Films 1895–1994* (Stuttgart: J. B. Metzler, 1995).
[6] Gerhard Bry, *Wages in Germany 1871–1945* (Princeton: Princeton University Press, 1960).
[7] Roth, 167.   [8] Hake, 53.

documentaries such as *Triumph of the Will* (1935) to burnish its reputation, and vilified its victims with slanderous works such as *The Eternal Jew* (1940). Hitler and Goebbels considered film so valuable in managing the public mood that they took a keen interest in the production of newsreels, often previewing them before approving their distribution countrywide.[9] Newsreels became a mandated element in film programs in October 1938. During World War II, the government ordered cinemas to lock their doors after the newsreel began so that no one could enter afterward to watch the movie without exposure to the propaganda.[10]

The state of preservation of interwar German film varies. The Federal Archives' Film Collection maintains and makes accessible numerous titles, but it is regrettable that most are lost or only left indirect evidence such as promotional materials, reviews, or censorship files. Just about one in ten Weimar motion pictures remain, and they were not necessarily popular, influential, or representative.[11] Some survive as fragments or export versions, or without audio. The run of 1920s newsreels is spotty; that from the 1930s is markedly fuller but by no means complete. These factors did not affect film as contemporary media but should be considered when used as historical sources.

Japan as Information

Newsreels were introduced shortly after the outbreak of World War I to inform the population of happenings around the nation and the world.[12] They had become an integral part of most cinematic experiences by 1920. Franz Hessel wrote, "For us [Berliners], the weekly newsreel makes up for all the world history that we did not get to live through."[13] Because a newsreel typically headed a program, it was likely the first film that moviegoers ever saw. When films came equipped with audio beginning in the early 1930s, the first sounds to greet audiences were frequently the announcement "Attention! Attention! You are watching and hearing Deulig Audio Newsreel."

[9] Jeremy Noakes, ed., *Nazism 1919–1945, Volume 4: The German Home Front in World War II* (Exeter: University of Exeter Press, 1998), 504.

[10] Ibid.; Hake, 64; Claudia Schmölders, *Hitler's Face: The Biography of an Image*, trans. Adrian Daub (Philadelphia: University of Pennsylvania Press, 2006), 120–122.

[11] Hake, 28.

[12] A previous version of this section appeared in: Ricky W. Law, "Beauty and the Beast: Japan in Interwar German Newsreels," in *Beyond Alterity*, 17–33.

[13] Franz Hessel, *Spazieren in Berlin*, in *Sämtliche Werke in fünf Bänden 3: Städte und Porträts*, ed. Bernhard Echte (Oldenburg: Igel Verlag, 1999), 131.

Deulig, Ufa, and Emelka/Bavaria produced most of the newsreels in Germany. Literally a "weekly show" (*Wochenschau*), a fresh newsreel lasting ten to twenty minutes was released every week to recount diverse doings of the previous seven or more days. A show's program normally did not have an overarching theme. Instead, it consisted of vignettes or trivialities, each a few minutes long. Despite aiming to be "living dailies," newsreels actually reported few time-sensitive events because breaking stories would long since have been announced in newspapers or on radio. Newsreels could suffer from substantial delays because weeks could pass before footage of an incident, particularly from overseas, made its way onto a screen. Smaller cinemas had to wait until larger ones were done showing the reels.[14] Above all, newsreels animated recent developments that spectators had already read or heard about in words. Partly as a result, and especially in the comparatively calm mid-1920s, newsreels mostly covered curiosities in politics, sports, culture, science, or foreign affairs.

Japan debuted as lighthearted information in newsreels in this relatively stable and relaxed atmosphere. Among extant newsreels from the 1920s, Japan or East Asia appeared only sporadically. Consistent with the peaceful times and playful tone of the medium, newsreels often portrayed the region as exotic and enigmatic. Viewers saw in 1925 the segment "Blue Jackets Visiting Famous Chinese Temples" that depicted German sailors traveling in China.[15] The sightseers were shown watching martial arts and smiling for photographs in front of a pagoda. The excursion in itself was hardly newsworthy, but the sheer alien quality of the scenery and the adventurous nature of the activity sufficed to catapult it onto screens.

Several shows from the late 1920s featured scenes of ordinary Japanese religious ceremonies. An Emelka newsreel introduced moviegoers to the spectacles of a Shinto festival in 1927.[16] It portrayed women in kimonos and men with straw hats chanting and parading a portable shrine through a town. The revelers pushed and beat a gigantic drum, though the silent reels could do justice to neither the singing nor drumbeat. Then in 1928, a Deulig newsreel brought to screens what it labeled a "Japanese Parish Fair."[17] It in fact captured a Bon festival, an annual Buddhist celebration recalling ancestors' spirits. Viewers again saw Japanese in festive costumes and stepping rhythmically to perform the Bon dance. A newsreel reported the same year that the city of Beppu had erected a 25-meter tall

---

[14] Schmölders, 121.   [15] BArch, *Emelka-Deulig-Wochenschau-Sujets*, c. October 1925.
[16] BArch, *Emelka-Wochenschau-Aufnahmen*, c. February 1927.
[17] BArch, *Deulig-Wochenschausugets* 17, c. June 1928.

Buddha statue.[18] Viewers were probably awed and amused by footage showing a few diminutive monks fitting comfortably into the colossus's cupped palms.

Although the opening of the Beppu Buddha was somewhat remarkable, Japan was already so peppered with large statues of deities that the completion of another would not have raised many eyebrows. Observance of a religious holiday somewhere took place so regularly that it usually did not warrant special attention. But portrayals of these mundane occurrences in Japan found their way as current affairs to German cinemas. That is, in the 1920s Japan often made news not for what it was but for being what it was thought to be. Far more happened in Japan than the construction of idols or celebration of festivals, but these activities conformed to the preexisting German imagination of Japan as a land of ageless traditions and arcane beliefs. Producers of newsreels furnished scenes of a certain Japan to fulfill consumers' expectations, thereby mutually reinforcing and perpetuating their communal stereotypes.

Newsreels began to highlight the modern aspects of Japanese life in the late 1920s. An Emelka program showcased the "Modern Woman in Japan" in 1929. It depicted kimonoed ladies awkwardly playing the imported game of billiards.[19] A Deulig clip in 1934 featured Japanese women taking off their kimonos to try on revealing Western bathing suits. The narrator used the moment to comment that "different times bring different custom. What was impossible 20 years ago is now a common sight: demonstrations of swimwear modeled on European fashion on a Japanese beach."[20]

This new Japan was powerful as well. A 1925 Deulig newsreel reported Japanese warships on tour reaching San Francisco.[21] The visiting and home flotillas saluted each other. The Japanese ships fired honorary shots. An American admiral boarded the Japanese flagship and was welcomed by disciplined, smartly uniformed seamen. This particular segment lasted longer than usual, with the camera lingering over the sleek Japanese ship and its smoking guns. The clip's pairing of the Japanese and the American ships creates an impression that the fleets enjoyed parity and that Japan was a military powerhouse beside Western nations. In an Ufa newsreel in 1936, the narrator declared "Cannon Thunder in New York" to lead a story on a Japanese squadron visiting

---

[18] BArch, *Ufa-Deulig-Opel-Wochenschau Sujets* 2, mid-1928.
[19] BArch, *Emelka-Woche* (hereafter: EW) 48, November 19, 1929.
[20] BArch, *Deulig-Tonwoche* (hereafter: DTW) 137, August 15, 1934.
[21] BArch, *Deulig-Woche, c.* December 1925.

the city.[22] The sequence parallels that in the 1925 clip: the guests and hosts hailed each other, Japanese sailors saluted the boarding party, and the shore battery and Japanese warships exchanged honorary salvos. But the inclusion of audio dramatically enlivened the footage's overall effect. Audiences no longer had to wonder what the scene sounded like but could hear for themselves the Japanese command given to the sailors to stand at attention and the cannons roaring. Thus film projectors and loudspeakers combined to demonstrate Japanese military might for German eyes and ears.

Much as technology and ideology transformed Germany and Japan's mutual perceptions in the press, as newsreels entered the era of sound and the turbulent 1930s their depiction of a Japan enticing for its Oriental mystique gave way to one dominated by firepower and forcefulness. Special occasions such as a luminary's death or an anniversary of Matthew C. Perry's "opening" of Japan still occupied screen time.[23] But even in some of these seemingly innocuous events the presence of a relentlessly rising Japan could still be felt. An Ufa newsreel in 1934 covered the funeral of Tōgō Heihachirō.[24] Tōgō had won fame in the West for defeating the Russian fleet in the Russo-Japanese War and launching Japan into the ranks of great powers. Also in 1934, a Deulig narrator used Perry's legacy to comment on contemporary Japan: "80 years ago Japan was still an island country cut off from the world and untouched by European and American civilization. American ships under Perry arrived in Shimoda in 1854. Japan became acquainted with modern civilization and henceforth it developed in an unusually rapid pace into today's world power."[25]

When military conflict erupted in Manchuria in 1931, weapons and warfare came to dominate Japan's filmic image. Newsreels already frequently carried stories on the world's armed forces in the mid-1920s, mostly peacetime maneuvers showcasing photogenic military hardware, especially naval exercises.[26] But East Asia stood out as the region that threatened to turn rumors of war into reality. For a few weeks in 1927 viewers saw scenes of skirmishes in China as part of its ongoing civil war.[27] Then in a 1929 Emelka segment, "Danger of War in the East," they watched Chinese troops preparing for a clash with their Russian counterpart.[28] Eventually, it was not the Soviet Union but Japan that

---

[22] BArch, *Ufa-Tonwoche* (hereafter: UTW) 314, September 9, 1936.
[23] BArch, UTW 277, December 25, 1935.   [24] BArch, UTW 200, July 4, 1934.
[25] BArch, DTW 125, May 23, 1934.   [26] BArch, EW 44, October 26, 1927.
[27] BArch, EW 32, August 3, 1927; BArch, EW 35, August 24, 1927.
[28] BArch, EW 28, July 3, 1929.

brought war to Asia in 1931 by seizing Manchuria. By the time fighting between Japan and China broke out in Shanghai on January 28, 1932, all three studios were ready and equipped to relay spectacular footage of the conflict. For most viewers, the coverage of the battle was their first opportunity to witness actual combat on screen, and it would define the presentation of Japan in newsreels for the rest of the decade.

Sights and sounds of war monopolized Japan's appearance for the duration of the battle until March 3. On February 10, just two weeks after the outbreak of fighting, *Deulig Audio Newsreel No. 6* was already featuring footage of combat. The narrator launched the segment: "Shanghai stands at the center of the world's concern today – Japan marching on East Asia's great commercial city of 2.7 million inhabitants."[29] As viewers gawked at aerial footage of the city, the narrator explained that the densely populated district of Chapei was set ablaze by Japanese bombs and artillery shells. In contrast to 1920s silent films that could not let footage "speak" for itself, in the 1930s audio newsreels on war came full of exploding bombs, buzzing warplanes, and wailing victims. The cotemporaneous advances in audio film and outbreak of war enabled the timely projection of the distant war before German audiences and rendered more real and concrete the power at Japan's command.

Subsequently, sights and sounds of war marked German cinemagoers' weekly rendezvous with Japan. Because a newsreel comprised segments on various topics, it could not devote an entire program to any single subject. The Sino-Japanese conflict thus effectively displaced all other stories on Japan. The Deulig newsreel relegated the ongoing Japanese incursion into Manchuria to "other news" after the headline assault on Shanghai. This segment featured Japanese soldiers in combat as they stormed the city of Harbin after heavy fighting. The filmmakers exercised an editorial touch and inserted generic sound effects not captured live but added afterward. Thus, the audience heard in the background unintelligible human voices that presumably stood for Japanese and drumbeat while Japanese troops marched past burning buildings as if they were in a triumphal parade. The artificial sounds, though incongruous in hindsight, animated the scene and led cinemagoers' imagination closer to the battlefield.

But this image of Japanese power, enhanced by film technology, clashed with Germany's ideological outlook. Newsreels in the last months of the Weimar Republic used the same technology to condemn Japanese violence. The rest of February witnessed the daily Japanese bombardment

---

[29] BArch, DTW 6, February 10, 1932.

of Shanghai and the newsreels' weekly bombardment of German movie-goers with footage of Japanese brutality. *Deulig Audio Newsreel No. 9* opened the segment on the war dramatically with sounds of gunfire and explosion, and closed it with images of Japanese armored cars passing urban ruins and burning buildings collapsing.[30] The following week, *Deulig Audio Newsreel No. 10* conveyed sympathy for the victims and contrasted Chinese helplessness with Japanese aggression.[31] The episode showed a Japanese caravan rumbling through streets lined with rubble while soldiers callously dispersed a crowd of refugees. The next scene ratcheted up the tension and focused on a woman carrying her infant and trudging wearily before heavily armed Japanese troops. The camera then switched to zoom in on a wounded Chinese man bemoaning his suffering. Interspersed with the man's sighs and cries, and breaking from the medium's normally staid tone, the narrator lamented that "the shelling of the city has visited the inhabitants with immense misery." As the camera panned from a throng of fleeing civilians to children in rags nibbling morsels on the ground, he continued, "Thousands upon thousands of refugees. Everyone is starving and has to rely on the public dole." *Emelka Audio Newsreel No. 77* that same week devoted screen time to the war and so guaranteed that most cinemagoers saw Japanese ruthlessness.[32] To open the segment "The Conflict in the East: The Latest Images from Shanghai," the announcer declared, "Chapei is burning."[33] The footage showed the harbor engulfed in smoke and flames, burning for three days and nights. He added that despite intercession by European powers the aggressors pressed on into the city and its outskirts, while the screen displayed streets littered with corpses. Thus, newsreels and their viewers bore witness to Japan's bombing of thickly populated areas.

The political and moral compasses of late Weimar newsreels remained sufficiently intact to discern that Japan's power would alienate other nations and ultimately isolate the country. The Emelka announcer pointed out that "although the Chinese regiments are resisting frantic-ally, they must still retreat steadily before the incomparably modern war machines of the Japanese." Yet later in the same program, viewers saw a special maneuver of the combined US Pacific and Atlantic Fleets near Hawai'i.[34] The armada of ships and warplanes dwarfed anything shown on screen thus far. The show of force was meant to remind Japan of

---

[30] BArch, DTW 9, March 2, 1932.   [31] BArch, DTW 10, March 9, 1932.
[32] That week's Ufa show is not extant, but it most likely contained a segment on the war like the Deulig and Emelka shows.
[33] BArch, *Emelka-Tonwoche* 77, March 10, 1932.
[34] BArch, DTW 8, February 24, 1932.

America's ability to project power afar and protect its interests in East Asia. China itself, too, seemed determined not to fall easy prey to Japanese expansion. *Deulig Audio Newsreel No. 10* concluded its coverage with the observation, "But China is hanging in there," and footage of a mass demonstration in Nanjing venting popular anger.[35] The final newsreel report on the conflict boded ill for further Japanese adventurism. In a rare feat for newsreels as a medium for capturing breaking news, *Deulig Audio Newsreel No. 23* played original footage of the attempted assassination of Japanese officials in Shanghai celebrating victory.[36] Though some Germans were impressed and won over by Japanese strength, others could see the damaging ramifications such exploits incurred for Japan.

As in the press, the depiction of Japan in newsreels illustrates transnational Nazism's accommodation and glorification of Japan soon after the Nazis' rise to power in January 1933. Instead of criticizing Japan's insatiable ambition, newsreels now used the Sino-Japanese conflict's intermittent nature to report Japan winning battle after battle. Japanese forces reprised their role as habitual victors in *Deulig Audio Newsreel No. 60* in early 1933.[37] The announcer explained that viewers were watching the first footage of the Japanese occupied city of Shanhaikwan on the Great Wall. He added that capturing the city, "the invasion gateway into the province of Jehol, is for Japan worth the withdrawal from the League of Nations." The segment ended with the demolition of the city's fortress by Japanese troops to visibly and audibly emphasize total Japanese domination.

Newsreels' coverage of Japan's domestic transformation likewise illustrates Nazis Germany's approving attitude toward Japanese militarism. The Great Wall, however fragile a barrier in the face of modern arms, provided a boundary marker between Manchukuo and China proper, and the basis for an uneasy ceasefire between 1933 and 1937. Rather than returning to the more innocent themes portrayed before Shanghai in 1932, newsreels zoomed in on the ascent of the military. "War Enthusiasm in Japan," proclaimed the narrator in *Deulig Audio Newsreel No. 57*, as footage showed ecstatic children, youngsters, and women seeing off a division headed for Manchuria.[38] Overflowing throngs of flag-waving well-wishers congested streets and lined the marching route of the soldiers and even the railroad for the troop transports. The scene was repeated at the dock, where the crowd nearly pushed itself into the sea in its eagerness to bid the warriors farewell. Absent was the normal

---

[35] BArch, DTW 10, March 9, 1932.   [36] BArch, DTW 23, June 9, 1932.
[37] BArch, DTW 60, February 22, 1933.   [38] BArch, DTW 57, February 1, 1933.

expression of sadness or worry when loved ones depart for deployment. The people actually seemed jubilant to see their sons and brothers leave to fight on foreign battlefields. Even though no major military action took place at the time, newsreels still described a martial Japan where the whole population supported the nation and military.

For the next few years, until the outbreak of full-scale war between Japan and China in 1937, newsreels maintained their focus on Japan's soldierly comportment. All Japan seemed geared for war. *Fox Audio Newsreel No. 38* showcased in September 1933 an air raid drill in Tokyo. Footage showed plumes of smoke billowing from the city, warplanes buzzing buildings and civilians, and flak firing into the air. The narrator commented: "The whole world is guarding against attacks from the air. Even a country so amply armed with aircraft like Japan runs air raid drills."[39] *Deulig Audio Newsreel No. 148* in October 1934 asked, "What does a Japanese schoolgirl do in her free time?" As cinemagoers watched Japanese teenage girls march with rifles to a firing range and shoot at targets, the voiceover continued, "They learn to shoot, not just a Tesching [handgun] or pistol ... Maybe one day she will stand by her man for real."[40] *Deulig Audio Newsreel No. 157* played a clip of Japanese boys mimicking soldiers and engaging as units in mock combat against one another. Some drilled with wooden sticks standing in for machine guns. Others crawled under and cut imaginary barbed wires. A few wriggled in painted boxes to simulate tanks. The narrator observed, "These tiny Japanese do not mess around with tin soldiers any more. Only the war game battlefield with machine guns and 'Jump up, march, march!' make the eight-year-old heart pound harder."[41] Viewers who maintained their Weimar sensibilities might have found this regimented Japan alarming, but Germany itself was marching in that direction through *Gleichschaltung* and preparations for rearmament and conscription.

The children's older brothers and fathers practiced war, too, just with real weapons. Spectators saw footage of a maneuver in Manchukuo attended by Puyi in *Ufa Audio Newsreel No. 227* in 1935.[42] The soldiers supposedly sported Manchurian colors, but their uniforms looked indistinguishable from those of Japanese troops in previous newsreels. And newspaper readers knew that Manchukuo was virtually a Japanese colony. *Deulig Audio Newsreel No. 174* reported later in the year that Puyi traveled to Japan to pay homage to his patron Hirohito.[43] The monarchs, in uniforms heavy with medals, were surrounded by other

[39] BArch, *Fox Tönende Wochenschau* VII 38, *c.* September 1933.
[40] BArch, DTW 148, October 31, 1934.   [41] BArch, DTW 157, January 2, 1935.
[42] BArch, UTW 227, January 9, 1935.   [43] BArch, DTW 174, May 1, 1935.

uniformed dignitaries as they saluted troops and sailors lining the streets. Again Japan appeared a land dominated by specialists in war. *Deulig Audio Newsreel No. 207* in late 1935 depicted Hirohito "on the white steed of the Mikado" and in full military garb presiding over a coordinated exercise of his armed forces involving masses of men, tanks, and warplanes.[44] In short, newsreels from 1933 chronicled Japan's metamorphosis into a mobilization society in which eight year olds and the emperor alike drilled for combat.

Newsreels' coverage of the Second Sino-Japanese War illustrates the impact of transnational Nazism. When Japan invaded China in July 1937, no attentive viewers would have been surprised. An Ufa program had already revealed in 1936 a Japanese troop build-up in "Turbulent Asia." A lone old lady's sobbing as she saw the soldiers off was drowned out by the crowd waving flags.[45] Of course, Germany and Japan had fundamentally realigned their relations with the Anti-Comintern Pact in 1936. Newsreels' portrayals of Japan, having already begun to glorify Japanese militarism, reflected the new diplomatic reality. Newsreel after newsreel from August 1937 replayed stories of the war, but with a perspective different from that in 1932. An Ufa narrator declared that "the situation in the Far East is again tense" and excused Japanese overreaction by faulting the Chinese for shooting a Japanese soldier.[46] As footage of Japanese troops entering Beijing rolled, a Bavaria newsreel announcer proclaimed, "The Japanese in Peking, to the rejoicing of their countrymen."[47] But in fact viewers saw poor, resigned Chinese sitting on dirt eyeing their conquerors indifferently. In case anyone still doubted where the Nazi regime's sympathy lay, *Ufa Audio Newsreel No. 368* coupled a story on Japanese troops puncturing a Chinese defense line in Shanghai with a segment on Japanese officers in Berlin observing an air raid drill.[48] Whereas in 1932 the newsreels detailed Chinese suffering, in 1937 they switched to trumpeting Japanese successes. Not only did Japan conquer more territory, it also gained more screen time at China's expense. An Ufa story titled "War Theater North China" focused only on Japanese soldiers in armored trains rolling into Beijing and not their impact on the Chinese populace.[49] *Ufa Audio Newsreel No. 374* in November displayed under the segment "China" mostly footage of Japanese offensive actions. Spectators saw the Japanese headquarters, Japanese soldiers using messenger dogs, and Japanese firing on camouflaged enemy

[44] BArch, DTW 207, December 18, 1935.   [45] BArch, UTW 302, June 17, 1936.
[46] BArch, UTW 362, August 11, 1937.
[47] BArch, *Bavaria-Tonwoche* 37, September 8, 1937.
[48] BArch, UTW 368, September 22–26, 1937.   [49] BArch, UTW 364, August 25, 1937.

positions – anything but "China."[50] Even the camera angle betrays a bias for Japan. In contrast to the newsreels in 1932 that zoomed in on individual suffering wrought by aerial bombing, in 1937 the camera literally sided with the attacker by shooting from the bombardier's point of view as he dropped bombs on faceless masses below.[51]

From early 1938, when Germany recalled its last military advisers from China, newsreels unambiguously expressed the Third Reich's preference for powerful Japan over helpless China. *Ufa Audio Newsreel No. 388* in February included footage of Japanese units in their "unstoppable advance" in China across the Yellow River.[52] The narrator spoke admiringly that although Chinese troops had blown up a bridge to hinder the invaders, the Japanese overcame the obstacle by quickly erecting a pontoon bridge. The newsreel stigmatized the Chinese government's training of female volunteer fighters as "following the Bolshevist model." But no such accusation had been raised when Japanese girls were shown learning to shoot. More poignant in demonstrating the filmic fusion of power and aesthetics, a sequence of Japanese cavalrymen charging toward the camera and so the screen would have left spectators with a deep impression of Japan's martial character. The action sequence was probably not captured during actual combat but carefully staged and choreographed – the camera had been strategically placed on the ground to dramatize the horsemen's speed and size.

Transnational Nazism caused the topical, stylistic, and rhetorical disparities between the newsreels on Japanese aggression in 1932 and 1937. Although the Japanese attack on Shanghai in 1937 mirrored that in 1932 – if anything, Japan far outdid itself the second time around – newsreels handled the two instances differently. In 1932, they channeled images of destruction of Chinese properties and lives. But five years later they captured only a triumphant Japan, with little regard for the collateral human costs. As far as can be established, German newsreels gave no coverage of the Nanking Massacre. It cannot be ascertained whether such footage was censored, but it strains credulity that interference by the Nazi regime did not play a role in keeping even a single scene from the six-week long atrocities from reaching the screen. The German embassy in China actually forwarded footage of the event to the Foreign Office and recommended that Hitler watch the material.[53] The changes in Japan's filmic portrayal were not triggered by Japan's actions but by Germany's

[50] BArch, UTW 374, November 5, 1937.   [51] BArch, UTW 372, October 10, 1937.
[52] BArch, UTW 388, February 9, 1938.
[53] *John Rabe: Der gute Deutsche von Nanking,* ed. Erwin Wickert (Stuttgart: Deutsche Verlags-Anstalt, 1997), 256–257.

weltanschauung. Germany had transformed from an internationally oriented republic to a unilateralist dictatorship in the intervening years. What the Weimar Republic had found inhumane, dangerous, and repulsive in Japan was in the Nazis' eyes decisive, powerful, and admirable. As Japan escalated its campaign against China in the 1930s, reports on the war hijacked the overall presentation of Japan, displacing the image of a quaint land of superstition and tradition in the 1920s. The crowd of religious revelers was replaced by the warmongering mob wishing troops good hunting. The villagers' pretty costumes were exchanged for military uniforms. Japan's descent into militarism and Nazism's rise in Germany enabled newsreels to depict Japanese violence beautifully. Had the alternative of a liberal democratic Germany survived, it would likely have continued to denounce Japanese brutality, and cooperation between Berlin and Tokyo would have remained the fantasy of a few ideologues.

Japan as Investigation

After the newsreel, moviegoers often watched an educational documentary (*Kulturfilm*). Ufa founded a culture section in 1918 to produce nonfiction short subjects, which soon became a mainstay category alongside newsreels and feature films. Like newsreels, documentaries conveyed facts and usually lasted no more than 30 minutes, though some spanned enough reels to be billed as full-length feature films. Unlike newsreels, documentaries investigated one theme rather than surveying many, and their contents did not always come across as timely. If newsreels just barely managed to relay current events, documentaries, given the time they spent in postproduction and censorship clearance, could not make any claim of immediacy. Breaking stories such as the Sino-Japanese conflict could force their way into newsreels, but documentarians usually had a specific topic in mind before setting out to shoot the first frame. Thus documentaries featured topics deemed ongoing and likelier to remain applicable even after lengthy editing and censorship processes. Owing to their investigative, exploratory nature and pedagogic mission, documentaries often highlighted subjects beyond the reach of ordinary viewers, such as a flight of the *Graf Zeppelin*.[54]

These peculiarities and limitations meant that documentaries, like newsreels, relied on familiar stereotypes to depict an unfamiliar Japan. Many works, especially from the Weimar years, emphasized the exotic aspects of the country and its inhabitants. In *Colin Ross with a Hand-Crank*

---

[54] BArch, *Graf Zeppelin*, Hamburg-Amerika-Linie, 1929.

Camera around the World, the travel writer took cinemagoers on a grand tour of China, the East Indies, Japan, and India.[55] In Japan, he undertook a grand tour of clichés: rickshaws in Tokyo, a temple in Kobe, cherry blossoms in Kyoto, and "Asia's symbol, the Buddha statue, smiles amicably and wisely over everything." Moviegoers watched in 1928 Japanese rice farmers and pearl divers ply their trades – neither a common sight in Germany. *Rice Cultivation in Japan* was set in a rural village.[56] The storyline revolved around a farmhouse, where peasants gathered and chatted around a low table. They wore outfits suited for agricultural work that Japanese urbanites would also have found strange, to say nothing of Germans sitting comfortably in a cinema. The film time-warped the planting season by displaying in succession the peasants selecting seeds, sowing them in rows, and applying pesticide to seedlings. Even the islands' climate, hot and humid enough to allow flooding the fields, could intrigue viewers only used to continental European weather.

Pearl Culture in Japan, directed by the adventurous photojournalist Martin Rikli, revealed another fascinating side.[57] The documentary portrayed fishermen harvesting pearls in shellfish grown from sand grains inserted earlier. It began on a coast, with several oarsmen rowing a boat away from a Shinto shrine's gate on the sea. The scene, idyllic to a fault, may depict a place other than that identified by the narrator, probably because the filmmaker thought viewers expected a certain iconic look of Japan exuding spirituality and tranquility. The narrator elaborated that natural pearls occur rarely but the Japanese had found a fantastic formula to farm them. Women undertook all pearl-diving and could stay underwater for a superhuman three minutes. Once again, to German cinemagoers, some of whom might not even have seen the sea, Japan appeared as a foreign place where people performed amazing deeds.

This habit of romanticizing and exoticizing Japan continued in the 1930s. Viewers got a more intimate look of Japan in the 1934 documentary *In Spring: A Film of Japanese Spring Festivals*, codirected by Wilhelm Prager and Kishi Kōichi.[58] The film opened with a kimonoed Japanese woman in a traditionally furnished room. It switched to close-up shots of cherry blossoms and then moved to a woman playing a samisen while the soprano Yuasa Hatsue sang in the background. The rest of the film jumped from a doll festival to the pleasure quarters in Kyoto, and from

---

[55] BArch, censorship file of *Colin Roß mit dem Kurbelkasten um die Erde*, dir. Colin Ross, Neumann-Film-Produktion, 1924.

[56] BArch, *Der Reisbau in Japan*, Deutsches Kali-Syndikat, 1928.

[57] BArch, *Perlenzucht in Japan*, dir. Martin Rikli, Ufa-Kulturabteilung, 1928.

[58] BArch, *Im Frühling: Ein Film von japanischen Frühlingsfesten*, dir. Kōichi Kishi and Wilhelm Prager, Ufa, 1934.

a costumed procession in Nara to the bizarre declaration that the Japanese went barefoot because they took pride in the beauty of their feet. Of course, the film mentioned the familiar yet unfamiliar geisha, "whom the European knows only from operetta," but who in fact performed the tea ceremony and practiced floral arrangement as well. The film, though supposedly educational, in reality consisted entirely of tired, predictable snapshots of Japan that spectators already knew from stories and operas from the nineteenth century.

Likewise, *Japan's Holy Volcano*, directed by Arnold Fanck during a cinematographic expedition to East Asia, played on the common stereotype of a traditional, mystic Japan.[59] The narrator pointed out correctly that the "Fujiyama" that everyone knew is actually called Fujisan, but added erroneously that the "holy volcano" amazingly remained snow-capped year-round even though it is further south than Mount Etna in Sicily. For good measure, the motion picture indulged in the standard list of Japanese subjects: toiling peasants, women weaving, cherry blossoms, and children in kimonos.

Japan also made important cameo appearances in two of the most influential full-length documentaries in the 1920s. Wilhelm Prager directed *Ways to Strength and Beauty*, a true "culture film" with the stated mission of enlightening the public. It promoted traditional Japanese lifestyle as an antidote for the ills of modern living.[60] The film began by waxing nostalgic over the ancient Greeks' appreciation of the linkages between aesthetics and health, as seen in their religious beliefs and sculptures. The segment on dancing as an expression of the body's instinct to move featured the dancers Ishii Baku and Ishii Konami performing a pantomime and a "dance of the seagulls." That on exercise crowned jiu-jitsu as Japan's most popular sport, which "needs no strength and is all cleverness." Jiu-jitsu could improve one's well-being not only as exercise but also self-defense – footage showed a jiu-jitsu master subdue his opponent with no force but only finesse. If anyone still needed to ask, "What is jiu-jitsu good for?," the film answered with staged combat in which a lone lady and a short gentleman taught respectively their male and armed would-be assailants a bodily lesson with jiu-jitsu. For Germans terrified by the turbulent early 1920s, the Japanese martial art might seem just the solution for navigating German cities. By elevating ordinary but allegedly quintessential Japanese activities to a secret path for Germans to acquire strength and beauty or at least a skill for surviving the present, the film idealized distant Japan just

---

[59] BArch, *Japans heiliger Vulkan*, dir. Arnold Fanck, Ufa, 1936/1941.
[60] BArch, *Wege zu Kraft und Schönheit*, dir. Wilhelm Prager, Ufa-Kulturabteilung, 1925.

as it idealized temporally distant antiquity. The documentary's pedagogic intention, which supposedly projected trustworthiness, in fact distorted the presentation of Japan through overstating or even mythicizing
the power of its culture and ability of its people.

The less preachy *Melody of the World*, the first feature-length German
talkie, discussed Japan as part of a symphony of global sounds.[61] The
documentary patched together clips of sights and sounds in a simulated
grand tour of the world. When the virtual globetrotter reached East Asia,
he encountered artisans painting paper umbrellas. The film juxtaposed
Japanese women in traditional garb on a richly decorated barge with
European ladies in Western clothes to underscore the foreignness of East
Asia. Cinemagoers also saw an exciting sumo bout and a judo master toss
around his opponent, as well as some Asians eating exotic food with their
even more exotic chopsticks. As the stay in Japan drew to a close, some
indispensable geisha saw the filmic tourist off with a parting dance. Even
when a longer documentary such as *Melody of the World* could devote
time to reveal facets of Japan beyond geisha and sumo wrestlers, it still
picked the path most traveled and stuck with familiar clichés. The truly
novel and dynamic developments in Japan, namely its modernization,
hardly received any attention. Although the documentarians supposedly
shouldered the responsibility of educating the public, they instead
indulged in stereotypes of a stagnant, unchanging Japan.

The primacy of politics in Germany in the early 1930s affected
documentaries' depiction of Japan. Works hawking the clichés did
not disappear, but a new batch of works emerged to investigate contemporary Asia. Colin Ross tried to raise German awareness of happenings in Asia in *Attention Australia! Attention Asia! The Two Faces of
the East.*[62] Ross was a student of geopolitics under Karl Haushofer
and impressed Hitler as an experienced authority on world affairs.[63]
He diagnosed what plagued Australia and Asia as "space without
people" and "people without space" – terms consonant with the Nazi
weltanschauung. The narrator explained that "Australia found a purely
materialist solution, Asia a spiritual one. Both solutions have great
historical significance." He predicted that the momentous changes in
Asia would eventually touch Germany, because once overcrowded

---

[61] BArch, *Melodie der Welt*, dir. Walter Ruttmann, Tobis, 1929.
[62] BArch, *Achtung Australien! Achtung Asien! Das Doppelgesicht des Ostens*, dir. Colin Ross, Ufa-Kulturabteilung, 1930.
[63] On Hitler's high esteem for Ross: see Hitler, *Monologe*, 254 (February 2, 1942); *Documents on German Foreign Policy, 1918–45*, series D, vol. 8 (Washington, DC: US Department of State, 1949), 910–913; Shirer, 683fn; Bailey, 216–227. Bailey was Ross's nephew-in-law.

China "manages to free itself from its past, it can certainly become a danger for Australia, maybe also for us."

Struggle for Manchuria: The World of the Yellow Race, codirected by Johannes Häussler and Gustav von Estorff, spelled out Germany's conundrum in Asia clearly.[64] Germany had to choose between Japan and China, both so-called peoples without space. The documentary stood out from its contemporaries by opening with images of a new Japan, an "adaptable modern civilization." It pointed out similarities between Japan and the West: "Tokyo, the capital of the Japanese Empire, has about 2 million inhabitants and is indistinguishable from a European and American metropolis." But soon footage of rickshaws, coolies, shrines, temples, gardens, and bonsai plants filled the screen. The narrator explained, "The old Japanese culture maintains its presence in art and religion ... Sitting on the floor, the Japanese eats with chopsticks, which he manipulates with only one hand." The film in fact devoted almost four out of its seven reels to show ageless and historical Japan and its lasting legacies.

The documentary built up its case gradually. The narrator mentioned that Japanese religiosity and geography made food shortage a problem, because "despite the [fishermen's] meager catch, the priest takes a tenth part in exchange for interceding with the gods," and that "every speck of land that can be irrigated is planted with rice, Japan's most important staple crop." So controlling Manchuria, "an enormous grain basket," was a matter of national survival. But "Manchuria is populated almost exclusively by the Chinese, who particularly in the last ten years flowed into the region and turned the steppes into productive fields with their frugality and hard work." So the film set the stage for the two nations to contest the area. Eight months after the documentary's release in January, Japan indeed seized Manchuria by force. The filmmakers made clear with which side they sympathized. As footage of destitute and toiling Chinese rolled, the narrator thundered, "Right next to the foreigners' irresponsible indulgence, the Chinese are barely scraping by. Chinese laborers, the cheapest in the world, are being ruthlessly exploited by the foreigners. Where is the morality of the so-called cultured nations that allows hundreds of thousands of Chinese in their most tender ages to waste away at [factory] machines?" It certainly helped that Germany, having lost its colonies, could claim the moral high ground and side with the Chinese to blast their imperialist overlords, in particular the British and the Japanese. The documentary concluded that while Japan took on

---

[64] BArch, *Kampf um die Mandschurei: Die Welt der gelben Rasse*, dir. Gustav von Estorff and Johannes Häussler, Herold-Filmgesellschaft, 1931.

the Western spirit with wonder, China was still struggling to build something new and powerful, but it would be only a question of time before the "yellow race" would succeed.

But this moral outrage did not last. Hitler came to power two years after the release of *Struggle for Manchuria*, in a sense the last Weimar documentary on Japan, and imposed a new political outlook. The Nazi Party affirmed Japan's martial prowess in *Disarmament*.[65] The film echoed a 1933 series in the *Völkischer Beobachter* mocking the Versailles–Washington powers' reluctance to disarm while Germany remained virtually defenseless. The documentary invoked Japan as an example of a great military power like America, Britain, and France. A lacuna separated *Disarmament* and the next extant documentaries on current affairs, *Winter Journey through South Manchuria* and *Imperial Buildings in the Far East*, both shot during Arnold Fanck's expedition in 1936 and released in 1938.[66] Fanck, whose legacy rests with the genre of mountain film, stumbled into the role of a major shaper of the German filmic portrayal of Japan. For financial rather than ideological reasons, Fanck, whose money troubles stemmed in part from his refusal to join the Nazi Party, undertook an expedition to East Asia at the invitation of the Japanese Ministry of Education. Fanck's trip coincided with the diplomatic rapprochement between the two countries, so that even his works reflect transnational Nazism. Whereas his *Japan's Holy Volcano* refrained from overt commentary, *Winter Journey* and *Imperial Buildings*, ostensibly travelogue documentaries, did not. Both motion pictures painted a satisfied, prosperous Manchukuo in its fate as a "Japanese protectorate." They highlighted Japan's ridding the countryside of bandits, outlawing opium to improve public health, and preserving China's former imperial residences in Jehol that the Chinese themselves had abandoned. They omitted the fact that Japan captured the palaces rather than rescued them from Chinese neglect, and urban combat damaged some structures. Of course, by 1938 political reality in Germany had much altered. Fanck, too, had to succumb and make film propaganda. Just as in newsreels, in documentaries the fantastic Japan in the 1920s was replaced by a more muscular one in the 1930s. In the same time span, Germany experienced a regime change that resulted in a leadership that valued strength and victory above all. These two separate strands,

---

[65] BArch, censorship file of *Abrüstung*, NSDAP/Reichspropagandaleitung, 1933.
[66] BArch, *Winterreise durch Südmandschurien: Aufnahmen der japanischen Fanck-Expedition*, dir. Arnold Fanck, Ufa, 1936/1938; BArch, *Kaiserbauten in Fernost: Aufnahmen der japanischen Fanck-Expedition*, dir. Arnold Fanck, Terra-Filmkunst, 1936/1938.

the militarization of Japan and Nazification of Germany, changed how the two countries viewed each other and bilateral collaboration.

The rest of the decade and early 1940s saw a retreat by most documentaries from portraying Japan in blatantly political terms. In a sign of the ideological reorientation under Nazi Germany, Johannes Häussler, a codirector of *Struggle for Manchuria*, now codirected *Great Power Japan*.[67] The title suggests that this lost film sang the praises of the aggressive Japan that he had eloquently denounced. If so, it would stand out as an exception because many documentaries avoided current affairs altogether and reverted to playing up a traditional, beautiful Japan. Fanck managed to extract three more works – all nature films – from the materials he had shot during his expedition: *Rice and Timber in the Land of the Mikado*, *Springtime in Japan*, and *Scenes from Japan's Seashores*.[68] The final feature-length documentary on Japan, *Nippon, the Land of the Rising Sun*, still paraded tired tropes of shrines, temples, kimonos, rice paddies, and cherry blossoms.[69] These motion pictures could still serve a propaganda role for the regime as escapist havens during the war.

For much of the interwar era, documentaries, rather than documenting Japan as it was, specialized in a quixotic mission to discover and romanticize a bygone, static Japan, the very Japan that many Japanese were determined to abandon through adopting Western styles and mores wholesale. Instead of highlighting a modern, dynamic Japan, the documentaries trained their lenses on the primitive, bizarre, and inexplicable. Certainly, some aspects of old Japan appeared because they played a notable, though not prevalent, role in society. But Germany itself had not managed to outrun its shadows from the past. Well into the twentieth century, pedestrians walked on cobblestone streets and shared roads with horse-drawn carriages, even in Berlin or Leipzig.[70] One did not have to look very hard to find an old Germany even though urban Germany arguably defined 1920s modernity. The documentarians, taking the genre's ethnographic if not downright voyeuristic perspective, set out to look for an old Japan and fulfilled their own prophesies by not looking at much else. They ventured to such familiar sites as volcanoes, forests, seashores, and fields – anywhere except where the Japanese actually

---

[67] *Großmacht Japan*, dir. Johannes Häussler and Ernst R. Müller, Rex-Film Bloemer & Co., 1938.

[68] BArch, *Reis und Holz im Lande des Mikado*, dir. Arnold Fanck, Ufa, 1936/1940; BArch, *Frühling in Japan*, dir. Arnold Fanck, Ufa, 1936/1941; BArch, *Bilder von Japans Küsten*, dir. Arnold Fanck, Ufa, 1936/1944.

[69] BArch, *Nippon, das Land der aufgehenden Sonne*, dir. Gerhard Niederstraß, Dr. Edgar Beyfuß-Film Nachf., 1942.

[70] VZ, June 15, 1932.

congregated: the cities. This preference for old Japan explains why none of the documentaries properly treated Tokyo as a subject matter. They turned a blind eye to the obvious and sought out "Japan" in the old imperial capital Kyoto or even ancient Nara. If Japan symbolically left the "feudal" for the modern age by moving the throne from Kyoto to Tokyo, German filmmakers seemed stubbornly stuck in the past with fantasies of an unchanging Japan. Thus many of the documentaries functioned more as animated slideshows of postcards depicting scenic Japan than a medium with a pedagogic mandate.

Japan as Imagination

At last, after sitting through the newsreel and documentary, spectators were treated to the marquee event, the feature film. Movies as historical sources bring with them particular baggage because they do not claim to be factual. The historian must decide how much of a film was meant to be taken as potentially plausible or purely fanciful. Because of their length, creative narratives, and popular appeal, they tended to spend more time in postproduction and censorship than documentaries or newsreels. But even the most fantastic of films must share assumptions with cinemagoers for the plot to resonate. So this section does not hold movies accountable for inaccurate portrayals of Japan but examines the role Japan played in Germany's filmic imagination – the representation rather than the presentation of Japan.

Early Weimar movies on Japan mostly toed storylines in nineteenth-century literature or performance art. The romantic comedy *The Maiden from Japan* relied on the familiar unfamiliar as shorthand to unfold its plot.[71] It revolved around the female lead Liesl maneuvering the male protagonist Ernst to give up his obsession with Japan and fall in love with her. Ernst, in rejecting Liesl, made a gesture indicating a short person and said, "I will not marry any of the boring European ladies! Only a Japanese maiden will be my wife." Just a flip of the hand and a spatter of words neatly pigeonholed all Japanese women as short, exotic, and different from European ones. Liesl then concocted a scheme to masquerade as a Japanese maid to lure her love interest. Wearing a kimono, heavy make-up, and her hair in knots, she reemerged as the daughter of a Japanese man named "Naga Hari," an allusion to the mysterious Mata Hari. The Dutch-born Mata Hari had nothing to do with Japan, but all Oriental exoticness could seem equally exotic anyway.

---

[71] BArch, *Das Mädel aus Japan*, dir. Toni Attenberger, Bayerische Filmindustrie, 1919.

Lifting but tweaking a scene from the musical *The Geisha*, the plot then had Liesl entreat Ernst to teach her kissing: "In Japan, I heard much about a peculiar German custom. It is called 'kissing.' Please show and learn [*sic*] it to me!"[72] As Ernst fell head over heels for Liesl's alter ego, Liesl broke the fourth wall and giddily confided to viewers, "What one cannot in German achieve, one can with Japanese deceive." Now firmly in charge, Liesl demanded that Ernst become Japanese and shave his beard and hair to resemble a samurai. She also had him put on a robe and pull her in a rickshaw, all chores meant to tire him of Japan. She then asked some itinerant Japanese acrobats, played by Caucasian actors in make-up, to help her cure Ernst of his "Japanese infection." Claiming to Ernst that they belonged to the "Green Dragon Society," they pretended to kidnap Liesl back to Japan. Ernst fought off the pseudo-assailants and declared: "I tell you all, not another word from Japan. I do not want to know anything more from it." On that cue, Liesl revealed her true identity and said, "It is very good then that I cannot speak Japanese." The lovers kissed, this time genuinely, as the curtains closed.

The Maiden from Japan embodies common Weimar stereotypes of Japan as exotic, impenetrable, and perhaps mildly threatening. The silent movie made the point of fabricating dialogues in gibberish in the subtitles and zooming in on the ransom note with illegible scribbles, all to underscore the strangeness of Japanese. The appearance and action of "the Japanese" invoked a uniform, robotic, and indistinguishable mass. All Japanese looked alike: hair in a knot, ghostly pale, and in flowing robes. Their stiff, slow corporeal movement, especially with arbitrary bowing, came across as unnatural and otherworldly. They exhibited little individuality or originality by acting in unison and following Liesl's order to rid Ernst of his Japanese disease. This obsequiousness was taken for granted by many Europeans as quintessentially Japanese.

Fritz Lang's *Harakiri* drew from a common pool of clichéd props, with a plot that closely followed that of *Madama Butterfly*.[73] But Lang injected his own vision and current artistic trends such as German Expressionism into the film. The Japanese characters, played by Europeans, moved in a slow, deliberate, and exaggerated manner. Yet viewers unfamiliar with avant-garde cinema might mistake it for typically Japanese behavior. A film critic lauded the movie: "It is uncanny how fully the Japanese subject lives up to the innermost essence of the film that spoken words are not missed even for a moment because one can imagine the life of the

---

[72] *The Geisha, a Story of a Tea House* was composed by Sidney Jones and Lionel Monckton, and first performed in London in 1896.
[73] BArch, *Harakiri*, dir. Fritz Lang, Decla-Film-Ges. Holz & Co., 1919.

Japanese with their excessively polite trifles as a kind of silent panto-mime."[74] Viewers saw plenty of rickshaws, prostrations on all fours, heavy make-up, hair in top knots, and sundry other supposedly Asian scenery such as temples and teahouses. Lang also introduced a visually appealing but fictitious "festival of falling leaves." The movie featured its own Mata Hari, an incongruously named Japanese prince who wooed O-Take-San, who rejected him to wait for her husband Olaf Anderson. When Anderson returned to Japan, now with his "real," Caucasian wife, O-Take-San stoically committed ritual suicide, because "to die with honor is better than to live in shame."

Several other period movies exploited similar themes. The titles of lost movies, including *The Geisha and the Samurai*, *The Kwannon of Oka Temple*, and *The Japanese Mask: The Bandit Nest on the Eagle Rock*, hint at a backdrop in traditional, static rather than new, dynamic Japan.[75] Two more works set in Japan were released in 1926: *Bushido, the Iron Code* and *The White Geisha*. *Bushido*, codirected by Heinz Karl Heiland and Kako Zanmu, was the first movie made jointly by Germans and Japanese.[76] The participation of a Japanese screenwriter did not result in a nuanced or less predictable plot. Indeed, the film indulged in old, exotic Japan with a story set in the sixteenth century. Viewers saw the obligatory checklist of hara-kiri, geisha, and samurai. Likewise, much of *The White Geisha*, codirected by Heiland and Valdemar Andersen, unfolded in Kyoto and its atmosphere of mystery and intrigue.[77] Few Japanese, real or represented, starred in the movie. Instead, the Caucasian female and male leads portrayed a geisha and a rickshaw puller. Together the two pseudo-Japanese foiled a European villain's plot. They then resumed their true identity and lived happily ever after.

To this point, Japan and its people appeared in German cinema specifically as Japanese, however anachronistically or quixotically, so that viewers could see conventional symbols and roles. Rather than individuals marked by individualities, the Japanese in movies were characters confined by characteristics. Their appearances hardly changed. Their traits remained constant. Their outlooks lacked room for development.

---

[74] *Berliner Börsenzeitung*, December 21, 1919; Lotte H. Eisner, *Fritz Lang* (London: Da Capo Press, 1976), 28.

[75] *Die Geisha und der Samurai*, dir. Carl Boese, Firmament-Film, 1919; *Die Kwannon von Okadera*, dir. Carl Froelich, Decla-Bioscop and Uco-Film, 1920; *Die japanische Maske I: Das Banditennest auf dem Adlerstein*, dir. Heinz Karl Heiland, Eiko-Film, 1921.

[76] *Bushido, das eiserne Gesetz*, dir. Heinz Karl Heiland and Zanmu Kako, Deutsch-Nordische Film-Union, 1926.

[77] BArch, *Die weiße Geisha*, dir. Heinz Karl Heiland and Valdemar Andersen, Deutsch-Nordische Film-Union, 1926.

The "Japanese" were condemned to fulfill, not act, certain roles with thoughts and behaviors defined and preprogrammed by their ethnicity. The Japanese in early Weimar movies, always in groups, interchangeable, and without distinguishable identities, were inserted into plots to "be Japanese." Europeans such as Liesl and Ernst could transform externally and internally, but the Japanese stayed the same throughout the plot and indeed early Weimar movies. This essentializing style was also used by much of the contemporary press.

Filmmakers imagined a different Japan to weave logical storylines from the late 1920s. Ufa released the espionage thriller *Spies* in 1928, directed by Fritz Lang and written by his wife Thea von Harbou.[78] The plot pioneered most elements in the spy film genre: a conspiratorial organization, an evil mastermind, a femme fatale, a dashing agent, and plenty of action and plot twists. In *Spies*, Haghi, intent on plunging the world into war, built a shadowy empire with tentacles everywhere. He learned that Japan had signed a secret treaty, "the most consequential in a century," and wanted to snatch it before it reached Japan. The Japanese diplomat Masimoto, wearing thick, black framed eyeglasses associated with the allegedly poor eyesight of the Japanese, took extra caution and assigned three separate couriers. He ordered, "Whoever fails to deliver his letter with the seal intact does not deserve to be called a Japanese!" Haghi had the carriers intercepted and killed, only to discover that they held decoy copies – Masimoto retained the original. But Haghi was not to be outwitted. He had already placed a seductress near Masimoto. She put on Japanese clothing and Masimoto, in a moment of weakness, gave in to her charms, and she duly made off with the document. The three agents' ghosts then appeared before Masimoto to return the diplomatic pouches and remind him of his own words. Deeply ashamed, Masimoto knelt down before a statue of Buddha and committed hara-kiri.

Though entertaining, the episode was only a sideshow in the larger plot, which could advance without mentioning Japan. Haghi was ultimately destroyed, his schemes thwarted, all without Japan's participation. Why then did Lang and Harbou add the subplot? Lang had shown his interest in Japan already in *Harakiri*. Then he named the nightclub in *Metropolis* "Yoshiwara," after the pleasure quarters of old Tokyo.[79] *Harakiri* did not show O-Take-San taking her own life, but *Spies* devoted several minutes to the sequence of Masimoto's ritual suicide. Lang must have become more knowledgeable about Japanese culture between the two movies. Moreover, Japan fitted well within a narrative of conspiracy.

---

[78] BArch, *Spione*, dir. Fritz Lang, Ufa, 1928.   [79] *Metropolis*, dir. Fritz Lang, Ufa, 1927.

The mysterious aura that had given traditional Japan its allure in early German films was transformed into secrecy as modern Japan began to appear on screen. Japan's threat stemmed precisely from a combination of supposedly Asian inscrutability with Western technology, a theme evident in late Weimar newsreels. That Japan had risen to match the West in industry and war unsettled many in Europe. So it made sense to invoke Japan, even tangentially, in a feature film on world domination.

This Japan, dangerous for its ambition and success in imitating the West, was even more clearly articulated in *Police File 909*, directed by Robert Wiene.[80] The movie opened with the theft of an experimental serum against plagues. But in unfinished form the serum posed a grave danger to the world. Detective Bninski suspected that some Asians had stolen the serum but needed more time to perfect the potion. So he asked a club singer to infiltrate the secretive coterie. She bewitched its ringleader Dr. Tokeramo with her charms, learned of the Asians' scheme, and passed on the information to Bninski. Tokeramo killed Bninski in a struggle. One of the cunning Asians attempted to take the blame so that Tokeramo could finish working on the serum. But an astute judge uncovered the truth in a courtroom and apprehended the whole clique. The serum was recovered and humanity rendered safe.

The film never specified that the "Asians" were Japanese, but it did not need to. Beyond such obvious clues as the clothing and bowing, cinemagoers could deduce that only Japan had the capacity and motive to pose a threat to the world. Like *Spies*, *Police File 909* assigned Japan a role because no other non-Western nation seemed as potentially menacing. This filmic vision of a dangerous Japan paralleled some literary imaginations. Ludwig Anton's science fiction *The Japanese Plague* described Japan readying itself for germ warfare against America.[81] Arnold Mehl's novel *Shadows of the Rising Sun* had Japan steal chemicals from Europe to attack the continent with poison gas.[82] *Police File 909* itself was adapted from Melchior Lengyel's 1913 play *Typhoon*.

But *Police File 909* reveals more outside than within its storyline. The movie had been slated to premiere in 1933 as *Typhoon*.[83] But the censorship board, now with a member from the new Ministry of Propaganda, found fault with what it called the relatively negative portrayal of

[80] BArch, *Polizeiakte 909*, dir. Robert Wiene, Camera-Film-Produktion, 1934.
[81] Ludwig Anton, *Die japanische Pest* (Bad Rothenfelde: J. G. Holzwarth, 1922).
[82] Arnold Mehl, *Schatten der aufgehenden Sonne* (Leipzig: Wilhelm Goldmann Verlag, 1935).
[83] There is apparently no extant copy of the remade *Police File 909*. The original *Typhoon*, though without audio, is available at the Federal Archives. The plot summary above is drawn from *Illustrierter Film-Kurier* 16, no. 2134 (1934).

Caucasians vis-à-vis Asians and the love affair between a European woman and an Asian man.[84] So editors renamed and substantially altered the narrative, and removed the offending parts. The movie won approval for release in 1934, but just barely. The *Völkischer Beobachter* review savaged its contrived storyline and the "still more embarrassing" interracial romance, and concluded that sensible viewers would want to be at the North Pole if the film played at the South.[85] The postproduction saga documents Germany's ideological transformation. In a sense, *Typhoon* was the last Weimar movie on Japan, *Police File 909* the first Nazi one. It also exemplifies the limit of Nazi accommodation of Japan: a powerful, even menacing, Japan was allowed on screen, but intimately embracing the Japanese was not.

Because feature films lacked newsreels' message nimbleness and currency, the first movie on Japan filmed under the Third Reich appeared only after the Anti-Comintern Pact. *Port Arthur*, released in December 1936, was set in the besieged harbor during the Russo-Japanese War.[86] The plot revolved around the conflicting loyalties of Boris Ranewsky, a Russian naval officer, and his Japanese wife Youki, the sister of a fanatical undercover agent. Squeezed between countries and families, the couple struggled to fulfill their national and family duties. With the stronghold about to fall to Japan, Boris and Youki attempted to break out of the blockade in a torpedo boat. Unsuccessful, they went down with the ship in each other's arms to uphold their honor and love.

Although the movie suffered from common ills such as portraying European actors as Asians, a Japanese as a spy, and romance between a white man and a Japanese woman, it departed from some well-trodden paths. Boris and Youki were married without ulterior motives and stayed together despite pressure from Boris's superior officer and Youki's brother. The Japanese exhibited individual personalities and outlooks rather than inherited Japanese attitudes: Youki refused her brother's demand that she betray Boris out of patriotism. The movie not only depicted an East Asian power triumph over a Western one, a rare sight in cinema, but it focused specifically on Japan defeating Russia. The movie was finished and approved for distribution in the same transnational Nazi atmosphere that facilitated German-Japanese rapprochement. It premiered opportunely about two weeks after the conclusion of the Anti-Comintern Pact implicitly targeting the Soviet Union.

---

[84] Uli Jung and Walter Schatzberg, *Beyond Caligari: The Films of Robert Wiene* (New York: Berghahn Books, 1999), 171–176.
[85] VB, July 31, 1934, NGE.
[86] *Port Arthur*, dir. Nicolas Farkas, F.C.L. and Slavia-Film AG, 1936.

Germany and Japan also articulated their realignment through film propaganda. *The Samurai's Daughter*, directed by Arnold Fanck and coproduced by the two countries, was released in March 1937.[87] The movie represents a regression of Japan's image on screen. Fanck sprinkled footage of urban, modern Japan throughout the movie, but the overall plot took place in a setting of clichés. Cinemagoers saw a volcanic eruption, an earthquake, coastlines, and straw-roofed huts in the opening minutes. The potentially iconoclastic spark – the flicker of interracial romance between the Japanese Teruo and the German Gerda – was smothered by the weight of Teruo's loyalty to his prearranged marriage and adoption into an old samurai family. The plot satisfied Fanck's propaganda bosses in Berlin and paymasters in Tokyo. In Germany, the film was billed as "national-politically and artistically valuable," not least because it implicitly repudiated the interracial liaisons in previous movies. The Nazi regime promoted the film with much fanfare, including arranging for the lead actress Hara Setsuko, "a delicate, exquisitely graceful young maiden – an enchanting Japanese woman," to sign autographs.[88] In Japan, the movie's skewed treatment of traditional and contemporary Japan coincided with the militarists' own campaign to reshape and glorify the past for present use. The motion picture depicted current Japan not much more faithfully than its 1920s predecessors, but in 1937 official Japan joined the filmmakers in advocating an idealized but distorted vision of the country. The movie ended with scenes of toiling rice farmers in Japan as a voiceover explained that there were now too many people for this speck of land. The next scene showed Teruo on a tractor plowing a field effortlessly while his Japanese wife and infant looked on – in Manchuria. An armed sentinel smiled and stood guard over the settler family. He then turned to stare resolutely in viewers' eyes as curtains closed. Transnational Nazi filmmaking could admire Japanese strength and aggression from afar, but not Germans and Japanese getting personally too close.

With the invocation of nature, traditional values, and history, *The Samurai's Daughter* returned the focus of the camera lenses to a version of the bygone, outdated Japan seen in the 1920s. Germany and Japan collaborated on one other film, *The Holy Goal*, set in Hokkaido in anticipation of the Winter Olympics in Japan.[89] The onset of World War II greatly reduced international travel and shipment of equipment

---

[87] BArch, *Die Tochter des Samurai*, dir. Arnold Fanck, Dr. Arnold Fanck-Film, 1937. In Japan, the film appeared as *Atarashiki tsuchi* (*New Earth*).
[88] BArch, promotional materials for *Die Tochter des Samurai*.
[89] BArch, *Das heilige Ziel*, dir. Kōshō Nomura, Cocco-Film, 1939.

and reels. *The Samurai's Daughter* was recycled, recensored, and rereleased in 1943 as *The Love of Mitsu* to reinforce the mirage of German-Japanese solidarity. Because the much ballyhooed Berlin-Tokyo Axis had few concrete results to show, reused footage would just have to do.

Transnational Nazism in Films

Around the time of Pearl Harbor in late 1941, German cinemagoers saw the Ufa documentary *Salt Harvesting in Japan*.[90] The narrator explained that Japan, unlike Europe, has no salt mines and so must extract salt from seawater. The process required intensive labor, as workers had to haul containers of seawater to fields and spray it over shallow pools. Machinery was used only toward the end to evaporate the last bit of water. Salt, he continued, had many uses, such as in producing soap, glass, and magnesium. The film closed with panoramic footage of a gleaming aircraft, while the narrator gloated that light metals drawn from sea salt went into constructing the machine. Here spectators were again fed the mixture of facts and fantasies that characterized the German filmic imagination of Japan. Japan did obtain chemicals from the sea for its war effort, but not in quantities that were large enough to make a difference.

Germany's presentation and representation of Japan in all film categories resemble a sentimental romance film writ large. Particularly in the 1920s, filmmakers were infatuated with a vision of Japan that only marginally corresponded with reality. Japan appeared as a faraway fableland, with its people living by inexplicable rituals and traditions. Germans' interest in Japan, as reflected on their screens, differed little from Olaf Anderson's interest in O-Take-San in *Harakiri* – intense at times but fundamentally superficial and cursory. All the interracial pairings in the movies ended in tragedy: humiliating betrayal and suicide in *Harakiri*, seduction for ulterior motives in *Spies* and *Police File 909*, death together in *Port Arthur*, and breakup in *The Samurai's Daughter*. But age-old cultural prejudice had more to do with the failures than Nazism's nasty biological racism. German motion pictures exhibit orientalism in tapping into the lingering Japonism and Chinoiserie from a previous age. They also show a measure of European arrogance in pigeonholing and objectifying an entire people as stock characters, such as geisha, samurai, monks, and rickshaw drivers.

---

[90] BArch, *Salzgewinnung in Japan*, Ufa, 1941.

Directors shot, and viewers watched, much footage on geisha, festivals, shrines and temples, kimonos, cherry blossoms, and Mount Fuji, but not many other topics. Germans could glean from films much knowledge of Japan, though in too confined an aspect. German cinema focused on a version of Japan that the Japanese themselves were largely leaving behind. Not only did the directors choose too narrow a lens to capture Japan, they also pointed their cameras in the wrong direction – backward. Just when the Japanese were reducing Kyoto to an open-air museum, German filmmakers flocked to the former imperial capital and country-side in search of "real Japan." Figuratively, as the Japanese collectively departed villages and Kyoto for factories and Tokyo, somewhere along the road they ran into camera-toting Germans traveling in the opposite direction and taking snapshots. That encounter, capturing a mostly traditional Japan with glimpses of the modern, branded the filmic infor-mation, investigation, and imagination of Japan for much of the interwar era.

Rather than revealing what might truly strike cinemagoers as novel, namely how Japan resembled Germany and other industrialized coun-tries, the filmmakers emphasized the familiar of the unfamiliar. Especially in the 1920s, documentaries and movies relied on widely shared stereo-types that stressed the foreign and mysterious qualities of Japan and its people. The spectators may be excused for not expecting more because they could not visit Japan, but the filmmakers, in their role as opinion makers, enhanced viewers' ignorance with scenes exoticizing Japan. The directors shirked their responsibility of enlightening the populace and merely perpetuated common caricatures. Instead of leading the public, the filmmakers joined it.

New technology and ideology in Germany in the early 1930s altered the portrayals of Japan. Newsreels shifted their focus from foreign curi-osities to war. Audio enabled newsreels and documentaries not just to chronicle but comment on current events. Many moviegoers saw and heard combat for the first time in the weekly shows on the fighting in Shanghai in 1932. Confronted by Japanese militarism and unrestrained by domestic politics, late Weimar newsreels and documentaries con-demned the aggressor and sympathized with the aggrieved. The Third Reich enforced new morals and attitudes, though transnational Nazism affected each of the film categories differently. Newsreels felt its impact immediately and starkly. They switched to admire the Japanese mobiliza-tion and militarism that they had denounced just months before. When Japan again attacked China in 1937, the newsreels sided with Japan in rhetoric and imagery. The events in 1932 and 1937 were similar but interpreted differently because of the transnational Nazi appreciation for

Japanese strength. Documentaries were less agile in responding to current events, though some managed to incorporate comments partial to Japan. Movies, slower still, propagated German-Japanese rapprochement only after the Anti-Comintern Pact. That the regimes used feature films to publicize and contextualize their alliance attests the perceived importance of the medium. New realities in international relations dictated a new purpose for cinema as a diplomatic space for joint productions.

But for ordinary viewers, these changes meant that they knew only two faces of Japan, the dainty one of geisha and cherry blossoms and the martial one of soldiers and grenades that displaced it. The Japanese mostly had predictably "Japanese" traits and little individuality in both cases. They wore either kimonos or uniforms. Even when they wore suits in *Spies* or *Police File 909*, they were still engaged in nefarious plots, so modern, liberal, and peaceful Japan never received proper screen time. The supposed mystery and inscrutability of Japan lent credibility to such storylines. Ironically, it was the Nazi regime that de-emphasized some old stereotypes, though it did so mostly to promote its own biases.

For someone who never set foot in Japan and likely did not meet a Japanese until the forty-first year of his life in 1930, Hitler did not lack fixed ideas about the land or its people. Even as a schoolboy in Austria in 1904, he had already formed his anti-Slavic worldview, so he rooted for Japan in the Russo-Japanese War.[1] In *Mein Kampf*, written two decades later, he denigrated the Japanese as a "culture carrying" folk suited only for aping the "culture generating" Aryans. But he also envied Japanese racial purity because Jewry could not infiltrate the "yellow Asiatics" as it had the white races.[2] Instead, the Jews would have to destroy Japan from the outside by manipulating Britain and America.[3] In his unpublished "second book," dictated in 1928, he lambasted the Kaiserreich for challenging and thus compelling Britain to form the Anglo-Japanese Alliance, when landlubbing Germany could have "played the role of Japan" to seafaring Britain.[4] The Führer pursued Anglo-German rapprochement after coming to power. But after failing to woo Britain, it was he who was left to settle for Japan as an ersatz ally.

As the leader of the strongest member state in the Anti-Comintern and Tripartite coalitions, Hitler had received numerous Japanese visitors and briefings about Japan by the 1940s. He esteemed some of the individuals he met, notably Ōshima Hiroshi, whom he praised lavishly.[5] He also spoke of Japan as a "first-rank military power" and the Berlin-Tokyo Axis as the "greatest guarantee of German security."[6] He even conceded that the German navy could learn from its Japanese counterpart.[7] Beyond admiration for Japan, his compliments conveyed discontent with conditions in Germany. He criticized German technicians for having laughed off Japanese midget submarines before Pearl Harbor. And he

---

[1] Hitler, *Mein Kampf*, 173; Hitler, *Monologe*, 64 (September 21, 1941).
[2] Hitler, *Mein Kampf*, 318–319.   [3] Ibid., 723–724.
[4] Adolf Hitler, *Hitlers zweites Buch: Ein Dokument aus dem Jahr 1928* (Stuttgart: Deutsche Verlags-Anstalt, 1961), 172.
[5] Hitler, *Monologe*, 177 (January 4–5, 1941).   [6] Ibid., 269–270 (February 6, 1942).
[7] Ibid., 181 (January 5–6, 1942).

used the Japanese emperor to illustrate the importance of unifying state authority and ideological power in one person.[8] Japan thus frequently served Hitler as a measuring stick for Germany.

Despite access to secret intelligence and Japanese personnel afforded by his position as Führer, much of Hitler's conceptualization of Japan remained the stale mix of prejudice and awe left over from his youth. He never got over Britain spurning his advances. If Britain would only accept German domination of Europe, he ranted, he never would have resorted to allying with Japan.[9] He pontificated that Germans could not have a deep relationship with the Japanese because "their culture and lifestyle are too alien to us."[10] In table talks during World War II, he thundered at Britain for refusing his outstretched hand and then either indulged in schadenfreude over the dismantling of the British Empire or regretted the white race's "loss" of the Far East to Japan.[11] And he did not stray far from his condescension toward Japanese creativity. The same night that he said that the German navy could learn from Japan, he also dispensed backhanded praise for Japan as a more discreet imitator than Russia. Then he likened a comparison between the ancient cultures of Greece and of Japan and China to one between Beethoven and screeching cats.[12] He held firm in his belief that the Japanese constituted a homogeneous race and so a natural enemy for Jewry.[13] Shortly after the attack on Pearl Harbor, the Führer reflected on Japan in an impromptu lecture that showcased the hodgepodge of personal impression, self-delusion, stereotypes, half-truths, and falsehood that characterized his understanding of the country and people:

The self-contained Japanese pose a danger to the Jews, who consequently agitated Britain and America to isolate Japan. Just as there have always been two Germanys, there have been two Japans: one capitalist and so Anglophilic; the other, the Japan of the Rising Sun, the realm of the samurai. The navy has always been excellent in this Japan. Those Japanese standing by us belong to the navy. But some attached to the royal court whom I met struck me as downright decadent. The Japanese never had a war in their own country in 2,600 years![14]

Although Hitler did not need to be a Japanologist, he should have known Germany's most important partner at least somewhat better by 1942. The Japanese army, not the navy, favored collaboration with Germany. He heard of the 2,600th anniversary in 1940 when the Japanese government celebrated with fanfare and propaganda Japan's mythical founding

---

[8] Ibid., 174 (January 3–4, 1942).   [9] Ibid., 240 (January 27, 1942).
[10] Ibid., 184 (January 7, 1942).   [11] Ibid., 156 (December 18, 1941).
[12] Ibid., 180 (January 5–6, 1942).   [13] Ibid., 280 (February 17, 1942).
[14] Ibid., 177 (January 4–5, 1942).

in 660 BC. Japan suffered several civil wars, fought by the very samurai whom he exalted in the same breath, though as a class they had been abolished well before his birth.

Exposure to confidential information and Japanese personalities hardly softened Hitler's long-ossified opinions of Japan and its populace. His adolescent preference for any enemy of the Slavs, including the Japanese, was rehashed in *Mein Kampf*. The dogmas on the Japanese racial make-up and intellect that he pronounced in the book resurfaced in monologues two decades later. Because Hitler did not have the means to learn about the Japanese firsthand until late in life, he derived his knowledge from the media such as newspapers and books. By all accounts, Hitler read avidly and kept a collection of books that grew with his status. When he became chancellor, he gained control of the chancellery library. But as in cultural history, it is difficult to prove which publications influenced his views. Hitler likely did not read all the books he owned. Many authors, some even from Japan, submitted their works to the Führer as presents. Only a portion of his personal library is extant, while the chancellery library was probably destroyed. Almost all the books on Japan found in his possession were published in the 1940s, long after his weltanschauung had taken shape.[15]

Yet the making of the Führer's views on Japan is of more than anecdotal interest. Until 1930, Hitler was one of many Germans who learned about distant places from authors. Hitler distrusted experts such as diplomats, academics, and high-ranking officers, but he did not dismiss expertise per se. In one monologue, he criticized his diplomats for failing to give him the information he wanted and said that he "got better intelligence from those like Colin Ross who traveled all over."[16] Most Germans did not have the luxury of choosing which groups of specialists to believe. After newspapers and films, they faced few options in acquiring further knowledge of Japan. Some might attend the handful of universities that offered Japan-related classes. Those in Berlin or Hamburg might join social clubs to make Japanese friends. But both institutions of higher education and binational associations maintained barriers to entry that excluded precisely the uninitiated who could benefit most from participation.

---

[15] Philipp Gassert and Daniel S. Mattern, *The Hitler Library: A Bibliography* (Westport: Greenwood Press, 2001); Ambrus Miskolczy, *Hitler's Library*, trans. Rédey Szilvia and Michael Webb (Budapest: Central European University Press, 2003); Timothy W. Ryback, *Hitler's Private Library: The Books That Shaped His Life* (New York: Alfred A. Knopf, 2008).

[16] Hitler, *Monologe*, 254 (February 2, 1942).

For the vast majority of Germans, the books in their local bookstores or libraries were the most accessible and authoritative source of information on Japan. Creative works such as novels and plays were undoubtedly popular – Hitler likely learned about samurai from a show or story rather than from a monograph. Yet literature's artificiality makes it a problematic historical source, so this chapter explores the depictions of Japan in nonfiction only. The German National Library in Leipzig preserves about 600 such publications from 1919 to 1937. Many, typically works in German published overseas, were unknown to contemporary readers because the sole copies were in Leipzig. This chapter concentrates on nonfiction accessible to general readers and with a claim to discuss Japan knowledgeably. Missionaries, scholars, travelers, and political commentators wrote on different aspects of Japan, but they shared a fundamental respect and appreciation for Japanese successes and exploits. Japan's perceived significance for Germany prompted them to study the country and share their findings with readers. Upheavals in Germany markedly affected the quantity, quality, and type of publications. Several authors who wrote about Japan had no firsthand exposure to the country and its population, or if they did, linguistic and practical barriers permitted only superficial generalizations. Thus works from the 1920s often seem indistinguishable from those a decade later, and many relied on stereotypes to depict Japan as a "country of juxtaposition." This descriptive trope allowed authors to selectively admire Japan. From the early 1930s, transnational Nazi writers highlighted features of Japan that suited their ideology, such as willingness to use force and defiance of the international order. Under the Third Reich's unconventional diplomatic posture, they advocated and even practiced German-Japanese convergence in their publications.

Japan According to Missionaries

Even when the interwar economy was at its best, the cost of transportation meant that only affluent Germans could afford a sojourn in East Asia. Expatriates in Japan had usually been dispatched by organizations for specific purposes such as trade, diplomacy, sports, or journalism. Especially in the early Weimar era, books by these professionals constituted an important source of information. Churches were one such institution with the wherewithal to send Germans – missionaries – to Japan and print books with little regard for financial gain. Missions played an outsized role in acquainting Germans with Japan after World War I because businesses and the government struggled to reestablish a foothold in the country. Although the hostilities did not leave a bitter legacy between Germany and Japan, Germans in Japan had suffered deportation and expropriation. Some petitioned the Japanese state for redress after the war but had only limited success.[17] Germany's official representation could offer little help because the embassy and consulates themselves needed to be restaffed. In a sign of the straitened times, as late as September 1922 the embassy was still using stationery of the "Imperial German Embassy," only with "Imperial" crossed out.[18]

In contrast to the recovering businesses and diplomatic stations, religious missions had not suffered severely and were better positioned to relay intelligence. The Japanese government had not imposed restrictions on German missionaries during the war. Afterward, they were admitted into Japan without hindrance.[19] At least one book on Japan or East Asia was published by a Christian press almost every year in the interwar era. Johannes Witte, a leading Protestant evangelist, reported in 1919 that Germany's heroic war effort had made a deep impression on the Japanese. He added that his mission was prepared to take advantage of the opportunity to inculcate a pro-German attitude among the populace.[20] The Catholic Church and many Protestant denominations proselytized in Japan. But the General Protestant Mission Association (Allgemeiner Evangelisch-Protestantischer Missionsverein, AEPM), an umbrella organization, dominated book production. Readers in Germany searching for current descriptions of Japan in the early 1920s could hardly miss those by the association. Other missions also published books on their activities in later years.

The missionaries generally praised Japan and the accomplishments of Japanese civilization. In *Japan: Country and People*, AEPM Inspector Emil Knodt described Japan as a healthy realm where the autumn sun bathed the land in light and natural beauty charmed visitors.[21] He admired Japan's development into a "cultured state" (*Kulturstaat*) and participation in the "modern life" through establishing excellent universities, a parliament, and a mighty military. Japan belonged to the great powers of the world.[22] He found the Japanese people "brave, hardworking, frugal, obedient and dutiful, sentimental, nature-loving and

---

[17] BArch, R 906/1699, estates of Johann Friedrich Heiderich, 1914–1930; PA AA, R 31245, Ostasiatischer Verein to Foreign Office, December 17, 1924.

[18] PA AA, R 85902, Renner to Foreign Office, September 18, 1922.

[19] PA AA, R 85953, report by Foreign Office, *c.* June 1920.

[20] BArch, R 57NEU/1045, Witte to Deutsches Ausland-Institut, February 10, 1919.

[21] Emil Knodt, *Japan: Land und Leute* (Berlin: Allgemeiner Evangelisch-Protestantischer Missionsverein, 1919), 4.

[22] Ibid., 7–8.

religious, very clever and very sensuous. They are outwardly very amiable, always smiling, friendly, collected, and peaceful in manner."[23]

Other religious writers echoed that glowing portrayal. AEPM Director Johannes Witte expressed similar sentiments in *Japan Today* in 1926. He proclaimed that few countries exceeded Japan in physical beauty. Specifically, Japan's sunny autumn impressed this German, too.[24] Nature posed some challenges to Japan, such as a shortage of resources and frequent disasters, but he could see the land's same charming, mild temperament in the people, at least in their public life.[25] Anton Ceska, a Catholic missionary, wrote in 1932 about the attractive Japanese landscape, one that could almost rival that of his beloved Austria.[26] He was fascinated by what he saw as the arrangement of Japanese society as one big family, in which "everyone builds in the same style, eats the same food, and celebrates the same festivals." Japan's strength, he reasoned, lay in this unity that provided a foundation for the state.[27] One must wonder how well the priest actually knew the place he called home for over 25 years. Even a newcomer would soon have recognized the diversity within Japan, especially the different local holidays and delicacies in which regions took so much pride. But the notion of the homogeneous "island nation of Japan" was so entrenched that even someone with much experience still used the cliché to articulate what he witnessed there.

The missionaries' appreciation for Japan extended even to religion. Diatribes against Shinto or Buddhism were absent. Instead, the proselytizers devoted much analytical effort to study local belief systems. Witte published *The Religions of East Asia: China and Japan* in 1926, an overview of Buddhism and Shinto that was free of derogatory remarks.[28] AEPM Superintendent Emil Schiller wrote *Shinto, the National Religion of Japan* in 1935. He discussed in erudite tones aspects of Shinto such as its relations with nature and reverence for the emperor and ancestors.[29] Another missionary linked to the AEPM, Wilhelm Gundert, wrote a dissertation in 1925 on the treatment of Shinto in Noh theater.[30]

---

[23] Ibid., 14.

[24] Johannes Witte, *Japan heute* (Berlin: Allgemeiner Evangelisch-Protestantischer Missionsverein, 1926), 5.

[25] Ibid., 7, 9.

[26] Anton Ceska, "Aus dem Lande des Nebeneinander," in *Von Japan und seinem Volke* (Vienna: Katholischer Akademischer Missionsverein, 1932), 18.

[27] Ibid., 20.

[28] Johannes Witte, *Die Religionen Ostasiens: China und Japan* (Leipzig: Quelle & Meyer, 1926).

[29] Emil Schiller, *Shinto, die Volksreligion Japans* (Berlin: Ostasien-Mission, 1935).

[30] Wilhelm Gundert, *Der Schintoismus im Japanischen Nō-Drama* (Hamburg: N.p., 1925).

Of course, the missionaries could take religious tolerance only so far. They subscribed to a faith with a monopolistic claim to truth. They ventured afar specifically to convert nonbelievers. The proselytizers were trained to work with their subjects without necessarily agreeing with them. A few missionaries even articulated their task in somewhat stark terms. Paul Schebesta, an Austrian Catholic, called missionary work "a struggle with the heathen world."[31] The Jesuit Georg Alfred Lutterbeck wrote a book in 1931 to teach young readers the church's hardships in sixteenth-century Japan.[32] Emil Schiller composed a booklet in 1924 on the history of martyrs in the previous 50 years.[33] The publication was slim, only 11 pages, because Meiji Japan stopped persecuting Christians in 1873. These few volumes on martyrdom notwithstanding, missionaries' publications on Japan stand out for their lack of confrontational language.

Why were these Christians so restrained? To convince the Japanese that Christianity could bring salvation, the proselytizers first had to understand the native faiths. Vitriol alone would not have won many followers. Conversion by force was out of the question. Insulting Shinto might turn off potential converts and even aggravate the Japanese state because the emperor functioned as chief Shinto priest. Unlike in China, where foreign missionaries enjoyed extraterritoriality, in Japan they operated under Japanese laws. So they trod carefully when dealing with Japanese beliefs. Even when Schiller came closest to criticizing Shinto, he only suggested rather hopefully that the true light of Christ would soon outshine that of the sun, worshipped by the Japanese as sacred.[34]

The missionaries attempted to gain followers by depicting Shinto and Buddhism as outdated superstitions and portraying Christianity as part of the rational Western civilization that Japan was adopting eagerly. In *Dawn in Japan*, Schiller first praised Japan for joining the modern world before asking, "Can the ancient religions satisfy today's Japan?" He then answered, "Japan needs Christianity."[35] In *In the Land of the Rising Sun*, Liebenzell missionaries first discussed "the meaning of Japan for the present" and then inquired, "Can the ancient religions calm the hunger

---

[31] Paul Schebesta, *Die Mission in Kampfe mit der Heidenwelt* (Vienna: Katholischer Akademischer Missionsverein, 1931).

[32] Georg Alfred Lutterbeck, *Die Jagd über die Inseln: Eine Erzählung aus den Kämpfen der japanischen Kirche* (Freiburg im Breisgau: Herder & Co., 1931).

[33] Emil Schiller, *Um Christi Willen! Eine Märtyrgeschichte aus Japan vor 50 Jahren* (Berlin: Allgemeiner Evangelisch-Protestantischer Missionsverein, 1924).

[34] Schiller, *Shinto*, 102.

[35] Emil Schiller, *Morgenröte in Japan* (Berlin: Allgemeiner Evangelisch-Protestantischer Missionsverein, 1926), 11, 17.

for God?"[36] Emil Knodt turned Japan's success in modernization as an argument for accepting Christianity. He packaged the religion as the essence of Western culture and the antidote for the spiritual emptiness brought by the industrial age.[37] Johannes Witte urged readers in Germany to invite Japanese expatriates into their homes and churches. He lamented that most Japanese in Germany learned only of factories, universities, theaters, and even some "bad locales" with questionable company. The Japanese should not only be introduced to the physical aspects of German civilization, but more important, the spiritual ones found in Christianity.[38]

This depiction of Japan as split between its backward beliefs and expectant Christianity fitted the overarching theme, seen in the press and some films, of Japan straddling two worlds: old and young, Asian and Western, unfamiliar and familiar. The phrase "the country of juxtaposition" recurred time and again in works on Japan. Anton Ceska titled his 1932 essay "From the Country of Juxtaposition," "where the new into the old collides, and the West and the East rub sides."[39] Witte wrote *Japan: Between Two Cultures* in 1928. It described Japan as a wrestling ring between the modern and ancient worlds.[40] Even some of the missionaries friendliest to Japan held the view that there were two Japans, one public and the other private. Knodt, after heaping compliments on the outwardly attractive attributes of the Japanese, remarked that a shadowy side of their character lurked just behind the smiles, or "as one would call it in good German, lies."[41]

If the missionaries could not be sure that they knew the "real" Japan, why did they find Japan so welcoming? The official Japanese tolerance of Christianity and proselytization played an important role in their positive conceptualization, especially in contrast to the unrest in China that often made life and work hazardous for Western proselytizers. In *China's Distress and Japan's Hope*, Otto Marbach, a Swiss member of the AEPM, concluded that China was mired in misery because it refused even to contemplate Christianity, but Japan had a path to eternal life because it was at least open to accepting Jesus as the savior.[42] Similarly, Paul

---

[36] *Im Land der aufgehenden Sonne: Aus der Arbeit der Liebenzeller Mission in Japan* (Bad Liebenzell: Buchhandlung der Liebenzeller Mission, 1935), 3, 8.

[37] Knodt, 19.   [38] Witte, *Japan heute*, 29.   [39] Ceska, 17.

[40] Johannes Witte, *Japan: Zwischen zwei Kulturen* (Leipzig: J. C. Hinrichs'sche Buchhandlung, 1928), 501.

[41] Knodt, 15.

[42] Otto Marbach, *Chinas Not und Japans Hoffnung: Erinnerungen eines Ostasienfreundes* (Bern: Paul Haupt, 1929). He expressed similar views in *Warum wollen die Japaner und die Chinesen das Christentum?* (Berlin: Allgemeiner Evangelisch-Protestantischer Missionsverein, 1920).

Schebesta stated that through the "infusion of European civilization" into the Japanese economy and commerce, traditional Asian culture might be undermined and its religion rendered unviable. He held out hope that someday this transformation would take place in Japan, but he thought the same would not happen in China for a long, long time.[43] In two separate books, *On Volcanic Ground: Travel Experiences in Japan and China* and *Summer Sunny Days in Japan and China: Travel Experiences in East Asia in the Year 1924*, Witte, too, wrote of his more favorable impressions of Japan than China.[44]

When Japan became a contested topic in Germany in late 1931, the missionaries' positive opinions morphed into political partisanship. The proselytizers mostly refrained from commenting on current events for much of the interwar era. But since Japan's seizure of Manchuria and the increasingly hostile stance toward Japan in the German media, some missionaries spoke out for Japan of their own volition. Ceska wrote in 1932 that he was personally convinced that many of the disapproving views of Japan among the German public stemmed from ignorance of the facts. Building on his theme of Japan as a big family, he stated that Japan could withstand any crisis because the Japanese stood firmly behind their state.[45] Schiller defended Japan in 1935 and cautioned readers that unfamiliarity with East Asia could lead them to misjudge events there and come to skewed conclusions.[46] He dispelled as "fables" speculation in the press that Japan had not only designs on China but also the Philippines, East Indies, and Australia.[47] A Liebenzell missionary excused the Japanese push overseas as an understandable response to the dearth of natural resources that plagued the homeland, so that "Japan has to explore opportunities for expansion."[48]

None of the missionaries appear to have criticized Japanese aggression in China.[49] Instead, they took Japan's side and voluntarily spoke for Japan in their publications. How did they come to adopt this pro-Japanese attitude? They liked Japan. They enjoyed the weather, people,

---

[43] Schebesta, 5.

[44] Johannes Witte, *Auf vulkanischem Boden: Reiseerlebnisse in Japan und China* (Berlin: Allgemeiner Evangelisch-Protestantischer Missionsverein, 1925); Johannes Witte, *Sommer-Sonnentage in Japan und China: Reise-Erlebnisse in Ostasien im Jahre 1924* (Göttingen: Vandenhoeck & Ruprecht, 1925).

[45] Ceska, 24.

[46] Emil Schiller, *Das Japan von heute* (Berlin: Ostasien-Mission, 1935), 5.   [47] Ibid., 7.

[48] *Im Land der aufgehenden Sonne*, 5.

[49] Only the Quaker Mission was mentioned as an advocate of peace between Japan and the outside world. Samuel John Umbreit, *Zwanzig Jahre Missionar in Japan: Erlebnisse und Beobachtungen in Missionsdienst der Evangelischen Gemeinschaft* (Stuttgart: Christliches Verlagshaus, 1929), 302.

and comfort offered by the country as a modern, cultured state. Some even internalized the Japanese government's rationale that the lack of resources necessitated and legitimized expansion abroad. Many writers noted the paucity of natural resources in the Japanese home islands and then described Japanese empire building, as if the former had to lead to the latter. Samuel John Umbreit, a Methodist bishop, even repeated a claim he heard in Japan that "one coal mine in China contains more coal than all the mines in Japan put together."[50] Reading these lines, Germans without access to alternative information sources might well have begun to accept Japan's actions.

Moreover, Japan seemingly promised opportunities for the missionaries. That Japan had been adopting aspects of Western civilization wholesale must have encouraged the missionaries trying to win converts in an alien place. They had good reasons to believe that articulating Christianity as integral to the rise of the West would persuade Japan to incorporate it as well. Converting Japan could also bring closer the prospect of saving the souls in an entire continent. Because Japan was recognized as the great power of Asia, if the missionaries managed to Christianize Japan, other Asians looking up to Japan might follow suit. Even if Japan failed to have an exemplary effect, because Japan was expected to dominate more of Asia, Christianized Japanese troops might still act as crusaders for the faith.[51] Especially in China, where Western missionaries could be loathed as agents of imperialism, the expansion of Japanese control and the concomitant room for proselytization created an opportunity. Self-interest led the missionaries to align themselves with Japan.

Also in China, Japan meant for the missionaries a bulwark against the spread of godless communism in Asia. The mere opening of Japan to Christianity elevated it to a far more appealing position in the missionaries' view than the closed Soviet Union and semi-closed China. The proselytizers failed to convert more than a sliver of the Japanese population, but the mere chance to perform religious activities safely and without obstruction made Japan a more acceptable nation. The Liebenzell missionary stressed the importance of Christianizing heathen Japan to secure it as a fortress against Bolshevism.[52] Schiller could thus justify the Japanese conquest of Manchuria as defense of its prerogatives against Chinese encroachment and a reaction to communist penetration in the region.[53] The missionaries did not see Japan as the lesser of two evils,

---

[50] Ibid., 298.
[51] Emily Anderson, *Christianity and Imperialism in Modern Japan: Empire for God* (London: Bloomsbury Academic, 2014).
[52] *Im Land der aufgehenden Sonne*, 6–7.   [53] Schiller, *Das Japan von heute*, 5.

but a solution to a far great evil – communism, the same evil that the Anti-Comintern Pact purported to combat.

Japan According to Scholars

As seen in Wilhelm Gundert's treatise on Shinto in Noh theater, new doctors of philosophy from German universities were another fount of knowledge and interpretations of Japan. In German academia, dissertations were published as paperbacks or booklets, typically 50 to 150 pages long, soon after the public defense as the last step in attaining a doctorate. Although many languished in university libraries, others attracted enough general interest that they warranted reissue in other formats. Gundert's dissertation was republished as a volume in a series on East Asian studies.[54]

Several such dissertations turned books on Japan appeared in almost every year from 1922 on. Some were composed by Japanese students finishing their degrees in Germany. Most were written by native graduates who went on to pursue careers in academia, business, government, and politics. Broadly speaking, these books focused on the arts and humanities, and the social sciences, especially politics and economics. That is, the researchers were particularly concerned with human endeavors in Japan such as culture and society, and less with the natural sciences. Unlike the missionaries, doctoral candidates at secular universities did not analyze Japanese civilization as part of a plan to transform it. Rather, they selected Japan as their own research subject.

Dissertations in the humanities and arts made up the minority of all dissertations and were generally written in the relatively tranquil 1920s and early 1930s. Gundert's was completed in 1925. Friedrich Perzyński, a recognized expert on Japanese art even before he earned his doctorate, wrote a dissertation on masks in Noh and Kyōgen dramas in 1924.[55] It was considered interesting enough that a mainstream scholarly press republished it in two hardcover volumes.[56] Other such dissertations included Martin Ramming's on eighteenth-century accounts of Russia by shipwrecked Japanese, Fritz Rumpf's on seventeenth-century

---

[54] Wilhelm Gundert, *Der Schintoismus im Japanischen Nō-Drama*, Mitteilungen der Deutschen Gesellschaft für Natur- und Völkerkunde Ostasiens 19 (Tokyo: Deutsche Gesellschaft für Natur- und Völkerkunde Ostasiens, 1925).

[55] Friedrich Perzyński, *Die Masken der japanischen Schaubühne* (Hamburg: N.p., 1924).

[56] Friedrich Perzyński, *Japanische Masken: Nō und Kyōgen* (Berlin: Walter de Gruyter, 1925).

woodblock illustrations, and Horst Hammitzsch's annotated translation of an ancient Shinto text.[57]

In contrast to the dissertations that highlighted facets of old Japan, the more numerous works in the social sciences tackled subjects with contemporary relevance or urgency. More such publications appeared as Japan drew attention in international affairs in the late 1920s and 1930s. A few dealt with Japanese law and diplomacy, such as the legal position of the emperor, Anglo-Japanese relations at the turn of the century, and the ramifications of Japan's withdrawal from the League of Nations for its Pacific mandates.[58]

By far the largest cluster of dissertations investigated the Japanese economy. Until the Anti-Comintern Pact, Japan meant much more for Germany as a counterparty in trade or competitor for markets or resources than as a model for imitation or as a diplomatic partner. Several projects dissected Japanese export policies. A dissertation surveyed modern German traffic to East Asia.[59] There was a dissertation that examined Japanese commerce, with an emphasis on trade and transportation links with Germany, in each of the successive periods of pre-unification Germany, the Kaiserreich, World War I, and the postwar years.[60] Japan's impact on the global economy also attracted scrutiny. Some dissertations underscored the Japanese urge to conquer commercially through analyzing Japanese penetration in the Chinese, Manchurian, and world markets

---

[57] Martin Ramming, *Rußland-Berichte schiffbrüchiger Japaner aus den Jahren 1793 und 1805 und ihre Bedeutung für die Abschließungspolitik der Tokugawa* (Berlin: Würfel-Verlag, 1930); Fritz Rumpf, *Das Ise-Monogatari von 1608 und sein Einfluß auf die Buchillustration des 17. Jahrhunderts in Japan* (Berlin: Würfel-Verlag, 1931); Horst Hammitzsch, *Yamato-hime no Mikoto Seiki: Bericht über den Erdenwandel ihrer Hoheit der Prinzessin Yamato* (Leipzig: N.p., 1937). Rumpf's work was later reprinted in book form.

[58] Alois Tichý, *Die staatsrechtliche Stellung des Kaisers von Japan unter besonderer Berücksichtigung des Kaiserlichen Hausgesetzes* (Ohlau: N.p., 1928); Anneliese Cramer, *Die Beziehungen zwischen England und Japan von 1894–1902* (Zeulenroda: N.p., 1935); Jacobus Reimers, *Das japanische Kolonialmandat und der Austritt Japans aus dem Völkerbund* (Quakenbrück: N.p., 1936).

[59] Kunibert Pauly, *Der deutsche Ueberseeverkehr mit dem Fernen Osten: Seine grundlegende Entwicklung vor dem Kriege, sein Wiederaufbau nach dem Kriege und seine Ausgestaltung in der neuesten Zeit unter besonderer Berücksichtigung des Verkehrs mit Japan und China* (Jülich: N.p., 1938).

[60] Ottmar Fecht, *Die Wahrung wirtschaftlicher und politischer Belange in Ostasien durch die Norddeutsche Bundesmarine: Ein Beitrag zur deutschen Marinegeschichte aus der Reichsgründungszeit* (Berlin: Mittler, 1937); Kurt Koepsel, *Die Entwicklung des japanischen Außenhandels, insbesondere der deutsch-japanischen Handelsbeziehungen vor dem Weltkriege* (Kassel: N.p., 1929); Amélie Reichelt, *Japans Außenhandel und Außenhandelspolitik unter dem Einfluß des Weltkrieges* (Cöthen: N.p., 1931); Erich Kiel, *Die handelspolitischen Beziehungen zwischen Deutschland und Japan in der Nachkriegszeit* (Münster: N.p., 1934).

in the twentieth century.[61] Another group of works analyzed the Japanese drive to free itself from the vicissitudes of trade through autarky, internal colonization, and self-sufficiency in raw materials.[62] When the world economic crisis plunged Germany into chaos and unemployment in the early 1930s, a couple of dissertations examined Japan's banking problems and industrialization as well.[63]

That doctoral candidates at various universities chose Japan as a topic indicates a sustained interest in Japan within learned circles in Germany. The overwhelming majority of these dissertations delved into the human, rather than the natural, features of the country, such as art, literature, government, and economy. This choice of themes reveals a fundamental appreciation and respect for the civilization and achievements of the Japanese. The scholars likely anticipated that Japan would remain relevant in world affairs for the foreseeable future, because no one would launch a career by toiling over a dissertation on a place that they believed would soon sink into oblivion.

The dichotomy between the arts and the social sciences also reflects the overall German imagination of a Japan with split personalities. The dissertations on the arts and humanities almost uniformly showcased a Japan of a bygone age. Although vestiges of Japanese pre-modern theater, woodblock prints, and ancient legends could still be found in the 1920s and 1930s, the Japanese also flocked to cinemas and baseball games, experimented with contemporary art, and composed modern literature. But a Japanese culture becoming more like a Western one might not have struck many humanities scholars as interesting. The inquisitive minds were trained to look for the foreign and make sense of the unknown. The known and the familiar, especially if viewed as derived from the West, needed no examination.

In contrast, students of the social sciences chose Japan precisely because it was behaving more like the West in commercial and imperialistic competitions. Some of the monographs described a pragmatic, even unscrupulous, Japan. Dissertations on Japan's participation in world trade often articulated its economic and political expansion as

---

[61] Waldemar Hazama Ohly, *Das wirtschaftliche Vordringen Japans in China seit dem Frieden von Portsmouth 5. September 1905* (Kiel: N.p., 1922); Erich Meyn, *Die japanische Wirtschaftspolitik in der Mandschurei* (Leipzig: N.p., 1938); Kurt Glück, *Japans Vordringen auf dem Weltmarkt* (Würzburg: N.p., 1937).

[62] Herbert Rosinski, *Studien zum Problem der Autarkie in Japan* (Berlin: N.p., 1930); Alfons Scheinpflug, *Die japanische Kolonisation in Hokkaido* (Leipzig: Hirt & Sohn, 1935); Wilhelm Mandl, *Das Streben nach Selbstversorgung und der Aussenhandel: Deutsches Reich, Grossbritannien, Frankreich, Britisch Indien, Japan* (Berlin: Limbach, 1939).

[63] Carl Kroll, *Die bankenkrisen in Japan* (Marburg: N.p., 1930); Karl Hahn, *Die Industrialisierung Japans* (Bochum-Langendreer: N.p., 1932).

"encroachment" (*Vordringen*). As a typical argument went, Japan used every advantage, such as cheap labor, a devalued currency, and export confederations, to enlarge its share in the world market.[64] Kurt Glück, a doctor of economics, warned in 1936 that if Japan succeeded in tapping the resources in China to support its export industries, the "Yellow Peril" would be felt in even more acute ways. He suggested that after Japan overran China, the British, French, and Dutch colonies would soon be threatened as well.[65] Amélie Reichelt, a scholar in political science, expressed virtually the identical opinion. She stated that Japan's imperialistic push into China would bring it into competition and confrontation with America.[66] That is, when the dissertations depicted a modern Japan with trappings familiar to Western readers such as imperialism and export-driven industrialization, it was ironically perceived as an alien power with suspect motives. The very adroitness with which Japan adopted modern technology and strategy made it appear all the more menacing to those Western powers with a substantial stake in Asia.

But not Germany. It was stripped of its colonial possessions during World War I, so Germany possessed nothing concrete for Japan to threaten. In fact, because, not in spite, of the consensus that Japan would soon dominate Asia, none of the dissertations advocated that Germany try to compete with Japan or dislodge it from its leadership position in Asia. Instead, it was felt that Germany should accept Japan's expansion as a fait accompli and leverage its own post-colonial position. Kunibert Pauly, an economist, quoted a German executive in the shipping industry to state that Japan would welcome German economic involvement in Asia more than that of Britain or America because it would not aim to pursue a political agenda.[67] Erich Kiel, a political scientist, argued that Germany and Japan had always maintained cordial relations, especially because Germany did not participate in the "opening" of Japan or harbor colonial ambitions toward the country. Germany should use its cultural capital in Japan to consolidate bilateral ties in areas such as the economy.[68] He also urged Germany to make peace with Japan's ascent and its goal of "Asia for the Asians under Japanese hegemony" so that Germany would not be shut out of East Asia altogether.[69] He completed his dissertation in 1934. Two years later, Germany would indeed through the Anti-Comintern Pact tacitly concede Japanese hegemony in Asia while hoping to maintain its economic stake in a Japan-dominated China.

---

[64] Glück, 107.   [65] Ibid., 102.   [66] Reichelt, 56.   [67] Pauly, 81.
[68] Kiel, 96–97.   [69] Ibid., 97.

Despite these insightful prognostications, many of these new doctors might not have known Japan very well. Each dissertation included a short biography summarizing the author's upbringing, education, military service, and occupation. These records reveal that only a handful of the doctoral candidates had any experience with Japanese civilization, and fewer still had any experience in Japan. In general, arts and humanities scholars commanded more firsthand knowledge of the country. Both Martin Ramming and Fritz Rumpf spent years in Japan. Wilhelm Gundert worked in Japan as a missionary and language teacher. These few individuals enjoyed cultural and linguistic training matched by few of their peers. None of the social scientists mentioned traveling to Japan. Only a few had studied Japanese. Most relied on sources in European languages or texts translated from Japanese. Moreover, because their projects were mostly concerned with contemporary events, sometimes of a sensitive nature such as diplomacy and export policies, they could not use the most relevant documents in Japanese government ministries, even if they could read the language or conduct research in the country.

This imbalance of knowledge between dissertations in the humanities and the social sciences can also be seen physically. Works on politics and economics tended to be shorter, rarely exceeding 100 pages. Those on art and literature could reach impressive lengths. Gundert's took up almost 300 pages. Perzyński's filled two volumes. Not only did these heftier oeuvres likely reflect a more profound understanding of Japan, they also helped launch their authors' careers. After receiving his doctorate, Gundert worked as manager of the Japanese-German Cultural Society in Tokyo. He returned to Germany in 1935 to become the professor of Japanology at the University of Hamburg. He rose to be *Rektor* of the university in 1938.[70] Ramming eventually taught at the University of Berlin and directed the Japan Institute. Horst Hammitzsch assumed the professorship of Japanology at the University of Leipzig in 1942. Whereas new doctors of philosophy in the arts and humanities usually entered academia, most of their colleagues in the social sciences pursued careers with little interaction with Japan. Research in art and literature favored topics in premodern Japan, so that Japanology in German universities was dominated by the likes of Gundert, Ramming, or Hammitzsch who wrote prolifically on a bygone Japan. Those who most needed firsthand and up-to-date experiences with Japan, the social scientists, lacked the opportunity to gain it. But those who enjoyed firsthand

---

[70] Gundert's rise had in part to do with his ties with the Nazi organization for professors. Michael Grüttner, *Biographisches Lexikon zur nationalsozialistischen Wissenschaftspolitik* (Heidelberg: Synchron, 2004), 67.

contact with modern Japan, the humanities scholars, turned their gaze to eras no longer accessible. Thus insights on Japan flowing from universities painted a somewhat skewed image with limited applicability for understanding the country in the 1920s and 1930s.

The cost of transportation kept the social scientists from researching in Japan. The authors' biographies indicate that almost all the doctoral candidates were raised in middle-class households. Their fathers worked in businesses, as civil servants, or for themselves, earning modest incomes that likely could not finance a sojourn in East Asia. Those scholars blessed with the opportunity to travel to Japan did so not as individuals but as members of an organization. Gundert went as a missionary. Rumpf served in a German garrison in China. Hammitzsch first ventured to Japan to work as a teacher only after he had earned his doctorate. In interwar Germany, having experience in faraway Japan set one apart from the rest of the population and endowed one with a fascinating tale to share.

Japan According to Travelers

Travelogues were thus another source of published knowledge of Japan, one far more appealing to the populace than recondite dissertations. Travelogues mentioning Japan were published in Germany in almost every year of the interwar era in varying numbers. Few new accounts appeared in the early 1920s. Readers therefore had to make do with those recounting journeys before World War I, such as that by Bernhard Kellermann, a bestselling author and correspondent for the *Berliner Tageblatt*.[71] As the German economy rebounded in the mid-1920s, several individuals and firms recovered enough financially to afford journeys abroad. These years witnessed the rise of large-than-life globe-trotters such as Colin Ross, whose scars and tans from misadventures overseas impressed Hitler far more than any diplomat's or professor's credentials. The number of travelogues ballooned, peaking in the late 1920s. Just then the world economic crisis struck and greatly diminished the means of Germans to venture afar. The outbreak of military conflict in East Asia made the region more hazardous and less open as a travel destination. The number of titles tapered off from the early 1930s and dropped markedly in the middle of the decade. In the years leading up to World War II in Europe, only a few travelogues appeared.

---

[71] Bernhard Kellermann, *Ein Spaziergang in Japan* (Berlin: Paul Cassirer, 1920).

These first-person accounts commanded very broad readerships. While the missionaries could count on churchgoers as consumers and the new doctors could boast an educated audience, travel writers relied on their fame and personality. The interwar world still abounded with unexplored deserts and unconquered mountains. Pioneers such as Hugo Eckener were hailed as heroes. Books by or about them drew great interest. Germany celebrated its share of such figures, several of whom wrote about Japan. Ross published a companion book in 1925 for his documentary *With a Hand-Crank Camera around the World*.[72] In 1929, he compiled a photo album of Asian scenery, *East Asia: China, Manchuria, Korea, and Japan*.[73] By then, Ross had firmly established his reputation as a premier adventurer and multimedia chronicler of foreign places in newspapers such as the *Vossische Zeitung* and films. He followed with another travelogue in 1940, *The New Asia*.[74] Another wanderer-writer and contributor to the *Vossische Zeitung*, the immensely popular Richard Katz, wrote two travelogues: *Sparkling Far East: Scenes in China, Korea, and Japan* in 1931, and *Japan of Today: Adventures of a Globetrotter* in 1933.[75] The thrill-seeker Kurt Faber had his achievements published posthumously in 1930 in *The Last Journeys and Adventure of a World Traveler: The Baltic, the Balkans, South Seas, Japan, Korea, China, Siberia, Moscow, Palestine, Syria, and Canada*.[76] Most of these books went through multiple printings and all these writers published other bestselling works that augmented their public voices and personas. For Ross, the accounts of his exploits earned Hitler's admiration and led to private audiences with the Führer. Faber, too, might have met Hitler because he joined the Nazi Party in 1925 and could have crossed paths with the Führer when the party was still relatively small. Faber – blond, brash, and bold – was precisely the type of man Hitler idolized.[77]

German travelers usually visited Japan as just one stop in much broader trips. A popular account from the early 1920s was called *Around the Earth: Scenes from America, Japan, Korea, China, India, and*

---

[72] Colin Ross, *Mit dem Kurbelkasten um die Welt* (Berlin: Gebr. Wolffsohn, 1925).

[73] Colin Ross, *Ostasien: China, Mandschurei, Korea, Japan* (Leipzig: E. A. Seemanns Lichtbildanstalt, 1929).

[74] Colin Ross, *Das Neue Asien* (Leipzig: F. A. Brockhaus, 1940).

[75] Richard Katz, *Funkelnder Ferner Osten: Erlebtes in China–Korea–Japan* (Berlin: Ullstein, 1931); Richard Katz, *Japan von heute: Erlebnisse eines Weltenbummlers* (Reutlingen: Enßlin & Laiblin, 1933).

[76] Kurt Faber, *Weltwanderers letzte Fahrten und Abenteuer: Baltikum, Balkan, Südsee, Japan, Korea, China, Sibirien, Moskau, Palästina, Syrien, Kanada* (Stuttgart: Robert Lutz Nachfolger Otto Schramm, 1930).

[77] VB, December 10, 1934, ME.

Arabia.[78] Another was titled *Sunny Worlds: East Asian Travel Sketches – Borneo, Java, Sumatra, India, Ceylon, and Japan.*[79] A 1937 work likewise contextualized Japan broadly as *Foray to Japan, Java, Bali, America, Africa, China, Ceylon, Sumatra, Celebes, Borneo, the Philippines, and Honolulu.*[80] Several others, though less expansive, included China, Korea, and India alongside Japan. While sojourners with a purpose such as missionaries, merchants, or diplomats traveled to Japan specifically, those who wandered for leisure or adventure tended to see Japan as one stop in a grand tour.

Japan appeared so often as one of many places because travelogues were written to make money. The titles were important marketing tools, especially because books in Germany, then as now, were not routinely adorned with very graphic covers. Titles encompassing many destinations made their authors seem more authoritative. Moreover, travelers could not go from Germany to Japan without traversing or visiting other places. Anyone spending the time and money to travel that far would want to take in as many sights as possible. So Japan was included as a stop on a crowded itinerary, one among many.

Whether visually or textually, the travel writers often began by remarking on how odd a place Japan struck them. Ross selected several photos for his album that paraded foreign scenes and landscapes, such as Mount Fuji, women in traditional garments, the Gion Festival in Kyoto, and even a room in a typical house.[81] But to German readers, the ordinary in Japan could seem extraordinary. Katz in *Sparkling Far East* titled a section "Different from Us" to highlight the stranger things he noticed in Japan. He was bemused by the Japanese' elaborately polite greetings and impressed by swarms of cyclists and pedestrians crisscrossing in every direction without colliding. He surmised that the Japanese must have a "sixth sense" for navigating traffic.[82] Faber wrote of the "fantastical Japanese script" as if it were a spell cast all over the country, "standing on walls, fluttering on banners, and dancing in lines in newspapers."[83] He sometimes wondered if the Japanese themselves could actually read the writing. In Japan, he marveled, even the Moon seemed to loom larger and the stars shine brighter.

---

[78] Eduard Büchler, *Rund um die Erde: Erlebtes aus Amerika, Japan, Korea, China, Indien und Arabien* (Bern: A. Francke, 1921). The book reached at least a third edition.

[79] Emil Selenka and Lenore Selenka, *Sonnige Welten: Ostasiatische Reise-Skizzen – Borneo, Java, Sumatra, Vorderindien, Ceylon, Japan*, 3rd ed. (Berlin: C. W. Kreidel, 1925).

[80] Ernst Josef Hoßdorf, *Streifzug nach Japan, Java, Bali, U.S.A., Afrika, China, Ceylon, Sumatra, Celebes, Borneo, Philippinen, Honolulu* (Frick: A. Fricker, 1937).

[81] Ross, *Ostasien*, 36–39.   [82] Katz, *Funkelnder Ferner Osten*, 206–207.

[83] Faber, 140.

As in films, some travelogues used the familiar unfamiliar to depict a known and unknown Japan, and delve into the causes of the strangeness one felt there. What made Japan so special to the travelers was its mixture of East and West, old and new. The travel writers recognized objects and elements that were like those found in Germany, but their appearance in a Japanese setting was unexpected and noteworthy. This parallel coexistence of different worlds in Japan made it a peculiar place in German eyes. The correspondent Alice Schalek chose a title for her travelogue to convey this theme – *Japan, the Country of Juxtaposition: A Winter Journey across Japan, Korea, and Manchuria.*[84] Another popular travel writer, Alfred E. Johann, named his work *Generals, Geisha, and Poems: Journeys and Adventures in Japan, from Sakhalin to Manchukuo.*[85]

Ross chose several photographs to illustrate visually the combination of past and present in Japan. One, titled "Wooden Huts and Skyscrapers in Tokyo," showed the stark contrast of modern buildings, which withstood the Great Kanto Earthquake, towering over hastily constructed barracks amid the ruins of old houses destroyed in the catastrophe. He wrote of the "lively and variegated" street traffic, in which automobiles, oxcarts, bicycles, and handcarts shared road space.[86] He noted, too, the struggle between old and new Japan. Despite some conservatives' efforts to revive ancient values, the country as a whole continued apace to "Japanize" European culture for its own purposes.[87]

Katz also described the blending, sometimes deceptively harmonious, between the ancient and modern in one place and time. He related an incident while traveling on an electrified express train in a "Pullmanesque" sleeping car. Just as he delighted in the "American" efficiency and amenities proffered by New Japan, Old Japan reared its head in another train car. Unbeknownst to Katz, a Japanese corvette captain took his own life by ritual suicide because he disapproved of the outcome of the London Naval Conference. Upon learning of the death, Katz mused that:

Here in Japan there is still always a seamless juxtaposition: the unfathomed dark green sea of the Asian soul and the immaculate offices of the new practicality. At day, iron and concrete prevail. But at night it is different. At night, the crusted wood reigns again, the same wood that houses the ancestral shrine. As the first stars begin to glisten, the chalk-white practicality submerges into the dark green sea. Asia awakes at night. Even in New Tokyo. Even in the sleeping car.[88]

---

[84] Alice Schalek, *Japan, das Land des Nebeneinander: Eine Winterreise durch Japan, Korea und die Mandschurei* (Breslau: Ferdinand Hirt, 1925).

[85] Alfred E. Johann, *Generäle, Geishas und Gedichte: Fahrten und Erlebnisse in Japan, von Sachalin bis Manchukuo* (Berlin: Ullstein, 1937).

[86] Ross, *Ostasien*, 44.   [87] Ibid., 45.   [88] Katz, *Funkelnder Ferner Osten*, 256.

Katz also found humor within Japan's split identity. He wrote that the Westernization of Asia could be considered a success in terms of hygiene and infrastructure, but when it came to the electric motor one should still pray to Buddha.[89] He mentioned that an American article gloated that Tokyo "has become as beautiful as a big American city," though he added dryly that Tokyo "is not quite so bad yet."[90] Although ancient Japan might never fade away entirely, Katz believed in the inexorable march of modern Japan. Like Ross, he depicted the near collision between old and new in street traffic, or more precisely the displacement of the old by the new. He pointed out that many roads in Tokyo were surfaced with asphalt so that vehicles no longer came and went in a dust cloud. Occasionally one might still see an oxcart or two, but the battle had been decided: wooden houses and oxcarts had lost.[91] The dark green sea of the "Asian soul" had been contained by white, concrete dams.

Other travelogues echoed this portrayal of Japan divided between the past and the future. Faber called Japan "the country of unlimited contradictions" where, as in other nations, some people pined for better bygone days in the face of progress.[92] He saw little chance of Japan turning back because the adoption of modern ways had advanced so much that Tokyo Central Station was built in the "Berlin style." He found the train service "really the best, cheapest, and most punctual in the world" – high praise from a German.[93] Alfred Johann articulated perhaps the most succinct summary of this Janus-faced Japan:

Our conception of Japan vacillates between two extremes. The first, older depiction sees in Japan nothing but a magical, fairytale-like country of cherry blossoms and geisha, the Japan of flowery kimonos, delicate woodcarving, and lacquer ware. The second, newer view describes Japan only as the violent rapist of defenseless China, the cunning, ruthless competitor in the world market that would stop at nothing to undercut trade rivals in order to drive them out of business.[94]

This conceptualization of Japan with multiple personalities affected the creation of German knowledge of Japan. Many of these impressions were superficial observations gathered from cursory stays. The globetrotters' grand tours meant that they spent a relatively brief time in Japan. Faber spent less than a month; Katz four months. The sightseeing nature of their journeys led them to predictable facilities and destinations. That both Katz and Faber wrote of their experiences with Japanese trains and hotels, and Kobe and Yokohama, is no coincidence. It should not have

---

[89] Ibid., 239.   [90] Ibid., 252.   [91] Ibid., 255.   [92] Faber, 141.
[93] Ibid., 141, 154.   [94] Johann, 171.

surprised them that they encountered a blend of civilizations there because hotels and port cities are designed to cater to foreigners. The language barrier prevented the travel writers from truly understanding the country and its people. None of the explorers could speak Japanese. Even some long-term residents there could not claim to know Japanese fluently. So the authors interacted only with the most Westernized Japanese individuals – those straddling the two worlds.

The description of Japan with elements of old and new was but a selective, self-centered understanding of the country. In Germany, too, one could see a mix of past and present. In fact, one likely had a much better chance of seeing something new in interwar Tokyo than Berlin because the Japanese capital was rebuilding after the earthquake. But because the writers had already decided that Japan was caught between old and new, they wrote their books to fit the conclusion.

The disagreement over what qualities characterized Japan allowed the authors to comment on conditions at home. The malleability and multiplicity of Japan's portrayals meant that the travel writers could choose the Japan with which to compare Germany. Katz opted to highlight the harmony he witnessed. As he was boarding a ship to depart Japan, he reflected on the pleasant dealings he had with "the yellow people," while everything that revolted him in Japan came from Caucasians. He concluded, "I believe firmly that they are better than we."[95] Faber, who seemingly spent most of his time in Japan on trains, wrote glowingly of the affordability of rail travel and the outrageous prices in Germany.[96] Ross perhaps went farthest in using Japan as a yardstick. In a caption for a photo of Osaka train station, he lamented that as Japan Westernized, "it has today the nouveau riche, the wartime and postwar profiteers, the grafters and usurers just like we do."[97] He complained about the rise of powerful industrial and financial concerns that controlled more and more of the national economy and were beginning to influence public opinion by acquiring newspapers. Meanwhile, a disgruntled working class was rising against the traditional belief in the sacrosanct imperial family. Ross's words against war profiteering, big businesses, and the restless proletariat sound virtually identical to Nazi rhetoric against the same forces in Germany. This ease – especially by Nazi-oriented writers such as Faber and Ross – in comparing and juxtaposing Germany with Japan also foreshadowed transnational Nazis' identification with Japan in the 1930s.

---

[95] Katz, *Funkelnder Ferner Osten*, 298.   [96] Faber, 141–142.   [97] Ross, *Ostasien*, 45.

But extensive political commentaries were rare among travelogues for much of the interwar era. When the writers felt compelled to discuss politics at home or in Japan, they did so in side remarks such as those discussed above. One author titled a section "Nothing More on Politics!!" just to insert a few paragraphs on the topic.[98] Even a diplomat devoted only about five pages in a chapter labeled "A Little Politics" to the subject.[99] Most travel writers, like the documentarians, did not delve into current events, preferring instead to discuss, sometimes in great detail, Japanese art, religion, and traditional architecture. The inattention to current events meant that the travelogues generally described little change in interwar Japan. Some writers' preference to seek out old Japan, in traditional theaters, shrines, and the countryside, resulted in a portrait of a timeless, static Japan. So such accounts written in the 1920s often differed little from those in the 1930s.

Japan According to Partisans

But around the early 1930s, ideology began to influence some travel accounts. Hans Thierbach described in 1933 his encounter the previous year with a group of Chinese while on his way from North America to East Asia. The Chinese passengers, returning home from studying abroad, complained bitterly to him about the Japanese attack on Shanghai. Thierbach wrote that, "Their hatred of the heavily armed Japanese aggressors who oppressed poor, defenseless China was genuine and thoroughly convincing to a German, who also belonged to a defenseless nation."[100] This late Weimar sympathy for China stemmed from nationalistic Germans' hostility toward the Versailles–Washington system. As the Nazis attained power, transnational Nazism altered Germany's stance toward China and Japan, just as Thierbach soon became a Nazi. Roland Strunk and Martin Rikli devoted many pages to happenings in Asia in *Attention! Asia Is Marching! A Factual Report* in 1934. The book differed from a typical travelogue because its main purpose was to relay and comment on current events. Strunk worked as a correspondent for the *Völkischer Beobachter*; Rikli made Nazi propaganda films. The book contrasted a hapless China incapable or unwilling to defend itself with a Japan claiming to be inspired by Germany.

---

[98] Arthur Holitscher, *Das unruhige Asien: Reise durch Indien – China – Japan* (Berlin: S. Fischer, 1926), 325.
[99] Hans Anna Haunhorst, *Das Lächeln Japans* (Leipzig: Georg Kummer, 1936), 97–101.
[100] Hans Thierbach, *Welt in der Wandlung: Eindrücke von einer Reise durch die Vereinigten Staaten, Japan und Sowjetrußland* (Berlin: Nachbarschafts-Verlag, 1933), 7.

A Chinese was quoted lamenting, "Why does China not defend itself like other peoples would? Why does the danger of foreign invasion not unite the feuding warlords?"[101] Later, the authors quoted a Japanese officer, "We are the Prussians of the East! We are convinced that the Germans, who taught us so much, will once again rediscover themselves. The fate of our two nations has much in common. No one would welcome more and understand better Germany's national regeneration than we would!"[102] Japanese transnational Nazis routinely used such rhetoric to identify with Germans. In turn, German transnational Nazis cited this affinity to accommodate and identify with the Japanese.

These politicized, opinionated travelogues emerged in the early 1930s in a rise of political commentaries on Japan and on Germany and Japan. Such works had a long pedigree. A cluster of books emerged to discuss current Japan in the years immediately after World War I. Some indulged in a retrospective, hypothetical refighting of the war. In *Mexico-Germany-Japan* in 1919, Ernst Schultze revisited the scheme proposed in the Zimmermann Telegram and argued that the true path for a German-Japanese connection should go through the Western Hemisphere.[103] Erich Ludendorff, too, mentioned Japan in his memoir. He faulted German diplomats for failing to prevent it from joining the Allies.[104] He spoke of Japan in the context of the Eastern Front – if Tokyo had sided with Berlin, Japan might have tied down enough Russian troops to make a difference for Germany. Not only did Ludendorff share with Hitler a contempt for diplomats, it is also conceivable that his perspective on the East influenced Hitler's worldview, given his close ties with the Nazis in the 1920s. At the same time, another group of works engaged in prospective conjectures about Japan. One warned of an "inevitable war" between Japan and America.[105] An astrologer, too, read from the stars a "coming world war" between the two powers.[106]

Early 1920s Germany did not lack in speculation about or proposals for coordination with Japan, but none of the schemes came near realization or serious consideration. In February 1919, barely three months

[101] Roland Strunk and Martin Rikli, *Achtung! Asien marschiert! Ein Tatsachenbericht* (Berlin: Drei Masken Verlag, 1934), 11.

[102] Ibid., 14.

[103] Ernst Schultze [Americanus, pseud.], *Mexico-Deutschland-Japan* (Dresden: Globus, 1919).

[104] Erich Ludendorff, *Meine Kriegserinnerungen 1914–1918* (Berlin: Mittler, 1919), 60.

[105] Friedrich Wencker-Wildberg, *Der unvermeidliche Krieg zwischen Japan und Amerika: Eine politische Studie* (Stuttgart: Neuer Stuttgarter Verlag, 1921).

[106] Hermann Leo, *Berechnung des kommenden Weltkrieges zwischen Amerika und Japan: Deutschlands Zusammenbruch und Deutschlands Aufstieg im astrologischen Lichte* (Freiburg im Breisgau: Peter Hofmann, 1920).

after the Armistice, Otto von Schwarzenegg argued in *Japan and We* that Germany and Japan should build a bloc stretching from Europe to Asia in conjunction with Russia as a counterweight to Anglo-American encirclement.[107] Paul Ostwald published *Germany and Japan* a year later to suggest an identical German-Russian-Japanese alignment. Ostwald, who also wrote newspaper articles on the topic, emphasized the need for Germany and Japan to utilize the Trans-Siberian Railway to increase bilateral trade. Only such a land-based European-Asian continental bloc, he projected, could counter the Anglo-Saxon control of the seas.[108] That same year, he published *Modern Japan*, a textbook for post-secondary institutions. There he explained that Germany should build a continental bloc with Russia and Japan to combat Anglo-Saxon world domination: "In terms of world politics and economy our interests lie with Japan."[109] Even a skeptic of such a scheme, Friedrich Klemann, acknowledged in 1921 that should his own preferred Anglo-German cooperation not come to fruition, Germany might find it expedient to work with Japan, just as Ostwald and the more famous geopolitics theorist Karl Haushofer argued.[110] A decade and a half later, Hitler's Germany would embark on this exact path.

These authors may seem extraordinarily far sighted, but at that time their arguments had little influence on debates or policies. Without the unpredictable rise of the Nazis, it seems unlikely that their schemes would have come to pass. True, Germany and Japan found much to dislike in the Versailles–Washington system, but none of the other powers involved claimed complete satisfaction with the postwar order. German and Japanese reactions differed in that Japan could live with the arrangement enough to participate in multilateral instruments, but Germany sought to change, redress, or undermine the system immediately. "Have-not" Germany worked with other losers of the settlement such as the Soviet Union and China in the 1920s. As far as Germany was concerned, Japan did not belong to the "have-not" club at that point.

Some of the schemes for alliance with Japan likely also resulted from a lack of choices. Many of the writers took pride in proclaiming that Germany fought against the whole world in the Great War. Afterward,

---

[107] Otto von Schwarzenegg, *Japan und wir* (Munich: Hugo Bruckmann, 1919), 44–45.
[108] Paul Ostwald, *Deutschland und Japan* (Berlin: Leonhard Simion Nachfolger, 1920), 31.
[109] Paul Ostwald, *Das moderne Japan*, Die Bücherei der Volkshochschule 2 (Leipzig: Velhagen & Klasing, 1920), 95. He wrote a third book with a similar argument. Paul Ostwald, *Japans Entwicklung zur modernen Weltmacht: Seine Kultur-, Rechts-, Wirtschafts- und Staatengeschichte von der Restauration bis zur Gegenwart* (Bonn: Kurt Schroeber, 1922).
[110] Friedrich Klemann, *Japan, wie es ist* (Leipzig: R. Voigtländer, 1921), 135.

the pariah nation had a difficult time finding an ally of worthwhile strength and heft. Japan, against which Germany did not hold a grudge, could appear a potential partner. The unsettled early 1920s created imaginative space for all sorts of wild schemes. An alliance with Japan was only one of many floated.

As German internal politics and external relations regained a semblance of normalcy in the mid-1920s, the number of works on Japanese politics or proposing German-Japanese convergence dwindled. The Weimar Republic pursued the "fulfillment" policy that answered Allied demands while seeking incremental redress of the Versailles Treaty and reintegration of Germany in the international community. Scholars interested in Japan regardless of its relevance to current affairs continued to produce fine studies. Two rising Japanologists were beginning to make their marks in the field. Hans Ueberschaar published a work on the nuances of state building in Japan.[111] Friedrich Max Trautz wrote a booklet on German-Japanese relations in the cultural and scholarly, rather than the political and diplomatic, realms.[112] Even Karl Haushofer, "father of geopolitics" and avid advocate of a continental bloc from Germany to Japan, did not devote much page space on this idea in his two publications on Japan in this period.[113]

The world economic crisis and the consequent collapse of the political order in Germany again led to a spike in the number of books on relations with Japan. Whereas travelogues enjoyed their heyday in the late 1920s, political books thrived in the turbulent early 1920s and 1930s. The breakdown of the economic and political systems, the second in about a decade, again freed minds to contemplate an unprecedented, more unconventional state of German-Japanese relations, much as in the immediate postwar period. What was different was that Japan walked out of the League of Nations in 1933 and renounced other multilateral instruments after the international community denounced its conquest of Manchuria. With the rise of the Hitler regime, which was willing to depart from established diplomatic practices, and Germany's own withdrawal from the league in October, partisan voices for bilateral rapprochement were received more favorably.

Yet despite the heightened interest, confusion and uncertainty were persistent features of discourse on Japan. Just as the publication trends of

[111] Hans Ueberschaar, *Die Eigenart der japanischen Staatskultur: Eine Einführung in das Denken der Japaner* (Leipzig: Theodor Weicher, 1925).

[112] Friedrich Max Trautz, *Japan: Was es uns war und was es uns ist* (Hamburg: N.p., 1929).

[113] Karl Haushofer, *Japan und die Japaner: Eine Landeskunde* (Leipzig: B. G. Teubner, 1923); Karl Haushofer, *Japans Reichserneuerung: Strukturwandlungen von der Meiji-Ära bis heute* (Berlin: Walter de Gruyter, 1930).

travelogues and partisan commentaries show an inverse relation, the experience and knowledge of their authors share a similar relationship. In contrast to the travel writers who saw Japan with their own eyes, many commentators on Japan in the mid-1930s had no ostensible connection to the country and relied solely on secondary sources. Even Haushofer, so prolific a proponent of convergence with Japan, spent less than two years in the country, from 1909 to 1910. It remains unclear whether he actually had functional command of the language. Some commentators seemed at a loss regarding Japan's rise to prominence on the world stage. Hugo Wilhelm von Doemming titled his book *What Does Japan Want?*[114] Johannes Stoye also titled his work with a question, *Japan: Danger or Model?*[115] Walther Funder wondered *Will the World Become Japanese?*[116] Even when Johannes Meyer did not use a question for his title, he still called his book *The Japanese Sphinx* to highlight the stereotypical "Asian inscrutability" of the Japanese.[117] Such confusion and doubts hint at the transition from Weimar's rejection of militarist Japan to the Nazis' acceptance.

The uncertainty caused Japan to appear yet again in books as a country with different personalities. A few publications underscored the threat that Japan posed. Fritz Bodinus was convinced that the end of the world, as predicted in the Book of Revelation, was near and Japan would be the agent. He was so motivated that he wrote a trilogy, "Christ and Antichrist on the Battlefield," on the topic.[118] He quoted a few times Wilhelm's warning of the "Yellow Peril" referring to Japan: "Nations of Europe, protect your most sacred things." Other writers worried that Japan would dominate the world market through its aggressive export policy. Walther Funder expressed concern that Japan would have a monopoly over soybeans. Ernst Schultze composed a two-part series to detail Japanese commercial expansion and its damaging ramifications for the white race.[119]

---

[114] Hugo Wilhelm von Doemming, *Was will Japan?* (Jena: Eugen Diederichs, 1934).

[115] Johannes Stoye, *Japan: Gefahr oder Vorbild?* (Leipzig: Quelle & Meyer, 1936).

[116] Walther Funder, *Wird die Welt japanische?* (Hamburg: Walther Funder, 1936).

[117] Johannes F. E. Meyer, *Die Japanische Sphinx: Ein Beitrag zum Verständnis des Landes und seiner Bewohner* (Frankfurt am Main: Karl Poths, 1936).

[118] Fritz Bodinus, *Japans Schatten über Deutschland* (Bielefeld: Hermann Mattenklodt, 1933); Fritz Bodinus, *Morgendämmerung? Das Gesicht Japans im Lichte der Offenbarung des Johannes und des Geheimdokument des Grafen Tanaka* (Bielefeld: Hermann Mattenklodt, 1934); Fritz Bodinus, *Der Vormarsch Japans: Die kommenden Ereignisse im Lichte der Offenbarung* (Constance: Huß Verlag W. Müsken, 1934).

[119] Ernst Schultze, *Die weisse und die gelbe Gefahr: Japans gewaltsame Erschliessung und wirtschaftliche Entwicklung*, Japan als Weltindustriemacht 1 (Stuttgart: W. Kohlhammer, 1935); Ernst Schultze, *Japan als Exportindustriestaat*, Japan als Weltindustriemacht 2 (Stuttgart: W. Kohlhammer, 1935).

But these criticisms only reiterated old fearmongering about Japan and were no longer persuasive to Germany's leaders in the mid-1930s. The ex-Kaiser's words carried little weight in Nazi Germany. Interpretations of Scripture did not move a state that scarcely hid its contempt for Christianity. Arguments about Japanese commercial and colonial expansion did not worry the new masters of Germany as they might have the previous republican and imperial governments. The Third Reich was more focused on independence from the world market. It saw its destiny in conquering living space in Eastern Europe – a prospect that Japan could help realize by pressuring the Soviet Union from East Asia.

In contrast to the smattering of hostile publications, a much larger cluster of books emerged to defend or promote Japan. Alfred Stoss, a corvette captain, wrote a trilogy: *The Plundering Raid against Japan! When Will Nations Finally Defend Themselves?* and *The Truth about Shanghai: The Attack of the World Leadership against the Last Free Nation, Japan* in 1932, and in 1934 *The Struggle between Judah and Japan: Japan as Champion of the Free National Economy*.[120] He imagined that there was a global conspiracy orchestrated by Jewry to use the League of Nations to subjugate the racially pure Japanese – a view Hitler also expressed in *Mein Kampf*. Despite the books' hyperbole and incendiary rhetoric, what stood out was an articulation of potential common ground between Germany and Japan as alleged targets of Jewish machinations. It mattered little that the Japanese government and public did not embrace anti-Semitism, but those Germans who viewed the world through a racial lens, such as Stoss and Hitler, identified with the Japanese as a "fellow antagonist" of Jewry. Transnational Nazis could accommodate Japan because racial hierarchy can only be maintained by racial purity.

More books appeared in the mid-1930s to discuss Germany and Japan in the same breath. Robert Mohl published a book in 1933 in a right-leaning series for young readers, and declared that "Japan is, like Germany, also a 'people without space.'"[121] Also in 1933, Haushofer wrote in a biography of the Meiji emperor that the inner pressure to expand was stronger in the Japanese Empire than Germany or Italy.[122] He advanced

---

[120] Alfred Stoss, *Der Raubzug gegen Japan! Wann endlich wehren sich die Völker?* (Munich: Ludendorffs Volkswarte-Verlag, 1932); Alfred Stoss, *Die Wahrheit über Shanghai: Der Angriff der Weltleitung gegen das letzte freie Volk Japan* (Hamburg: Selbstverl., 1932); Alfred Stoss, *Der Kampf zwischen Juda und Japan: Japan als Vorkämpfer freier Volkswirtschaft* (Munich: Ludendorffs Verlag, 1934).

[121] Robert Mohl, *Der Japaner*, Deutsche Jugendbücherei 482 (Berlin: Hermann Hillger, 1933), 31.

[122] Karl Haushofer, *Mutsuhito, Kaiser von Japan*, Colemans kleine Biographien 36 (Lübeck: Charles Coleman, 1933), 50.

a similar argument in *Japan's Development as a Military Power and Empire*.[123] Hugo Wilhelm von Doemming, whose book asked "What does Japan want?," answered that Japan belonged to the same group of nations as Germany and Italy that needed and wanted to consolidate themselves internally in politics, religion, and race to form a "national bloc of steel."[124]

From 1935, some publications began to discuss collaboration between Germany and Japan to guard against a specific threat perceived to jeopardize both countries. Ernst Otto Hauser pointed out that "Germany stood on the side of Japan against the assembled nations at Geneva, and Germany was like Japan the natural opponent of the Soviet Union."[125] Gustav Fochler-Hauke, a colleague of Haushofer, also linked the fates of Berlin and Tokyo through Moscow. A geographer, he speculated that Germany would one way or another be tied to events in East Asia. Should the Soviet Union suffer defeat in East Asia, it would inevitably shift its attention westward; or if it won a victory in the East, it would certainly be emboldened to strengthen pressure in the West, too.[126] Heinz Corazza, a Nazi propagandist who went on to write about samurai in SS publications, unambiguously illustrates in *Japan: Wonder of the Sword* the transnational Nazi accommodation of and identification with Japan:

The same forces that encircled Germany in 1914 are feverishly baiting and mobilizing against Germany and Japan 20 years later. Germany and Japan are natural allies because they are inspired by the same ideas of death-defying, heroic philosophy on leader and loyalty, maintenance of racial purity, attention to ancestral heritage, and ceaseless work toward peace for the people and nation. Even if these two great hero nations do not conclude paper agreements with each other in the future, as dead set enemies of liberal-Bolshevik materialism they are still the strong bulwarks of Western and Asian idealism today and the entire twentieth century![127]

Corazza's fixation on the samurai sword was so extreme that the philosophy professor Tomoeda Takahiko attempted to provide a corrective in the foreword. He reminded readers that to properly understand Japanese

---

[123] Karl Haushofer, *Japans Werdegang als Wehrmacht und Empire* (Berlin: Walter de Gruyter, 1933).

[124] Doemming, 308–309.

[125] Ernst Otto Hauser, *Gefährlicher Osten: Japan und die Mächte* (Zurich: Max Niehans, 1935), 110–111.

[126] Gustav Fochler-Hauke, *Der Ferne Osten: Macht- und Wirtschaftskampf in Ostasien* (Leipzig: B. G. Teubner, 1936), 69.

[127] Heinz Corazza, *Japan: Wunder des Schwertes* (Berlin: Klinkhardt & Biermann, 1935), 151.

culture, they should not ignore "the two other sacred treasures of our people, which embody justice and benevolence ... both traits of the Japanese character."[128] Much as Japanese transnational Nazis interpreted National Socialism selectively, their German counterparts emphasized aspects of Japanese civilization for their own political needs. In particular, the belief in Japanese racial purity enabled Corazza, Hitler, and Nazi Germany to enshrine Japan in a logically consistent niche within their ideology.

If Corazza and Tomoeda disagreed on a balanced portrayal of Japan, such difference was absent in *Japan and Germany, the Two Enigmas of the World*, published in April 1936. The book resulted from German-Japanese collaboration. It was coauthored by Eduard von Pustau, a naval officer, and "Okanouye-Kurota." The latter was described as a representative of the *Ōsaka asahi* and referred certainly to the correspondent Kuroda Reiji, born Okanoe Morimichi. The book argued that the two countries, out of their inner conviction and without prior arrangement or formal compacts, had come together to fight against the twin hegemonies of international capital and Marxism. Not only did the two governments make known their intention to combat Bolshevism, but the two peoples had also closed ranks for the struggle as no nation run by squabbling political parties could.[129] As in Japan, several months before the two regimes signed the Anti-Comintern Pact, a union against Bolshevism had already been suggested by advocates from civil societies on both sides.

Transnational Nazism in Nonfiction

Even if you are young and do not understand much of politics, you would still grasp that there is great tension here in the Far East. Another fact would be clear to you: how similar Japan's situation is to ours. We, too, are a nation with a long, glorious past and yet full of fresh vigor of youth. Only three years separated Japan's national restoration and Bismarck's national foundation. Both peoples are animated by the same national zeal and selfless devotion to a purposeful national leadership. The same industriousness and energy drive both nations. But the two peoples also have to fight hard for their living space,

---

[128] Takahiko Tomoeda, foreword to Corazza, 5. The three sacred treasures of Japan comprise a sword, mirror, and jewel.

[129] Eduard von Pustau and Okanouye-Kurota, *Japan und Deutschland, die beiden Welträtsel: Politische, wirtschaftliche und kulturelle Entwicklung* (Berlin: Deutscher Verlag für Politik und Wirtschaft, 1936), 202.

and they stand together in defense against the destructive power of Bolshevism. Would it have been surprising, if these two – as one of the leading German statesmen put it – spiritually related people had early on begun to work together?[130]

So wrote in 1937 Alfred Bohner, who had lived in Japan in the 1920s along with his two brothers as German teachers. The political atmosphere after the Anti-Comintern Pact facilitated the publication of some nonfiction but hindered other works. Those that depended on a peaceful environment and international traffic, such as missionaries' accounts and travelogues, virtually disappeared in the late 1930s. The production of dissertations continued apace, though as more young men and women were consumed by the war effort, fewer doctoral candidates were left to write dissertations. Only works with a partisan political message thrived, their opinions showing little diversity and often mere propaganda. Paul Ostwald, who first wrote a book called *Germany and Japan* in 1920, published a second work with the identical title in May 1941. He had every reason to feel vindicated: both Germany and Japan had concluded nonaggression pacts with the Soviet Union, and the continental bloc seemed stronger than ever.[131] Little did he know that in a month or so Operation Barbarossa would turn his vision into a chimera.

There was often talk of some sort of collaboration between the two countries in the interwar era. Such publications blossomed especially in the early 1920s. But nothing came of such proposals until the mid-1930s when developments within Germany readied the government to act on the idea of rapprochement. Germany was taken over by a radical regime with no interest in following the policy inherited from its republican predecessor. Some historians see the German-Japanese alliance as realization of the continental bloc promoted by Haushofer and other students of geopolitics, but most such schemes needed the inclusion of Russia in the union. When Hitler attacked the Soviet Union in June 1941, he destroyed all prospects of such a dream. In fact, the Weimar Republic implemented the concept of continental bloc much more profitably than the Third Reich ever did. It benefited far more and for far longer from its cooperation with the Soviet Union and China than Nazi Germany ever managed with Japan.

The books discussed in this chapter fostered an intellectual environment in which German-Japanese cooperation became plausible. They

---

[130] Alfred Bohner, *Japan und die Welt* (Berlin: Julius Beltz, 1937), 130.
[131] Paul Ostwald, *Deutschland und Japan: Eine Freundschaft zweier Völker* (Berlin: Junker und Dünnhaupt, 1941), 146.

portrayed Japan as a Westernized "cultured state" capable of self-preservation and advancement, and with which Germany could deal on an equal footing. Transnational Nazi nonfiction valued Japanese strength more than sympathy for China, and prioritized Japanese racial purity over Asiatic racial inferiority. But German books on Japan stood out far more for the dearth of biological, racist remarks than the occasional stereotypical clichés about the "inscrutable" Asians.

The overarching image of Japan was that of a competent, energetic, and industrious nation that belonged to the same group of great powers as Germany. Japan was never meant to be the perfect partner for Germany. No doubt Hitler was never fully satisfied with Japan. Ever since childhood he kept a vision of Japan that blended multiple sentiments – envy and admiration, underestimation and heroization, misinformed bigotry and misguided fascination. In many ways, the question "Japan: danger or model?" posed by Johannes Stoye was one that Hitler himself would have asked. Just as Stoye answered that Japan was a danger and a model, Hitler's Germany likewise reached the same conclusion that Japan was at once threatening and instructive. If Westernized Japan presented a danger, Germany might also take advantage of that threat to the liberal democratic West and the Soviet Union. Economic rationality might have argued for cooperation with China, but such reasoning also argued against attacking the Soviet Union, declaring war on America, or persecuting Jews. Romance, not sensible trade or production figures, appealed to the Nazis. Transnational Nazis did not need to embrace Japan, they just needed to accept it as good enough.

8   Japan in Voluntary Associations

One German, a philosopher. Two Germans, an association. Three Germans, a war.
                                                                  – Aphorism

The Motorist

In 1937, Rome joined the Anti-Comintern Pact forged originally by Berlin and Tokyo. Shortly thereafter, Eberhard Ponndorf, a native of Weimar recently dispatched to lead the unit of the National Socialist Motor Corps (Nationalsozialistisches Kraftfahrkorps, NSKK) in East Prussia, thought he found a way out of the fringe region. A member of the Nazi Party and SA since 1931, Ponndorf knew that the path upward in the polycratic Third Reich required him to "work toward the Führer" proactively by anticipating Hitler's wishes and acting accordingly.[1] So he wrote to his superior in Munich, Erwin Kraus, to plump for a motorcycle and automobile rally from Berlin via Rome to Tokyo.

Far from being outright insane, Ponndorf pleaded, the proposal had merit. The SS had long been burnishing its image through horsemanship, fencing, and other activities, so the NSKK should do the same: "But why should we not do something for once, something to show off to the public the grit and determination of the NSKK?"[2] Ponndorf envisioned a nine-month expedition starting from Germany, traversing Switzerland, Italy, North Africa, the Middle East, India, Southeast Asia, and finishing in Japan. The tour would achieve an international propaganda coup for Germany and its automobile industry. But even more crucial it would cement once and for all the predominance of the NSKK in all things automotive versus other institutions within Nazi Germany. He believed that the NSKK would not be burdened financially because

---

[1] Ian Kershaw, *Hitler, 1889–1936: Hubris* (New York: W. W. Norton, 1999), 529–591.
[2] BArch, NS 24/255, Ponndorf to Kraus, February 11, 1938.

carmakers such as BMW would sponsor the undertaking if Hitler and Hermann Göring expressed excitement. "I myself would like to lead the expedition," he added hopefully. Ponndorf was apparently rejected as deranged. He evidently received no response. The motor rally never took off. He remained in East Prussia. By the end of 1938, he seems no longer to have belonged to the NSKK.[3] The episode had no effect on German-Japanese relations, but it illustrates the influence Japan exercised in associational life in interwar Germany as well as the impact of Nazism on interpersonal, cultural, and political dynamics.

Japan might not have improved the fortune of Ponndorf or the NSKK, but it made the careers of other individuals and provided the raison d'être for several organizations. Interest clubs were a specialized means for Germans striving to familiarize themselves with Japan, but they were also much less accessible than newspapers, films, and books. Almost all Germans lacked the means to travel to East Asia. Universities, normally the fount and disseminator of the nation's collective knowledge, furnished only limited information beyond dissertations. Germany's 23 universities together could boast only three professorships of Japanology as of 1935.[4] Hamburg had the first and only chair. Leipzig and Berlin each had a regular professorship. For comparison, there were twenty professors of Indology, seven of Sinology, fifteen of Semitology, four of Islamic studies, eight of Egyptology, one of Assyriology, sixteen of Oriental studies, two of East Asian studies (both focusing on China), and one of Near Eastern studies. In contrast to German language study in Japan and courses such as Seminar Germania, finding a venue to study Japanese was a challenge. Only four universities (Berlin, Hamburg, Bonn, and Leipzig) regularly offered Japanese classes.[5] Their instruction could be quite innovative, for example the use of gramophones to teach pronunciation at the Oriental Seminar at Berlin, but only a tiny sliver of the population enjoyed access to higher education.[6] In 1931, the interwar

---

[3] Ponndorf (1897–1980) became *Gruppenführer* of NSKK-Motorgruppe Ostland in late 1936. Some sources report that he was out of the NSKK by late 1938, though SA documents from 1941 still indicate that he was an NSKK-Gruppenführer, in BArch, SA 108B. He remained in Königsberg as a Reichstag deputy for East Prussia until 1945.

[4] BArch, R 64IV/38, Wilhelm Burmeister to Paul Behncke, June 7, 1935. In addition, there was one lecturer in Jena, one (a Japanese national) in Frankfurt, and in Bonn one lecturer and an honorary professor from Japan.

[5] BArch, R 64IV/38, Behncke to Bernhard Rust, June 12, 1935. The lecturers in Jena and Frankfurt sometimes taught language courses.

[6] BTH, February 14, 1932, supplement.

year with the highest number of matriculants, there were 103,912 university students among Germany's population of roughly 65 million.[7] Unlike the effort by some Japanese to teach themselves German, attempts to teach oneself Japanese would have struck Germans as quixotic and bizarre. And the main textbook still in use in the 1920s had been written more than 30 years earlier.[8]

Under these circumstances, interest clubs in Germany had the opportunity and latitude to shape knowledge of Japan and advocate bilateral rapprochement. Voluntary associations had long performed key functions in public and personal lives in modern Germany.[9] By one count in 1930, there were over 5,000 registered societies in Berlin alone, while many others remained informal and unincorporated.[10] This chapter analyzes the influence that voluntary associations exercised in maintaining German-Japanese relations. Because the Weimar Republic's many crises kept the state from pursuing vigorous diplomacy vis-à-vis Japan, German civil society, with substantial initiative and support from some Japanese, had to step into the vacuum to manage relations through the available and familiar instrument of voluntary associations. In the 1920s and early 1930s, the individuals guiding the groups mostly concerned themselves with cultural and scholarly ties with Japan; the few activists agitating for political convergence operated in the margins. The ascent of Nazism triggered structural and ideological changes in Japanese studies in Germany. The most relentlessly political individuals were given unprecedented opportunities to promote Japan and insert themselves in Japan-related affairs. But the Nazification of German society introduced rank amateurs to leadership positions in voluntary associations, politicized knowledge of Japan, and prioritized dogmatism and party loyalty over truth and pragmatism. Through this duality, voluntary associations illustrate more clearly than other forms of media the possibilities and limits of transnational Nazism's accommodation of and identification with Japan.

---

[7] Michael Grüttner, *Studenten im Dritten Reich* (Paderborn: Ferdinand Schöningh, 1995), 487.

[8] Rudolf Lange, *Lehrbuch der japanischen Umgangsprache I: Formenlehre und die wichtigsten Regeln der Syntax*, 3rd ed. (Berlin: Walter de Gruyter, 1922).

[9] David Blackbourn, "The Discreet Charm of the Bourgeoisie: Reappraising German History in the Nineteenth Century," in *The Peculiarities of German History: Bourgeois Society and Politics in Nineteenth-Century Germany*, by David Blackbourn and Geoff Eley (New York: Oxford University Press, 1984), 190–205.

[10] JTM, November 13, 1930.

The Chemist

Most historical accounts trace the origins of German-Japanese associations to the Wa-Doku Kai (Japanese-German Society). It was established by the Japanese philosopher Inoue Tetsujirō in Berlin in 1888 and was reputedly the first binational organization in Germany in which members of both nationalities enjoyed equal standing.[11] It counted about 150 members at its peak, mostly Japanese students in Berlin and Germans who had experienced or were otherwise knowledgeable about Japan. The group published a journal, *East Asia*, and hosted lectures and gatherings to raise the awareness of Japan among the German public. Despite its outreach efforts, the organization had negligible impact outside its immediate circles. It dissolved in about 1912.[12]

World War I and its aftermath reduced Germany to such chaos that as far as the Weimar Republic was concerned far more urgent priorities eclipsed fostering ties with Japan, beyond negotiating a peace treaty and reestablishing diplomatic representation in 1920. The central government, preoccupied with reintegrating Germany with the world and softening the blows of Versailles, could do little to support Ambassador Wilhelm Solf. Thus Solf had to rely on his celebrity in the Japanese media to advocate for Germany through publicity and cultural associations. It took until mid-1927 for Berlin and Tokyo to conclude the new commerce treaty even though it behooved both parties to have done so sooner. Germany enjoyed a trade surplus vis-à-vis Japan, while Japan needed to acquire German patents.[13]

In this near absence of official attention, private individuals became caretakers of foreign relations. They conducted bilateral exchanges through associational activities. Initiatives by elements within German civil society to revive and encourage interactions with Japan bore fruit even before the commerce treaty was signed. After an enthusiastically

---

[11] Günther Haasch, ed., *Die Deutsch-Japanischen Gesellschaften von 1888 bis 1996* (Berlin: Wissenschaftsverlag Volker Spiess, 1996), xxiii. There is some discrepancy among German and Japanese sources in translating names of bilateral associations. German works tend to call them "German-Japanese" and Japanese ones "Japanese-German." I translate the titles into English based on the original word order and perhaps the location of the organization.

[12] Ibid., 11–66; Günther Haasch, "Die Wa-Doku-Kai (1888–1912) als Vorläuferin der Deutsch-Japanischen Gesellschaft Berlin," in *Berlin–Tôkyô im 19. und 20. Jahrhundert*, ed. Japanisch-Deutsches Zentrum (Berlin: Springer Verlag, 1997), 79–82; Bert Becker, *Japan an der Spree: Deutsch-Japanische Beziehungen im Spiegel Berlins und Brandenburgs* (Berlin: Ausländerbeauftragte des Senats, 1996), 22.

[13] BArch, R 5/6662, negotiations for commerce treaty, 1924–1927; BArch, R 43I/1099, Memorandum to Treaty of Commerce and Navigation, July 20, 1927.

received tour in Japan in 1924, Fritz Haber began publicly urging stronger scholarly and cultural bonds with the country.[14] He delivered speeches and wrote newspaper columns for his cause. He gathered like-minded figures, especially notable German Japanologists and expatriate Japanese academics, for their input, endorsement, and collaboration in founding a new organization. His energetic leadership and his colleagues' preparation culminated in the opening of the Japan Institute as a registered association in Berlin in 1926.[15] A year later, Solf and Japanese luminaries helped found the Japanese-German Cultural Society as the Japan Institute's counterpart in Tokyo.

Haber's reputation, as well as those of the major figures in Japanese studies whom he mobilized, conferred much prestige on the institute and made it the premier German-Japanese association into the early 1930s.[16] Its honorary members included Viscount Gotō Shinpei, former ambassador to Germany Honda Kumatarō, and Solf. The officers, headed by Haber as chairman, included representatives highly placed in academia and bureaucracy.[17] The board of trustees read like a who's who of Japanese studies in Germany. It featured Karl Florenz, the first and at the time only professor of Japanology in Germany; Otto Kümmel, director of East Asian art at the Berlin State Museum; Ludwig Riess, an authority on Japanese history and the final head of Wa-Doku Kai; Karl Haushofer, a proponent of geopolitics and convergence with Japan; and Clemens Scharschmidt, the lecturer of Japanese at the University of Berlin. Almost everyone who was anyone in the field in Germany had something to do with the Japan Institute, a far cry from the open and informal Wa-Doku Kai.

These trustees were all employees of the state in one fashion or another, but their involvement did not mean the government controlled the organization. Germany had no private universities, so all academics and many researchers were civil servants by definition, with Haber, the

---

[14] Margit Szöllösi-Janze, *Fritz Haber 1868–1934: Eine Biographie* (Munich: C. H. Beck, 1998), 560–580; Dietrich Stoltzenberg, *Fritz Haber: Chemist, Nobel Laureate, German, Jew* (Philadelphia: Chemical Heritage Press, 2004), 263–269.

[15] Eberhard Friese, *Japaninstitut Berlin und Deutsch-Japanische Gesellschaft Berlin: Quellenlage und ausgewählte Aspekte ihrer Politik 1926–1945* (Berlin: East Asian Institute, Free University of Berlin, 1980); Eberhard Friese, "Wir brauchen den Austausch geistiger Güter!," in *Berlin–Tôkyô im 19. und 20. Jahrhundert*, 233–244; Haasch, ed., *Die Deutsch-Japanischen Gesellschaften*, 73–77.

[16] Haber (1868–1934) is known for inventing the process that extracts atmospheric nitrogen, which enables the production of fertilizer or explosives without any need for natural nitrate deposits. He won the Nobel Prize in Chemistry in 1918. He led the Kaiser Wilhelm Institute for Physical Chemistry and Electrochemistry until 1933.

[17] PA AA, R 85969, constitution of the Japan Institute, 1926.

director of a Kaiser Wilhelm Institute, as the prime example. Their participation in the Japan Institute did not fall within their official capacities but were their private, extracurricular activities, particularly for Haber the chemist. Although the Foreign Office and especially Solf welcomed the idea of the institute, German officialdom only played a passive role in its establishment and activities. The government issued no directives and did not demand specific outcomes. Its involvement consisted only of providing office space for the institute and its library in the Berlin City Palace, and an annual subsidy of 61,000 RM after 1926.[18] In the preparatory stage, the seed money was almost entirely donated by the Japanese pharmaceutical entrepreneur Hoshi Hajime, who admired Haber so much that he invited the Nobel laureate to visit Japan in 1924. Interaction with Japan, to the extent that it attracted any interest among the German populace, posed no divisive political issues that provoked strong debate. Anyone vaguely familiar with German-Japanese relations could agree that encouraging the flow of goods and technology to Japan could only enrich a Germany impoverished by war, reparations, and isolation.

In the development of the Japan Institute, advancing Japanese studies in Germany and facilitating bilateral scholarly communication superseded foreign-policy considerations. In his inaugural speech, Haber envisioned the association playing an independent role for Germany in cultural and scientific exchange similar to those of embassies in diplomacy or chambers of commerce in trade.[19] Similarly, Friedrich Max Trautz, an emerging talent in Japanology appointed as the institute's German codirector, had already in 1923 tried to persuade the authorities that abstract knowledge of Japan could translate into concrete benefits.[20] He cited an incident after the war when an international commission was drawing the new German-Polish boundary in Upper Silesia, but Germany could not find anyone to translate documents for the Japanese commissioner. He added that scientific expertise was the only card Germany could play after the ruinous war and hyperinflation. Even the organization's registered title, "Institute for the Promotion of Reciprocal Knowledge of the Intellectual Life and Public Institutions in Japan and Germany" (Institut zur Förderung der wechselseitigen Kenntnis des

---

[18] BArch, R 64IV/224, table of the institute's funding, May 15, 1936.
[19] PA AA, R 85969, speech by Haber, December 4, 1926.
[20] PA AA, R 85969, memorandum by Trautz to Foreign Office, 1923. Trautz (1877–1952) received his doctorate in Japanology in 1921 and earned his *Habilitation* in 1927. In 1933, he became the professor of Japanology at the University of Berlin. He moved to Japan in 1931 and led the German Research Institute in Kyoto until his return to Germany in 1938. BArch, NS 9/Box 4, list of Nazi Party members in Japan, 1945.

geistigen Lebens und der öffentlichen Einrichtungen in Japan und Deutschland), made no reference to aspirations for engaging in official affairs.

On paper, the institute commanded formidable human and material resources to pursue its mission. Its officers held high posts in academia and society. Its reading room boasted a sizable collection of journals and reference books in Japanese.[21] But in reality, it had to operate within inflexible constraints. The German populace as a whole was, or at least was perceived to be, far more concerned about and sympathetic to China than Japan. Berliners encountered more resident Chinese than Japanese in more parts of the city in the 1930s.[22] They could even explore Chinatowns of sorts near Jannowitzbrücke or on Kantstrasse.[23] Especially dispiriting for those striving to promote Japan through associational activities, more organizations in Germany concentrated on interpreting China than Japan, even though the chaos in China made it a less lucrative, more difficult subject, with little financial or political support from China.[24] In the face of China's greater popularity, Trautz wrote in 1928 to Wilhelm Gundert, manager of the Japanese-German Cultural Society, that the Japan Institute must take measures to counter the "Germans' generally widespread preference for China and comparatively low regard for Japan."[25] He had as early as 1922 tried to use this interest in China to inveigle the Foreign Office to support an institute for Japanology. He argued circuitously that "Japan is the world's oldest and most successful researcher of China and Sinologist."[26] Moreover, the institute's very excellence and formality might have intimidated people only casually curious about Japan. Because perhaps only a few dozen Germans, scattered across the country, could read Japanese without difficulty, most of the institute's periodicals and

---

[21] BArch, R 57NEU/1043, list of participants of Japan Institute, n.d.; PA AA, R 85970, inventory of library, December 24, 1929.

[22] In 1936, 665 Chinese nationals were registered to be living in Berlin versus 356 Japanese, in *Statistisches Jahrbuch der Stadt Berlin 1937* (Berlin: Statistisches Amt der Reichshauptstadt Berlin, 1938), 99. Most Chinese in Berlin lived in Charlottenburg, Lichtenberg, and Schöneberg. The Japanese congregated overwhelmingly in Schöneberg. More Japanese than Chinese visited Berlin, though only for short periods of various lengths.

[23] JTM, January 10, 1934.

[24] There were the China-Studien-Gesellschaft, Verband für den Fernen Osten (renamed Deutsch-Chinesischer Verband in 1943), Verein zur Förderung der deutsch-mandschurischen Wirtschaftsbeziehungen, and China-Institut.

[25] PA AA, R 85970, Trautz to Gundert, October 3, 1928.

[26] PA AA, R 85969, memorandum by Trautz, January 1922.

books probably gathered dust at its library ensconced on the fourth floor of the ex-Kaiser's City Palace.[27] Despite Trautz's rhetoric of broadening Germans' awareness of Japan, the institute was never intended to speak to or engage with the man in the street, at least not as its top priority. Its outreach efforts, though not very thoroughly documented in the early years, comprised public lectures and exhibitions. Laypeople were probably charmed by an exhibition of artwork by Japanese pupils. But talks on more arcane subjects such as "Japanese attitudes toward European music," "medical and ethical matters from Japan," or "Zen-Buddhist meditation" probably did not attract large audiences.[28] The institute's management seemed content to host presentations on narrow themes in small gatherings rather than attempt to attract larger crowds. Although Germans could hardly avoid coverage of Japan's seizure of Manchuria in the early 1930s, the institute maintained an uncharacteristic silence about the conflict. The institute likely wanted to avoid upsetting its Japanese participants and patrons. It stayed away from the topic precisely because the Sino-Japanese conflict polarized public opinions among Germans.

The Philosopher

The institute's contentment with its specialist character, restricted membership, and, in particular, political irrelevance spurred the emergence of a splinter group led by Kanokogi Kazunobu.[29] A philosopher of religion, Kanokogi had played a role in conceptualizing the Japan Institute and nominated members for its board of trustees.[30] He suggested that an action-oriented subcommittee be formed within but separate from the deliberative and cumbersome board. After the institute came into existence, he served as the Japanese codirector for about two years until the end of his visiting professorship at Berlin in early 1929. But he seems not to have participated in its activities with much regularity or great enthusiasm. His attitude made such a poor impression to some that in

---

[27] Trautz mentioned the paucity of Germans able to read Japanese in Friedrich Max Trautz, "'Kulturbeziehungen' und 'Kulturaustausch' zwischen Deutschland und Japan," *Ostasiatische Rundschau* 9, no. 2 (1928), 42–44.

[28] PA AA, R 85971, report of meeting, June 23, 1932.

[29] Kanokogi (1884–1949) studied philosophy and completed a dissertation in Germany. His political views drifted increasingly toward nationalism and xenophobia in the 1930s. In Japan, he helped found a party modeled on the Nazi Party and published widely on Pan-Asianism. He was arrested as a Class A war criminal in 1945. Christopher W. A. Szpilman, "Kanokogi Kazunobu: 'Imperial Asia,' 1937," in *Pan-Asianism*, 123–126.

[30] PA AA, R 85969, Kanokogi to Haber, April 27, 1926.

1934 Trautz still felt the need to describe Kanokogi sarcastically as the "so-called" Japanese codirector.[31]

Kanokogi had envisioned a more ambitious, activist bilateral association from the outset, so he was disappointed by the Japan Institute. When he recommended the trustees to Haber, Kanokogi articulated his goal for the institute to concern itself not merely with "retrospective Japan research. It should instead strive to be a living institution for bilateral spiritual exchange in the realm of culture and civilization as a whole."[32] To further this end, Kanokogi even invited Chancellor Wilhelm Marx to a lecture he was giving in 1927.[33] He evidently made a nuissance of himself by agitating for the institute's leadership to steer the organization into more political waters. Trautz became so alarmed that he ranked the thwarting of Kanokogi's endeavors to "pull the rug from under the scientific and cultural Japan Institute and to drag it toward the political and economic" as its second objective behind popularizing Japan in Sinophilic Germany.[34] Trautz fumed privately that Kanokogi seemed reluctant to work within the institute's framework and was plotting to exploit it as a vehicle for his own aggrandizement. Still later, Trautz complained to the Kobe–Osaka chapter of the Nazi Party that while he tried to lead the institute in the "German tradition and for German interests," Kanokogi attempted to hijack it to serve the purposes of Japanese propaganda.[35] Kanokogi's behavior, even if not quite so egregious as described, infuriated Trautz, who always considered himself the *Urvater* of the institute – rightfully so, because he had been lobbying the government to sponsor such a group since the early 1920s.

So in July 1928, not even two years after the Japan Institute opened, Kanokogi resorted to launching the German-Japanese Study Group (Deutsch-Japanische Arbeitsgemeinschaft, DJAG). He had already proposed in 1926 a distinct "society of friends of Japan research" for promoting Japanese studies, while the institute focused on supporting Japanology.[36] That is, the society would function as a public relations arm for the institute and perhaps Japan. His idea met either rejection or silence, which together with his dissatisfaction with the institute, prompted him to strike out on his own.

---

[31] PA AA, R 85961, confidential report by Trautz, June 7, 1934.
[32] PA AA, R 85969, Kanokogi to Haber, April 27, 1926.
[33] BArch, R 43II/1454, Reich Chancellery to Verband für den Fernen Osten, November 21, 1927.
[34] PA AA, R 85970, Trautz to Gundert, October 3, 1928.
[35] PA AA, R 85961, confidential report by Trautz, June 7, 1934.
[36] PA AA, R 85969, Kanokogi to Haber, April 27, 1926.

The DJAG reflected Kanokogi's idea of a bilateral association.[37] Whereas the institute specifically ruled out political or economic entanglements, the DJAG had as its expressed mission "the collective investigation of the cultural, political, and economic problems of Japan, and the propagation of accurate presentations of Japan to the German public."[38] In his opening remarks, he stated unambiguously that the DJAG was founded on the idea that "an Eastward orientation could play a greater role in German politics instead of the current unilateral commitment to the West and that Japan should also make a stronger entrance into the German political consciousness."[39] The philosopher Kanokogi's fingerprints on the DJAG were also evident in the group's stated interest in exploring Japan's "national psyche," which diverged from the institute's generally academic orientation. Unlike the institute's all-star officers, the DJAG had to make do with figures less well established in Japanology, cochaired by Kanokogi and the artist Fritz Rumpf.[40] As part of its strategy to put a positive spin on Japan, the DJAG published a journal, *Yamato*, the sort of communication the institute pointedly abjured.

But the institute and the DJAG were not adversaries. Rather, they operated in distinct but related and increasingly overlapping areas. Within a year of founding the DJAG, Kanokogi departed for Japan, followed not long afterward by Trautz. The two took their feud to Japan and so removed their interpersonal enmity from the two organizations.[41] Meanwhile, Wilhelm Solf retired from his ambassadorship to Japan and took over the institute at Haber's request. Solf also became the honorary German cochairman of the DJAG, thus bridging the leaderships of both groups. The DJAG resolved to formalize itself in early 1930 as a registered association called the German-Japanese Association (Deutsch-Japanische Gesellschaft, DJG). Besides Solf, Japan Institute board members like Otto Kümmel and Clemens Scharschmidt assumed supervisory roles in the DJG. While the two entities formally maintained a

---

[37] Haasch, ed., *Die Deutsch-Japanischen Gesellschaften*, 78–94.

[38] Statutes §1 and §2 of DJAG quoted in Haasch, ed., *Die Deutsch-Japanischen Gesellschaften*, 80.

[39] *Deutsche Tageszeitung*, August 26, 1928.

[40] There was eventually some overlap in the institute's and DJAG's memberships, but in the DJAG's early years it was led by several individuals with no ties to the institute.

[41] Kanokogi and Momo Minosuke appointed themselves protectors of a German seeking to join the Nazi Party's Kobe–Osaka chapter in 1934. The young man's mother, backed by the two Japanese professors, accused Trautz of sabotaging her son's application out of envy. Trautz counterclaimed that Kanokogi was maneuvering to accumulate more power, in PA AA, R 85961, confidential report by Trautz, June 7, 1934. For more on German Nazis in Japan: see Nakamura Ayano, *Tōkyō no Hākenkuroitsu: Higashi Ajia ni ikita Doitsujin no kiseki* (Tokyo: Hakusuisha, 2010).

division of labor – the institute focusing on research and scholarship, the DJG on politics, economy, and public relations – they began cohosting events. In a sign of their convergence, the institute moved out of its perch in the City Palace to Schöneberg district in 1931, closer to the Japanese colony in Berlin.

Still, the DJG nearly monopolized the cultivation of bilateral personal bonds.[42] The DJG's Statute §1 stated the group's mission: "collective research on the cultural, political, and economic problems of Japan, propagation of accurate presentations of Japan in the German public sphere, as well as the maintenance of personal relations between Japanese and Germans."[43] Factors that once seemingly disadvantaged the DJG vis-à-vis the Japan Institute, such as its nonacademic character, less restrictive membership, and more publicity-minded outlook, actually recommended it as the preferred venue for Germans and Japanese to mingle without intellectual expectations. The DJG used the Japan Institute's facilities to organize regular "German-Japanese gentlemen's evenings," and for ladies lessons on Japanese floral arrangements.[44] For Germans mildly interested in Japan, the DJG offered the rare opportunity to meet some Japanese, a feat that not even many German universities could claim.

By the end of 1932, both the specialists at the Japan Institute and the activists at the DJG could be optimistic about raising Japan's profile in Germany. The government continued to provide a stipend to the institute, even if reduced to 44,000 RM in the 1931–1932 fiscal year.[45] Far more important, a new department of Japanese studies opened in 1932 at the University of Leipzig, despite the national economic meltdown and political paralysis. Its endowment of 110,000 RM was mostly supplied by Japanese donors in Osaka, including ¥15,000 from Motoyama Hikoichi, president of the *Ōsaka mainichi*, and 25,000 gold yen from the fertilizer manufacturer Nippon Chisso. Sata Aihiko, president of the Osaka City Medical Academy and a member of the Japanese-German Cultural

---

[42] Other associations included the Japanischer Verein in Deutschland, which was a gathering venue for the Japanese in Berlin rather than a place for exchange. There was also the Deutsche Gesellschaft für Natur- und Völkerkunde Ostasiens (also known as Ostasiatische Gesellschaft), but it was based in Japan. The Gesellschaft für ostasiatische Kunst busied itself mainly with art and not only with Japan but East Asia. In Hamburg there were also a few associations with East Asia as a focus, such as the Ostasiatischer Verein Hamburg-Bremen.

[43] PA AA, R 104900, statutes of the DJG, March 19, 1930.

[44] PA AA, R 85971, report of meeting, June 23, 1932.

[45] BArch, R 64IV/224, table of the institute's funding, May 15, 1936.

Society, raised 60,000 RM.[46] The professorship of Japanology, the second in Germany, was assumed by Hans Ueberschaar. He had lived in Japan for two decades and was a highly promising scholar among his cohort of Japanologists. In the 15 years or so that he spent teaching around Osaka, he cultivated personal ties to luminaries that ultimately bore fruit for Germany's production of knowledge of Japan. Even before his new appointment, Ueberschaar already improved bilateral exchange in 1930 by raising ¥6,000 from the *Mainichi* for a pair of two-year scholarships for German students to study in Kyoto.[47] In the unofficial atmosphere that characterized much of the interaction between interwar Germany and Japan, international relations comprised the aggregate of interpersonal relations. Without personalities such as Haber, Solf, Trautz, Kanokogi, and Ueberschaar and his Japanese friends, German-Japanese collaboration in associations would have been much diminished.

The Admiral

Although Kanokogi and Trautz clashed over the proper purpose of knowledge of Japan in Germany, Trautz seems to have undergone an ideological conversion by late 1932 and adopted views approximating his rival's. In August, Trautz sent Hitler – then still a private individual – a newspaper clipping from Japan with a photo of the Nazi leader.[48] He wrote to Hitler again in May 1933 to report on a play about the Führer that he saw in Kyoto and the enthusiastic reaction it elicited from the spectators, one of whom supposedly told Trautz that Japan, too, needed a Hitler. Trautz also sent two of his works on Japan, which entered Hitler's personal library. And he stated that he and some like-minded individuals were working on Hitler's behalf in Japan.

Why did Trautz, who previously had showed no tendency to politicize Japan in Germany, now try to curry favor with the Nazis? The year 1933 ushered in a new era not just for Germany but also for individuals such as Trautz and associational activities centering on Japan, though not necessarily in predictable ways. Upon taking power, the Nazis went about transforming the country according to their weltanschauung.

---

[46] TN, October 3, 1931; Universitätsarchiv Leipzig (hereafter: UAL), Phil.Fak D1/17:07, Akten der Philosophischen Fakultät zu Leipzig betr. Stiftung: Deutsch-Japanisches Studentenheim, 1932; UAL, PA1008, Dean of the School of Philosophy to Saxon Ministry of Education, July 27, 1931; UAL, PA1008, Saxon Ministry of Education to Saxon Foreign Ministry, November 27, 1931.
[47] PA AA, R 85963, Otto von Erdmannsdorff to Foreign Office, June 28, 1930.
[48] BArch, R 43II/1454, Trautz to Hitler, May 30, 1933.

People deemed unworthy of the Nazi national community, such as non-Aryans (Jews especially), communists, and eventually gays and other social outcasts, were excluded through legal or extralegal means from Germany's civic, social, economic, and cultural life. In practice, the Nazi regime unleashed *Gleichschaltung* to implement totalitarian rule by suppressing pluralism in entities from hobby clubs to the Reichstag. The regime at times enforced uniformity from above, though often the population Nazified itself, as when groups forced out members incompatible with Nazism. The long arm of *Gleichschaltung* even reached across Eurasia, as Trautz began working toward the Führer in Japan.[49]

At first glance, Nazism, with its ideology of Aryan supremacy, would seem to defeat the purpose of the Japan Institute and particularly the DJG, whose missions were the scholarly appreciation and the political advocacy of a foreign people. There certainly were anecdotes of overzealous Nazis harassing Japanese nationals in Germany. Besides the previously mentioned incidents involving the correspondent Suzuki Tōmin and constitutional scholar Minobe Tatsukichi, the hygienist Akano Rokurō quit Germany abruptly after witnessing students at the University of Berlin express disapproval of Erwin Bälz, the Meiji emperor's physician, marrying a Japanese.[50] Tokyo protested at language in Germany's new legislation that categorically discriminated against all non-Aryans in the civil service. The Japanese embassy requested in October 1933 that the German government clarify "colored" in its proposed reform to the criminal law code.[51] The *Japan Times* reported "the dismissal of a German professor from a post which he had honorably held for many years merely because he happened to be of mixed German and Japanese blood."[52] Yet these objections stood mostly on principled, not empirical ground, because very few Japanese were working for the German state. In fact, several Japanese nationals continued to be employed by German universities, including one hired after the passage of the civil service law.[53] The dismissed professor was thus "guilty" of being mixed-race rather than Japanese. Few Japanese could have been inconvenienced by the Nazi ascent. Just 350–400 Japanese lived in Berlin

---

[49] Trautz was admitted into the Nazi Party in April 1934. BArch, NS 9/Box 4, Nazi Party membership records, 1946.

[50] Geheime Staatsarchiv Preußischer Kulturbesitz, Rep. 76 Va Sekt. 1 JiA. XII No. 42 Bd. II, Heinrich Zeiss to Ministry of Interior, September 25, 1934.

[51] Harumi Furuya, "Japan's Racial Identity in the Second World War: The Cultural Context of the Japanese Treatment of POWs," in *Japanese Prisoners of War*, eds. Philip Towle, Margaret Kosuge, and Yōichi Kibata (London: Hambledon and London, 2000), 123; Fox, 83–93.

[52] JTM, October 22, 1933.   [53] JTM, October 7, 1933.

during the 1930s.[54] No SA thugs stood outside Japanese restaurants and shops to berate potential customers. Very few Japanese residents or visitors had to endure the trauma of physical harm. The *Vossische Zeitung* reported in January 1934 that a German man was sentenced to prison for nine months for cursing and hitting a Chinese traveler. The punishment was made exemplary because the perpetrator was deemed to have sullied Germany's reputation.[55] Japanese expatriates, mostly academics, diplomats, officers, and merchants, moved in respectable circles of colleagues that ruled out boorish behaviors toward guests from so far away. The unpleasantness experienced by the Japanese mentioned above came at the hands of strangers from outside the victims' social milieus – random onlookers in the case of Suzuki, fellow passengers in the case of Minobe, and university students in the case of Akano. At least from the racial standpoint, the Nazi regime raised no objections to Japanese belonging to binational associations. The DJG, at the request of its Japanese participants, even refrained from specifying that its German members had to be Aryans, a rarity in the Third Reich and clear illustration of the transnational Nazi accommodation of Japan.[56]

Yet the DJG was not untouched by the wholesale Nazification of society. Some Japanese in Berlin opened the door for the DJG's *Gleichschaltung* in April 1933. They complained to the authorities that the DJG had a Jewish chairman, Wilhelm Haas, and board member, Alexander Chanoch, who were allegedly vilifying Germany to impressionable new Japanese arrivals – a reminder that the Japanese, especially transnational Nazis, did not identify with other "fellow victims" of Nazism.[57] The DJG's entire leadership was made to step down, even though Haas had led the DJAG after Kanokogi's departure and Chanoch had belonged to the organization since its days as a lowly splinter group. A coterie of opportunistic amateurs only marginally involved in German-Japanese

[54] *Statistisches Jahrbuch der Stadt Berlin*, 1930–1939.   [55] VZ, January 12, 1934.
[56] BArch R 64IV/231, Friedrich Wilhelm Hack to Kümmel, September 19, 1933.
[57] PA AA, R 104900, Artur Görlitzer to Kurt Daluege, April 24, 1933. Annette Hack conjectures that the accusers were not Japanese but one or more of the Germans scheming to take over the DJG: see Haasch, ed., *Die Deutsch-Japanischen Gesellschaften*, 113. I think there is no reason to doubt the content of the document. In his letter to Commissioner for Special Duties Daluege, Deputy Gauleiter Görlitzer stated that the Japanese lodged the complaint to him personally. He had no motive to lie to Daluege. Görlitzer's explanation that the Japanese were troubled that the chairman was sowing hatred of Germany to those Japanese just coming to the country, if true, would have concerned the local Japanese. If some German members wanted to target the Jews they could have done so directly and taken credit for it. That the denunciation was made indirectly to outside authorities indicates that it originated from the Japanese, whose cultural background and status as guests in Germany deterred them from speaking out openly.

exchange so far inserted itself to make over the association in compliance with the new ideological climate.[58] The details of this local seizure of power are shrouded in some uncertainty, but the outcome is clear.[59]

Foremost, the DJG adopted a new set of statutes and a new management structure.[60] In accordance with the Nazi leadership principle, the German and Japanese cochairmanships were replaced by a sole presidency, assumed by retired admiral Paul Behncke.[61] The post of secretary was reserved for SS-Obersturmbannführer (lieutenant colonel) Herbert Scholz, who compensated for his clerical deficiencies with political connections. He held a position in the liaison staff of the Nazi Party and was a foreign policy consultant for the SA leadership. His close relations with Rudolf Hess could attract a powerful patron for the DJG. The architects of the new DJG even planned to invite Göring and Foreign Minister Konstantin von Neurath to the honorary steering committee, but they had to "settle for" Wilhelm Solf and the Japanese ambassador.[62] The board was cleansed of people distasteful to the new regime. Because the DJG did not explicitly exclude non-Aryans, at least one individual, Otto Kümmel, was approached confidentially to identify "definite" and "possible" Jews and "hence left-wing radicals" among the members.[63] A large advisory committee, consisting of prominent representatives from the bureaucracy, military, academia, and businesses, was created to lend clout to the organization.

The far more consequential seizure of power was the displacement of the Japan Institute by the DJG. The two organizations already shared some members and functions before 1933. Political developments afterward hastened their convergence, or more precisely the subordination of

---

[58] Fox, 179. The mastermind behind the DJG's *Gleichschaltung* was Friedrich Wilhelm Hack, owner of a trading firm with business ties to East Asia who once lived in Japan. He engaged in rogue diplomacy on behalf of Ribbentrop in the mid-1930s. His contribution to the Anti-Comintern Pact was as a go-between for the Ribbentrop Office and the Japanese army. Another busybody was Hans Musa, who in early 1934 was in Japan on a self-appointed diplomatic mission but only managed to antagonize the local Nazis: see PA AA, R 85961, Dirksen to Foreign Office, April 24, 1934.

[59] Haasch, ed., *Die Deutsch-Japanischen Gesellschaften*, 106–122. The description of the takeover as a "coup" is accurate, but the DJG was not alone. While the coup at the DJG unfolded in its particular manner, other associations underwent a similar process that involved the ousting of those found unsuitable and the promotion of those whose main qualification was their devotion to Nazism or at least eagerness to jump onto the bandwagon.

[60] BArch, R 64IV/3, statutes of DJG, November 20, 1933.

[61] Behncke (1866–1937) spent two years in East Asia as the captain of a gunboat. After World War I, he became head of the naval command, retiring in 1924. BArch, RW 59/2161, Personalakte Admiral Behncke.

[62] PA AA, R 104900, draft of proposed members of the DJG, *c.* 1933.

[63] BArch, R 64IV/231, Hack to Kümmel, September 19, 1933.

the institute to the DJG. The institute had drifted about for some time. Haber and Trautz's departures deprived it of sustained, energetic guidance. Its apolitical outlook and unwieldy leadership structure proved inadequate to negotiate the vicissitudes in the early 1930s, much as Kanokogi had foreseen. Most damning, the institute was "tainted" for having Haber as its founder. In early 1934, six years after Haber vacated the chairmanship and months after his self-imposed exile from Germany, Trautz still had to fend off accusations of having collaborated with a Jew.[64]

By contrast, the more agile and less scrupulous DJG reinvented itself to take advantage of the regime change to amass political power. Although *Gleichschaltung* effectively destroyed pluralistic Germany through marginalizing organizations not explicitly affiliated with Nazi ideology, groups willing to conform and transform as the DJG did could thrive. The DJG jettisoned its human baggage soon after Hitler became chancellor and installed a new management in touch with the new masters of Germany. It adopted new bylaws to anoint itself the epicenter of German-Japanese relations. Statute §1 of the reformed DJG now claimed its mission was "to cultivate relations between Germany and Japan, to bolster the knowledge of Japan in Germany, and to provide advice and assistance to those Japanese staying in Germany."[65] The association's rapidly expanding ambitions threatened to outgrow its budget. But through appealing to the DJG's own SS officer, Behncke could wangle more funds from other institutions and the government. Behncke mentioned in his request that the reduced means of the Japan Institute could no longer support and serve the DJG. The supersession of the DJG over the Japan Institute soon became unmistakable. In addition to his chief appointment as DJG President, Behncke became head of the institute. Symbolically, the DJG and the institute moved next door to each other in Schöneberg.

The DJG assiduously courted allies near the center of political power to fortify its position. It created new posts to accommodate "advisers" with no knowledge of or prior interest in Japan, just substantial connections that helped the association attract other influential individuals. Businesses, too, could become corporate members. As a result of the DJG's recruitment drive, membership had swollen sevenfold to about 350 by early 1934.[66] The DJG was determined to cultivate the ascendant SS. In late 1934, not even a full year after its reorganization, the DJG was

---

[64] PA AA, R 85961, Sofie Leo to Wilhelm Brückner, March 27, 1934.
[65] BArch, R 64IV/3, statutes of DJG, November 20, 1933.
[66] PA AA, R 104900, Behncke to Rudolf Graf Strachwitz, February 23, 1934.

self-assured enough to invite Reichsführer-SS Heinrich Himmler to its events. Himmler apparently never attended any DJG functions but felt obliged to dispatch high-ranking underlings in his stead. After failing to land Himmler, the DJG expanded its guest list to include other SS chiefs. It worked equally hard to associate itself with officials in other branches of the party and government. Behncke boasted at a DJG lecture in late 1935 that he had the honor to welcome Ambassador Joachim von Ribbentrop, the mayor of Berlin Heinrich Sahm, and representatives from the military, party, government, and city authorities.[67]

With Behncke at the helm, the DJG navigated resolutely into the realm of power politics. Despite its bombast about a radical break from the past, the Nazi regime, like its republican predecessor, did not devote much effort to improving official ties with Japan, especially because traditional conservatives still ran the Foreign Office and War Ministry in the early years. The DJG stepped in to play the part of a semi-official entity capable of addressing foreign dignitaries, and state, party, and military bureaucracies on an equal footing. It assigned itself the responsibilities of an advocacy group, mediation firm, and liaison agency for all things German-Japanese. Behncke's rank proved convenient when a Japanese naval squadron visited Europe in mid-1934. The DJG hosted a reception for the Japanese officers and German state and party functionaries. He used the occasion to trumpet "true Prussianism and the old national spirit of Japan" and proclaim that the two peoples "are now fighting the same battle for honor and equality rights."[68] The Japanese admiral reciprocated and declared that "the Japanese and German nations have in common ability, bravery and endurance, and thanks further to their love of country, Germany and Japan occupy a special place among the nations." The DJG had acquired such stature in bilateral relations by mid-1935 that when the publication of two books critical of Japanese trade policies upset the Japanese community in Berlin and threatened to trigger protests from the Japanese embassy, the Foreign Office itself contemplated using Behncke's good offices to ease the tension.[69]

Such forays into unofficial diplomacy emboldened the DJG to dream of a grander future. It submitted to the Foreign Office a breathtaking list of demands and goals in December 1934.[70] Most concerned public relations and propaganda. The DJG planned to publish a German-Japanese

[67] BArch, R 64IV/257, speech by Behncke, October 29, 1935.   [68] JTM, June 27, 1934.
[69] PA AA, R 85964, note to State Secretary Bülow, May 24, 1934. The books were written by Ernst Schultze.
[70] PA AA, R 85981, Rudolf Strobl Edler von Ravelsberg to Hermann Katzenberger, December 4, 1934.

newsletter and had already identified four correspondents deemed sympathetic to Japan as potential editors. It added that German Protestant and Catholic missionaries in Japan should also contribute to the publication. It recommended that illustrated magazines in Germany feature more photographs of Japan and issue a "Germany and Japan" number as the *Japan Times* did in 1934. It aimed to host photographic exhibitions, film exchanges, and athletic events. The DJG also claimed leadership in managing relations with Japanese expatriates in Germany. Its long-term goal was to launch a German-Japanese academy that would offer medical and technical courses. It called on the German Academic Exchange Service to produce informational material for Germans and Japanese interested in studying in each other's country. Finally, the DJG planned to give itself the power to create an office for certifying German-Japanese translations.

Before this ambitious vision could materialize, the DJG missed no chance to enhance its relevance by addressing matters trivial and profound. Behncke acted as a referee for Kuroda Reiji in 1934 when the *Asahi* correspondent sought an interview with Hitler.[71] In November 1935, Behncke called for establishing chairs of Japanese studies at the universities of Berlin and Munich. He pointed out that whereas 18 Germans were teaching at Japanese universities, there were only three professorships of Japanology in Germany.[72] The DJG even took up the cause of a Japanese restaurateur whose business suffered because he could not obtain an alcohol license. The DJG contacted the Schöneberg district authorities on his behalf and depicted the local matter in foreign-policy terms. It suggested that the borough police department should take into account "German interests" in considering the restaurant's application because the Japanese chef and patrons could construe rejection as national affront.[73]

The DJG also did not shirk more sensitive problems. It interceded for the few people of mixed German and Japanese ancestry ensnared as bycatch in the Nazi dragnet trawling for non-Aryans. The regime did not launch any campaign against Japanese nationals, who as guests could and did not seek integration in the Third Reich. But the biracial Japanese Germans presented a peculiar dilemma. Their partial Germanness entitled them to stake a claim to membership in the national community

[71] BArch, R 43II/1454, Kuroda to Hitler, November 22, 1934.
[72] BLA, November 29, 1935.
[73] BArch, R 64IV/239, Strobl to Police Department of Schöneberg-Wilmersdorf, January 28, 1936.

and thus rendered them a threat to its racial purity.[74] They were not persecuted as the Jews were, but they experienced humiliation and hindrance in their everyday lives. A few lost jobs. Some were barred from the Nazi Party or affiliated organizations. Others were expelled from universities. Many fell afoul of the authorities when they applied to marry "full Aryans." In desperation and faced with few options for redress, about a dozen victims turned to the DJG for assistance.[75] Individual DJG members vouched for the character of some of the Japanese Germans. Hans Ueberschaar, who as a party member commanded more credibility, single-handedly interceded for at least three.[76] The DJG corresponded copiously on the victims' behalf with various party and government agencies. But the DJG's mediation in such delicate matters was a thankless quest. As far as can be ascertained, the petitions for relief from Aryan laws were mired in delay and indecision. Although the regime narrowed its target for discrimination from non-Aryans to Jews in the 1935 Nuremberg Laws, the Nazi Office of Racial Policy stood its ground on refusing to consider the Japanese Aryans.[77] A few of the Japanese Germans even cited the Führer lauding the Japanese as "honorary Aryans" to support their petitions, but the phrase was merely a quip and carried no legal weight. In a supreme irony, licenses for matrimonies between Aryans and Japanese Germans were grudgingly granted out of foreign-policy considerations until the eve of the Tripartite Pact in September 1940. Hitler then intervened to halt the practice, dictating that race would trump diplomacy and that the Japanese, too, would appreciate his preserving their racial purity. With Germany and Japan having closed ranks, Hitler felt less obliged to tend to Japanese sensibilities.[78] To avoid the appearance of abrupt shifts in policy, such marriage applications were henceforth handled dilatorily and denied after a year.[79] Transnational Nazism had limits – the honorary Aryans were only honorary.

On the surface, the DJG had little to gain in lending a hand to helpless individuals, but by representing them it created for itself a reputation as a

---

[74] These people referred to themselves as "German Japanese" (*Deutsch-Japaner*). I translate them as "Japanese Germans" because they identified as Germans. Their Japaneseness was an attribute.

[75] Furuya, "Japan's Racial Identity," 123–127.

[76] BArch, R 64IV/31, notes on conversation between Behncke and Fujii Keinosuke, November 21, 1933; BArch, R 64IV/31, Helmut Werner to Ueberschaar, March 18, 1935.

[77] Fox, 92; Harumi Shidehara Furuya, "Nazi Racism toward the Japanese: Ideology vs. Realpolitik," *Nachrichten der Gesellschaft für Natur- und Völkerkunde Ostasien (NOAG)* 157–8 (1995): 33–36.

[78] Furuya, "Nazi Racism," 53.

[79] BArch, R 43II/1456a, memorandum by Hans Lammers, September 21, 1940.

peer of official institutions. The DJG used transnational Nazism's respect for Japan as a tool to defend and expand its turf in the Nazi polycratic jungle throughout the 1930s. Behncke offered Education Minister Bernhard Rust the DJG's services in fostering German-Japanese relations in 1935. He explained that now that Japan had risen to become a world power, it behooved Germany to get to know the country better.[80] He suggested that the DJG could encourage cultural, intellectual, and scientific traffic; bilateral networking among political and military leaders; and mutual propagation of information for the German and Japanese public. The DJG also lobbied for resources for Japanese studies in Germany through more professorships of Japanology, exchanges of students and teachers, and improved and broadened instructions of Japanese.

The Japanese language gave the DJG an opening to wedge itself into the armed forces. It helped that transnational Nazis admired Japan as a military power and the DJG was commanded by an admiral who could address military leaders on personal and equal terms. Behncke, as he did with Rust, pressed War Minister Werner von Blomberg in October 1935 to teach Japanese in the military.[81] The admiral once again invoked Japan's great power status. He also underlined the deplorable level of knowledge of Japan in the armed forces: not even the military and naval attachés at the Tokyo embassy knew the language. By one count in 1936, only three officers in the army and two in the navy could speak any Japanese.[82] Behncke proposed that the DJG rectify the situation and arrange to have junior officers enroll in language classes or to train students in Japanology to become cadets. When the army chief, citing various difficulties, declined the offer, Behncke then suggested that the DJG could recruit Germans in Japan already fluent in the language. The army again demurred, but through sheer persistence and prestige Behncke persuaded the less conservative navy and air force to spare a few officers to study Japanese.[83] Japan's reputation in the Nazi worldview as a sea and air power likely played a constructive role.

By the end of 1936, the DJG could look back on many achievements and forward to more opportunities. Early in the year, Japan awarded Behncke the First Class Order of the Rising Sun for promoting German-Japanese rapprochement.[84] In October, it hosted Ambassador Herbert

---

[80] PA AA, R 104900, Behncke to Rust, June 12, 1935.
[81] BArch, R 64IV/60, Behncke to Werner von Blomberg, October 10, 1935.
[82] BArch, R 64IV/60, Behncke to Robert Matthiass, May 26, 1936. Matthiass was head of C. Illies & Co., an important trading firm founded by German merchants in Japan in 1859.
[83] BArch, R 64IV/60, Heinz Eduard Menche to Behncke, November 18, 1935.
[84] JTM, May 21, 1936.

von Dirksen before his return to Japan.[85] In November, Germany and Japan concluded the Anti-Comintern Pact. To be sure, the DJG as a voluntary association played no direct role in the negotiations behind the pact – they were guarded jealously by Ribbentrop from all potential interlopers. But at least one DJG member had served as an early go-between for Ribbentrop and some like-minded Japanese. The pact promised an even brighter future for the DJG and its leadership. Days after the pact's conclusion, Behncke, as president of the Japan Institute, sent an honorary telegram to Hitler on the occasion of the organization's tenth anniversary.[86] The Führer obliged by reciprocating with a message thanking and encouraging the institute in its endeavor in German-Japanese collaboration.[87] The *Völkischer Beobachter* published the exchange.[88] When Behncke died days into 1937, another admiral, the newly retired chief of the fleet Richard Foerster, dully filled the DJG presidency. The group's continued status as a powerbroker and access to the highest reaches of the government, party, and military was thus guaranteed.[89] Enabled and empowered by *Gleichschaltung*, the DJG overtook the Japan Institute in almost every aspect of German-Japanese interaction. It consolidated its position as the all-purpose intermediary in Germany for dealings with Japan. Government ministries, party organizations, and the armed forces had to acknowledge the semi-official niche the DJG had carved for itself. Even before the diplomatic accord, the DJG helped pioneer and intensify the politicization of Japan's image in Germany by boosting it and widening its relevance in the public. As Japan's fortune rose so did that of the association, which drew its very essence and legitimacy from its self-proclaimed mastery of the previously apolitical, undervalued subject of Japan.

The Exile

The DJG thus seemed more robust than ever by the mid-1930s. Well beyond the dreams of its founders, its ranks grew into the hundreds and eventually over a thousand. Himmler, Ribbentrop, and other dignitaries and firms had either joined or would soon do so. The DJG pulled off another political and publicity coup shortly into Foerster's tenure. It oversaw the Berlin premiere of *The Samurai's Daughter*, even though it

---

[85] JTM, October 9, 1936.   [86] JTM, December 7, 1936.
[87] VB, December 6, 1936, NGE.   [88] VB, December 5, 1936, ME.
[89] Richard Foerster (1879–1952) commanded the cruiser *Emden* on its voyage around the world in 1926–1928. He was chief of the fleet from 1933 and had retired from active service by the end of 1936. BArch, Pers 6/2321, Personalakte Admiral a. D. Richard Foerster; BArch, R 64IV/258, résumé of Foerster, *c.* 1939.

had played no role in producing the movie.[90] From the late 1930s, the DJG embarked on an expansion spree that eventually established branches in Leipzig, Hamburg, and Munich. It captured the ultimate prize in February 1939 when the Führer and his entourage visited an exhibition of ancient Japanese art at the Pergamon Museum.[91]

But besides marking a high point of the DJG's sway, this episode symbolizes an ailment plaguing the creation of knowledge of Japan under Nazism. Hitler visiting an event by the DJG meant that an amateur was hosted by an amateur association. Although the curator, Otto Kümmel, certainly qualified as an art connoisseur, the DJG was run by charlatans with little expertise on Japan. As late as 1944, only two among the staff of 15 at the DJG's Berlin main office commanded any usable Japanese.[92] Neither Behncke nor Foerster studied the country or its language. As the membership swelled, it inevitably admitted individuals with no knowledge of or prior interest in Japan. All the while, the more studious Japan Institute languished in the DJG's shadows.

The DJG was not alone in being overrun by dilettantes with negligible skills, education, or experience except political acumen, opportunism, sycophancy, and ruthlessness. In a sense, the Nazi "seizure of power" imposed amateurization on Germany. The former chicken breeder Himmler took over the police. The one-time champagne salesman Ribbentrop became foreign minister. Göring, who last commanded fighter squadrons, now headed the entire air force and coordinated the country's economic mobilization for war. Most egregious, the ill-educated, barely employed drifter and ex–lance corporal Hitler was elevated to the chancellorship and commander of the armed forces. With few exceptions, the Nazification of an institution led to unprofessionalism, cronyism, corruption, and an exodus of talent.

The DJG's claim of knowledge of Japan enabled it to act as a counterparty to other outfits in the Third Reich, but the relentless quest for power weakened the quality of the association's human capital. The "original sin" of the reconstituted DJG entailed the expulsion of two Jewish members who were sufficiently interested in Japan to help found and manage the humble DJAG. The DJG in its pursuit of politically connected figures even scratched individuals from its membership roster once they ceased to be useful to the organization regardless of their curiosity about Japan or eagerness to continue to participate. It replaced a reservist lieutenant colonel with two active-duty officers in 1939 for no

---

[90] BArch, R 64IV/67, notes on invitees to the screening, March 17, 1937.
[91] BArch, R 64IV/92, minutes of Hitler's visit, February 27, 1939.
[92] BArch, R 64IV/241, appendix on DJG employees, August 9, 1944.

other reason than his recent retirement from the leadership of the veterans' federation.[93] The DJG had little use for the common people. It might not have officially discriminated against members by race or pedigree, but it certainly favored the politically connected.

Outside the DJG, Nazi ideology inflicted much harm on German-Japanese interactions. Some Japanese Germans experienced discrimination or suffered injury despite their claims to German ancestry under a regime that was increasingly intolerant of minorities. Haber, the father of the Japan Institute, left Germany after unsuccessfully interceding for his Jewish colleagues. His plight at the Nazis' hands made unfavorable headlines in Japan. Solf, who restored and enhanced German respectability in Japan, became persona non grata for his criticism of Nazism. The Jewish pianist Leonid Kreutzer, who lectured on "Japanese attitudes toward European music" at a DJG–Japan Institute event, fled Germany and found refuge in Japan, never to return.[94] It did not satisfy the Nazi authorities that the musician emigrated and no longer jeopardized the national community. The German embassy spied on him and other exiles in Japan.[95] Kreutzer's plight is particularly galling. The very same embassy glowingly reported to Berlin in 1931 his success in solidifying the position of German music in Japan through his tour across the country, performances before luminaries, and commendation by the emperor for training numerous Japanese musicians.[96]

Ironically, Nazism dealt its heaviest blow to Japanese studies in Germany precisely when the country most needed accomplished Japanologists to interpret contemporary Japan, after the conclusion of the Anti-Comintern Pact in November 1936. The next month, the Nazi Party expelled Hans Ueberschaar, and the University of Leipzig then suspended him from his teaching responsibilities.[97] Ueberschaar was not Jewish. He qualified as a party "old fighter" (*Alter Kämpfer*) – he had joined the Nazi Party shortly after his repatriation from Japan in 1932, before the Nazis entered government. He was active in local party organizations concerned with culture and education, and delivered several

---

[93] BArch, R 64IV/251, notes on membership of Freiherr von Maltzahn, September 9, 1939. Maltzahn later attempted to rejoin the DJG as a private individual. BArch, R 64IV/250, Maltzahn to Werner, May 5, 1940.
[94] K, February 8, 1934.   [95] PA AA, R 85961, report by Dirksen, April 13, 1934.
[96] PA AA, R 85978, Erdmannsdorff to Foreign Office, May 20, 1931; TN, February 28, 1931.
[97] Ueberschaar (1885–1965) received his doctorate from the University of Leipzig with a dissertation on the constitutional status of the emperor in Japan. He taught German in the Osaka region from 1911. Between 1914 and 1920, he stayed in captivity as a prisoner of war. Upon his release, he returned to teaching and worked from 1925 as a lecturer at Kyoto Imperial University.

public lectures on Japan. He voluntarily signed the "German Professors' vow of allegiance to Hitler and the Nazi state" in November 1933.[98] As a civil servant, he swore an oath of personal loyalty to the Führer in late 1934.[99] As the head and only regular faculty member of Japanese studies at Leipzig, he exceeded all expectations. He offered standard classes on Japanese language and literature, and seminars relevant to current events.[100]

Why did the Nazi regime turn on one of its own and deprive itself of one of its most accomplished Japanologists just when Germany and Japan's destinies became more intertwined than ever? What did Ueberschaar do to incur the authorities' wrath? He was accused of violating Paragraph 175 of the Penal Code that criminalized "unnatural fornication between men." Although the Nazi regime expanded the scope of the law in 1935 (promulgated in 1871) and escalated its persecution of gays, its motivations for targeting Ueberschaar, and the vindictiveness with which it did so, remain unclear. It is impossible to prove that he engaged in any homosexual acts. The charges were dropped in April 1937, before a trial, but the damage had been done.[101] The Saxon Ministry of Education used the allegation to launch a case against him for committing "the grossest misconduct and violating his obligations as a university teacher and educator of German youth."[102] It also fired him from his professorship of Japanology. Ueberschaar did not wait to see how his fate would be settled. Fearing extrajudicial detention by the Gestapo, he fled to Japan in mid-1937.[103] Even his exile could not mollify his tormentors, who in early 1939 resorted extraordinarily to revoking his doctorate in absentia to discredit his achievements.[104] Even much more stubborn foes of Nazism did not always receive such punishment, one that went far beyond any prescribed by Paragraph 175. The ferociousness with which he was attacked might well have been fueled by a personal vendetta or ulterior motives.

The Nazi regime's proscription of Ueberschaar decapitated Japanology at Leipzig and wreaked havoc with the creation of knowledge of Japan.

---

[98] *Bekenntnis der Professoren an den deutschen Universitäten und Hochschulen zu Adolf Hitler und dem nationalsozialistischen Staat* (Dresden: W. Limpert, 1933), 136.

[99] UAL, PA1008, Ueberschaar's signed oath, November 1, 1934.

[100] Universität Leipzig, *Verzeichnis der Vorlesungen* (Leipzig: Universitäts-Buchhändler, 1934–1936).

[101] UAL, PA1008, report on withdrawal of case, April 25, 1937.

[102] UAL, PA1008, order to institute proceedings, May 25, 1937.

[103] Steffi Richter, "Japanologie in Leipzig – was war, was sein wird" (lecture, Ostasiatisches Institut, Japanologie at Leipzig University), November 1996.

[104] UAL, PA1008, Werner Studentkowski to Artur Knick, March 23, 1939.

The department did not recover. The number and variety of courses decreased precipitously. The haste with which the authorities pursued Ueberschaar left no time for a search for a replacement. In the end, the university settled for a series of lecturers from Japan who mostly taught just the language. Not until January 1942 was Horst Hammitzsch installed as professor. He taught for one semester before being conscripted into the army. The Saxon government still petitioned the Education Ministry for elevating the professorship to a chair in October 1943. The request was rejected in January 1944 for being "not compellingly important for the war."[105] Leipzig University reopened its Japanese Studies Department only in 1996.

The Ueberschaar episode exposes the shallowness of the 1936 German-Japanese compact. Neither the real shortage of experts capable of interpreting Japan for the public and government nor the appearance of care for advancing Japanology in Germany could mitigate his plight. The "crime" in question was never proven. The Japanese Consulate in Leipzig expressed concern for Ueberschaar and the impact of his legal troubles on Japanese studies at the university, especially because the professorship and department were funded largely by Japanese donors personally acquainted with Ueberschaar. Some professors at Leipzig also worried that Ueberschaar's dismissal would lead to damaging repercussions overseas.[106] The dean of the School of Philosophy submitted a statement supporting Ueberschaar, citing his academic excellence and work in building the department from scratch.[107] All these appeals fell on deaf ears. Even the normally ubiquitous DJG, so ready to intervene in such matters, was caught off guard by the prosecution, which unfolded at such speed in the overzealous hands of the Saxon government that the Berlin-based DJG still planned to invite Ueberschaar to the premiere of *The Samurai's Daughter* in March 1937. In any case, some powerful, politically connected elements were so determined to undo Ueberschaar that it seems doubtful whether the DJG could have shielded him. Despite the known negative consequences to German-Japanese exchange and Japan learning in Germany, in persecuting Ueberschaar the regime placed dogma before reason, ideology before diplomacy, and Nazism before transnational Nazism.

---

[105] BArch, R 2/22127, Hellmuth Schwender to Rust, October 9, 1943; BArch, R 2/22127, Abteilung IV to Abteilung I A, January 27, 1944; UAL, PA528, Otto Vossler to Schwender, February 24, 1944.
[106] UAL, PA1008, Heinrich Junker to Erich Bräunlich, May 13, 1937.
[107] UAL, PA1008, statement by Bräunlich, June 5, 1937.

Transnational Nazism in Voluntary Associations

In July 1942, Germany and Japan were fighting their wars of destiny. The retired admiral Foerster knew the global conflict had cut off most vital communications and traffic between the two countries, but he decided to work toward the Führer by floating the idea of rehabilitating Ueberschaar. Like the NSKK's Eberhard Ponndorf, Foerster wrote to the authorities:

Professor Hans Ueberschaar occupied the professorship of Japanology at the University of Leipzig until 1937. He faced certain legal proceedings against him in Leipzig at the time, though he avoided their execution by accepting a position at a Japanese university in Kobe-Osaka, where he has been leading a reclusive life ever since. He keeps no contact whatsoever with Germans living in Japan, though he is endorsed and sought after for collaboration by prominent Japanese professors. Because Ueberschaar is one of the few German Japanologists, it would greatly benefit Japanology in this country if his expertise and knowledge could once again be tapped. In view of his outstanding qualifications, it is regrettable that this strength can at this time not be adequately used.[108]

Foerster asked the Education Ministry about the possibility of reinstating the exiled professor. He did not receive a response, so in October he sent another inquiry, which also went unanswered.[109] Foerster's letter seems to mark the end of the archival trail for Ueberschaar, who remained and taught German at various colleges and universities in the Osaka–Kobe area.[110] He never returned to Germany.

The DJG continued to operate until the end of the war despite Germany's and Japan's increasingly dire circumstances. After lengthy deliberations, the National Student Directorate (Reichsstudentenführung) and DJG unveiled with much fanfare in January 1941 an essay contest between German and Japanese university students, with a yearlong scholarship in Japan as the top prize for the German winner.[111] Promotion of the event was hindered by a struggle for control between the two organizations (Figure 8.1).[112] Germany's invasion of the Soviet Union in June severed

---

[108] BArch, R 64IV/241, Foerster to Heinrich Dahnke, July 29, 1942. It was written in the margin that Professor Martin Ramming of the Japan Institute also supported the proposal.

[109] BArch, R 64IV/241, Rudolf Trömel to Dahnke, October 9, 1942.

[110] *The Japan Times*, December 9, 1957. I also had the good fortune of corresponding with Iwamoto Akira, one of Ueberschaar's students in the early 1950s, who shared with me his fond memories of the demanding teacher.

[111] BArch, NS 38/4646, announcement of contest at University of Berlin, January 20, 1941; BArch, R 64IV/130, description of contest, c. early 1941; VB, January 21, 1941, NGE.

[112] BArch, Plak 003-022-008/Albert Herr, 1941.

Figure 8.1 A poster by the National Student Directorate promoting the German-Japanese student competition, jointly administered with the DJG. Contestants can write on the features of German and Japanese state building, the meaning of the new order in Europe and East Asia, or another theme in German and Japanese intellectual history relevant to the current German-Japanese situation. Three prize winners will receive a scholarship to study in Japan for a year, including transportation costs and a monthly stipend of ¥230. The deadline for submission is July 31, 1941. Original in color. Bundesarchiv, Plak 003-022-008/Albert Herr, 1941.

the rail link to East Asia. Anticipating victory, the DJG proposed similar competitions in 1942 and 1943, which both fell through. Finally, it administered its own scaled-down essay contest in 1944.[113] In the meantime, the

[113] BArch, R 64IV/130, Werner to Erich Otto, March 17, 1942; BArch, R 64IV/130, Trömel to Fritz Kubach, January 25, 1943; Haasch, ed., *Die Deutsch-Japanischen Gesellschaften,* 337–349; Sarah Panzer, "Prussians of the East: The 1944 *Deutsch-*

DJG persevered in hosting presentations, film screenings, and exhibitions on topics such as ikebana and Shinto.[114] One of the last lectures was delivered in January 1945 by Herbert von Dirksen, ambassador to Japan at the time of the Anti-Comintern Pact, on "Japan and the USA in War and Peace."[115]

The historian Carol Gluck remarks that in more than a century of German-Japanese interactions, the two countries were probably farthest apart during the Axis years.[116] The history of binational voluntary associations in Germany bears her out. Nowadays, the several German-Japanese Societies and similar groups resemble their pre-1945 predecessor – not ancestor – only in their geographical distribution throughout Germany. Whereas branches of the centralized DJG were subordinates of the headquarters in Berlin, each of the postwar associations answers only to its local members. Unlike the DJG, they operate in the cultural, social, academic, and interpersonal spheres, with no political ambition or agenda of self-aggrandizement. They inherited their inspiration and mission from the Wa-Doku Kai and Japan Institute. Seen from the long-term development of German-Japanese relations, the Nazified, power-political DJG, as well as the Axis that it contextualized, was an evolutionary dead-end.

From the 1920s to the early 1930s, the friendly, mutually beneficial ties that Germany and Japan maintained were not a foreign-policy priority for either country, nor did either side see them as a stepping stone to a strategic partnership. Civil organizations in Germany and Japan had much latitude to foster cooperation and propagate public opinion through mobilizing and organizing those individuals most knowledgeable and experienced in the other country. The Japan Institute was satisfied with hosting scholarly audiences at small events. But the DJG sought ways to translate its exclusive claim to understand "great power Japan" into political and bureaucratic power. When the Nazi regime instituted *Gleichschaltung*, the DJG opened its doors to politically connected amateurs to advance and expand under the polycratic regime.

Japanische Gesellschaft's Essay Contest and the Transnational Romantic," in *Beyond Alterity: German Encounters with Modern East Asia*, eds. Qinna Shen and Martin Rosenstock (New York: Berghahn Books, 2014), 52–69.

[114] BArch, R 64IV/253, invitation to lecture by W. Hautz on June 7, 1944; BArch, R 64IV/245, invitation to lecture by T. Murata on August 9, 1944.

[115] BArch, R 64IV/252, invitation to lecture by Dirksen on January 10, 1945.

[116] Carol Gluck, "What a Difference 120 Years Make: Germany, Japan, the World" (lecture, conference "Von, über und mit Japan reden: 120 Jahre Japan-Forschung in Berlin" at the Berlin-Brandenburgische Akademie der Wissenschaften, Berlin), October 15, 2007.

Transnational Nazism offered the DJG opportunities to acquire power and rise to heights unmatched by other binational organizations in Germany. Its leaders mingled with dignitaries in the bureaucracy, party, and military. It inserted itself in areas of propaganda and public diplomacy such as films, lectures, exhibitions, essay competitions, personal exchanges, and reception of Japanese visitors. It established branches across Greater Germany and was accepted by other government agencies as a counterparty in negotiations. It relentlessly promoted itself by exploiting the transnational Nazi admiration for Japan as a military great power that Germany would ignore at its peril. It introduced a political dimension to the image of Japan in Germany that did not exist before and has not since. *Gleichschaltung* provided the DJG with the political environment to thrive, while Japanese aggression and expansion furnished the continued raison d'être. In short, the DJG was a product of Nazism in Germany and militarism in Japan.

Yet the same Nazi ideology inflicted substantial damage to German-Japanese interactions. The reconstituted DJG took part in *Gleichschaltung* through the "initiation rite" of deposing its Jewish chairman and board member. Haber and Solf, who each contributed mightily to interwar German-Japanese reconciliation, were respectively driven into exile or shunned. The limits, tension, and contradiction of transnational Nazism soon became clear. The power of the DJG to advocate for an alien people under a xenophobic ideology proved only illusory. When biracial Japanese Germans trapped in a system with no consideration for them appealed to the DJG for assistance, the association could do little beyond rephrasing their appeals in bureaucratic prose on official-looking letterheads. The DJG's voluminous correspondences with government and party agencies responsible for racial matters seldom brought good news or even a definitive rejection. Its other schemes, such as the instruction of Japanese to German officers, were received with ambivalence if not outright opposition. When the authorities sought to unmake Ueberschaar, one of the DJG's most prominent members and accomplished scholars, the association was not even informed of the situation. In the end, although the DJG itself fed off and thrived under Nazism, the ideology also inflicted irreparable harm to the overall creation of German knowledge of Japan.

Conclusion

Official Japanese-German solidarity was tested and found wanting within a year of the Anti-Comintern Pact. Japan launched an all-out war against China in July 1937. Oskar Trautmann, Germany's ambassador to China, tried to mediate between Berlin's ideological ally and pragmatic partner. But Hitler purged the senior ranks of the Foreign Office and War Ministry in February 1938. Germany then recalled Trautmann and its military advisers from China and downgraded its diplomatic representation. In placing politics over practicality, the Third Reich abandoned not only China but also German interests there. Several Germans in Japan-dominated China suffered property damage or personal injury. Missionaries felt that their facilities were singled out for attack. At least four missions in different cities reported bombings by Japanese warplanes even though their hospitals, orphanages, and schools were prominently marked by large, purpose-made Nazi swastika flags.[1] An incensed Catholic bishop denounced Japan's "act of terrorism" specifically targeting Germans.[2] Nor did Nazi Party membership offer much protection, as two Germans touring the Great Wall discovered when they were stopped and beaten by Japanese sentries. The German Legation in China alternately warned its Japanese interlocutor that "no German of honour – both gentlemen are members of the N.S.D.A.P. – can meekly submit to being hit in the face and to wilful bodily attack" or invoked the "very cordial relations existing between our Governments and countries." But it only extracted an admission that "this unfortunate incident happened and that, by mutual misunderstanding, the affair led to German visitors being hit."[3] German Nazis and Japanese militarists could get along as long as each stayed out of the other's way.

---

[1] BArch, R 9221/1–4, correspondence with German Embassy in Tokyo, 1938–1939.
[2] BArch, R 9221/1, Hermann Schoppelrey to Heinz Lautenschlager, September 11, 1938.
[3] PA AA, R 104881, Hans Bidder to Horiuchi Tateki, August 17, 1938 and October 12, 1938.

Transnational Nazism, as well as the Japanese-German convergence that it fostered, was made possible by distance. Nazi Germany and militarist Japan were both aggressive, xenophobic, and expansionist. They needed space to accomplish their goals of resource autarky and territorial hegemony. The strategic alliance they built, starting with the Anti-Comintern Pact and culminating in the Tripartite Pact, rested on the tacit agreement that they would maintain disparate spheres of influence. Space, and the concomitant limited capacity of interwar communications and transportation to overcome it, also enabled opinion makers in each country to depict the other according to their ideological and cultural penchants. Space between Japan and Germany was needed for the understanding, misunderstanding, projection, imagination, delusion, accommodation, and identification that undergirded the bilateral rapprochement.

In Japan, the media treated Germany overwhelmingly positively. Newspapermen across the political spectrum studied Germany's politics, culture, economy, science, and technology. Their personality-driven journalism nurtured a human, intimate familiarity with individual German subjects. This sentiment manifested itself in the steadfast concern for the ex-Kaiser and acute excitement for the *Graf Zeppelin*. But it also lured the dailies to sympathize with colorful figures such as Wilhelm, Hindenburg, and Hitler. Lecturers and pamphleteers offered different levels of knowledge to consumers in distinct social strata. Patrician listeners enjoyed firsthand access to expert speakers who engaged or studied Germany professionally. Plebeian readers mostly made do with less-qualified, sensationalist writers eager to profit from stirring emotions. That both formats covered Germany indicates widespread demand for tidings from the country. Nonfiction translators and authors shared insights on and knowhow from Germany. Government and civil society translators introduced German expertise in numerous areas. Writers dissected Germany in genres from anthologies to biographies. Developments in Germany attracted such interest that they were even reflected in publication trends. Linguists and textbook authors touted learning German and learning from Germany as paths for individual and national advancements. German functioned as the standard language in several academic and professional fields, and an institutionalized barrier to higher education and career promotion. German studies exposed participants to German current events and gave Germanists a sizable, reliable, and impressionable readership. The language teachers as key opinion leaders potentially influenced the attitudes toward Germany of their students, many of whom went on to attain powerful positions in the media, academia, military, or government.

As Hitler and the Nazi Party became increasingly prominent in the early 1930s, every layer of the Japanese media began to espouse transnational Nazism. Newspapers, after some initial criticisms of Nazi irredentism and anti-Semitism, successively moved to admire the man and his ideology. Their preexisting fixation on a charismatic personality leading a rightist Germany was particularly suited to trumpet the Hitler phenomenon. Even leftist newsmen became advocates of the Third Reich. Lectures and pamphlets reacted to Nazi Germany in accordance with their social outlooks. The affluent establishment chose to prioritize Hitler's anticommunism and policy successes and to disregard Nazi violence and bombast. The lower classes eagerly embraced Nazi populism as the solution for Japan in the extraordinary times. Nativized National Socialism was ambiguous, superficial, and literal enough to win over adherents in various segments of Japanese society. Nonfiction publishers affirmed their belief in the Third Reich's stability and popularity by issuing Hitler biographies and encyclopedic anthologies. Translators unquestioningly rendered Nazi concepts and legislations into Japanese. Nazi aesthetics even affected the appearance of books. Language textbooks, already partial to monarchy, nation, and war, shifted smoothly to politicize German lessons and inculcate a Nazi-speak. Without any pressure or incentives from Germany, linguists inserted Nazi phrases and passages in their works in an instance of voluntary *Gleichschaltung*. Generally, most Japanese opinion makers were impressed by Nazism or made their peace with it, but in every layer a few unwavering liberals and leftists remained openly critical until the Anti-Comintern Pact. The similar, simultaneous transitions to acclaim for Hitler and Nazism throughout the media illustrate transnational Nazism's universal appeal. Nazi racism was not much of a factor because the Nazis did not persecute the few Japanese in Germany and the Japanese did not think of themselves as its victims.

In Germany, the media also perceived Japan favorably, though with some peculiarities. Journalists of all political persuasions appreciated Japan as a powerful, modern nation worthy of attention and respect. Japan's participation and exploits in Western-dominated diplomacy, commerce, culture, and sports elevated the country to the status of Germany's peer. Ideology drove the press to takes sides in and fight over Japan's conquest of Manchuria with passion and intensity. But it also imprisoned the dailies in parallel political universes. Filmmakers regularly chose Japan as a topic for all categories of motion pictures. Newsreels and documentaries presented basic facts on Japan. Feature films used popular images and expectations of Japan to advance their plots. But almost all films relied on a version of the familiar unfamiliar to pigeonhole and stereotype Japan. Missionaries, scholars, travelers, and political pundits wrote nonfiction works on Japan. Although they focused on diverse aspects, they agreed overall that Japan was a cultured state with features readily recognizable to Germans. The type, quality, and quantity of publications fluctuated with conditions in Germany and Japan. In addition, voluntary associations were founded by engaged citizens to strengthen civil society ties to Japan. They hosted exhibitions, lectures, film screenings, and other events to heighten Germans' awareness of Japan as an important nation. They filled the void left by the state in bilateral exchanges. Under the right circumstances, these groups could even assume semi-official functions and conduct informal foreign relations.

The ascendancy of Hitler and the Nazi regime fundamentally altered the ideation of Japan on every level of the media through the propagation of transnational Nazism. The *Völkischer Beobachter* reigned as the predominant newspaper nationwide. It not only glorified Japanese achievements in sports, diplomacy, and military affairs, but it also imbued them with ideological significance. So the Japanese appeared a racially pure, physically fit, and politically resolute people in newsprint. The party organ even engaged in press diplomacy to establish its own bonds with like-minded Japanese. Films did not abandon their clichés but activated only ideologically applicable ones to cosmeticize Japan. Newsreels most thoroughly adopted filmic transnational Nazism and nimbly switched sides in the Sino-Japanese conflict. Movies spotlighted a potent, victorious Japan and were used to implement German-Japanese collaboration through joint productions. Book authors selected facets of Japanese culture such as martial ethos, homogeneity, and anticommunism. German and Japanese writers worked together on a publication to express solidarity even before the Anti-Comintern Pact. The voluntary association DJG pushed with much fanfare and some successes the self-interested argument that Japan was a strong, rising world power that Germany could not afford to ignore and the association as the best channel to reach it. The DJG thrived on Nazism in Germany and militarism in Japan. Generally, rightists in every layer of the media maintained a far more affirmative, partisan posture toward Japan. The rapprochement was made imaginable through the wholesale silencing of liberal and leftist voices hostile to Japanese militarism. It was also made ideologically consistent by the Nazi emphasis on Japan's racial purity over its non-Aryan identity and de-emphasis on reclaiming Germany's former Asian-Oceanic colonies. That multiple, competing arms of the Nazi media – Rosenberg's *Völkischer Beobachter*, newsreels and movies censored by Goebbels's Propaganda Ministry, books for the SS by Heinz Corazza, and the

DJG after *Gleichschaltung* – all accommodated and identified with Japan denotes that transnational Nazism was not limited to Hitler or Ribbentrop.

The symmetrical approach adopted in this book serves as a basis for comparison and contrast. Confronted with the obstacle of physical distance, the Japanese and the German media each developed a shorthand of cultural types and stereotypes to portray and explain the other country. These descriptive and interpretive devices predated the interwar era. Like all generalizations, they contained a kernel of truth and were reasonably useful and harmless during the Weimar and Taisho years. But in the 1930s they effortlessly mutated into tools for ushering in transnational Nazism.

In Japan, opinion makers put stock in the German national character and its ability to save Germany. They had faith that this national essence – never comprehensively defined but whose presence was never doubted – would lift the country out of its postwar troubles, just as it supposedly did after previous German defeats. This belief in an inevitable revival misled them into anticipating the restoration of the Kaiserreich at every turn of events and dismissing the Weimar Republic as transient. From 1933, they applied this malleable national character to welcome the Third Reich as the latest iteration of Germany's historical recoveries. "Resurgent Germany" became a set phrase in countless publications and the formula for assessing Hitler's deeds. Another trope was Germany as a model and inspiration for Japan. Cultural intermediaries from reporters to language teachers watched Germany intently to mine lessons for Japan, including traits of the German national character. This mindset originated in the Meiji era but still permeated the interwar years and transcended political outlooks. Communists, liberals, fascists, and apolitical Japanese all sought to benefit from learning from Germany. But this uncontested assumption hid dangerous pitfalls: very few commentators paused to ask whether Japan should absorb anything from Nazi Germany. Instead, they incorporated the Third Reich's rhetoric, imagery, and tenets as a matter of course and thereby turned Nazism transnational.

In Germany, opinion makers likewise employed rehearsed narratives to explain Japan. One was the consensus on Japan as a great power. Germany had considered Japan such since at least the Russo-Japanese War. World War I markedly enhanced Japan's international status by providing easy conquests and hollowing rival empires such as Russia, Britain, France, and Germany. "Great power Japan" was a recurrent phrase and filter for analyzing Japanese developments. Japan's stances both for and against the Versailles–Washington system were seen as worthy of German notice. Nazi publicists in the 1930s did not need to work to elevate Japan in the public sphere but only to change the angle from which to view it. Potentially deplorable acts such as quitting the League of Nations and arms limitation regimes, and annexing neighboring territories were celebrated and then reenacted by Germany. More important, the prevalent storyline of Japan as a "country of juxtaposition" gave pundits flexibility to depict it as agreeable, whatever their ideological or cultural preferences. The Weimar media, orientalist but apolitical, picked geisha, beauty, and harmony from the nineteenth-century catalog of stereotypes. Nazi propagandists from the avid Heinz Corazza to the reluctant Arnold Fanck did not have to invent a new portrayal. They simply chose familiar tropes such as samurai, fighting spirit, and national unity. Japan's old–young, East–West, and danger–model dualities were nebulous enough to earn it enshrinement in transnational Nazism.

A distinct asymmetry marks the mutual appreciation of interwar Japan and Germany. Japan's knowledge landscape concerning Germany was much broader, deeper, more variegated, and more richly detailed. Far more Japanese knew more about Germany than Germans did Japan. The average Japanese newspaper reader was exposed to and familiar with the names of several Germans. Bayer, Bosch, Röntgen, and Zeppelin were everyday household names in Japan, but no Japanese brand was in Germany. For all its flaws, Japanese newsmen's personality-driven style gave readers more-relatable stories and required of them closer engagement with Germany. Meanwhile, the German press largely treated the Japanese as an anonymous mass. It was the Nazi Party organ that began to profile individual Japanese in the mid-1930s. German cinemagoers were entertained by domestically produced movies set in Japan with representations of Japanese characters. Japanese filmmakers seemed not to have made movies about Germany. Instead, Japanese spectators watched films from Germany. Some bought companion texts so they could better follow and comprehend German talkies. Germany, especially under Nazism, was a sufficiently popular subject in Japan to draw audiences for lecturers and to make money for pamphleteers. Momo Minosuke could continuously capitalize on just a single meeting with the Führer. The only comparably emotional moment in the German media was the strong reactions to Japan's seizure of Manchuria. The best German nonfiction books were as good as Japanese works, but there were far fewer of them. Japanese nonfiction featured more, and more diverse, information in more genres. Readers could choose titles among biographies, travel guides, and encyclopedic anthologies, in addition to monographs on politics, literature, and the economy. Germany had no equivalent of Japan's translation industry that imported reams of knowhow. And the mass phenomenon that trained the translators, learning the other's language, was altogether absent in Germany. Conquering German could ensure one's upward social mobility and open doors in Japan. Mastering Japanese offered no similar advantages in Germany. Few Germans considered the idea of teaching themselves Japanese, unlike the many Japanese who labored on their own to master German. Fundamentally, interwar Japanese-German relations were unequal and mostly one way: by and large Japanese traveled to Germany to learn and trade, while Germans headed to Japan to teach and preach. Transnational Nazism embodied this inequality and traffic flow. Japanese transnational Nazis gravitated toward the Führer and National Socialism. German transnational Nazis controlled whom to admit and accommodate in their weltanschauung.

Historical transnational Nazism was extinguished in 1945 with the downfalls of Nazi Germany, militarist Japan, and the Axis. After World War II, the two countries each built a stable, prosperous liberal democracy. Bilateral relations are not a top foreign-policy priority. Japan is still trying to maneuver between China and America, and Germany is once again adjusting its role in Europe. There are no more Nazis to officially determine ideological orthodoxy or anyone's belongingness. But transnational Nazism's other strain, the cross-cultural resonance of Hitler and Nazism, has proved stubbornly resilient and communicable, in spite but also perhaps because of the Third Reich's legacy of war and genocide, as well as the taboo and mystery surrounding it. Hitler's image and Nazi symbolism continue to be casually adapted and appropriated, often by youths seeking to jest, demand attention, shock, or rebel. Some of these sentiments are behind the minor but recurring "Nazi chic" fad in Asia, including Japan, South Korea, Taiwan, Hong Kong, China, India, Indonesia, and Thailand.[4] Nazi uniforms inspire fashion design and costumes. Red-white-black props with eagles clutching swastikas decorate restaurants and shops. Hitler's face and name appear on storefronts, merchandise, and advertisements. These uses are ill advised but usually not ill willed. They reflect the generally low awareness of Nazi atrocities among many in Asia who, now as then, do not see themselves as victims of Nazi discrimination.[5] They also recall the Japanese bicycle maker's

---

[4] Mark Hay, "Nazi Chic: The Asian Fashion Craze That Just Won't Die," *Vice*, February 12, 2015, www.vice.com/en_us/article/xd5bdd/nazis-chic-is-asias-offensive-fashion-craze-456 (accessed August 21, 2018).

[5] Yenni Kwok, "Raising Asian Awareness of the Holocaust," *The New York Times*, January 26, 2014, www.nytimes.com/2014/01/27/world/asia/raising-asian-awareness-of-the-holocaust.html (accessed August 21, 2018); Ilaria Maria Sala, "Asia's Disturbing Embrace of 'Nazi Chic' Is Prompting a Nonprofit to Teach Holocaust History,"

1934 application to trademark "Hitler" but are less excusable because we now know what the Hitler dictatorship was ultimately capable of.

More serious than the kitschy, cultish fascination with the Führer is the widespread surge of nativist populism in the early twenty-first century. Some variants are explicitly derived from National Socialism.[6] Ultra-nationalists in Mongolia, Japan, and India are selectively adopting Nazi trappings and messages, much like historical transnational Nazis.[7] Neo-Nazis in the West used to fetishize Nazi rites and paraphernalia in obscurity and isolation but have become more visible, vocal, and galvanized.[8] Many of these groups interact, organize, and recruit via social media. They operate their own news outlets on the internet to propagate their worldviews and communicate with followers. Away from the fringes, individuals and causes espousing nativism and populism have swept into power or effected policy changes.[9] These nativists and populists in different countries have incompatible goals and often understand one another only vaguely. But some of them have developed a sense of connectedness across borders so that success in one place can lead to celebration and imitation in another. In light of transnational Nazism, this "transnational nativist populism" is not as incongruous as it may first seem. The two phenomena incubated in similar political and media climates. Ideology and technology shaped the media in both the interwar period and the early twenty-first century. The ends of the Great War and the Cold War inaugurated a moment of triumphalist internationalism and liberalism. Breakthroughs in communications technology – radios and films in the 1920s and 1930s, and computers and the internet in the 2000s – gave the masses more channels for information. The freer political atmospheres allowed people to associate, physically or virtually. But a world economic crisis terminated each era. Authoritarians rose

---

Quartz, March 9, 2017, https://qz.com/928440/asias-disturbing-embrace-of-nazi-chic-is-prompting-a-nonprofit-to-teach-holocaust-history/ (accessed August 21, 2018).

[6] Cf. Federico Finchelstein, *From Fascism to Populism in History* (Oakland: University of California Press, 2017).

[7] Chetan Bhatt, *Hindu Nationalism: Origins, Ideologies and Modern Myths* (Oxford: Berg Publishers, 2001); Jairus Banaji, ed., *Fascism: Essays on Europe and India* (New Delhi: Three Essays Collective, 2016).

[8] Gavriel D. Rosenfeld, *The Fourth Reich: The Specter of Nazism from World War II to the Present* (New York: Cambridge University Press, 2019); Andrea Mammone, *Transnational Neofascism in France and Italy* (New York: Cambridge University Press, 2015).

[9] Paul D. Kenny, *Populism and Patronage: Why Populists Win Elections in India, Asia, and Beyond* (Oxford: Oxford University Press, 2017); Roger Eatwell and Matthew Goodwin, *National Populism: The Revolt against Liberal Democracy* (London: Pelican, 2018); Pippa Norris and Ronald Inglehart, *Cultural Backlash: Trump, Brexit, and Authoritarian Populism* (New York: Cambridge University Press, 2018).

to power by manipulating social and cultural angst and obfuscating the truth. It turned out that access to diverse media sources did not necessarily improve one's knowledge. Instead, it merely enabled many to live in their own multimedia ideological echo chambers and socialize only with like-minded others. Far-flung right-wing groups used the media and freedoms of speech and association to imagine a transnational community. The lessons of transnational Nazism may thus shed light on similar dynamics in extreme ideology and media technology in the present and future.

Bibliography

Archives and Libraries

Bundesarchiv, Berlin, Germany
Bundesarchiv-Bildarchiv, Koblenz, Germany
Bundesarchiv-Filmarchiv, Berlin, Germany
Bundesarchiv-Militärarchiv, Freiburg im Breisgau, Germany
Deutsche Lufthansa AG Firmenarchiv, Frankfurt am Main, Germany
Friedrich-Ebert-Stiftung, Bonn, Germany
Geheime Staatsarchiv Preußischer Kulturbesitz, Berlin, Germany
German National Library, Leipzig, Germany
Landesarchiv Berlin, Germany
National Diet Library, Tokyo, Japan
Politisches Archiv des Auswärtigen Amts, Berlin, Germany
Staatsbibliothek zu Berlin, Germany
Universitätsarchiv Leipzig, Germany

Newspapers

8-Uhr-Abendblatt
B.Z. am Mittag
Berliner Börsenzeitung
Berliner Lokal-Anzeiger: Zentral-Organ für die Reichshauptstadt
Berliner Tageblatt und Handels-Zeitung
Deutsche Allgemeine Zeitung
Deutsche Tageszeitung
Germania: Zeitung für das deutsche Volk
Illustrierter Film-Kurier
The Japan Times
The Japan Times and Mail
Jewish Daily Bulletin
Königsberger Allgemeine Zeitung
Kokumin shinbun
Neue Preußische (Kreuz)-Zeitung
The Osaka Mainichi & The Tokyo Nichi Nichi
Ōsaka mainichi shinbun
Rheinisch-Westfälische Zeitung

Die Rote Fahne: Zentralorgan der Kommunistischen Partei Deutschlands
Sekki
Tōkyō asahi shinbun
Tōkyō nichinichi shinbun
*Völkischer Beobachter: Kampfblatt der nationalsozialistischen Bewegung
     Großdeutschlands*
*Vorwärts: Berliner Volksblatt, Zentralorgan der Sozialdemokratischen Partei
     Deutschlands*
Vossische Zeitung: Berlinische Zeitung von Staats- und gelehrten Sachen
Yomiuri shinbun

Films

Newsreels

Bavaria-Tonwoche
Deulig-Tonwoche
Deulig-Woche
Emelka-Tonwoche
Emelka-Woche
Fox Tönende Wochenschau
Ufa-Tonwoche

Documentaries

Abrüstung (NSDAP/Reichspropagandaleitung, 1933)
Achtung Australien! Achtung Asien! Das Doppelgesicht des Ostens (Dir. Colin Ross,
     Ufa-Kulturabteilung, 1930)
Bilder von Japans Küsten (Dir. Arnold Fanck, Ufa, 1936/1944)
Colin Roß mit dem Kurbelkasten um die Erde (Dir. Colin Ross, Neumann-Film-
     Produktion, 1924)
Frühling in Japan (Dir. Arnold Fanck, Ufa, 1936/1941)
Graf Zeppelin (Hamburg-Amerika-Linie, 1929)
Großmacht Japan (Dir. Johannes Häussler and Ernst R. Müller, Rex-Film
     Bloemer & Co., 1938)
Im Frühling: Ein Film von japanischen Frühlingsfesten (Dir. Kōichi Kishi and
     Wilhelm Prager, Ufa, 1934)
Japans heiliger Vulkan (Dir. Arnold Fanck, Ufa, 1936/1941)
Kaiserbauten in Fernost: Aufnahmen der japanischen Fanck-Expedition (Dir. Arnold
     Fanck, Terra-Filmkunst, 1936/1938)
Kampf um die Mandschurei: Die Welt der gelben Rasse (Dir. Gustav von Estorff and
     Johannes Häussler, Herold-Filmgesellschaft, 1931)
Melodie der Welt (Dir. Walter Ruttmann, Tobis, 1929)
Nippon, das Land der aufgehenden Sonne (Dir. Gerhard Niederstraß, Dr. Edgar
     Beyfuß-Film Nachf., 1942)
Perlenzucht in Japan (Dir. Martin Rikli, Ufa-Kulturabteilung, 1928)

Reis und Holz im Lande des Mikado (Dir. Arnold Fanck, Ufa, 1936/1940)
Der Reisbau in Japan (Deutsches Kali-Syndikat, 1928)
Salzgewinnung in Japan (Ufa, 1941)
Wege zu Kraft und Schönheit (Dir. Wilhelm Prager, Ufa-Kulturabteilung, 1925)
Why We Fight: Prelude to War (Dir. Frank Capra, Department of War, 1943)
Winterreise durch Südmandschurien: Aufnahmen der japanischen Fanck-Expedition (Dir. Arnold Fanck, Ufa, 1936/1938)

Feature Films

Bushido, das eiserne Gesetz (Dir. Heinz Karl Heiland and Zanmu Kako, Deutsch-Nordische Film-Union, 1926)
Die Geisha und der Samurai (Dir. Carl Boese, Firmament-Film, 1919)
Harakiri (Dir. Fritz Lang, Decla-Film-Ges. Holz & Co., 1919)
Das heilige Ziel (Dir. Kōshō Nomura, Cocco-Film, 1939)
Die japanische Maske I: Das Banditennest auf dem Adlerstein (Dir. Heinz Karl Heiland, Eiko-Film, 1921)
Die Kwannon von Okadera (Dir. Carl Froelich, Decla-Bioscop and Uco-Film, 1920)
Das Mädel aus Japan (Dir. Toni Attenberger, Bayerische Filmindustrie, 1919)
Metropolis (Dir. Fritz Lang, Ufa, 1928)
Polizeiakte 909 (Dir. Robert Wiene, Camera-Film-Produktion, 1934)
Port Arthur (Dir. Nicolas Farkas, F.C.L. and Slavia-Film AG, 1936)
Spione (Dir. Fritz Lang, Ufa, 1928)
Die Tochter des Samurai (Dir. Arnold Fanck, Dr. Arnold Fanck-Film, 1937)
Die weiße Geisha (Dir. Heinz Karl Heiland and Valdemar Andersen, Deutsch-Nordische Film-Union, 1926)

Pre-1945 Publications

Abe Jirō. *Yūō zakki: Doitsu no maki.* Tokyo: Kaizōsha, 1933.
Adachi Kenzō. *Nachisu no shinsō.* Tokyo: Arusu, 1933.
Akamatsu Kotora. "Hittorā undō wo kataru." In *Shakai kyōiku panfuretto 189.* Tokyo: Shakai Kyōiku Kyōkai, 1934: 1–44.
Akimoto Kikuo. *Shōkai shin Doitsu gogaku.* Tokyo: Kōgakukan Shoten, 1926.
Anton, Ludwig. *Die japanische Pest.* Bad Rothenfelde: J. G. Holzwarth, 1922.
Aoki Ichirō. *Meikai Dokubunten.* Tokyo: Nanzandō Shoten, 1936.
    Shin Doitsu bunpō-dokuhon. Tokyo: Nanzandō Shoten, 1941.
    Shin Doitsu shō-dokuhon. Tokyo: Nanzandō Shoten, 1943.
    Sūgaku butsurigaku kagaku wo manabu hito no Doitsugo kontei. Tokyo: Tōkyō Butsuri Gakkō Dōsōkai, 1935.
Aoki Kazuo. "Doitsu no baishō mondai ni tsuite." In *Indoyō kōenshū*, edited by Shimazu Tsunesaburō. Kyoto: Shimazu Tsunesaburō, 1921: 20–71.
Aoki Shigetaka. *Doitsu shinbun no yomikata.* Tokyo: Daigaku Shorin, 1941.
Aoki Shōkichi. *Doitsu bungaku to sono kokumin shisō.* Tokyo: Shun'yōdō, 1924.
    Shokyū shō Dokubunten. Tokyo: Nanzandō Shoten, 1937.

Ashida Hitoshi. "Zāru kizoku mondai to Ōshū seikyoku no zento." In *Keizai Kurabu kōen 79*. Tokyo: Tōyō Keizai Shuppanbu, 1935: 1–21.

Baba Hisayoshi. *Teikoku daigaku juken jūyō hissu Doitsugo tangoshū 5000-go*. Tokyo: Nichi-Doku Shoin, 1930.

Bekenntnis der Professoren an den deutschen Universitäten und Hochschulen zu Adolf Hitler und dem nationalsozialistischen Staat. Dresden: W. Limpert, 1933.

Bodinus, Fritz. *Japans Schatten über Deutschland*. Bielefeld: Hermann Mattenklodt, 1933.

Morgendämmerung? Das Gesicht Japans im Lichte der Offenbarung des Johannes und des Geheimdokument des Grafen Tanaka. Bielefeld: Hermann Mattenklodt, 1934.

Der Vormarsch Japans: Die kommenden Ereignisse im Lichte der Offenbarung. Constance: Huß Verlag W. Müsken, 1934.

Bohner, Alfred. *Japan und die Welt*. Berlin: Julius Beltz, 1937.

Büchler, Eduard. *Rund um die Erde: Erlebtes aus Amerika, Japan, Korea, China, Indien und Arabien*. Bern: A. Francke, 1921.

Ceska, Anton. "Aus dem Lande des Nebeneinander." In *Von Japan und seinem Volke*. Vienna: Katholischer Akademischer Missionsverein, 1932: 17–24.

Chōsen Sōtokufu, ed. *Kyū Doku-ryō Pōrando tōchi gaikan 1*. Chōsa shiryō 9. Keijō: Chōsen Sōtokufu, 1924.

Corazza, Heinz. *Japan: Wunder des Schwertes*. Berlin: Klinkhardt & Biermann, 1935.

Cramer, Anneliese. *Die Beziehungen zwischen England und Japan von 1894–1902*. Zeulenroda: N.p., 1935.

Doemming, Hugo Wilhelm von. *Was will Japan?* Jena: Eugen Diederichs, 1934.

Doitsu no keizai kokka kanri ni kansuru kinkyū hōki 1–2. Sangyō keizai shiryō 7–8. Tokyo: Zenkoku Sangyō Dantai Rengōkai Jimukyoku, 1932.

Doitsu rōdō hokenhō. Translated by Okada Kashinosuke. Shinagawa-chō: Kawaguchi Insatsujo Shuppanbu, 1930.

Doitsu shin yonkanen keikaku kenkyū shiryō 1. Tokyo: Nichi-Man Zaisei Keizai Kenkyūkai, 1937.

Doitsukoku senkyohō yakubun. Ōshū seijō kenkyū shiryō 22. Tokyo: Gaimushō Ōbeikyoku Dainika, 1924.

Dokubun Sekai Shichō Henshūbu, ed. *Doitsu shinbun no yakkai*. Tokyo: Tachibana Shoten, 1933.

Dōmei oyobi Rengōkoku to Doitsukoku no heiwa jōyaku narabini giteisho. Tokyo: Chōyōkai, 1920.

Domizlaff, Karl, and Eugen Friedrich Wolfgang Freiherr von Liebig. *Ippan kasai hoken yakkan*. Translated by Kan'i Hokenkyoku. Tokyo: Kan'i Hokenkyoku, 1925.

Enomoto Tsunetarō, and Kurotsuka Juichi. *Doitsugo ronbun sakuhō kenkyū*. Tokyo: Taiyōdō Shoten, 1932.

Faber, Kurt. *Weltwanderers letzte Fahrten und Abenteuer: Baltikum, Balkan, Südsee, Japan, Korea, China, Sibirien, Moskau, Palästina, Syrien, Kanada*. Stuttgart: Robert Lutz Nachfolger Otto Schramm, 1930.

Fecht, Ottmar. *Die Wahrung wirtschaftlicher und politischer Belange in Ostasien durch die Norddeutsche Bundesmarine: Ein Beitrag zur deutschen Marinegeschichte aus der Reichsgründungszeit.* Berlin: Mittler, 1937.

Feder, Gottfried. *Nachisu kōryō.* Translated by Kido Hiroo. Doitsu shōronbun taiyaku sōsho 2. Tokyo: Daigaku Shorin, 1934.

Fochler-Hauke, Gustav. *Der Ferne Osten: Macht- und Wirtschaftskampf in Ostasien.* Leipzig: B. G. Teubner, 1936.

Frank, Hans, ed. *Nachisu no hōsei oyobi rippō kōyō keihō oyobi keiji soshōhō.* Translated by Shinotsuka Haruyo. Shihō shiryō 211. Tokyo: Shihōshō Chōsaka, 1936.

Fujii Shin'ichi. *Shin Doitsu kenpō seiji.* Tokyo: Yūhikaku, 1929.

Fukkōkyoku, ed. *Toshi keikaku ni kansuru Doitsu hōsei oyobi gyōsei.* Tokyo: Fukkōkyoku Keikakuka, 1924.

Funada Naka. *Tazan no ishi: Haisen Doitsu kara Daisan Teikoku kensetsu e.* Kokusei isshin ronsō 21. Tokyo: Kokusei Isshinkai, 1937.

Funder, Walther. *Wird die Welt japanisch?* Hamburg: Walther Funder, 1936.

Futara Yoshinori. "Nachisu Doitsu no seishōnen undō." In *Minshū bunko 86.* Tokyo: Shakai Kyōiku Kyōkai, 1934: 1–33.

Gaimushō Rinji Chōsabu, ed. *Kakumeigo no Doitsu seijō.* Tokyo: Gaimushō Rinji Chōsabu, 1919.

Glück, Kurt. *Japans Vordringen auf dem Weltmarkt.* Würzburg: N.p., 1937.

Godō Takuo. "Doitsu shisatsudan." In *Keizai Kurabu kōen 121.* Tokyo: Tōyō Keizai Shuppanbu, 1936: 1–39.

Doitsu shisatsudan. Keizai Renmei kōen 81. Tokyo: Nihon Keizai Renmeikai, 1936.

Doitsu wa doko e iku. Nihon kōen tsūshin 318. Tokyo: Nihon Kōen Tsūshinsha, 1936.

Gonda Yasunosuke. *Doitsu shinbun kenkyū.* Doku-Wa taiyaku shōbin bunko 2. Tokyo: Yūhōdō Shoten, 1929.

Gonda Doku-Wa shin jiten. Tokyo: Yūhōdō, 1937.

Kijun Doitsu bunpō. Tokyo: Yūhōdō Shoten, 1931.

Kijun Dokubun Wayakuhō. Tokyo: Yūhōdō Shoten, 1933.

Saishin Doitsugo kōza 1–2. Tokyo: Yūhōdō Shoten, 1931.

Gorai Kinzō. *Hittorā to Mussorīni.* Nihon kōen tsūshin 158. Tokyo: Nihon Kōen Tsūshinsha, 1932.

"Ōshū seikyoku no zento to fasshizumu." In *Keizai Kurabu kōen 14.* Tokyo: Tōyō Keizai Shuppanbu, 1932: 1–60

Gotō Shinpei. "Kaikai no ji." In *Nichi-Doku bunka kōenshū 1.* Tokyo: Nichi-Doku Bunka Kyōkai, 1927: 1–2.

Gräf, Erich. *Rōdō hōshi seido no hōritsu genri.* Translated by Tōkyō-fu Gakumubu Shakaika. Shitsugyō taisaku shiryō 6. Tokyo: Tōkyō-fu Gakumubu Shakaika, 1934.

Gundert, Wilhelm. *Der Schintoismus im Japanischen Nō-Drama.* Hamburg: N.p., 1925.

Der Schintoismus im Japanischen Nō-Drama. Mitteilungen der Deutschen Gesellschaft für Natur- und Völkerkunde Ostasiens 19. Tokyo: Deutsche Gesellschaft für Natur- und Völkerkunde Ostasiens, 1925.

Haber, Fritz. *Nichi-Doku keizai teikei no hitsuyōnaru yuen.* Tokyo: Kōseikai Shuppanbu, 1925.

"Wirtschaftlicher Zusammenhang zwischen Deutschland und Japan." Lecture, Verein zur Wahrung der Interessen der chemischen Industrie Deutschlands e. V., Frankfurt a. Main, June 11, 1925.

Hahn, A., and Sawai Yōichi. *Seiongaku hon'i Dokubun shinkai.* Tokyo: Nichi-Doku Shoin, 1924.

Hahn, Karl. *Die Industrialisierung Japans.* Bochum-Langendreer: N.p., 1932.

Hamada Saburō, and Takahashi Toshio. *Doku-Wa taiyaku: Shinsatsu mondō.* Tokyo: Nichi-Doku Shoin, 1936.

Hammitzsch, Horst. *Yamato-hime no Mikoto Seiki: Bericht über den Erdenwandel ihrer Hoheit der Prinzessin Yamato.* Leipzig: N.p., 1937.

Haruta Ikuzō. *Doitsugo nyūmon sōsho 3: Seiji keizai Doitsugo nyūmon.* Tokyo: Hakusuisha, 1935.

Hashimoto Fumio. *Shin Doitsu bunpō.* Tokyo: Shōbundō, 1936.

Hashimoto Kichirō. *Kagaku yōgo shin jiten.* Tokyo: Taiyōdō Shoten, 1927.

Hashimoto Tadao. *Doitsugo no shūjiteki kōsei.* Tokyo: Nankōdō Shoten, 1933.

Hata Toyokichi. *Berurin Tōkyō.* Tokyo: Okakura Shobō, 1933.

Kōshoku Doitsu onna. Tokyo: Bungei Shunjū Shuppanbu, 1928.

Haunhorst, Hans Anna. *Das Lächeln Japans.* Leipzig: Georg Kummer, 1936.

Hauser, Ernst Otto. *Gefährlicher Osten: Japan und die Mächte.* Zurich: Max Niehans, 1935.

Haushofer, Karl. *Japan und die Japaner: Eine Landeskunde.* Leipzig: B. G. Teubner, 1923.

Japans Reichserneuerung: Strukturwandlungen von der Meiji-Ära bis heute. Berlin: Walter de Gruyter, 1930.

Japans Werdegang als Wehrmacht und Empire. Berlin: Walter de Gruyter, 1933.

Mutsuhito, Kaiser von Japan. Colemans kleine Biographien 36. Lübeck: Charles Coleman, 1933.

Hayakawa Bun'ya. *Kan'yō Doitsu bunten.* Tokyo: Nanzandō Shoten, 1927.

Heigensha, ed. *Doitsugo ABC kōza.* Tokyo: Heigensha, 1941.

Higuchi Reiyō. *Doitsu no Nihon shinnyū.* Tokyo: Dokuritsu Shuppansha, 1918.

Shiberia yori Tōkyō e. Tokyo: Dokuritsu Shuppansha, 1920.

Hirose Hikota. *Doitsu sensuikan no daikatsuyaku: Emono wo motomete.* Tokyo: Kaigun Kenkyūsha, 1928.

Hitaka Kinji. "Doitsu haisen no kyōkun to waga kokubō no shōrai." In *Matsush-ima kōenshū,* edited by Kozai Sutetarō. Tokyo: Kokusan Shōreikai, 1919: 168–186.

Hitler, Adolf. *Hitorā no shishiku: Shinkō Doitsu no eiyū Adorufu Hitorā Shushō enzetsushū.* Edited by Joseph Goebbels. Translated by Taki Kiyoshi. Tokyo: Nihon Kōensha, 1933.

Mein Kampf. Munich: Franz Eher Nachf., 1927.

Waga tōsō. Translated by Murobuse Kōshin. Tokyo: Daiichi Shobō, 1940.

Yono tōsō: Doitsu Kokumin Shakai Shugi undō. Translated by Sakai Takaji. Tokyo: Naigaisha, 1932.

Hoeppner, Ernst von. *Ōshū taisen ni okeru Doitsu kūgun no katsuyaku.* Translated by Rikugun Kōkūbu. Tokyo: Fuji Shoin, 1923.

Holitscher, Arthur. *Das unruhige Asien: Reise durch Indien–China–Japan*. Berlin: S. Fischer, 1926.

Hoßdorf, Ernst Josef. *Streifzug nach Japan, Java, Bali, U.S.A., Afrika, China, Ceylon, Sumatra, Celebes, Borneo, Philippinen, Honolulu*. Frick: A. Fricker, 1937.

Ida Iwakusu. *Nichi-Doku Bōkyō Kyōtei ze ka hi ka*. Tokyo: Kokusai Shisō Kenkyūkai Jimushitsu, 1936.

Iida Toyoji. *Shōnen Hittorā den*. Tokyo: Kōa Shobō, 1939.

Iinuma Hajime. *Denki kiso Doitsugo*. Tokyo: Rajio Kagakusha, 1940.

Iizawa Shōji, ed. *Hittorā seiken no hyōri*. Tokyo: Teikoku Shuppan Kyōkai, 1936.

Ikeda Nobumasa. *Hittorā*. Tokyo: Kaiseisha, 1941.

Ikeda Ringi. *Hittorā*. Tokyo: Taiyōsha, 1933.

Shinkō Doitsu-damashii. Tokyo: Banrikaku Shobō, 1930.

Ikumi Takuichi. *Puroretaria gogaku sōsho 1: Doitsugo hen*. Tokyo: Nanboku Shoin, 1932.

Ikushima Hirojirō. "Doitsu baishōkin shiharai riron no kōsatsu." In *Shōgyō Kenkyūjo kōenshū 50*. Kobe: Kōbe Shōgyō Daigaku Shōgyō Kenkyūjo, 1931: 1–39.

Im Land der aufgehenden Sonne: Aus der Arbeit der Liebenzeller Mission in Japan. Bad Liebenzell: Buchhandlung der Liebenzeller Mission, 1935.

Imasato Katsuo. *Hittorā no kokumin kakumei*. Tokyo: San'yōkaku, 1933.

Inahara Katsuji. *Saikin no Doitsu*. Tsūzoku kokusai bunko 1. Tokyo: Gaikō Jihōsha Shuppanbu, 1919.

Intourist. *Der transsibirische Express ist der kürzeste, bequemste und billigste Weg zwischen Europa und dem fernen Osten*. Moscow: Wneschtorgisdat, 1935.

Ishikawa Renji. *Doitsugo hatsuon kenkyū*. Daigaku Shorin bunkō 14. Tokyo: Daigaku Shorin, 1939.

Isobe Kōichi. *Doitsu ibun no kakikata*. Tokyo: Daigaku Shorin, 1932.

Rika Doitsu gohō kyōtei. Tokyo: Kanehara Shoten, 1933.

Iwamoto Tsunemaru. *Doitsu bunpō yōketsu: Sankō jishū*. Tokyo: Daigaku Shorin, 1930.

Izeki Takao. *Hittorā: Shinkō Doitsu no kyojin*. Tokyo: Senshinsha, 1931.

The Japan-Manchoukuo Year Book 1937. Tokyo: The Japan-Manchoukuo Year Book Co., 1937.

Johann, Alfred E. *Generäle, Geishas und Gedichte: Fahrten und Erlebnisse in Japan, von Sachalin bis Manchukuo*. Berlin: Ullstein, 1937.

Kada Tetsuji. "Fasshizumu ni tsuite." In *Keizai Kurabu kōen 21*. Tokyo: Tōyō Keizai Shuppanbu, 1933: 1–41.

Kagawa Tetsuo. *Hoshū Doitsu ibun kaishakuhō*. Tokyo: Nanzandō Shoten, 1930.

Kajima Morinosuke. "Doitsu no Rokaruno Jōyaku haiki to Ōshū no anzen hoshō mondai." In *Keizai Kurabu kōen 117*. Tokyo: Keizai Kurabu, 1936: 1–30.

Kamei Tōtarō. *Jitsuyō Doitsu bunpō kōgi*. Tokyo: Kanasashi Hōryūdō, 1931.

Kan'i Hokenkyoku, ed. *Berurin ni okeru kōeki jūtaku kenchiku jigyō*. Tsumitatekin un'yō shiryō 7. Tokyo: Kan'i Hokenkyoku, 1926.

Kanokogi Kazunobu. *Yamato kokoro to Doitsu seishin*. Tokyo: Min'yūsha, 1931.

Kanokogi Koruneria, and Koide Naosaburō. *Doitsugo kan'yōku 2000*. Tokyo: Taimusu Shuppansha, 1939.

Kasuya Mahiro. *Kasuya Doitsu jishū bunten.* Tokyo: Kōbundō Shoten, 1922.

Katayama Masao. *Gendai Doitsu bungakukan.* Tokyo: Bunken Shoin, 1924.

Sōkai Doku-Wa daijiten. Tokyo: Nankōdō Shoten, 1927.

Sōkai Doku-Wa daijiten. 6th ed. Tokyo: Nankōdō Shoten, 1929.

Katayama Takashi. *Dokusai sannin otoko: Sonogo no Hittorā Shōkaiseki Mussorīni.* Tokyo: Morita Shobō, 1936.

Katsumoto Seiichirō. "Nachisu shihaika ni okeru Doitsu no genjō wo chūshin toshite." In *Keizai Kurabu kōen 52.* Tokyo: Tōyō Keizai Shuppanbu, 1934: 43–76.

Katsuya Arito, ed. *Shakai kagaku Doitsugo kenkyū.* Tokyo: Ryūshōkaku, 1933.

Katz, Richard. *Funkelnder Ferner Osten: Erlebtes in China–Korea–Japan.* Berlin: Ullstein, 1931.

Japan von heute: Erlebnisse eines Weltenbummlers. Reutlingen: Enßlin & Laiblin, 1933.

Kawasaki Minotarō. *Waga seimeisen wo obiyakasu sekka no Kyokutō hōijin: Nichi-Doku kyōtei ze ka hi ka.* Tokyo: Rakutensha, 1937.

Kellermann, Bernhard. *Ein Spaziergang in Japan.* Berlin: Paul Cassirer, 1920.

Kiel, Erich. *Die handelspolitischen Beziehungen zwischen Deutschland und Japan in der Nachkriegszeit.* Münster: N.p., 1934.

Kimura Hikoemon. *Senpai no Doitsu wo rekiyū shite.* Osaka: Suzuya Shoten, 1921.

Kinoshita Hanji, ed. *Shakai kagaku tangoshū: Nichi-Doku-Futsu-Ei-Ro taishō.* Tokyo: Daigaku Shorin, 1934.

Kinoshita Kōtarō. *Hittorā to Doitsu Fashizumu undō.* Tokyo: Naigaisha, 1932.

Kita Reikichi. *Saikakumei no Doitsu.* Sekai no ima asu sōsho 8. Tokyo: Heibonsha, 1933.

Kitagami Ken. *Nachisu Doitsu.* Tokyo: Gakuji Shoin, 1935.

Kitahara Toshiko. *Kodomo no mita Yōroppa.* Tokyo: Hōbunkan, 1926.

Klemann, Friedrich. *Japan, wie es ist.* Leipzig: R. Voigtländer, 1921.

Knodt, Emil. *Japan: Land und Leute.* Berlin: Allgemeiner Evangelisch-Protestantischer Missionsverein, 1919.

Knorr, Karl. "Doitsu-gawa yori mitaru baishōkin mondai." In *Nichi-Doku bunka kōenshū 7.* Tokyo: Nichi-Doku Bunka Kyōkai, 1931: 31–52.

Kobayashi Ryōsei, ed. *Shin Doitsu seiji keizai goi.* Tokyo: Nikkō Shoin, 1942.

Kobayashi Yasutarō. *Hikōki kikai no chishiki.* Doitsugo bunko. Tokyo: Shōbundō, 1936.

Koepsel, Kurt. *Die Entwicklung des japanischen Außenhandels, insbesondere der deutsch-japanischen Handelsbeziehungen vor dem Weltkriege.* Kassel: N.p., 1929.

Koide Jōyū. *Doitsu wa nani wo watakushi ni oshieshiya.* N.p.: Koide Jōyū, 1928.

Koizumi Eiichi. *Berurin yawa.* Tokyo: Waseda Daigaku Shuppanbu, 1925.

Kokusai Kankōkyoku, ed. *Doitsu seinen shukuhakujo renmei gaikan.* Tokyo: Kokusai Kankōkyoku, 1931.

Komura Minoru. *Beruringo.* Tokyo: Daigaku Shorin, 1935.

Ikeru Doitsugo kaiwa. Tokyo: Taiyōdō Shoten, 1937.

Shin Doitsu bunpō: 24-jikan seiri. Tokyo: Taiyōdō Shoten, 1933.

Kondō Harubumi. "Nachisu Doitsu chika ni okeru seishōnen undō toshite no Hittorā Yūgendo ni tsuite." In *Teikoku Shōnendan Kyōkai sōsho 4.* Tokyo: Teikoku Shōnendan Kyōkai, 1935: 1–43.

Kondō Keisuke. *Bakudan otoko Hittorā no zenbō: Zen Ōshū wasen no kagi.* Tokyo: Yūkōsha, 1936.

Kōno Mitsu. "Sekai kakkoku fukeiki taisaku 2." In *Shakai kagaku kōza 4.* Tokyo: Seibundō, 1931: 14–24.

Kozai Sutetarō, ed. *Matsushima kōenshū.* Tokyo: Kokusan Shōreikai, 1919.

Kroll, Carl. *Die bankenkrisen in Japan.* Marburg: N.p., 1930.

Kunze Haruko. *Nihonjin muki no Doitsu katei ryōri.* Nagoya: Ichiryūsha, 1934.

Kuroda Reiji. *Dokusaiō Hittorā.* Tokyo: Shinchōsha, 1936.

——— *Haitei zengo.* Tokyo: Chūō Kōronsha, 1931.

——— *Nichi-Doku Bōkyō Kyōtei no igi.* Nichi-Doku Dōshikai shōsasshi 1. Tokyo: Nichi-Doku Dōshikai, 1937.

——— *Nichi-Doku dōmeiron: Bōkyō Kyōtei wo sarani ippo mae e!* Nichi-Doku Dōshikai panfuretto 1. Tokyo: Nichi-Doku Dōshikai, 1936.

Kuroki Shōma. *Nichi-Doku Bōkyō Kyōtei no kentō: Sekai no kanshin no yobu hatashite Kominterun no katsudō wo fusegu ka.* Tokyo: Kyōzaisha, 1936.

——— *Nichi-Doku dōmei no kiun: Sono hitsuzensei no kentō.* Tokyo: Kyōzaisha, 1936.

Lange, Rudolf. *Lehrbuch der japanischen Umgangsprache I: Formenlehre und die wichtigsten Regeln der Syntax.* 3rd ed. Berlin: Walter de Gruyter, 1922.

Leo, Hermann. *Berechnung des kommenden Weltkrieges zwischen Amerika und Japan: Deutschlands Zusammenbruch und Deutschlands Aufstieg im astrologischen Lichte.* Freiburg im Breisgau: Peter Hofmann, 1920.

Liebig, Eugen Friedrich Wolfgang Freiherr von. *Doitsu ni okeru kasai hoken seido.* Translated by Kan'i Hokenkyoku. Tokyo: Kan'i Hokenkyoku, 1925.

Ludendorff, Erich. *Meine Kriegserinnerungen 1914–1918.* Berlin: Mittler, 1919.

Lutterbeck, Georg Alfred. *Die Jagd über die Inseln: Eine Erzählung aus den Kämpfen der japanischen Kirche.* Freiburg im Breisgau: Herder & Co., 1931.

Maita Minoru. *Echiopia no haisen ni tomonau Ōshū no seikyoku.* Nihon kōen tsūshin 317. Tokyo: Nihon Kōen Tsūshinsha, 1936.

Mandl, Wilhelm. *Das Streben nach Selbstversorgung und der Aussenhandel: Deutsches Reich, Grossbritannien, Frankreich, Britisch Indien, Japan.* Berlin: Limbach, 1939.

Marbach, Otto. *Chinas Not und Japans Hoffnung: Erinnerungen eines Ostasienfreundes.* Bern: Paul Haupt, 1929.

——— *Warum wollen die Japaner und die Chinesen das Christentum?* Berlin: Allgemeiner Evangelisch-Protestantischer Missionsverein, 1920.

Marx, Karl Heinrich. *Chinrōdō to shihon.* Translated by Hirono Toshikama. Doitsu shōronbun taiyaku sōsho 2. Tokyo: Daigaku Shorin, 1933.

Masui Mitsuzō. "Doitsu no gaishi shunyū to baishō shiharai no shōrai." In *Shōgyō Kenkyūjo kōenshū 51.* Kobe: Kōbe Shōgyō Daigaku Shōgyō Kenkyūjo, 1931: 1–48.

Masumoto Yoshirō, ed. *Shinkō Doitsu no shōkai 2.* Koganei-mura: Shinkō Doitsu Kenkyūkai, 1934.

Matsumoto Kunpei. *Kaizaru Kōtei to kaiken: Ikin to suru Ōshū wo mite.* Tokyo: Seinen Kyōdan, 1928.

Matsunami Jirō. *Nachisu no ugoki.* Tokyo: Nōgeisha, 1934.

Matsuoka Binkō. *Shōkei Dokubun shoho.* Tokyo: Shōbundō, 1933.

——— *Sōyō Doitsu bunten.* Tokyo: Shōbundō, 1932.

Matsuoka Yōsuke. *Nichi-Doku Bōkyō Kyōtei no igi.* Daiichi Shuppan jikyoku sōsho 1. Tokyo: Daiichi Shuppansha, 1937.

———. *Nichi-Doku Bōkyō Kyōtei no igi to waga gaikō no kaiko.* Man'ichi sōsho 7. Dairen: Manshū Nichinichi Shinbunsha, 1937.

Mehl, Arnold. *Schatten der aufgehenden Sonne.* Leipzig: Wilhelm Goldmann Verlag, 1935.

Meyer, Johannes F. E. *Die Japanische Sphinx: Ein Beitrag zum Verständnis des Landes und seiner Bewohner.* Frankfurt am Main: Karl Poths, 1936.

Meyn, Erich. *Die japanische Wirtschaftspolitik in der Mandschurei.* Leipzig: N.p., 1938.

Michibe Jun. *Dokushūsha no Doitsugo: Ei-Doku taishō hatsuon yakudoku bunpō shōkai.* Tokyo: Ikubundō Shoten, 1926.

Miki Rin. *Doitsu wa danzen kyōsan shugi e sensensu: Hitorā Doitsu Sōtō netsuben Pio Rōma Hōō rikisetsu seien.* Tokyo: Tsūzoku Seidan Kenkyūkai, 1936.

Minami Manshū Tetsudō Kabushiki Kaisha Shomubu Chōsaka, ed. *Doitsu gyōshōnin seido no kenkyū to Doitsu bōeki no shinkō ni kōkenseru chōya no shokikan.* Translated by Ōta Sankō and Nakamura Hisashi. Dairen: Minami Manshū Tetsudō Shomubu Chōsaka, 1923.

Minobe Tatsukichi. "Doitsu saikin no keizai jōsei." In *Keizai Kurabu kōen 69.* Tokyo: Tōyō Keizai Shuppanbu, 1934: 29–56.

Mishima Yasuo. *Nichi-Doku wa naze dōmei shita ka: Kyōsan shugi e no kyōdō sensen.* Tokyo: Kyō no Mondaisha, 1936.

Mitsuma Shinzō. *Doitsu hōritsu ruigo idōben.* Tokyo: Yūhikaku, 1935.

Miura Kichibee, ed. *Kōdō Doitsugo kōza 1.* Tokyo: Daigaku Shorin, 1931.

Miyazawa Toshiyoshi. *Doitsu kenpō no dokusaika.* Tokyo: Tōkyō Chūō Kōenkai, 1934.

Mohl, Robert. *Der Japaner.* Deutsche Jugendbücherei 482. Berlin: Hermann Hillger, 1933.

Momo Minosuke. "Hittorā to Nachisu wo kataru." In *Keizai Kurabu kōen 94.* Tokyo: Tōyō Keizai Shuppanbu, 1935: 1–39.

Momonoi Tsuruo. *Doitsugo hatsuon no kenkyū.* Tokyo: Taiyōdō Shoten, 1936.

Mori Toshio. *Doitsugo yonshūkan.* Tokyo: Kashiwaba Shobō, 1929.

Murobuse Kōshin. *Hittorā to Hittorā undō.* Tokyo: Heibonsha, 1932.

Mushakōji Kintomo. "Hittorā seiken to Doitsu no kokujō." In *Keizai Kurabu kōen 101.* Tokyo: Tōyō Keizai Shuppanbu, 1935: 1–30.

Nachisu no keihō. Translated by Shihōshō Chōsaka. Shihō shiryō 184. Tokyo: Shihōshō Chōsaka, 1934.

Nagai Matsuzō. "Nachisu seikenka ni okeru Doitsu no genjō to shōrai." In *Keizai Kurabu kōen 79.* Tokyo: Tōyō Keizai Shuppanbu, 1935: 51–66.

Nagata Kenzō. *Sekai jinrui no teki kyōsantōin e bakudan—Nichi-Doku Bōkyō Kyōtei no yurai.* Tokyo: Aikoku Shinbunsha Shuppanbu, 1936.

Nagura Mon'ichi. *Kyōwakoku Doitsu.* Tokyo: Ōsaka Yagō Shoten, 1922.

Naikaku Tōkeikyoku, ed. *Nihon Teikoku tōkei nenkan.* Tokyo: Tōkyō Tōkei Kyōkai, 1919–1937.

Naitō Hachirō. *Iyō gaikokugo nyūmon: Doitsugo Ratengo yomikata.* Nagoya: Nagoya-shi Ishikai Fuzoku Kango Fusanba Gakkō, 1933.

Nakagawa Shigeru. *Hittorā.* Ijin denki bunko 67. Tokyo: Nihonsha, 1935.

Nakama Teruhisa, ed. *Sekai chiri fūzoku taikei 11*. Tokyo: Shinkōsha, 1931.

Nakayama Hisashi, ed. *Nichi-Doku Shoin Doitsugo zensho 1: Butsuri to kagaku*. Tokyo: Nichi-Doku Shoin, 1934.

Naruse Mukyoku. *Saikin Doitsu bungaku shichō*. Tokyo: Hyōgensha, 1924.

Nichi-Doku Bōkyō Kyōtei ni tsuite. Tokyo: Gaimushō Jōhōbu, 1937.

Nichi-Doku Shoin, ed. *Shiken mondai Doitsugo shōkai*. Tokyo: Nichi-Doku Shoin, 1925.

Zenkoku teidai nyūgaku shiken Doitsugo mondai to sono kaitō: Jukensha no tame ni 1932. Tokyo: Nichi-Doku Shoin, 1932.

Nihon Bunka Kenkyūkai Doitsugobu, ed. *Doitsugo-dokuhon 5*. Tanbaichi-chō: Tenri Jihōsha, 1941.

Nihon Denpō Tsūshinsha, ed. *Doitsu taikan 1936*. Tokyo: Nihon Denpō Tsūshinsha, 1936.

Doitsu taikan 1937–38. Tokyo: Nihon Denpō Tsūshinsha, 1937.

Nihon Hōsō Kyōkai, ed. *Nihon Hōsō Kyōkai shi*. Tokyo: Nihon Hōsō Kyōkai, 1939.

Nihon Hōsō Kyōkai Kantō Shibu, ed. *Rajio Doitsugo kōza*. Tokyo: Tōkyō Chūō Hōsōkyoku, 1927.

Nikolai, Walter. *Taisenkan Doitsu no chōhō oyobi senden*. Translated by Sanbō Honbu. Tokyo: Naikaku Jōhōbu, 1938.

Nishiki Masao. *Shōnen sekai chiri bunko 7*. Tokyo: Kōseikaku Shoten, 1930.

Nojiri Momoki. Introduction to *Indoyō kōenshū*, edited by Shimazu Tsunesaburō. Kyoto: Shimazu Tsunesaburō, 1921: 1–3.

Nussbaum, Arthur. *Doitsu shin keizaihō*. Translated by Shihōshō Chōsaka. Shihō shiryō 33. Tokyo: Shihōshō Chōsaka, 1923.

Doitsu teitō seidoron. Translated by Miyazaki Kazuo. Tokyo: Shimizu Shoten, 1932.

Obama Toshie. "Shoninkyū shirabe." *Chūō kōron 45*, no. 7 (1930): 295–301.

Obara Shizuto. *Doitsugo henka zenpyō*. Tokyo: Daigaku Shorin, 1935.

Ohly, Waldemar Hazama. *Das wirtschaftliche Vordringen Japans in China seit dem Frieden von Portsmouth 5. September 1905*. Kiel: N.p., 1922.

Ohta, M. [Masataka Ōta]. *Society and the Newspaper*. Tokyo: Hōchi Shinbun Shuppanbu, 1923.

Oikawa Shigenobu. *Doitsu kahei botsuraku monogatari*. Tokyo: Banrikaku, 1931.

"Doitsu no kinkyō." In *Keimeikai kōenshū 22*. Tokyo: Keimeikai, 1927: 2–54.

Oka Minoru. "Saikin Ō-Bei keizaikai to waga kuni." In *Kōbe Keizaikai kōenshū 5*. Kobe: Kōbe Keizaikai, 1923: 1–14.

Okada Kashinosuke. *Doitsu oyobi sonota shokoku shitsugyō hoken oyobi shitsugyō kyūsai*. Shinagawa-chō: Kawaguchi Insatsujo Shuppanbu, 1930.

Okada Kenzō. *Hakodate chūtō Doitsu Ryōji Hābā-shi sōnanki*. Hakodate sōsho 4. Hakodate: Hakodate Hābā Kinenkai, 1924.

Okada Shun'ichi. *Okada Doitsugo kōza*. Tokyo: Heigensha, 1937.

Okamoto Shūsuke. *Gendai Doitsu bunpō kōwa: Hinshiron*. Tokyo: Sanseidō, 1937.

Ōmura Jintarō, Yamaguchi Kotarō, and Taniguchi Hidetarō. *Doitsu bunpō kyōkasho 1*. Tokyo: Nichi-Doku Shoin, 1927.

Ōno Yūji. *Senryō seizō kagaku: Kagaku kōgyō.* Doitsugo bunko. Tokyo: Shōbundō, 1932.

Osada Arata. *Doitsu dayori: Saiyūki.* Tokyo: Meguro Shoten, 1931.

Ōsaka Mainichi Shinbunsha, ed. *Doitsu no bakudan sengen to senritsu no Ōshū.* Osaka: Ōsaka Mainichi Shinbunsha, 1935.

——— ed. *Ōshū kankōki.* Osaka: Ōsaka Mainichi Shinbunsha, 1928.

Ōshima Muneharu. *Doitsugo dokushū.* Tokyo: Doitsugo Gakkai, 1919.

Ōshima Shun'ichirō. *Jitsuyō Doitsu shōgyō tsūshinbun.* Tokyo: Ōkura Shoten, 1929.

Ostwald, Paul. *Deutschland und Japan.* Berlin: Leonhard Simion Nachfolger, 1920.

——— *Deutschland und Japan: Eine Freundschaft zweier Völker.* Berlin: Junker und Dünnhaupt, 1941.

——— *Japans Entwicklung zur modernen Weltmacht: Seine Kultur-, Rechts-, Wirtschafts- und Staatengeschichte von der Restauration bis zur Gegenwart.* Bonn: Kurt Schroeber, 1922.

——— *Das moderne Japan.* Die Bücherei der Volkshochschule 2. Leipzig: Velhagen & Klasing, 1920.

Ōtake Torao. "Taidoku baishō mondai ni tsuite." In *Nichi-Doku bunka kōenshū 7.* Tokyo: Nichi-Doku Bunka Kyōkai, 1931: 1–30.

Ōtomo Shingo. *Nihon Doitsu Itaria to Kokusai Renmei.* Tokyo: Kokusai Jijō Kenkyūkai, 1935.

Ōtsuka Torao. *Nachi Doitsu wo yuku.* Tokyo: Ari Shoten, 1936.

Ōuchi Kazuta. Introduction to *Mēmeru mondai to Hittorā Sōtō,* by Sugiyama Akira. Tokyo: Kyōzaisha, 1935: 1–2.

Oyanagi Tokuji. *Shumi no Dokugo nyūmon.* Tokyo: Nichi-Doku Shoin, 1929.

Pauly, Kunibert. *Der deutsche Ueberseeverkehr mit dem Fernen Osten: Seine grundlegende Entwicklung vor dem Kriege, sein Wiederaufbau nach dem Kriege und seine Ausgestaltung in der neuesten Zeit unter besonderer Berücksichtigung des Verkehrs mit Japan und China.* Jülich: N.p., 1938.

Perzyński, Friedrich. *Japanische Masken: Nō und Kyōgen.* Berlin: Walter de Gruyter, 1925.

——— *Die Masken der Japanischen Schaubühne.* Hamburg: N.p., 1924.

Pustau, Eduard von, and Okanouye-Kurota. *Japan und Deutschland, die beiden Welträtsel: Politische, wirtschaftliche und kulturelle Entwicklung.* Berlin: Deutscher Verlag für Politik und Wirtschaft, 1936.

Radbruch, Gustav. *Doitsukoku shōnen saibanshohō.* Translated by Shihōshō Chōsaka. Shihō shiryō 31. Tokyo: Shihōshō Chōsaka, 1923.

——— *Rajio tekisuto sokusei Doitsugo: Kaki.* Tokyo: Nihon Hōsō Kyōkai, 1938.

Ramming, Martin. *Rußland-Berichte schiffbrüchiger Japaner aus den Jahren 1793 und 1805 und ihre Bedeutung für die Abschließungspolitik der Tokugawa.* Berlin: Würfel-Verlag, 1930.

Reichelt, Amélie. *Japans Außenhandel und Außenhandelspolitik unter dem Einfluß des Weltkrieges.* Cöthen: N.p., 1931.

Reimers, Jacobus. *Das japanische Kolonialmandat und der Austritt Japans aus dem Völkerbund.* Quakenbrück: N.p., 1936.

Remarque, Erich Maria. *Seibu Sensen ijō nashi.* Translated by Hata Toyokichi. Tokyo: Chūō Kōronsha, 1929.

Rosinski, Herbert. *Studien zum Problem der Autarkie in Japan.* Berlin: N.p., 1930.

Ross, Colin. *Mit dem Kurbelkasten um die Welt.* Berlin: Gebr. Wolffsohn, 1925.

Das Neue Asien. Leipzig: F. A. Brockhaus, 1940.

Ostasien: China, Mandschurei, Korea, Japan. Leipzig: E. A. Seemanns Lichtbildanstalt, 1929.

Rumpf, Fritz. *Das Ise-Monogatari von 1608 und sein Einfluß auf die Buchillustration des 17. Jahrhunderts in Japan.* Berlin: Würfel-Verlag, 1931.

Saigō Keizō. *Shin Doitsugo yonshūkan.* Tokyo: Shōbundō, 1930.

Saitō Seijirō, "Ōshū senran ni okeru Doitsu haisen no riyū." In *Fukyō kenkyūkai kōenshū 9,* edited by Honganji Kyōmubu. Kyoto: Honganji Kyōmubu, 1920: 194–205.

Saitō Yoichirō. *Doitsu gakusei kishitsu.* Hakodate Toshokan sōsho 10. Hakodate: Shiritsu Hakodate Toshokan, 1931.

Sakakibara Yoshio. *Doitsu ni okeru yobōteki keisatsu kōryū seido.* Shihō kenkyū hōkokusho 21 (12). Tokyo: Shihōshō Chōsaka, 1937.

Sakuma Masakazu. *Doitsugo shin kyōten.* Tokyo: Ikubundō Shoten, 1940.

Sakurada Tsunehisa. *Doitsugo nyūshi mondai kaitō.* Tokyo: Shōbundō, 1937.

Sakurai Waichi. *Doitsugo wahō no kenkyū.* Tokyo: Daigaku Shorin, 1934.

Sassa Kōkichi. *Rōkai Daiei Teikoku wo taose: Nichi-Doku-I no teikei ni yorite sekai ryōdo no saibunkatsu jitsugen wo kantetsu seyo.* Tokyo: Kokusai Jijō Kenkyūkai, 1935.

Satō Sankichi. Introduction to *Igaku Doitsugo kenkyū: Kiso iga hen,* by Takizawa Yuzuru. Tokyo: Mokuseisha Shoin, 1931: 1–2.

Satō Tsunehisa, ed. *Doitsugo kyōhon ongaku gakkōyō.* Tokyo: Musashino Ongaku Gakkō, 1941.

Satō Yoshisuke, ed. *Sekai genjō taikan 2.* Tokyo: Shinchōsha, 1930.

Sawada Ken. *Hittorā den.* Tokyo: Dai Nihon Yūbenkai Kōdansha, 1934.

Schalek, Alice. *Japan, das Land des Nebeneinander: Eine Winterreise durch Japan, Korea und die Mandschurei.* Breslau: Ferdinand Hirt, 1925.

Schebesta, Paul. *Die Mission in Kampfe mit der Heidenwelt.* Vienna: Katholischer Akademischer Missionsverein, 1931.

Scheinpflug, Alfons. *Die japanische Kolonisation in Hokkaido.* Leipzig: Hirt & Sohn, 1935.

Schenzinger, Karl Aloys. *Heigensha tōkī shirīzu A(12): Hittorā seinen Doku-Wa taiyaku.* Tokyo: Heigensha, 1934.

Schiller, Emil. *Das Japan von heute.* Berlin: Ostasien-Mission, 1935.

Morgenröte in Japan. Berlin: Allgemeiner Evangelisch-Protestantischer Missionsverein, 1926.

Shinto, die Volksreligion Japans. Berlin: Ostasien-Mission, 1935.

Um Christi Willen! Eine Märtyrgeschichte aus Japan vor 50 Jahren. Berlin: Allgemeiner Evangelisch-Protestantischer Missionsverein, 1924.

Schultze, Ernst. *Japan als Exportindustriestaat.* Japan als Weltindustriemacht 2. Stuttgart: W. Kohlhammer, 1935.

Die weisse und die gelbe Gefahr: Japans gewaltsame Erschliessung und wirtschaftliche Entwicklung. Japan als Weltindustriemacht 1. Stuttgart: W. Kohlhammer, 1935.

Schultze, Ernst [Americanus, pseud.]. *Mexico-Deutschland-Japan*. Dresden: Globus, 1919.

Schwarzenegg, Otto von. *Japan und wir*. Munich: Hugo Bruckmann, 1919.

Sekiguchi Tsugio. *Doitsugo daikōza 1–6*. Tokyo: Gaikokugo Kenkyūsha, 1934–1935.

Hyōjun Doitsu bunpō. Tokyo: Shōbundō, 1933.

Hyōjun shotō Doitsugo kōza I–III. Tokyo: Tachibana Shoten, 1933.

Nyūmon kagakusha no Doitsugo 1. Tokyo: Sanshūsha, 1943.

Sekkin suru Nihon to Doitsu. Tokyo: Taimusu Tsūshinsha, 1935.

Selenka, Emil, and Lenore Selenka. *Sonnige Welten: Ostasiatische Reise-Skizzen— Borneo, Java, Sumatra, Vorderindien, Ceylon, Japan*. 3rd ed. Berlin: C. W. Kreidel, 1925.

Senzen oyobi sengo ni okeru waga taidoku bōeki jōkyō narabini Doitsu sangyō fukkō no waga kuni ni oyobosubeki eikyō. Tokyo: Nihon Ginkō Chōsakyoku, 1925.

Setsudō. *Sekaisen ni okeru Doitsu no sakusen oyobi gaikō hihan*. Tokyo: Miyamoto Burindō, 1919.

Shakai Rōdōbu, ed. *Doitsu rōdō hogo hōan narabini riyūsho*. Rōdō hogo shiryō 34. Tokyo: Shakaikyoku Rōdōbu, 1932.

Shibata Yoshihisa. *Nichi-Doku kyōtei to Nihon no yakushin*. Tokyo: Nihon Jiji Tsūshinsha, 1936.

Shihō jimu no keihi setsugen kan'ika oyobi sokushin: Doitsu saibansho shoki dōmei no kaikakuan. Translated by Shihōshō Chōsaka. Shihō shiryō 169. Tokyo: Shihōshō Chōsaka, 1932.

Shimada Masami, and Kokubu Shirō. *Shika Doitsugo dokushūsho*. Tokyo: Kanehara Shoten, 1929.

Shinomiya Kyōji. *Nachisu*. Kyoto: Seikei Shoin, 1934.

Shō Naokazu. *Jishū Doitsu bunpō shōkai*. Tokyo: Taiyōdō Shoten, 1940.

Snyder, Louis Leo [Nordicus, pseud.]. *Hittorā shugi*. Translated by Kizaki Masaru. Tokyo: Kaizōsha, 1932.

Solf, Wilhelm. "Daijō Bukkyō no shimei." In *Nichi-Doku bunka kōenshū 1*. Tokyo: Nichi-Doku Bunka Kyōkai, 1927: 91–110.

Statistisches Jahrbuch der Stadt Berlin 1937. Berlin: Statistisches Amt der Reichshauptstadt Berlin, 1938.

Stellrecht, Helmut. *Doitsu rōdō hōshi seido*. Translated by Tōkyō Chihō Shitsugyō Bōshi Iinkai and Tōkyō-fu Gakumubu Shakaika. Shitsugyō taisaku shiryō 3. Tokyo: Tōkyō Chihō Shitsugyō Bōshi Iinkai, 1934.

Stoss, Alfred. *Der Kampf zwischen Juda und Japan: Japan als Vorkämpfer freier Volkswirtschaft*. Munich: Ludendorffs Verlag, 1934.

Der Raubzug gegen Japan! Wann endlich wehren sich die Völker? Munich: Ludendorffs Volkswarte-Verlag, 1932.

Die Wahrheit über Shanghai: Der Angriff der Weltleitung gegen das letzte freie Volk Japan. Hamburg: Selbstverl., 1932.

Stoye, Johannes. *Japan: Gefahr oder Vorbild?* Leipzig: Quelle & Meyer, 1936.

Strunk, Roland, and Martin Rikli. *Achtung! Asien marschiert! Ein Tatsachenbericht*. Berlin: Drei Masken Verlag, 1934.

Sugiyama Akira. *Hokushi wo meguru Ei-Yudaya zaibatsu no inbō*. Jikyoku panfuretto 1. Tokyo: Kōtsū Tenbōsha, 1937.

318   Bibliography

Kakudai suru hainichi no yōun: Kyokutō wo nerau Ei-Bei-So. Kōtōkaku panfuretto 3. Tokyo: Kōtōkaku, 1936.

Mēmeru mondai to Hittorā Sōtō. Tokyo: Kyōzaisha, 1935.

Nichi-Doku dōmei no kiun. Tokyo: Kyōzaisha, 1935.

Sumi Hidesuke. *Shokyū Doitsugo-dokuhon.* Tokyo: Nanzandō Shoten, 1942.

Suzuki, Bunshirō. *Japanese Journalism.* Tokyo: The Japanese Council Institute of Pacific Relations, 1929.

Suzuki Hidesuke. *Nichi-Doku kyōtei to kakkoku no dōkō: Sekima no kyōi ni kōsō.* Tokyo: Morita Shobō, 1936.

Suzuki Tōmin. "Doitsu fasshisuten to sono undo." In *Shakai kagaku kōza 4.* Tokyo: Seibundō, 1931: 1–12.

Nachisu no kuni wo miru. Tokyo: Fukuda Shobō, 1934.

Tabata Tamehiko. "Hītorā no jinbutsu kaibō." In *Nihon kōen tsūshin 170.* Tokyo: Nihon Kōen Tsūshinsha, 1932: 1–36.

Tada Motoi. *Hyōjun Doitsugo daiippo.* Tokyo: Gakushūdō, 1934.

Tagawa Daikichirō. "Doitsu no Kokusai Renmei dattai to sono kokusai seikyoku ni oyobosu eikyō." In *Keizai Kurabu kōen 41.* Tokyo: Tōyō Keizai Shuppanbu, 1933: 1–34.

Kaizō tojō no Ō-Bei shakai kenbutsu. Tokyo: Nihon Hyōronsha Shuppanbu, 1920.

Taisen tōsho Doitsu no torero senji zaisei keizai hōsaku: Doitsu Teikoku kōbunsho yōyaku. Chōsa shiryō 11. Tokyo: Shūgiin Chōsabu, 1938.

Takagi Seiji. Introduction to *Kagaku Doitsugo kenkyū*, by Nakayama Hisashi. Tokyo: Mokuseisha Shoin, 1930: 1.

Takakura Shinobu. "Hittora to sono ittō." In *Minshū bunko 76.* Tokyo: Shakai Kyōiku Kyōkai, 1933: 1–34.

Takakusu Junjirō. "Doitsu no kinkyō." In *Keimeikai kōenshū 2.* Tokyo: Keimeikai, 1920: 1–40.

Takakuwa Sumio. *Teiyō Doitsu shōbunten.* Tokyo: Nanzandō Shoten, 1936.

Takarada Tsūgen. *Shinkō Doitsu no genjō.* Gakugei Kōen Tsūshinsha panfuretto 32. Tokyo: Gakugei Kōen Tsūshinsha, 1926.

Takatori Junsaku. *Ō-Bei man'yūki: Bankoku Giin Kaigi sanretsu.* Tokyo: Takatori Jimusho, 1926.

Takekoshi Yosaburō. Introduction to *Shinbungaku: Ō-Bei shinbun jigyō*, by Matsumoto Kunpei. Tokyo: Hakubunkan, 1899: 1–7.

Takeo Hajime. *Naniyue no Nichi-Doku Bōkyō Kyōtei ka: Kinpaku jōtai no So-Doku kankei to Kōkoku Nihon no tachiba.* Kōtōkaku panfuretto 4. Tokyo: Kōtōkaku, 1936.

Takimoto Jirō. *1500-en sankagetsukan Ō-Bei kenbutsu annai.* Tokyo: Ō-Bei Ryokō Annaisha, 1929.

Takizawa Yuzuru. *Igaku Doitsugo kenkyū: Kiso iga hen.* Tokyo: Mokuseisha Shoin, 1931.

Tanaka Kōichi. *Doitsu bunpō kyōkasho.* Tokyo: Hakusuisha, 1935.

Tanaka Mitsuharu. *Yoku wakaru shonensei no Doitsu bunpō.* Tokyo: Taiyōdō Shoten, 1939.

Teikoku Keiba Kyōkai, ed. *Doitsukoku keiba shikō kitei.* Tokyo: Keiba Kyōkai, 1929.

Teishinshō Kansenkyoku Sen'yōhin Kensajo, ed. *1906-nen Doitsu sentō shaken kisoku shōyaku.* Kenkyū shiryō 3. Tokyo: Teishinshō Kansenkyoku, 1921.

Tenri Daini Chūgakkō Doitsugoka, ed. *Chūtō Doitsu-dokuhon 1.* Tanbaichi-chō: Tenri Daini Chūgakkō Doitsugoka, 1940.

Tetsudōshō Un'yukyoku, ed. *Shiberia keiyu Ōshū ryokō annai.* Tokyo: Tetsudōshō Un'yukyoku, 1929.

Tetsudōshō Un'yukyoku Kokusaika, ed. *Doitsu shin tetsudō unsō kitei.* Tokyo: Tetsudō Un'yukyoku, 1928.

Thierbach, Hans. *Welt in der Wandlung: Eindrücke von einer Reise durch die Vereinigten Staaten, Japan und Sowjetrußland.* Berlin: Nachbarschafts-Verlag, 1933.

Tichý, Alois. *Die staatsrechtliche Stellung des Kaisers von Japan unter besonderer Berücksichtigung des Kaiserlichen Hausgesetzes.* Ohlau: N.p., 1928.

Tōa Keizai Chōsakyoku, ed. *Doitsu ni okeru kōdantai no keizaiteki katsudō.* Tōa shōsatsu 13. Tokyo: Tōa Keizai Chōsakyoku, 1933.

Tobari Chikufū, ed. *Shinshiki Doku-Wa daijiten.* 32nd ed. Tokyo: Ōkura Shoten, 1919.

Tōkyō Hōsōkyoku, ed. *Rajio kōenshū 1.* Tokyo: Nihon Rajio Kyōkai, 1925.

Tōkyō Shisei Chōsakai Shiryōka, ed. *Doitsu ni okeru tochi kukaku seiri no jitsurei.* Tokyo: Tōkyō Shisei Chōsakai, 1924.

Tomita Kumao. *Doitsugo wa tanoshimi da.* Tokyo: Seikōsha Shoten, 1941.

Tomoeda Takahiko. "Doitsu Daisan Kokka ni tsuite." In *Nichi-Doku bunka kōenshū 10.* Tokyo: Nichi-Doku Bunka Kyōkai, 1936: 1–30.

Toyosaki Zennosuke. *Fu-Futsu Sensō igo no Doitsu keizai.* Tokyo: Kōgyō no Nihonsha, 1920.

Trautz, Friedrich Max. *Japan: Was es uns war und was es uns ist.* Hamburg: N.p., 1929.

"'Kulturbeziehungen' und 'Kulturaustausch' zwischen Deutschland und Japan." *Ostasiatische Rundschau* 9, no. 2 (1928): 42–44.

Tsuboi Michizō, and Okabe Noboru. *Kikai Doitsugo kaishaku kenkyū.* Tokyo: Taiyōdō Shoten, 1935.

Tsukamoto Yoshitaka. *Saishin no Doitsu wo hōzu: Tsepperin hikōsen ni takushite.* Osaka: Shinbun Rengōsha Ōsaka Shisha, 1929.

Tsurumi Sakio. Introduction to "Saikin no Doitsu," in *Keimeikai kōenshū 37,* by Nagaoka Harukazu. Tokyo: Keimeikai, 1930: 1–2.

Tsuzumi Tsuneyoshi. *Katsuyō Doitsu bunpō.* Tokyo: Daigaku Shorin, 1934.

Kihon Doitsu bunpō. Tokyo: Daigaku Shorin, 1933.

Shōkai Doitsu bunten. Tokyo: Ōkura Shoten, 1921.

Uchida Eizō, and Tada Motoi. *Doitsugo seibatsu.* Tokyo: Ōkura Kōbundō, 1932.

Uchida Mitsugi. *Doitsu shin bunten.* Tokyo: Ikubundō Shoten, 1930.

Tōkei ni motozuku hyōjun Doitsu tango 6000. Tokyo: Ikubundō Shoten, 1938.

Uchiyama Toshio. *Chūsei Doitsu doreishi.* Shakai mondai sōsho 5. Tokyo: Fukunaga Shoten, 1920.

Über Kanada nach Ostasien und Australien: Der neue Expreßdienst mit Riesenschnelldampfern. Hamburg: Canadian Pacific, 1934.

Überfahrts- und Gepäckbestimmungen: Ostasien, Niederländisch-Indien, Australien. Hamburg: Hamburg-Amerika-Linie, 1939.

Ueberschaar, Hans. *Die Eigenart der japanischen Staatskultur: Eine Einführung in das Denken der Japaner.* Leipzig: Theodor Weicher, 1925.

Uenishi Hanzaburō. *Mottomo jissaitekina shinbun Doitsugo no yomikata*. Tokyo: Taimusu Shuppansha, 1932.

Umbreit, Samuel John. *Zwanzig Jahre Missionar in Japan: Erlebnisse und Beobachtungen im Missionsdienst der Evangelischen Gemeinschaft*. Stuttgart: Christliches Verlagshaus, 1929.

Universität Leipzig. *Verzeichnis der Vorlesungen*. Leipzig: Universitäts-Buchhändler, 1934–1936.

Utley, Freda. "Germany and Japan." *The Political Quarterly* 8, no. 1 (1937): 51–65.

Japan's Feet of Clay. New York: W. W. Norton, 1937.

Wagatsuma Sakae. *Nachisu no hōritsu*. Tokyo: Nihon Hyōronsha, 1934.

Watanabe Kakuji. *Tei-Doitsugo kenkyū*. Tokyo: Daigaku Shorin, 1943.

Wencker-Wildberg, Friedrich. *Der unvermeidliche Krieg zwischen Japan und Amerika: Eine politische Studie*. Stuttgart: Neuer Stuttgarter Verlag, 1921.

Wessels, Heinrich. *Doitsu kōei kasai hoken seido. Edited and translated by Kan'i Hokenkyoku*. Tokyo: Kan'i Hokenkyoku, 1925.

Wildes, Harry Emerson. *The Press and Social Currents in Japan*. Chicago: University of Chicago Press, 1927.

Witte, Johannes. *Auf vulkanischem Boden: Reiseerlebnisse in Japan und China*. Berlin: Allgemeiner Evangelisch-Protestantischer Missionsverein, 1925.

Japan heute. Berlin: Allgemeiner Evangelisch-Protestantischer Missionsverein, 1926.

Japan: Zwischen zwei Kulturen. Leipzig: J. C. Hinrichs'sche Buchhandlung, 1928.

Die Religionen Ostasiens: China und Japan. Leipzig: Quelle & Meyer, 1926.

Sommer-Sonnentage in Japan und China: Reise-Erlebnisse in Ostasien im Jahre 1924. Göttingen: Vandenhoeck & Ruprecht, 1925.

Woytinsky, Wladimir S. *Zehn Jahre neues Deutschland: Ein Gesamtüberblick in Zahlen*. Berlin: Rudolf Mosse Buchverlag, 1929.

Yamada Junjirō. *Doitsu shin kenpō ni arawaretaru shakaiteki shisō*. Tokyo: Ganshōdō Shoten, 1923.

Yamada Kiichi. *Sengo no Ō-Bei man'yūki*. Nishisugamo-machi: Hōten Gijuku, 1920.

Yamada Kōzaburō. *Doitsugo hattatsushi*. Tokyo: Daigaku Shorin, 1935.

Doitsugo kanshi no kenkyū. Tokyo: Daigaku Shorin, 1937.

Jishū shin Doitsugo. Tokyo: Taiyōdō Shoten, 1930.

Yamagishi Mitsunobu. *Doitsu bunka gairon*. Tokyo: Kanasashi Hōryūdō, 1927.

Gendai no Doitsu gikyoku 1. Tokyo: Ōmura Shoten, 1920.

ed. *Shin Doitsugo kōza 1*. Tokyo: Doitsugo Kenkyūsha, 1934.

Shotō Doitsu bunten. Tokyo: Kashiwaba Shobō, 1929.

Yamaguchi Miki. *Doitsugo kaitei*. Tokyo: Kanasashi Hōryūdō, 1931.

Yamaguchi Miki, and Okakura Ichirō. *Jitsuyō Doku-Wa kaiwa hen*. Kobe: Kawase Nisshindō Shoten, 1926.

Yanagisawa Ken. "Bunka gaikō to kakkoku no bunka jigyō ni tsuite." In *Keizai Kurabu kōen 79*. Tokyo: Tōyō Keizai Shuppanbu, 1935: 23–50.

Yūki Shintarō. *Sokushū Doitsugo kōza 3*. Tokyo: Taiyōdō Shoten, 1942.

Post-1945 Publications

Abel, Jessamyn R. *The International Minimum: Creativity and Contradiction in Japan's Global Engagement, 1933–1964.* Honolulu: University of Hawai'i Press, 2015.

Adluri, Vishwa, and Joydeep Bagchee. *The Nay Science: A History of German Indology.* New York: Oxford University Press, 2014.

Akahata: Hi gōhō jidai no Nihon Kyōsantō chūō kikanshi. Kyoto: San'ichi Shobō, 1954.

Anderson, Benedict R. *Imagined Communities: Reflections on the Origin and Spread of Nationalism.* Rev. ed. New York: Verso, 1991.

Anderson, Emily. *Christianity and Imperialism in Modern Japan: Empire for God.* London: Bloomsbury Academic, 2014.

Araki Shigeo, Manabe Ryōichi, and Fujita Sakae, eds. *Sekiguchi Tsugio no shōgai to gyōseki.* Tokyo: Sanshūsha, 1967.

Arvidsson, Stefan. *Aryan Idols: Indo-European Mythology as Ideology and Science.* Translated by Sonia Wichmann. Chicago: University of Chicago Press, 2006.

Bailey, George. *Germans: The Biography of an Obsession.* New York: The Free Press, 1991.

Bain, Peter, and Paul Shaw, eds. *Blackletter: Type and National Identity.* New York: The Cooper Union and Princeton Architectural Press, 1998.

Balsamo, William M. "Japan's Contribution to the World of Opera." *Kenmei Joshi Gakuin Tanki Daigaku kenkyū kiyō: Beacon* 37 (2002): 15–26.

Banaji, Jairus, ed. *Fascism: Essays on Europe and India.* New Delhi: Three Essays Collective, 2016.

Baranowski, Shelley. *Nazi Empire: German Colonialism and Imperialism from Bismarck to Hitler.* Cambridge: Cambridge University Press, 2010.

Bartels-Ishikawa, Anna. *Theodor Sternberg: Einer der Begründer des Freirechts in Deutschland und Japan.* Berlin: Duncker & Humblot, 1998.

Bartholomew, James R. *The Formation of Science in Japan: Building a Research Tradition.* New Haven: Yale University Press, 1989.

Baskett, Michael. *The Attractive Empire: Transnational Film Culture in Imperial Japan.* Honolulu: University of Hawai'i Press, 2008.

Bauerkämper, Arnd, and Grzegorz Rossoliński-Liebe, eds. *Fascism without Borders: Transnational Connections and Cooperation between Movements and Regimes in Europe from 1918 to 1945.* New York: Berghahn Books, 2017.

Becker, Bert. *Japan an der Spree: Deutsch-Japanische Beziehungen im Spiegel Berlins und Brandenburgs.* Berlin: Ausländerbeauftragte des Senats, 1996.

Beer, Lawrence Ward. *Freedom of Expression in Japan: A Study in Comparative Law, Politics, and Society.* Tokyo: Kodansha International, 1984.

Bergholz, Max. "Thinking the Nation: *Imagined Communities: Reflections on the Origin and Spread of Nationalism,* by Benedict Anderson." *The American Historical / Review* 123, no. 2 (April 2018): 518–528.

Berman, Nina, Klaus Mühlhahn, and Patrice Nganang, eds. *German Colonialism Revisited: African, Asian, and Oceanic Experiences.* Ann Arbor: University of Michigan Press, 2014.

Bhatt, Chetan. *Hindu Nationalism: Origins, Ideologies and Modern Myths*. Oxford: Berg Publishers, 2001.

Bieber, Hans-Joachim. *SS und Samurai: Deutsch-japanische Kulturbeziehungen 1933–1945*. Munich: Iudicium, 2014.

Blackbourn, David. "The Discreet Charm of the Bourgeoisie: Reappraising German History in the Nineteenth Century." In *The Peculiarities of German History: Bourgeois Society and Politics in Nineteenth-Century Germany*, by David Blackbourn and Geoff Eley. New York: Oxford University Press, 1984: 159–292.

Boyd, Carl. *The Extraordinary Envoy: General Hiroshi Ōshima and Diplomacy in the Third Reich, 1934–1939*. Washington, DC: University Press of America, 1980.

Hitler's Japanese Confidant: General Ōshima Hiroshi and MAGIC Intelligence, 1941–1945. Lawrence: University Press of Kansas, 1993.

Brightwell, Erin L. "Refracted Axis: Kitayama Jun'yū and Writing a German Japan." *Japan Forum* 27, no. 4 (2015): 431–453.

Brockmann, Stephen. *A Critical History of German Film*. Rochester: Camden House, 2010.

Brooker, Paul. *The Faces of Fraternalism: Nazi Germany, Fascist Italy, and Imperial Japan*. New York: Oxford University Press, 1991.

Browning, Christopher R. *Ordinary Men: Reserve Police Battalion 101 and the Final Solution in Poland*. Rev. ed. New York: Harper Perennial, 2017.

Brückenhaus, Daniel. *Policing Transnational Protest: Liberal Imperialism and the Surveillance of Anticolonialists in Europe, 1905–1945*. New York: Oxford University Press, 2017.

Bry, Gerhard. *Wages in Germany 1871–1945*. Princeton: Princeton University Press, 1960.

Burkman, Thomas W. *Japan and the League of Nations: Empire and World Order, 1914–1938*. Honolulu: University of Hawai'i Press, 2008.

Burleigh, Michael. *The Third Reich: A New History*. New York: Hill and Wang, 2000.

Burleigh, Michael, and Wolfgang Wippermann. *The Racial State: Germany 1933–1945*. Cambridge: Cambridge University Press, 1991.

Chapman, John W. M. *Ultranationalism in German-Japanese Relations, 1930–45: From Wenneker to Sasakawa*. Folkestone: Global Oriental, 2011.

Cho, Joanne Miyang, Eric Kurlander, and Douglas T. McGetchin, eds. *Transcultural Encounters between Germany and India: Kindred Spirits in the Nineteenth and Twentieth Centuries*. New York: Routledge, 2014.

Cho, Joanne Miyang, and Douglas T. McGetchin, eds. *Gendered Encounters between Germany and Asia: Transnational Perspectives since 1800*. New York: Palgrave Macmillan, 2017.

Cho, Joanne Miyang, Lee Roberts, and Christian W. Spang, eds. *Transnational Encounters between Germany and Japan: Perceptions of Partnership in the Nineteenth and Twentieth Centuries*. New York: Palgrave Macmillan, 2016.

Christensen, Peter H. *Germany and the Ottoman Railways: Art, Empire, and Infrastructure*. New Haven: Yale University Press, 2017.

Collins, Sandra. *The 1940 Tokyo Games: The Missing Olympics*. London: Routledge, 2008.

Conrad, Sebastian. *What Is Global History?* Princeton: Princeton University Press, 2016.

Coons, Lorraine, and Alexander Varias. *Tourist Third Cabin: Steamship Travel in the Interwar Years*. New York: Palgrave Macmillan, 2003.

Coox, Alvin D. *Nomonhan: Japan against Russia, 1939*. Stanford: Stanford University Press, 1985.

Crack, Angela M. *Global Communication and Transnational Public Spheres*. New York: Palgrave Macmillan, 2008.

De Syon, Guillaume. *Zeppelin! Germany and the Airship, 1900–1939*. Baltimore: The Johns Hopkins University Press, 2002.

Deakin, F. W. *The Brutal Friendship: Mussolini, Hitler, and the Fall of Italian Fascism*. New York: Harper & Row, 1962.

Dennis, David B. *Inhumanities: Nazi Interpretations of Western Culture*. New York: Cambridge University Press, 2012.

Dickinson, Frederick R. *War and National Reinvention: Japan in the Great War, 1914–1919*. Cambridge: Harvard University Press, 1999.

  World War I and the Triumph of a New Japan, 1919–1930. New York: Cambridge University Press, 2013.

DiNardo, Richard L. *Germany and the Axis Powers: From Coalition to Collapse*. Lawrence: University Press of Kansas, 2005.

Dobson, Hugo. "The Failure of the Tripartite Pact: Familiarity Breeding Contempt between Japan and Germany, 1940–45." *Japan Forum* 11, no. 2 (1999): 179–190.

Documents on German Foreign Policy, 1918–45. Series D. Vol. 8. Washington, DC: US Department of State, 1949.

Dower, John W. *War without Mercy: Race and Power in the Pacific War*. New York: Pantheon Books, 1986.

Drechsler, Karl. *Deutschland-China-Japan, 1933–1939: Das Dilemma der deutschen Fernostpolitik*. [East] Berlin: Akademie-Verlag, 1964.

Durham, Martin, and Margaret Power, eds. *New Perspectives on the Transnational Right*. New York: Palgrave Macmillan, 2010.

Eatwell, Roger. *Fascism: A History*. New York: Viking Penguin, 1996.

Eatwell, Roger, and Matthew Goodwin. *National Populism: The Revolt against Liberal Democracy*. London: Pelican, 2018.

Einstein, Albert. *The Travel Diaries of Albert Einstein: The Far East, Palestine, and Spain, 1922–1923*, edited by Ze'ev Rosenkranz. Princeton: Princeton University Press, 2018.

Eisner, Lotte H. *Fritz Lang*. London: Da Capo Press, 1976.

Fascism: Journal of Comparative Fascist Studies 2, no. 2 (2013).

Finchelstein, Federico. *From Fascism to Populism in History*. Oakland: University of California Press, 2017.

  Transatlantic Fascism: Ideology, Violence, and the Sacred in Argentina and Italy, 1919–1945. Durham: Duke University Press, 2010.

Fletcher, William Miles. *The Search for a New Order: Intellectuals and Fascism in Prewar Japan*. Chapel Hill: The University of North Carolina Press, 1982.

Fliess, Peter J. *Freedom of the Press in the German Republic, 1918–1933.* Baton Rouge: Louisiana State University Press, 1955.

Fousek, John. *To Lead the Free World: American Nationalism and the Cultural Roots of the Cold War.* Chapel Hill: The University of North Carolina Press, 2000.

Fox, John P. *Germany and the Far Eastern Crisis 1931–1938: A Study in Diplomacy and Ideology.* Oxford: Clarendon Press, 1985.

Framke, Maria. *Delhi–Rom–Berlin: Die indische Wahrnehmung von Faschismus und Nationalsozialismus 1922–1939.* Darmstadt: Wissenschaftliche Buchgesellschaft, 2012.

Freyeisen, Astrid. *Shanghai und die Politik des Dritten Reiches.* Würzburg: Königshausen und Neumann Verlag, 2000.

Friese, Eberhard. *Japaninstitut Berlin und Deutsch-Japanische Gesellschaft Berlin: Quellenlage und ausgewählte Aspekte ihrer Politik 1926–1945.* Berlin: East Asian Institute, Free University of Berlin, 1980.

——— "'Wir brauchen den Austausch geistiger Güter!'" In *Berlin–Tôkyô im 19. und 20. Jahrhundert*, edited by Japanisch-Deutsches Zentrum. Berlin: Springer Verlag, 1997: 233–244.

Fritzsche, Peter. *A Nation of Fliers: German Aviation and the Popular Imagination.* Cambridge: Harvard University Press, 1992.

Fuechtner, Veronika, and Mary Rhiel, eds. *Imagining Germany Imagining Asia: Essays in Asian-German Studies.* Rochester: Camden House, 2013.

Fuhrmann, Malte. *Der Traum vom deutschen Orient: Zwei deutsche Kolonien im Osmanischen Reich 1851–1918.* Frankfurt am Main: Campus Verlag, 2006.

Fulda, Bernhard. *Press and Politics in the Weimar Republic.* New York: Oxford University Press, 2009.

Furuya, Harumi. "Japan's Racial Identity in the Second World War: The Cultural Context of the Japanese Treatment of POWs." In *Japanese Prisoners of War*, edited by Philip Towle, Margaret Kosuge, and Yōichi Kibata. London: Hambledon and London, 2000: 117–134.

Furuya, Harumi Shidehara. "Nazi Racism toward the Japanese: Ideology vs. Realpolitik." *Nachrichten der Gesellschaft für Natur- und Völkerkunde Ostasiens (NOAG)* 157–8 (1995): 17–75.

Gassert, Philipp, and Daniel S. Mattern. *The Hitler Library: A Bibliography.* Westport: Greenwood Press, 2001.

Gluck, Carol. "What a Difference 120 Years Make: Germany, Japan, the World." Lecture, conference "Von, über und mit Japan reden: 120 Jahre Japan-Forschung in Berlin" at the Berlin-Brandenburgische Akademie der Wissenschaften, Berlin, October 15, 2007.

Glynn, Paul. *A Song for Nagasaki: The Story of Takashi Nagai – Scientist, Convert, and Survivor of the Atomic Bomb.* San Francisco: Ignatius Press, 2009.

Goebbels, Joseph. *Die Tagebücher von Joseph Goebbels: Teil I, Band 3/I*, edited by Elke Fröhlich. Munich: K. G. Saur, 2005.

Goldman, Stuart D. *Nomonhan, 1939: The Red Army's Victory That Shaped World War II.* Annapolis: Naval Institute Press, 2012.

Goodman, David G., and Masanori Miyazawa. *Jews in the Japanese Mind: The History and Use of a Cultural Stereotype.* Lanham: Lexington Books, 2000.

Gordon, Andrew. *Labor and Imperial Democracy in Prewar Japan*. Berkeley: University of California Press, 1987.

Gorman, Daniel. *The Emergence of International Society in the 1920s*. New York: Cambridge University Press, 2012.

Griffin, Roger. *The Nature of Fascism*. New York: Palgrave Macmillan, 1991.

Grüttner, Michael. *Biographisches Lexikon zur nationalsozialistischen Wissenschaftspolitik*. Heidelberg: Synchron, 2004.

Studenten im Dritten Reich. Paderborn: Ferdinand Schöningh, 1995.

Guettel, Jens-Uwe. *German Expansionism, Imperial Liberalism, and the United States, 1776–1945*. New York: Cambridge University Press, 2012.

Gulyás, Réka. *Von der Puszta will ich träumen...: Das Ungarn-Bild im deutschen Spielfilm 1929–1939*. Innsbruck: Inst. für Sprachwiss., 2000.

Gumperz, John J., and Stephen C. Levinson, eds. *Rethinking Linguistic Relativity*. Cambridge: Cambridge University Press, 1996.

Haasch, Günther, ed. *Die Deutsch-Japanischen Gesellschaften von 1888 bis 1996*. Berlin: Wissenschaftsverlag Volker Spiess, 1996.

"Die Wa-Doku-Kai (1888–1912) als Vorläuferin der Deutsch-Japanischen Gesellschaft Berlin." In *Berlin–Tôkyô im 19. und 20. Jahrhundert*, edited by Japanisch-Deutsches Zentrum. Berlin: Springer Verlag, 1997: 79–82.

Hake, Sabine. *German National Cinema*. 2nd ed. New York: Routledge, 2008.

Hansen, Janine. *Arnold Fancks Die Tochter des Samurai: Nationalsozialistische Propaganda und japanische Filmpolitik*. Wiesbaden: Harrassowitz, 1997.

"Celluloid Competition: German-Japanese Film Relations, 1929–45." In *Cinema and the Swastika: The International Expansion of Third Reich Cinema*, edited by Roel Vande Winkel and David Welch. New York: Palgrave Macmillan, 2007: 187–197.

Haruki Takeshi. *Sangoku Dōmei no hyōka*. Tokyo: Aoyama Gakuin Daigaku Hōgakukai, 1964.

Hasegawa Shin'ichi. *Japan Taimuzu monogatari: Bunkyū gannen (1861) kara gendai made*. Tokyo: Japan Taimuzu, 1966.

Hathaway, Oona A., and Scott J. Shapiro. *The Internationalists: How a Radical Plan to Outlaw War Remade the World*. New York: Simon & Schuster, 2017.

Havens, Thomas R. H. *Valley of Darkness: The Japanese People and World War II*. New York: W. W. Norton, 1978.

Hay, Mark. "Nazi Chic: The Asian Fashion Craze That Just Won't Die." *Vice*, February 12, 2015. www.vice.com/en_us/article/xd5bdd/nazis-chic-is-asias-offensive-fashion-craze-456 (accessed August 21, 2018).

Hayashi Shigeru. *Nihon no rekishi 25: Taiheiyō Sensō*. Tokyo: Chūō Kōronsha, 1967.

Hempenstall, Peter J., and Paula Tanaka Mochida. *The Lost Man: Wilhelm Solf in German History*. Wiesbaden: Harrassowitz, 2005.

Hepp, Michael, ed. *Die Ausbürgerung deutscher Staatsangehöriger 1933–45 nach den im Reichsanzeiger veröffentlichten Listen: Band I*. Munich: K. G. Saur, 1985.

Herde, Peter. *Der Japanflug: Planungen und Verwirklichung einer Flugverbindung zwischen den Achsenmächten und Japan 1942–1945*. Stuttgart: Franz Steiner Verlag, 2000.

Herren, Madeleine. "Fascist Internationalism." In *Internationalisms: A Twentieth-Century History,* edited by Glenda Sluga and Patricia Clavin. Cambridge: Cambridge University Press, 2017: 191–212.

Herzog, Rudolph. *Dead Funny: Humor in Hitler's Germany.* Translated by Jefferson Chase. New York: Melville House, 2011.

Hessel, Franz. *Spazieren in Berlin.* In *Sämtliche Werke in fünf Bänden 3: Städte und Porträts,* edited by Bernhard Echte. Oldenburg: Igel Verlag, 1999.

Walking in Berlin: A Flaneur in the Capital. Translated by Amanda DeMarco. Cambridge: The MIT Press, 2017.

Hitler, Adolf. *Hitler's Table Talk 1941–1944: His Private Conversations.* Translated by Norman Cameron and R. H. Stevens. New York: Enigma Books, 2000.

Hitlers zweites Buch: Ein Dokument aus dem Jahr 1928. Stuttgart: Deutsche Verlags-Anstalt, 1961.

Monologe im Führerhauptquartier 1941–1944, edited by Werner Jochmann. Munich: Orbis Verlag, 2000.

Hoenicke Moore, Michaela. *Know Your Enemy: The American Debate on Nazism, 1933–1945.* New York: Cambridge University Press, 2010.

Hofmann, Reto. *The Fascist Effect: Japan and Italy, 1915–1952.* Ithaca: Cornell University Press, 2015.

Hoppner, Inge, and Fujiko Sekikawa, eds. *Brückenbauer: Pioniere des japanisch-deutschen Kulturaustausches.* Munich: Iudicium Verlag, 2005.

Horn, Elija. *Indien als Erzieher: Orientalismus in der deutschen Reformpädagogik und Jugendbewegung 1918–1933.* Bad Heilbrunn: Verlag Julius Klinkhardt, 2018.

Hosoya, Chihiro. "The Japanese-Soviet Neutrality Pact." In *The Fateful Choice: Japan's Advance into Southeast Asia, 1939–1941,* edited by James William Morley. New York: Columbia University Press, 1980: 13–114.

"The Tripartite Pact, 1939–1940." In *Deterrent Diplomacy: Japan, Germany, and the USSR 1935–1940,* edited by James William Morley. New York: Columbia University Press, 1976: 179–258.

Hoston, Germaine A. *Marxism and the Crisis of Development in Prewar Japan.* Princeton: Princeton University Press, 1990.

Hüttenberger, Peter. "Nationalsozialistische Polykratie." *Geschichte und Gesellschaft: Zeitschrift für Historische Sozialwissenschaft* 4 (1976): 417–442.

Huffman, James L. *Creating a Public: People and Press in Meiji Japan.* Honolulu: University of Hawai'i Press, 1997.

Hutton, Christopher M. *Linguistics and the Third Reich: Mother-Tongue Fascism, Race and the Science of Language.* London: Routledge, 1999.

Ike, Nobutaka. *Japan's Decision for War: Records of the 1941 Policy Conferences.* Stanford: Stanford University Press, 1967.

Ikeuchi Osamu. *Kotoba no tetsugaku: Sekiguchi Tsugio no koto.* Tokyo: Seidosha, 2010.

Iklé, Frank. *German-Japanese Relations, 1936–1940.* New York: Bookman Associates, 1956.

"Japanese-German Peace Negotiations during World War I." *The American Historical Review* 71, no. 1 (October 1965): 62–76.

"Japan's Policies toward Germany." In *Japan's Foreign Policy, 1868–1941: A Research Guide*, edited by James W. Morley. New York: Columbia University Press, 1974: 265–339.

Inabe Kojirō. *Ikki to Reikichi: Kita kyōdai no sōkoku*. Niigata: Niigata Nippō Jigyōsha, 2002.

Iriye, Akira. *Global and Transnational History: The Past, Present, and Future*. London: Palgrave Macmillan, 2013.

Power and Culture: The Japanese-American War, 1941–1945. Cambridge: Harvard University Press, 1981.

Iwamura Masashi. *Senzen Nihonjin no tai Doitsu ishiki*. Tokyo: Keiō Gijuku Daigaku Shuppankai, 2005.

Jervis, Robert. *How Statesmen Think: The Psychology of International Politics*. Princeton: Princeton University Press, 2017.

Perception and Misperception in International Politics. New ed. Princeton: Princeton University Press, 2017.

Johnson, Chalmers. *An Instance of Treason: Ozaki Hotsumi and the Sorge Spy Ring*. Expanded ed. Stanford: Stanford University Press, 1990.

Jones, F. C. *Japan's New Order in East Asia: Its Rise and Fall, 1937–45*. London: Oxford University Press, 1954.

Jones, Peter. *Track Two Diplomacy in Theory and Practice*. Stanford: Stanford University Press, 2015.

Jung, Uli, and Walter Schatzberg. *Beyond Caligari: The Films of Robert Wiene*. New York: Berghahn Books, 1999.

Kamimura Naoki. *Kindai Nihon no Doitsugo gakusha*. Suwa: Chōeisha, 2008.

"Meijimatsu no Gokō no Doitsugo kyōshitachi." In *Kyūshū no Nichi-Doku bunka kōryū jinbutsushi*. Kumamoto: Kumamoto Daigaku, 2005: 102–103.

Kasza, Gregory J. *The State and the Mass Media in Japan, 1918–1945*. Berkeley: University of California Press, 1988.

Katō Tetsurō. *Waimāruki Berurin no Nihonjin: Yōkō chishikijin no hantei nettowāku*. Tokyo: Iwanami Shoten, 2008.

Kaufmann, Wolfgang. *Das Dritte Reich und Tibet: Die Heimat des "östlichen Hakenkreuzes" im Blickfeld der Nationalsozialisten*. Ludwigsfelde: Ludwigsfelder Verlagshaus, 2009.

Keizai Kurabu 50-nen. Tokyo: Keizai Kurabu, 1981.

Kennedy, Malcolm D. *The Estrangement of Great Britain and Japan, 1917–35*. Berkeley: University of California Press, 1969.

Kenny, Paul D. *Populism and Patronage: Why Populists Win Elections in India, Asia, and Beyond*. Oxford: Oxford University Press, 2017.

Kershaw, Ian. *Hitler, 1889–1936: Hubris*. New York: W. W. Norton, 1999.

The "Hitler Myth": Image and Reality in the Third Reich. Oxford: Clarendon Press, 1987.

Kersten, Rikki. "Japan." In *The Oxford Handbook of Fascism*, edited by R. J. B. Bosworth. New York: Oxford University Press, 2009: 526–544.

Kim, Hoi-eun. *Doctors of Empire: Medical and Cultural Encounters between Imperial Germany and Meiji Japan*. Toronto: University of Toronto Press, 2014.

Kimmich, Christoph M. *German Foreign Policy, 1918–1945: A Guide to Current Research and Resources*. 3rd ed. Lanham: Scarecrow Press, 2013.

Kirby, William C. *Germany and Republican China*. Stanford: Stanford University Press, 1984.

Kocka, Jürgen. "Asymmetrical Historical Comparison: The Case of the German *Sonderweg*." *History and Theory* 38, no. 1 (February 1999): 40–50.

Koltermann, Till Philip. *Der Untergang des Dritten Reiches im Spiegel der deutsch-japanischen Kulturbegegnung 1933–1945*. Wiesbaden: Harrassowitz, 2009.

Kontje, Todd. *German Orientalisms*. Ann Arbor: University of Michigan Press, 2004.

Kott, Sandrine and Kiran Klaus Patel, eds. *Nazism Across Borders: The Social Policies of the Third Reich and Their Global Appeal*. Oxford: Oxford University Press, 2019.

Krämer, Hans Martin. *Unterdrückung oder Integration? Die staatliche Behandlung der katholischen Kirche in Japan, 1932 bis 1945*. Marburg: Förderverein Marburger Japan-Reihe, 2002.

Kramer, Paul A. "Power and Connection: Imperial Histories of the United States in the World." *The American Historical Review* 116, no. 5 (December 2011): 1348–1391.

Krebs, Gerhard, ed. *Japan und Preußen*. Munich: Iudicium Verlag, 2002.

Krebs, Gerhard, and Bernd Martin, eds. *Formierung und Fall der Achse Berlin-Tōkyō*. Munich: Iudicium Verlag, 1994.

Kreiner, Josef, ed. *Deutschland-Japan: Historische Kontakte*. Bonn: Bouvier, 1984.

Kreiner, Josef, and Regine Mathias, eds. *Deutschland-Japan in der Zwischenkriegszeit*. Bonn: Bouvier, 1990.

Krug, Hans-Joachim, Yōichi Hirama, Berthold J. Sander-Nagashima, and Axel Niestlé. *Reluctant Allies: German-Japanese Naval Relations in World War II*. Annapolis: Naval Institute Press, 2001.

Kudō, Akira. *Japanese-German Business Relations: Cooperation and Rivalry in the Inter-War Period*. London: Routledge, 1998.

Kudō Akira, and Tajima Nobuo, eds. *Nichi-Doku kankeishi 1890–1945*. 3 vols. Tokyo: Tōkyō Daigaku Shuppankai, 2008.

Kudō, Akira, Nobuo Tajima, and Erich Pauer, eds. *Japan and Germany: Two Latecomers on the World Stage, 1890–1945*. 3 vols. Folkestone: Global Oriental, 2009.

Kurlander, Eric. *Hitler's Monsters: A Supernatural History of the Third Reich*. New Haven: Yale University Press, 2017.

Kwok, Yenni. "Raising Asian Awareness of the Holocaust." *The New York Times*, January 26, 2014. www.nytimes.com/2014/01/27/world/asia/raising-asian-awareness-of-the-holocaust.html (accessed August 21, 2018).

Large, Stephen S. "Oligarchy, Democracy, and Fascism." In *A Companion to Japanese History*, edited by William M. Tsutsui. Malden: Blackwell Publishing, 2007: 156–171.

Law, Ricky W. "Beauty and the Beast: Japan in Interwar German Newsreels." In *Beyond Alterity: German Encounters with Modern East Asia*, edited by Qinna Shen and Martin Rosenstock. New York: Berghahn Books, 2014: 17–33.

"Between the State and the People: Civil Society Organizations in Interwar Japan." *History Compass* 12, no. 3 (2014): 217–225.

"Runner-Up: Japan in the German Mass Media during the 1936 Olympic Games." *Southeast Review of Asian Studies* 31 (2009): 164–180.

Lebow, Richard Ned. *A Cultural Theory of International Relations.* New York: Cambridge University Press, 2010.

Lee, Jung Bock. *The Political Character of the Japanese Press.* Seoul: Seoul National University Press, 1985.

Linhart, Sepp. *"Dainty Japanese" or Yellow Peril? Western War Postcards 1900–1945.* Vienna: LIT Verlag, 2005.

Low, Morris, ed. *Building a Modern Japan: Science, Technology, and Medicine in the Meiji Era and Beyond.* New York: Palgrave Macmillan, 2005.

Macklin, Graham, and Fabian Virchow, eds. *Transnational Extreme Right Networks.* New York: Routledge, 2018.

Maltarich, Bill. *Samurai and Supermen: National Socialist Views of Japan.* New York: Peter Lang, 2005.

Mammone, Andrea. *Transnational Neofascism in France and Italy.* New York: Cambridge, 2015.

Manjapra, Kris. *Age of Entanglement: German and Indian Intellectuals across Empire.* Cambridge: Harvard University Press, 2014.

Marchand, Suzanne L. *German Orientalism in the Age of Empire: Religion, Race, and Scholarship.* New York: Cambridge University Press, 2009.

Martin, Bernd. *Japan and Germany in the Modern World.* New York: Berghahn Books, 1995.

——— ed. *Japans Weg in die Moderne: Ein Sonderweg nach deutschem Vorbild?* Frankfurt: Campus Verlag, 1987.

Maruyama, Masao. *Thought and Behavior in Modern Japanese Politics,* edited by Ivan Morris. Expanded ed. London: Oxford University Press, 1963.

Matthäus, Jürgen, and Frank Bajohr. *The Political Diary of Alfred Rosenberg and the Onset of the Holocaust.* Lanham: Rowman & Littlefield, 2015.

McGetchin, Douglas T. *Indology, Indomania, and Orientalism: Ancient India's Rebirth in Modern Germany.* Madison: Fairleigh Dickinson University Press, 2009.

Medzini, Meron. *Under the Shadow of the Rising Sun: Japan and the Jews during the Holocaust Era.* Boston: Academic Studies Press, 2016.

Meffert, Jeffrey J. "Key Opinion Leaders: Where They Come from and How That Affects the Drugs You Prescribe." *Dermatological Therapy* 22, no. 3 (2009): 262–268.

Meskill, Johanna Menzel. *Hitler and Japan: The Hollow Alliance.* New York: Atherton Press, 1966.

Michalka, Wolfgang. "From the Anti-Comintern Pact to the Euro-Asiatic Bloc: Ribbentrop's Alternative Concept of Hitler's Foreign Policy Programme." In *Aspects of the Third Reich,* edited by H. W. Koch. New York: St. Martin's Press, 1985: 267–284.

——— *Ribbentrop und die deutsche Weltpolitik, 1933–1940: Aussenpolitische Konzeption und Entscheidungsprozesse im Dritten Reich.* Munich: W. Fink, 1980.

Mimura, Janis. *Planning for Empire: Reform Bureaucrats and the Japanese Wartime State.* Ithaca: Cornell University Press, 2011.

Miskolczy, Ambrus. *Hitler's Library.* Translated by Rédey Szilvia and Michael Webb. Budapest: Central European University Press, 2003.

Mitchell, Richard H. *Censorship in Imperial Japan.* Princeton: Princeton University Press, 1983.

——— *Thought Control in Prewar Japan.* Ithaca: Cornell University Press, 1976.

Miyake Masaki. "Hitorā seiken no shōaku to Nihon no rondan—zasshi *Kaizō* to *Chūō kōron* wo chūshin to suru kōsatsu." In *Berurin Wīn Tōkyō: 20-seiki zenhan no Chūō to Higashi Ajia*, edited by Miyake Masaki. Tokyo: Ronsōsha, 1999: 191–249.

Nichi-Doku seiji gaikōshi kenkyū. Tokyo: Kawade Shobō Shinsha, 1996.

Nichi-Doku-I Sangoku Dōmei no kenkyū. Tokyo: Nansōsha, 1975.

Miyanaga Takashi. *Nichi-Doku bunka jinbutsu kōryūshi*. Tokyo: Sanshūsha, 1993.

Mochida Yukio, ed. *Kindai Nihon to Doitsu: Hikaku to kankei no rekishigaku*. Kyoto: Mineruva Shobō, 2007.

Moore, Aaron Stephen. *Constructing East Asia: Technology, Ideology, and Empire in Japan's Wartime Era, 1931–1945*. Stanford: Stanford University Press, 2013.

Moore, Barrington, Jr. *Social Origins of Dictatorship and Democracy: Lord and Peasant in the Making of the Modern World*. Boston: Beacon Press, 1966.

Morinaga Takurō. *Bukka no bunkashi jiten: Meiji Taishō Shōwa Heisei*. Tokyo: Tenbōsha, 2009.

Morison, Stanley. *Politics and Script: Aspects of Authority and Freedom in the Development of Graeco-Latin Script from the Sixth Century B.C. to the Twentieth Century A.D.* Oxford: Clarendon Press, 1972.

Morris, David Stuart, and Robert H. Haigh. "Japan, Italy, Germany and the Anti-Comintern Pact." In *Rethinking Japan, Volume II: Social Sciences, Ideology and Thought*, edited by Adriana Boscaro, Franco Gatti, and Massimo Raveri. New York: St. Martin's Press, 1990: 32–42.

Mugikura Tatsuo. *Nichi-Doku ryōminzoku no jikankan: Toki no hyōgen ni miru gengo jijitsu wo fumaete*. Okayama: Daigaku Kyōiku Shuppan, 2001.

Murphy, Mahon. *Colonial Captivity during the First World War: Internment and the Fall of the German Empire, 1914–1919*. New York: Cambridge University Press, 2018.

Myers, Perry. *German Visions of India, 1871–1918: Commandeering the Holy Ganges during the Kaiserreich*. New York: Palgrave Macmillan, 2013.

Nagl, Tobias. *Die unheimliche Maschine: Rasse und Repräsentation im Weimarer Kino*. Munich: edition text + kritik, 2009.

Nakamura Ayano. *Tōkyō no Hākenkuroitsu: Higashi Ajia ni ikita Doitsujin no kiseki*. Tokyo: Hakusuisha, 2010.

Nakano Yoshiyuki. *Doitsujin ga mita Nihon: Doitsujin no Nihonkan keisei ni kansuru shiteki kenkyū*. Tokyo: Sanshūsha, 2005.

Narashino-shi Kyōiku Iinkai, ed. *Doitsu heishi no mita Nippon: Narashino Furyo Shūyōjo 1915–1920*. Tokyo: Maruzen, 2001.

Nichi-Doku Kōryūshi Henshū Iinkai, ed. *Nichi-Doku kōryū 150-nen no kiseki*. Tokyo: Yūshōdō Shoten, 2013.

Nish, Ian Hill. *Japanese Foreign Policy in the Interwar Period*. Westport: Praeger Publishers, 2002.

Noakes, Jeremy, ed. *Nazism 1919–1945, Volume 4: The German Home Front in World War II*. Exeter: University of Exeter Press, 1998.

Noakes, Jeremy, and Geoffrey Pridham, eds. *Nazism 1919–1945, Volume 2: State, Economy and Society 1933–1939*. Exeter: University of Exeter Press, 2000.

Norris, Pippa, and Ronald Inglehart. *Cultural Backlash: Trump, Brexit, and Authoritarian Populism*. New York: Cambridge University Press, 2018.

Ōhata, Tokushirō. "The Anti-Comintern Pact, 1935–1939." In *Deterrent Diplomacy: Japan, Germany and the USSR 1935–1940*, edited by James William Morley. New York: Columbia University Press, 1976: 1–112.

Okamoto, Ippei. "Albert Einstein in Japan: 1922." Translated by Kenkichiro Koizumi. *American Journal of Physics* 49, no. 10 (October 1981): 930–940.

Olstein, Diego. *Thinking History Globally.* New York: Palgrave Macmillan, 2015.

Orbach, Danny. "Japan through SS Eyes: Cultural Dialogue and Instrumentalization of a Wartime Ally." *Yōroppa kenkyū* 7 (2008): 115–132.

O'Shaughnessy, Nicholas. *Marketing the Third Reich: Persuasion, Packaging and Propaganda.* New York: Routledge, 2018.

Selling Hitler: Propaganda and the Nazi Brand. London: Hurst & Company, 2016.

Osuga, William M. "The Establishment of State Shintō and the Buddhist Opposition." MA thesis, University of California, Berkeley, 1949.

Owen, John M., IV. *The Clash of Ideas in World Politics: Transnational Networks, States, and Regime Change, 1510–2010.* Princeton: Princeton University Press, 2010.

Oyama, Hideko Tamaru. "Setsuro Tamaru and Fritz Haber: Links between Japan and Germany in Science and Technology." *The Chemical Record* 15, no. 2 (April 2015): 535–549.

Pantzer, Peter. "Deutschland und Japan vom Ersten Weltkrieg bis zum Austritt aus dem Völkerbund (1914–1933)." In *Deutschland-Japan: Historische Kontakte*, edited by Josef Kreiner. Bonn: Bouvier, 1984: 141–160.

Panzer, Sarah. "Prussians of the East: The 1944 *Deutsch-Japanische Gesellschaft*'s Essay Contest and the Transnational Romantic." In *Beyond Alterity: German Encounters with Modern East Asia*, edited by Qinna Shen and Martin Rosenstock. New York: Berghahn Books, 2014: 52–69.

Panzer, Sarah Jordan. "The Prussians of the East: Samurai, Bushido, and Japanese Honor in the German Imagination, 1905–1945." PhD diss., University of Chicago, 2015.

Pauer, Erich. "Die wirtschaftlichen Beziehungen zwischen Japan und Deutschland 1900–1945." In *Deutschland-Japan: Historische Kontakte*, edited by Josef Kreiner. Bonn: Bouvier Verlag, 1984: 161–210.

Paxton, Robert O. *The Anatomy of Fascism.* New York: Alfred A. Knopf, 2004.

Payne, Stanley G. *A History of Fascism, 1914–1945.* Madison: University of Wisconsin Press, 1995.

Pegelow Kaplan, Thomas. *The Language of Nazi Genocide: Linguistic Violence and the Struggle of Germans of Jewish Ancestry.* New York: Cambridge University Press, 2009.

Pendas, Devin O., Mark Roseman, and Richard F. Wetzell. *Beyond the Racial State: Rethinking Nazi Germany.* New York: Cambridge University Press, 2017.

Peng, Xunhou. *China in the World Anti-Fascist War.* Beijing: China Intercontinental Press, 2005.

Petzina, Dietmar, Werner Abelshauser, and Anselm Faust, eds. *Sozialgeschichtliches Arbeitsbuch Band III: Materialien zur Statistik des Deutschen Reiches 1914–1945.* Munich: C. H. Beck, 1978.

Prawer, Siegbert Salomon. *Between Two Worlds: The Jewish Presence in German and Austrian Film, 1910–1933*. New York: Berghahn Books, 2005.

Presseisen, Ernst L. *Germany and Japan: A Study in Totalitarian Diplomacy, 1933–1941*. The Hague: Martinus Nijhoff, 1958.

Prinzler, Hans Helmut. *Chronik des deutschen Films 1895–1994*. Stuttgart: J. B. Metzler, 1995.

Rabe, John. *John Rabe: Der gute Deutsche von Nanking*, edited by Erwin Wickert. Stuttgart: Deutsche Verlags-Anstalt, 1997.

Reynolds, E. Bruce, ed. *Japan in the Fascist Era*. New York: Palgrave Macmillan, 2004.

Richter, Sabine. "Einblick in ein kunstpädagogisches Skizzenbuch. Leben und Werk von Eva Eyquem." PhD diss., University of Erlangen-Nuremberg, 2016.

Richter, Steffi. "Japanologie in Leipzig – was war, was sein wird." Lecture, Ostasiatisches Institut, Japanologie at Leipzig University, November 1996.

Roberts, Lee M., ed. *Germany and the Imagined East*. Newcastle upon Tyne: Cambridge Scholars Publishing, 2009.

Roberts, Lee M. *Literary Nationalism in German and Japanese Germanistik*. New York: Peter Lang, 2010.

Rodogno, Davide, Bernhard Struck, and Jakob Vogel, eds. *Shaping the Transnational Sphere: Experts, Networks and Issues from the 1840s to the 1930s*. New York: Berghahn Books, 2014.

Rössler, Patrick. *The Bauhaus and Public Relations: Communication in a Permanent State of Crisis*. New York: Routledge, 2014.

Rosenfeld, Gavriel D. *The Fourth Reich: The Specter of Nazism from World War II to the Present*. New York: Cambridge University Press, 2019.

Roth, Joseph. *What I Saw: Reports from Berlin 1920–1933*. Translated by Michael Hofmann. New York: W. W. Norton, 2003.

Ryback, Timothy W. *Hitler's Private Library: The Books That Shaped His Life*. New York: Alfred A. Knopf, 2008.

Saaler, Sven, Akira Kudō, and Nobuo Tajima, eds. *Mutual Perceptions and Images in Japanese-German Relations, 1860–2010*. Leiden: Brill, 2017.

Sachsenmaier, Dominic. *Global Perspectives on Global History: Theories and Approaches in a Connected World*. New York: Cambridge University Press, 2011.

Saint-Amour, Paul K. *Tense Future: Modernism, Total War, Encyclopedic Form*. New York: Oxford University Press, 2015.

Sala, Ilaria Maria. "Asia's Disturbing Embrace of 'Nazi Chic' Is Prompting a Nonprofit to Teach Holocaust History." *Quartz*, March 9, 2017. https://qz.com/928440/asias-disturbing-embrace-of-nazi-chic-is-prompting-a-nonprofit-to-teach-holocaust-history/ (accessed August 21, 2018).

Scalapino, Robert A. *Democracy and the Party Movement in Prewar Japan: The Failure of the First Attempt*. Berkeley: University of California Press, 1953.

Schlosser, Horst Dieter. *Sprache unterm Hakenkreuz: Eine andere Geschichte des Nationalsozialismus*. Cologne: Böhlau Verlag, 2013.

Schmalenbach, Paul. *German Raiders: A History of Auxiliary Cruisers of the German Navy, 1895–1945*. Annapolis: Naval Institute Press, 1979.

Schmölders, Claudia. *Hitler's Face: The Biography of an Image*. Translated by Adrian Daub. Philadelphia: University of Pennsylvania Press, 2006.

Schneider, Wolfgang, ed. *Alltag unter Hitler*. Berlin: Rowohlt, 2000.

Schweller, Randall L. *Deadly Imbalances: Tripolarity and Hitler's Strategy of World Conquest*. New York: Columbia University Press, 1998.

Seidensticker, Edward. *Tokyo from Edo to Showa 1867–1989: The Emergence of the World's Greatest City*. Rutland: Tuttle Publishing, 2010.

Seidman, Michael. *Transatlantic Antifascisms: From the Spanish Civil War to the End of World War II*. New York: Cambridge University Press, 2018.

Shen, Qinna, and Martin Rosenstock, eds. *Beyond Alterity: German Encounters with Modern East Asia*. New York: Berghahn Books, 2014.

Shirer, William L. *The Rise and Fall of the Third Reich: A History of Nazi Germany*. New York: Simon & Schuster, 1990.

Shūkan Asahi, ed. *Nedanshi nenpyō: Meiji Taishō Shōwa*. Tokyo: Asahi Shinbunsha, 1988.

Sluga, Glenda. *Internationalism in the Age of Nationalism*. Philadelphia: University of Pennsylvania Press, 2013.

Sommer, Theo. *Deutschland und Japan zwischen den Mächten, 1935–1940: Vom Antikominternpakt zum Dreimächtepakt, eine Studie zur diplomatischen Vorgeschichte des Zweiten Weltkriegs*. Tübingen: J. C. B. Mohr, 1962.

Sottile, Joseph P. "The Fascist Era: Imperial Japan and the Axis Alliance in Historical Perspective." In *Japan in the Fascist Era*, edited by E. Bruce Reynolds. New York: Palgrave Macmillan, 2004: 1–48.

Spang, Christian W. *Karl Haushofer und Japan: Die Rezeption seiner geopolitischen Theorien in der deutschen und japanischen Politik*. Munich: Iudicium, 2013.

Spang, Christian W., and Rolf-Harald Wippich, eds. *Japanese-German Relations, 1895–1945: War, Diplomacy and Public Opinion*. London: Routledge, 2006.

Sprengard, Karl Anton, Kenchi Ono, and Yasuo Ariizumi, eds. *Deutschland und Japan im 20. Jahrhundert: Wechselbeziehungen zweier Kulturnationen*. Wiesbaden: Harrassowitz, 2002.

Steinhoff, Patricia G. *Tenkō: Ideology and Societal Integration in Prewar Japan*. New York: Garland, 1991.

Steinmetz, George. *The Devil's Handwriting: Precoloniality and the German Colonial State in Qingdao, Samoa, and Southwest Africa*. Chicago: University of Chicago Press, 2007.

Stoltzenberg, Dietrich. *Fritz Haber: Chemist, Nobel Laureate, German, Jew*. Philadelphia: Chemical Heritage Press, 2004.

Streeck, Wolfgang, and Kozo Yamamura. *The Origins of Nonliberal Capitalism: Germany and Japan in Comparison*. Ithaca: Cornell University Press, 2001.

Sutton, Donald S. "German Advice and Residual Warlordism in the Nanking Decade: Influences on Nationalist Military Training and Strategy." *China Quarterly* 91 (September 1982): 386–410.

Szöllösi-Janze, Margit. *Fritz Haber 1868–1934: Eine Biographie*. Munich: C. H. Beck, 1998.

Szpilman, Christopher W. A. "Fascist and Quasi-Fascist Ideas in Interwar Japan, 1918–1941." In *Japan in the Fascist Era*, edited by E. Bruce Reynolds. New York: Palgrave Macmillan, 2004: 73–106.

"Kanokogi Kazunobu: 'Imperial Asia,' 1937." In *Pan-Asianism: A Documentary History, Volume 1: 1850–1920*, edited by Sven Saaler and Christopher W. A. Szpilman. Lanham: Rowman & Littlefield, 2011: 123–126.

"'Misunderstood Asianism' and 'The Great Mission of Our Country,' 1917." In *Pan-Asianism: A Documentary History, Volume 1: 1850–1920*, edited by Sven Saaler and Christopher W. A. Szpilman. Lanham: Rowman & Littlefield, 2011: 297–303.

Tajima Nobuo. *Nachizumu Kyokutō senryaku: Nichi-Doku Bōkyō Kyōtei wo meguru chōhōsen*. Tokyo: Kōdansha, 1997.

Nihon Rikugun no taiso bōryaku: Nichi-Doku Bōkyō Kyōtei to Yūrashia seisaku. Tokyo: Yoshikawa Kōbunkan, 2017.

Tankha, Brij. *Kita Ikki and the Making of Modern Japan: A Vision of Empire*. Folkestone: Global Oriental, 2006.

Tansman, Alan. *The Aesthetics of Japanese Fascism*. Berkeley: University of California Press, 2009.

Thompson, Mark R. "Japan's 'German Path' and Pacific Asia's 'Flying Geese.'" *Asian Journal of Social Science* 38, no. 5 (2010): 697–715.

Tomita Hiroshi. *Bandō Furyo Shūyōjo: Nichi-Doku Sensō to zainichi Doitsu furyo*. Tokyo: Hōsei Daigaku Shuppankyoku, 2006.

Tsutsui, William M, and Michael Baskett, eds. *The East Asian Olympiads, 1934–2008: Building Bodies and Nations in Japan, Korea, and China*. Leiden: Brill, 2011.

Unger, J. Marshall. *The Role of Contact in the Origins of the Japanese and Korean Languages*. Honolulu: University of Hawai'i Press, 2008.

Vagts, Alfred. *A History of Militarism: Civilian and Military*. Rev. ed. New York: The Free Press, 1967.

Vietsch, Eberhard von. *Wilhelm Solf: Botschafter zwischen den Zeiten*. Tübingen: Wunderlich Verlag, 1961.

Wachtel, Joachim. *As Time Flies By: The History of Lufthansa since 1926*. Rev. ed. Frankfurt am Main: Deutsche Lufthansa AG, 2002.

Wada Hirofumi, Shindō Masahiro, Nishimura Masahiro, Miyauchi Junko, and Wada Keiko. *Gengo toshi Berurin 1861–1945*. Tokyo: Fujiwara Shoten, 2006.

Waltz, Kenneth N. *Theory of International Politics*. New York: McGraw-Hill, 1979.

Ward, Max M. *Thought Crime: Ideology and State Power in Interwar Japan*. Durham: Duke University Press, 2019.

Weber-Schäfer, Peter. "Verspätete Demokratie: Parlamentarismus in Japan und Deutschland." In *Japan und Deutschland im 20. Jahrhundert*, edited by Klaus Kracht, Bruno Lewin, and Klaus Müller. Wiesbaden: Harrassowitz, 1984: 137–149.

Weinberg, Gerhard L. "Die geheimen Abkommen zum Antikominternpakt." *Vierteljahrshefte für Zeitgeschichte* 2 (1954): 193–201.

Hitler's Foreign Policy 1933–1939: The Road to World War II. New York: Enigma Books, 2010.

Weinstein, Valerie. "Reflecting Chiral Modernities: The Function of Genre in Arnold Fanck's Transnational *Bergfilm, The Samurai's Daughter* (1936–37). In *Beyond Alterity: German Encounters with Modern East Asia*, edited by Qinna Shen and Martin Rosenstock. New York: Berghahn Books, 2014: 34–51.

Weiss, John. *The Fascist Tradition: Radical Right-Wing Extremism in Modern Europe*. New York: Harper & Row, 1967.

Wennberg, Rebecca. "Ideological Incorrectness Beyond 'Political Religion': Discourse on Nazi Ideology among Scandinavian National Socialist Intellectuals." PhD diss., Royal Holloway, University of London, 2015.

Wiskemann, Elizabeth. *The Rome-Berlin Axis: A Study of the Relations between Hitler and Mussolini*. London: Collins, 1966.

Yanagisawa, Osamu. *European Reformism, Nazism and Traditionalism: Economic Thought in Imperial Japan, 1930–1945*. Frankfurt am Main: Peter Lang, 2015.

Yellen, Jeremy A. "Into the Tiger's Den: Japan and the Tripartite Pact, 1940." *Journal of Contemporary History* 51, no. 3 (2016): 555–576.

Yoshimi, Yoshiaki. *Grassroots Fascism: The War Experience of the Japanese People*. Translated and edited by Ethan Mark. New York: Columbia University Press, 2015.

Young, Louise. *Japan's Total Empire: Manchuria and the Culture of Wartime Imperialism*. Berkeley: University of California Press, 1998.

Zachariah, Benjamin. "A Voluntary Gleichschaltung? Perspectives from India towards a Non-Eurocentric Understanding of Fascism." *Transcultural Studies* 5, no. 2 (2014): 63–100.

Zimmerman, Andrew. *Alabama in Africa: Booker T. Washington, the German Empire, and the Globalization of the New South*. Princeton: Princeton University Press, 2010.

Index

For EU product safety concerns, contact us at Calle de José Abascal, 56–1°,
28003 Madrid, Spain or eugpsr@cambridge.org.

www.ingramcontent.com/pod-product-compliance
Ingram Content Group UK Ltd.
Pitfield, Milton Keynes, MK11 3LW, UK
UKHW020401140625
459647UK00020B/2590